W9-AMZ-782

АННА АХМАТОВА
Полное собрание стихотворений

ТОМ ПЕРВЫЙ

ИЗДАТЕЛЬСТВО «ЗЕФИР»
1990

The Complete Poems of
ANNA AKHMATOVA, v.1

VOLUME I

Translated by
JUDITH HEMSCHEMEYER

Edited and with an Introduction by
ROBERTA REEDER

ZEPHYR PRESS
Somerville, Massachusetts, U.S.A.
1990

Acknowledgement is gratefully made to the following periodicals, in which some of these translations initially appeared: *Agni Review, Boulevard, Calyx, Frank* (Paris, France), *Gargoyle* (Washington, D.C.), *Green House, The Hudson Review, Kalliope, MUNDUS ARTIUM, The Nantucket Review, New England Review and Bread Loaf Quarterly, New Letters, Northwest Review, Pequod, Ploughshares, Poetry Now, Prism International* (University of British Columbia, Vancouver, Canada), *rara avis, Room, Southern Review* (University of Adelaide, Australia), *The Southern Review, Stand* (Newcastle-upon-Tyne, U.K.), *TriQuarterly.*

ISBN 0-939010-13-5
Library of Congress Catalogue Card No. 88-51831

Second Printing

The paper used in this book meets the minimum requirements of the American National Standard of Permanence of Paper for Printed Library Materials Z39.48-1984.

ZEPHYR PRESS
13 Robinson Street
Somerville, Massachusetts 02145, U.S.A.

Project Coordinator
Ed Hogan

Editor for "Mirrors and Masks"
Leora Zeitlin

Copyediting
Hugh Abernethy, Leora Zeitlin

Design
Ed Hogan

Publication of this edition was assisted by support from
The Bydale Foundation
The Literature Program of the National Endowment for the Arts
The Sagan Foundation
It was funded in part by the Massachusetts Council on the
Arts and Humanities, a state agency.

Photographs and illustrations were supplied or are reproduced by kind permission of the following:

Volume I: Ardis (20, 23, 24, 97, 123 [top], 154, 156); Curtis Brown Ltd. (111 [lower right]); Boris A. Filipoff (35, 59, 149 [top], 493, 535); Amanda Haight (71, 79, 81, 103, 108, 114, 122, 128, 129, 149 [lower left]); Amanda Haight and Oxford University Press (32, 58, 140); Fernand Rude (83, 100, 105, 533); Vsesoyuznoe Agentstvo Po Avtorskim Pravam (VAAP) (frontispiece, 27, 28, 33, 101, 111 [top left], 123 [bottom], 127 [bottom] 139, 147, 210, 298, 372, 494, 536); YMCA Press (37, 62, 74, 127 [top], 155, 371, 534). Photographs or illustrations on pages 39, 55, 201–208, and 289–296 are from pre-1973 Soviet publications. The photograph on page 153 is from *The Theme of Time in the Poetry of Anna Axmatova* by Kees Verheul, and is reprinted by permission of Mouton de Gruyter, Publishers.

Volume II: Isaiah Berlin (24); Ardis (481, 484, 557); Boris A. Filipoff (frontispiece, 151, 556); Amanda Haight (67, 323); Fernand Rude (149, 644, 742); Vsesoyuznoe Agentstvo Po Avtorskim Pravam (VAAP) (69, 148, 150, 322, 558); YMCA Press (46, 68, 395, 592). Photographs or illustrations on pages 139–144, 147, and 620 are from pre-1973 Soviet publications.

Keyboarded on a Vendex Turbo-888-XT
microcomputer and output in Bembo on Compugraphic equipment
at Type for U, ZephyrType, and LeGwin Associates,
all in Cambridge, Massachusetts.
Supplementary Russian typesetting by
Any Phototype, New York, N.Y.

Printed in the United States of America
by Cushing-Malloy, Inc.

*We dedicate this edition
to the memory of
Amanda Haight (1939–1989)*

Содержание

List of Illustrations   *xxxiii*
Acknowledgements   *xxxv*
Translator's Preface   1

INTRODUCTION

Mirrors and Masks: The Life and Poetic works of Anna
    Akhmatova   *Roberta Reeder*   21

Chronology   185
Index to Poems—By Source   191

ВЕЧЕР

Portfolio: TSARSKOYE SELO
    (ЦАРСКОЕ СЕЛО)   199

I.

Любовь   212
В ЦАРСКОМ СЕЛЕ
    1. «По аллее проводят лошадок...»   212
    2. «...А там мой мраморный двойник...»   214
    3. «Смуглый отрок бродил по аллеям...»   214
«И мальчик, что играет на волынке...»   216
«Любовь покоряет обманно...»   216
«Сжала руки под темной вуалью...»   218
«Память о солнце в сердце слабеет...»   220
«Высоко в небе облачко серело...»   220
«Дверь полуоткрыта...»   222
«Хочешь знать, как все это было?»   224
Песня последней встречи   224
«Как соломинкой пьешь мою душу...»   226
«Я сошла с ума, о мальчик странный...»   228
«Мне больше ног моих не надо...»   228

II.

ОБМАН
    1. «Весенним солнцем это утро пьяно...»   230
    2. «Жарко веет ветер душный...»   232
    3. «Синий вечер. Ветры кротко стихли...»   232
    4. «Я написала слова...»   234
«Мне с тобою пьяным весело...»   236
«Муж хлестал меня узорчатым...»   238

«Сердце к сердцу не приковано...»   238
Песенка   240
«Я пришла сюда, бездельница...»   242
Белой ночью   242
«Под навесом темной риги жарко...»   244
«Хорони, хорони меня, ветер!»   244
«Ты поверь, не змеиное острое жало...»   246

III.

Музе   248
АЛИСА
    1. «Все тоскует о забытом...»   250
    2. «Как поздно! Устала, зеваю...»   252
Маскарад в парке   254
Вечерняя комната   256
Сероглазый король   258
Рыбак   258
Он любил...   260
«Сегодня мне письма́ не принесли...»   262
Надпись на неоконченном портрете   262
«Сладок запах синих виноградин...»   264
Подражание И. Ф. Анненскому   266
«Туманом легким парк наполнился...»   266
«Я живу, как кукушка в часах...»   268
Похороны   268
Сад   270
Над водой   272
«Три раза пытать приходали...»   274

⟨ДОПОЛНЕНИЯ⟩

«Молюсь оконному лучу...»   276
ДВА СТИХОТВОРЕНИЯ
    1. «Подушка уже горяча...»   276
    2. «Тот же голос, тот же взгляд...»   278
ЧИТАЯ «ГАМЛЕТА»
    1. «У кладбища направо пылил пустырь...»   278
    2. «И как будто по ошибке...»   280
«И когда друг друга проклинали...»   280
Первое возвращение   282
«Я и плакала и каялась...»   282

«Меня покинул в новолунье...» — 284
«Мурка, не ходи, там сыч...» — 284

Ч Е Т К И

Portfolio: PETERSBURG (ПЕТЕРБУРГ) — 287

I.

СМЯТЕНИЕ
   1. «Было душно от жгучего света...» — 300
   2. «Не любишь, не хочешь смотреть?» — 300
   3. «Как велит простая учтивость...» — 300
Прогулка — 302
Вечером — 304
«Все мы бражники здесь, блудницы...» — 304
«После ветра и мороза было...» — 306
«...И на ступеньки встретить...» — 308
«Безвольно пощады просят...» — 308
«Покорно мне воображенье...» — 310
Отрывок — 312
«Настоящую нежность не спутаешь...» — 312
«Не будем пить из одного стакана...» — 314
«У меня есть улыбка одна...» — 316
«Столько просьб у любимой всегда!» — 316
«В последний раз мы встретились тогда...» — 318
«Здравствуй! Легкий шелест слышишь...» — 318

II.

«Цветов и неживых вещей...» — 320
«Каждый день по-новому тревожен...» — 322
«Мальчик сказал мне: «Как это больно!» » — 322
«Высокие своды костела...» — 324
«Он длится без конца — янтарный,
   тяжкий день!» — 326
Голос памяти — 326
«Я научилась просто, мудро жить...» — 328
«Здесь всё то же, то же, что и прежде...» — 328
Бессонница — 330
«Ты знаешь, я томлюсь в неволе...» — 332
«Углем наметил на левом боку...» — 332

III.

«Помолись о нищей, о потерянной...»   334
«Вижу выцветший флаг над таможней...»   336
«Плотно сомкнуты губы сухие...»   336
«Дал Ты мне молодость трудную...»   338
8 ноября 1913   340
«Ты пришел меня утешить, милый...»   340
«Умирая, томлюсь о бессмертьи...»   342
«Ты письмо мое, милый, не комкай...»   342
Исповедь   344
«В ремешках пенал и книги были...»   346
«Со дня Купальницы-Аграфены...»   346
«Я с тобой не стану пить вино...»   346
«Вечерние часы перед столом...»   348

IV.

«Как вплелась в мои темные косы...»   350
«Я пришла тебя сменить, сестра...»   350
СТИХИ О ПЕТЕРБУРГЕ
    1. «Вновь Исакий в облаченьи...»   354
    2. «Сердце бьется ровно, мерно...»   354
«Знаю, знаю — снова лыжи...»   356
Венеция   358
«Протертый коврик под иконой...»   358
Гость   360
«Я пришла к поэту в гости...»   362

⟨ДОПОЛНЕНИЯ⟩

«Проводила друга до передней...»   364
«Простишь ли мне эти ноябрьские дни?»   364
«Я не любви твоей прошу...»   364
«Горят твои ладони...»   366
«Будешь жить, не зная лиха...»   368

Б Е Л А Я   С Т А Я

I.

«Думали: нищие мы, нету у нас ничего...»   374
«Твой белый дом и тихий сад оставлю...»   374
Уединение   376
Песня о песне   376
«Слаб голос мой, но воля не слабеет...»   378

«Был он ревнивым, тревожным и нежным...» 380
«Тяжела ты, любовная память!» 380
«Потускнел на небе синий лак...» 382
«Вместо мудрости — опытность, пресное...» 382
«А! это снова ты. Не отроком влюбленным...» 384
«Муза ушла по дороге...» 384
«Я улыбаться перестала...» 386
«Они летят, они еще в дороге...» 386
«О, это был прохладный день...» 388
«Я так молилась: «Утоли...» 388
«Есть в близости людей заветная черта...» 390
«Всё отнято: и сила, и любовь...» 392
«Нам свежесть слов и чувства простоту...» 392
Ответ 394
«Был блаженной моей колыбелью...» 394

II.

9 декабря 1913 года 396
«Как ты можешь смотреть на Неву...» 398
«Под крышей промерзшей пустого жилья...» 398
«Целый год ты со мной неразлучен...» 398
Киев 400
«Еще весна таинственная млела...» 402
Разлука 404
«Чернеет дорога приморского сада...» 404
«Не в лесу мы, довольно аукать...» 404
«У тебя заботы другие...» 406
«Господь немилостив к жнецам и садоводам...» 406
«Все обещало мне его...» 408
«Как невеста, получаю...» 408
«Божий ангел, зимним утром...» 410
«Ведь где-то есть простая жизнь и свет...» 410
«Подошла. Я волненья не выдал...» 412
Побег 412
«О тебе вспоминаю я редко...» 416
«Царскосельская статуя 416
«Вновь подарен мне дремотой...» 418
«Все мне видится Павловск холмистый...» 420

«Бессмертник сух и розов. Облака...»   422

III.

«Майский снег   424
«Зачем притворяешься ты...»   424
«Пустых небес прозрачное стекло...»   426
ИЮЛЬ 1914
    1. «Пахнет гарью. Четыре недели...»   426
    2. «Можжевельника запах сладкий...»   428
«Тот голос, с тишиной великой споря...»   428
«Мы не умеем прощаться...»   430
Утешение   432
«Лучше б мне частушки задорно выкликать...»   432
Молитва   434
«Где, высокая, твой цыганенок...»   434
«Столько раз я проклинала...»   436
«Ни в лодке, ни в телеге...»   438
«Вижу, вижу лунный лук...»   438
«Бесшумно ходили по дому...»   440
Моей сестре   442
«Так раненого журавля...»   444
«Буду тихо на погосте...»   446
«Высокомерьем дух твой помрачен...»   446
«Приду туда, и отлетит томленье...»   448
Памяти 19 июля 1914   448

IV.

«Перед весной бывают дни такие...»   450
«То пятое время года...»   452
«Выбрала сама я долю...»   452
Сон   452
Белый дом   454
«Долго шел через поля и села...»   456
«Широк и желт вечерний свет...»   458
«Я не знаю, ты жив или умер...»   460
«Нет, царевич, я не та...»   460
«Из памяти твоей я выну этот день...»   462
«Не хулил меня, не славил...»   464
«Там тень моя осталась и тоскует...»   464
«Двадцать первое. Ночь. Понедельник...»   466

«Небо мелкий дождик сеет...»   466
«Я знаю, ты моя награда...»   468
Милому   470
«Судьба ли так моя переменилась...»   470
«Как белый камень в глубине колодца...»   472
«Первый луч — благословенье Бога...»   474

⟨ДОПОЛНЕНИЯ⟩

«И мнится — голос человека...»   474
«Когда в мрачнейшей из столиц...»   476
«Как площади эти обширны...»   478
«Для того ль тебя носила...»   480
«Родилась я ни поздно, ни рано...»   480
«Мне не надо счастья малого...»   482
«Город сгинул, последнего дома...»   482
«О, есть неповторимые слова...»   484
«Стал мне реже сниться, слава Богу...»   484
«Не тайны и не печали...»   486
«Будем вместе, милый, вместе...»   488
«Черная вилась дорога...»   488
«Как люблю, как любила глядеть я...»   490

П О Д О Р О Ж Н И К

«Сразу стало тихо в доме...»   496
«Ты — отступник: за остров зеленый...»   496
«Просыпаться на рассвете...»   498
«И в тайную дружбу с высоким...»   500
«Словно ангел, возмутивший воду...»   500
«Когда о горькой гибели моей...»   500
«А ты теперь тяжелый и унылый...»   502
«Пленник чужой! Мне чужого не надо...»   502
«Я спросила у кукушки...»   504
«По неделе ни слова ни с кем не скажу...»   504
«В каждых сутках есть такой...»   506
«Земная слава как дым...»   508
«Это просто, это ясно...»   508
«О нет, я не тебя любила...»   510
«Я слышу иволги всегда печальный голос...»   512

«Как страшно изменилось тело…»   512
«Я окошка не завесила…»   514
«Эта встреча никем не воспета…»   514
«И вот одна осталась я…»   516
«Чем хуже этот век предшествующих? Разве…»   516
«Теперь никто не станет слушать песен…»   518
«По твердому гребню сугроба…»   518
«Теперь прощай, столица…»   520
«Ждала его напрасно много лет…»   522
Ночью   522
«Течет река неспешно по долине…»   524
«На шее мелких четок ряд…»   524
Песенка   526
«И целый день, своих пугаясь стонов…»   528
«Ты мог бы мне сниться и реже…»   528
«Когда в тоске самоубийства…»   528

⟨ДОПОЛНЕНИЕ⟩
За́ре   530

ANNO DOMINI MCMXXI

I. ПОСЛЕ ВСЕГО

Петроград, 1919   538
Бежецк   540
Предсказание   540
ДРУГОЙ ГОЛОС
    1. «Я с тобой, мой ангел, не лукавил…»   542
    2. «В тот давний год, когда зажглась
        любовь…»   542
«Сказал, что у меня соперниц нет…»   544
«Земной отрадой сердца не томи…»   544
«Не с теми я, кто бросил землю…»   546
ЧЕРНЫЙ СОН
    1. «Косноязычно славивший меня…»   546
    2. «Ты всегда таинственный и новый…»   548
    3. «От любви твоей загадочной…»   550
    4. «Проплывают льдины, звеня…»   550
    5. Третий Зачатьевский   552
    6. «Тебе покорной? Ты сошел с ума!»   552

«Что ты бродишь неприкаянный…»   554
«Веет ветер лебединый…»   554
«Ангел, три года хранивший меня…»   556
«Шепчет: «Я не пожалею…»   558
«Слух чудовищный бродит по городу…»   558
«Заболеть бы как следует, в жгучем бреду…»   560
«За озером луна остановилась…»   560
«Как мог ты, сильный и свободный…»   562
БИБЛЕЙСКИЕ СТИХИ
   1. Рахиль   564
   2. Лотова жена   566
   3. Мелхола   568
Причитание   570
«Вот и берег северного моря…»   572
«Хорошо здесь: и шелест, и хруст…»   572
Сказка о черном кольце   574
«Небывалая осень построила купол высокий…»   578

      II. MCMXXI
«Всё расхищено, предано, продано…»   578
«Путник милый, ты далече…»   580
«Сослужу тебе верную службу…»   582
«Нам встречи нет. Мы в разных станах…»   582
«Страх, во тьме перебирая вещи…»   584
«Ты мне не обещан ни жизнью, ни Богом…»   584
«О, жизнь без завтрашнего дня!»   586
«Кое-как удалось разлучиться…»   588
«А, ты думал — я тоже такая…»   588
«Пусть голоса орга́на снова грянут…»   590
«Чугунная ограда…»   592
«А Смоленская нынче именинница…»   592
«Пророчишь, горькая, и руки уронила…»   594
«Не бывать тебе в живых…»   594
«Пока не свалюсь под забором…»   596
«На пороге белом рая…»   598
«Я гибель накликала милым…»   598
«Долгим взглядом твоим истомленная…»   600
Клевета   600

III. ГОЛОС ПАМЯТИ

«Широко распахнуты ворота...» 602
«Почернел, искривился бревенчатый мост...» 604
«Тот август как желтое пламя...» 606
Призрак 608
ТРИ СТИХОТВОРЕНИЯ
   1. «Да, я любила их, те сборища ночные...» 610
   2. «Соблазна не было. Соблазн в тиши
       живет...» 610
   3. «Не оттого ль, уйдя от легкости проклятой...» 610
Колыбельная 612
«Заплаканная осень, как вдова...» 612
«Буду черные грядки холить...» 614
Новогодняя баллада 616
«О, знала ль я, когда в одежде белой...» 616
Многим 618

Notes to the Poems 621
Index of Proper Names 645

Table of Contents

List of Illustrations   *xxxiii*
Acknowledgements   *xxxv*
Translator's Preface   *Judith Hemschemeyer*   1

INTRODUCTION
Mirrors and Masks: The Life and Poetic Works
   of Anna Akhmatova   *Roberta Reeder*   21

Chronology   185
Index to Poems—By Source   191

EVENING

Portfolio: TSARSKOYE SELO   199

I.

Love   213
IN TSARSKOYE SELO
   1. "They're leading the horses..."   213
   2. "...And there's my marble double..."   215
   3. "A dark-skinned youth wandered..."   215
"The boy who plays the bagpipes..."   217
"Love conquers by deception..."   217
"Under her dark veil she wrung her hands..."   219
"The heart's memory of the sun grows faint..."   221
"High in the sky a small cloud grayed..."   221
"The door is half open..."   223
The Song of the Last Meeting   225
"As if with a straw..."   227
"Oh, strange boy, I lost my head..."   229
"I don't need legs anymore..."   229

II.

DECEPTION
   1. "This morning is drunk with spring sun..."   231
   2. "The wind blows stifling hot..."   233
   3. "Dark blue evening..."   233
   4. "I finally wrote down the words..."   235
"When you're drunk it's so much fun..."   237
"My husband whipped me..."   239
"One heart isn't chained to another..."   239
A Song   241

"I came here, an idler. . ."   243
On a White Night   243
"Under the dark roof of the threshing shed. . ."   245
"Bury me, bury me, wind!"   245
"Believe me, not the serpent's sharp sting. . ."   247

III.

To the Muse   249
ALISA
   1. "Everything mourns for the forgotten. . ."   251
   2. "How late it is! I'm tired, I'm yawning. . ." 253
Masquerade in the Park   255
Evening Room   257
The Gray-Eyed King   259
The Fisherman   259
He Loved. . .   261
Inscription on an Unfinished Portrait   263
"The smell of blue grapes is sweet. . ."   265
Imitation of I. F. Annensky   267
"The park was filled with light mist. . ."   267
"I live like a cuckoo in a clock. . ."   269
Funeral   269
The Garden   271
Over the Water   273
"Three times it came to torment me. . ."   275

(ADDITIONS)
"I pray to the sunbeam from the window. . ."   277
TWO POEMS
   1. "Both sides of the pillow. . ."   277
   2. "That same voice, that same gaze. . ."   279
READING *HAMLET*
   1. "Dust rose from the vacant lot. . ."   279
   2. "And as if by mistake. . ."   281
"And when we had cursed each other. . ."   281
First Return   283
"I wept and repented. . ."   283
"At the new moon he abandoned me. . ."   285
"Moorka, don't go. . ."   285

R O S A R Y

Portfolio: PETERSBURG   287

I.

CONFUSION
   1. "It was stifling in the burning light..."   301
   2. "Don't you love me..."   301
   3. "As simple civility demands..."   301
Outing   303
In the Evening   305
"We are all carousers and loose women here..."   305
"After the wind and the frost..."   307
"...And they didn't come out with lanterns..."   309
"Helplessly, my eyes ask mercy..."   309
"My imagination obeys me..."   311
Fragment   313
"One would not mistake true tenderness..."   313
"We will not drink, from the same glass..."   315
"I have a certain smile..."   317
"How many demands the beloved can make!"   317
"We met for the last time..."   319
"Hello! Do you hear the light rustling..."   319

II.

"In this house there's a pleasant smell..."   321
"Each day is anxious all over again..."   323
"The boy said to me: 'How this hurts!'"   323
"The high vaults of the Polish church..."   325
"It drags on forever—this heavy, amber day!"   327
The Voice of Memory   327
"I've learned to live simply, wisely..."   329
"Here everything is the same as before..."   329
Insomnia   331
"You know, I languish in captivity..."   333
"He made a charcoal mark on the left side..."   333

III.

"I ask you to pray for my poor...living soul..."   335
"I see the faded flag above the customhouse..."   337
"The dry lips are tightly closed..."   337

"You gave me a difficult youth..."   339
November 8, 1913   341
"You've come to comfort me, darling..."   341
"Dying, I am tormented by immortality..."   343
"Darling, don't crumple my letter..."   343
Confession   345
"With my pencil case and books in a bookstrap..."   347
"Since Agrafena-Kupalnitsa's..."   347
"I won't start drinking wine with you..."   347
"Evening hours at the desk..."   349

IV.

"Intertwined in my dark braids..."   351
"'I came to take your place, sister...'"   351
VERSES ABOUT PETERSBURG
     1. "Once more St. Isaac's wears robes..."   355
     2. "My heart beats calmly, steadily..."   355
"I know, I know—the skis will crunch..."   357
Venice   359
"Under the icon, a threadbare rug..."   359
The Guest   361
"I visited the poet..."   363

(ADDITIONS)

"I led my lover out to the hall..."   365
"Can you forgive me these November days?"   365
"I'm not asking for your love..."   365
"'The palms of your hands are burning...'"   367
"You will live without misfortune..."   369

W H I T E   F L O C K

I.

"We thought: we are beggars, we have nothing..."   375
"I will leave your white house and tranquil garden..."   375
Solitude   377
Song about a Song   377
"Weak is my voice..."   379
"He was jealous, troubled and tender..."   381
"Memory of love, you are painful!"   381

"The sky's dark blue lacquer has dimmed..." 383
"Instead of wisdom..." 383
"Ah! It's you again..." 385
"The Muse fled down the road..." 385
"I no longer smile..." 387
"They are flying, they are still on their way..." 387
"Oh, it was a cold day..." 389
"This was my prayer..." 389
"There is a sacred boundary between those who
    are close..." 391
"Everything has been cut off..." 393
"For us to lose freshness of words..." 393
The Reply 395
"My blissful cradle was a dark city..." 395

II.

December 9, 1913 397
"How can you bear to look at the Neva?" 399
"Under the freezing roof..." 399
"All year you've been inseparable from me..." 399
Kiev 401
"The mysterious spring still thrills..." 403
Separation 405
"The road by the seaside garden darkens..." 405
"We're not in the forest..." 405
"The Lord is not merciful to reapers and gardeners..." 407
"Everything promised him to me..." 409
"Like a fiancée, I receive..." 409
"The angel of God..." 411
"Somewhere there is a simple life..." 411
"She approached. I didn't betray my agitation..." 413
Flight 413
"I seldom think about you now..." 417
Statue in Tsarskoye Selo 417
"Drowsiness takes me back again..." 419
"I can still see hilly Pavlovsk..." 421
"The everlasting is rosy and dry..." 423

III.

May Snow	425
"Why do you pretend to be..."	425
"The pellucid glass of the empty heavens..."	427
JULY 1914	
1. "It smells of burning..."	427
2. "The sweet smell of juniper..."	429
"That voice opposing total silence..."	429
"We don't know how to say good-bye..."	431
Comfort	433
"I should have raucously screeched little folk tunes..."	433
Prayer	435
"'Tall woman, where is your little gypsy..."	435
"How many times I've cursed..."	437
"It's impossible to get here..."	439
"I see, I see the moon's bended bow..."	439
"Noiselessly they walked about the house..."	441
To My Sister	443
"Just as the other cranes..."	445
"Under an oaken slab in the churchyard..."	447
"Your spirit is clouded by arrogance..."	447
"I will go there and weariness will fly away..."	449
In Memoriam, July 19, 1914	449

IV.

"Before spring there are days like these..."	451
"This fifth season of the year..."	453
"I myself chose the fate..."	453
Dream	453
The White House	455
"For a long time he walked through fields and villages..."	457
"Broad and yellow is the evening light..."	459
"I don't know if you're living or dead..."	461
"No, tsarevitch, I am not the one..."	461
"I will root out this day from your memory..."	463
"He didn't mock me, he didn't praise..."	465
"There my shadow remained, and it grieves..."	465
"The twenty-first. Night. Monday..."	467

"The sky sows a fine rain..."   467
"I know that you are my reward..."   469
To the Beloved   471
"Has my fate changed so much..."   471
"Like a white stone in the depths of a well..."   473
"The first ray of light—God's blessing..."   475

(ADDITIONS)

"And it seems—a human voice..."   475
"When, in the gloomiest of capitals..."   477
"How steep and resounding these bridges are..."   479
"Why then did I used to hold you in my arms..."   481
"I was born neither too early nor too late..."   481
"I don't need much happiness..."   483
"The city disappeared..."   483
"Oh, there are unique words..."   485
"I dream of him less often now, thank God..."   485
"Not mystery and not grief..."   487
"We will be together, darling, together..."   489
"The dark road twisted..."   489
"How I love, how I loved to look..."   491

P L A N T A I N

"Suddenly it's become still in the house..."   497
"You are an apostate..."   497
"To wake at dawn..."   499
"And into secret friendship..."   501
"Like the angel moving upon the water..."   501
"When he finally hears the news..."   501
"And now you are depressed and despondent..."   503
"Someone else's captive?"   503
"I asked the cuckoo..."   505
"All week I don't say a word to anyone..."   505
"In every twenty-four hours there is one..."   507
"Earthly fame is like smoke..."   509
"It is simple, it is clear..."   509
"Oh no, it wasn't you I loved..."   511
"I am listening to the orioles' ever mournful voice..."   513
"How terribly the body has changed..."   513

"I haven't covered the little window..."   515
"No one sang about that meeting..."   515
"And here, left alone..."   517
"Has this century been worse..."   517
"Now no one will listen to songs..."   519
"Over the snowdrift's hard crust..."   519
"Now farewell, capital..."   521
"Long years I waited for him in vain..."   523
At Night   523
"The river flows slowly through the valley..."   525
"Around the neck is a string of fine beads..."   525
Little Song   527
"And all day, terrified by its own moans..."   529
"You shouldn't be in my dreams so often..."   529
"When in suicidal anguish..."   529

(ADDITION)

To Zara   531

ANNO DOMINI MCMXXI

I. AFTER EVERYTHING

Petrograd, 1919   539
Bezhetsk   541
Prophecy   541
THE VOICE OF ANOTHER
    1. "I didn't mean to trick you, my angel..." 543
    2. "In that year long ago, when love flared..." 543
"He said that I have no rivals..."   545
"Don't torment your heart with earthly joys..."   545
"I am not with those who abandoned their land..." 547
DARK DREAM
    1. "Praising me inarticulately..."   547
    2. "You are always novel and mysterious..."   549
    3. "Because of your enigmatic love..."   551
    4. "Ice floes float by, resounding..."   551
    5. Number Three, Zachatevsky   553
    6. "Submissive to you? You're out of your mind!" 553
"Why do you wander restlessly?"   555
"The wind of swans is blowing..."   555

"The angel who for three years watched over me..." 557
"He whispers: 'I'm not sorry...'" 559
"A monstrous rumor roams the city..." 559
"Falling ill, just as expected..." 561
"The moon stalled behind the lake..." 561
"How could you, strong and free..." 563
BIBLICAL VERSES
  1. Rachel 565
  2. Lot's Wife 567
  3. Michal 569
Lamentation 571
"Here is the shore of the northern sea..." 573
"It is good here..." 573
The Tale of the Black Ring 575
"The fantastic autumn constructed a high cupola..." 579

II. MCMXXI
"Everything has been plundered..." 579
"Dear traveler, you are far away..." 581
"Certainly I'll do you a good turn..." 583
"We won't meet. We are in different camps..." 583
"Terror, fingering things in the dark..." 585
"You were promised to me neither by life nor
  by God..." 585
"Oh, life without tomorrow's day!" 587
"Somehow we've managed to part..." 589
"Ah—you thought I'd be the type..." 589
"Let the voice of the organ against burst forth..." 591
"Cast-iron fence..." 593
"Today is the nameday of Our Lady of Smolensk..." 593
"You prophecy, bitter one..." 595
"You are no longer among the living..." 595
"Until I collapse by the fence..." 597
"On the white threshold of paradise..." 599
"I brought disaster to my dear ones..." 599
"Exhausted by your long, fixed gaze..." 601
Slander 601

III. THE VOICE OF MEMORY
"The gates are thrown wide open..." 603

"The log bridge is blackened and twisted..."   605
"That August was like a yellow flame..."   607
Apparition   609
THREE VERSES
   1. "Yes, I loved them, those nightly gatherings..."   611
   2. "There was no temptation..."   611
   3. "Isn't it to escape from this damned easy life..." 611
Lullaby   613
"The tear-stained autumn, like a widow..."   613
"I will tend these rich, black beds..."   615
New Year's Ballad   617
"Oh, if only I'd known, when, dressed in white..."   617
To the Many   619

Notes to the Poems   621
Index of Proper Names   645

List of Illustrations

Akhmatova, 1910s or 1920s . . . . Frontispiece
Akhmatova, 1924. Photo by Moses Nappelbaum 20
Inna Erazmovna Gorenko 23
Victor and Anna Gorenko, ca. 1892 24
Anna Gorenko, ca. 1904 27
Anna Gorenko. Evpatoriya, 1905 28
Nikolay Gumilyov, ca. 1910 32
Anna Gorenko with brothers Andrey, Victor and sister
    Iya. In center, mother Inna. Kiev, 1909 33
Akhmatova by Modigliani 35
Anna Akhmatova, ca. 1910. 37
Alexander Blok, 1907 39
Vladimir Mayakovsky, 1918 55
Osip Mandelstam, Korney Chukovsky, Benedikt Livshits,
    Yury Annenkov. 1914 58
Akhmatova. Painting by Natan Altman, ca. 1914 59
Akhmatova and Olga Sudeikina, 1924 62
Gumilyov and Akhmatova with their son, Lev. 1915
    or 1916 71
Nikolay Nedobrovo 74
Vladimir Shileiko 79
Artur Lourié 81
Akhmatova. Drawing by Yury Annenkov, 1921 83
Akhmatova with Nikolay Punin, 1926 97
Georgy Chulkov, Maria Petrovykh, Akhmatova 100
Akhmatova and Mandelstam. 1934 101
Vladimir Garshin 103
Marina Tsvetaeva 105
Boris Pasternak 108
Akhmatova with "my neighbor, the Leningrad boy,
    Valya Smirnov," 1940 111
Olga Berggolts 111

Karl Marx Street, Tashkent 114
Akhmatova reciting her poems, 1946 122
Akhmatova and Pasternak, 1946 123
Delegation of Leningrad poets: Pavel Antokolsky,
    Olga Berggolts, Mikhail Dudin, Akhmatova, and
    Nikolay Tikhonov 123
Akhmatova, Nadezhda Mandelstam, Emma
    Gershtein. 1950s 127
Akhmatova, end of the 1950s. Collection of
    L. Ya. Ginzburg 127
Akhmatova's work table at Komarovo. 1960s 128
Joseph Brodsky and Anatoly Naiman at Komarovo 129
Vsevolod Knyazev 139
Olga Sudeikina, 1922 140
Akhmatova receives Etna-Taormina literary prize.
    Catania, Italy, 1964 147
At the conferral of the Honorary Doctorate of Oxford
    University 149
Salomea Halpern, Akhmatova, and Amanda Haight.
    London, 1965 149
Akhmatova. Photo by Nika Glen 153
10 March 1966: Anatoly Naiman, Evgeny Rein, Dmitry
    Bobyshev, Joseph Brodsky, Era Korobova 154
10 March 1966 155
Lev Gumilyov at grave of Akhmatova 156
Portfolio: TSARSKOYE SELO 199
Original title page, *Evening* 210
Portfolio: PETERSBURG 287
Original title page, *Rosary* 298
Akhmatova, ca. 1916 371
Original title page, *White Flock* 372
Akhmatova and Her Muse. Painting by
    Kuzma Petrov-Vodkin 493
Original title page, *Plantain* 494
Akhmatova, 1921. Gouache by Yury Annenkov 533
Akhmatova, 1920s 534
1920s. Photo by Moses Nappelbaum 535
Original title page, *Anno Domini MCMXXI* 536

Acknowledgements

I wish to acknowledge my indebtedness to the Princeton University Council of the Humanities for awarding me the Hodder Fellowship for the academic year 1981–82. The fellowship enabled me to complete the first draft of most of the translations.

I also wish to acknowledge a research grant of $5,000 from the Division of Sponsored Research, University of Central Florida, for the summer of 1983.

The list of individuals to whom I am deeply grateful is long indeed. Ann Wilkinson of Santa Barbara Community College provided me with literal translations of the first 300 poems and Natasha Gurfinkel of Princeton provided me with literal translations of 355 more poems, including *Poem Without a Hero*. Roberta Reeder supplied literals for the remaining poems.

Dmitry Bobyshev read the entire manuscript and made many emendations and suggestions. Others who contributed to the historical context and idiomatic accuracy of specific poems include Ellen Chances, Tamara Chapro, Sarah Hirschman, Wassily Leontief, Vladimir Ussachevsky and Eugenia Zhiglevich.

I am also grateful for the emotional support and encouragement I received through my years of work on this translation from Alice Crozier, Paula Deitz, Estelle and Wassily Leontief, Frederick Morgan, my children Stephanie Rosenfeld and David Rosenfeld and my friend Anne Richardson Goode (1933–1989).

Judith Hemschemeyer

I would like to thank the following, without whom *Mirrors and Masks* could not have been written: Amanda Haight for her insightful criticism and generous sharing of her knowledge, especially that which was based on her personal relationship with Anna Akhmatova; the Harvard Ukrainian Research Institute, which gave me access to Harvard University and Widener Library's vast resources on Akhmatova and her era; Valerie Kukharenko, who provided valuable information on Akhmatova's Ukrainian background; Sheila Rosalyn Deitchman and Karen Yilmaz for their moral support; Ed Hogan and Leora Zeitlin for their patient collaboration on a difficult but rewarding manuscript, and Zephyr Press for making this work possible; and Anatoly Naiman and Dmitry Bobyshev who shared with me their extensive knowledge of Russian culture as well as their personal recollections of Akhmatova.

Roberta Reeder
November 28, 1989

This edition could not have been completed without the assistance of many people. We would like in particular to express our appreciation to the following.

Isaiah Berlin provided editorial advice concerning certain poems, as well as kind permission to reprint his remarkable memoir of meetings with Akhmatova. Dmitry Bobyshev has been a willing consultant, and also read a draft of *Mirrors and Masks*. Anatoly Naiman provided helpful suggestions concerning the manner of presentation of certain texts. His "poet's introduction" to Akhmatova appears, in Russian and in English, in VOLUME II. We also acknowledge his kind permission to reprint an excerpt from *Rasskazy o Anne Akhmatovoi* (English title: *The End of the First Half of the Twentieth Century*).

We were all saddened by the untimely death of Amanda Haight, Akhmatova's eminent biographer. The many comments, corrections, and insights she has shared with us during the past three years were invaluable, particularly with regard to her careful critique of *Mirrors and Masks*.

Miriam Sagan, a former (and founding) editor of Zephyr Press, has, during the past six years, lent us all manner of support—editorial, emotional, and financial. We also acknowledge her early critical reading of the entire draft translation.

Dr. Arcadi Nebolsine, President of the American Society for the Preservation of Russian Monuments and Culture, helped us to identify and contact consultants on whose assistance we have relied. We thank Warwick J. Rodden for his early enthusiasm and considerable assistance in obtaining useful photographic and other materials.

We are especially grateful to the Bydale Foundation for financial assistance without which this edition could not have been published in its present form; and to an anonymous benefactor whose initial encouragement and financial support gave us the courage to undertake it. We also acknowledge major assistance from the National Endowment for the Arts Literature Program, the Massachusetts Council on the

Arts and Humanities, and the Sagan Foundation.

The valuable comments and suggestions of June Gross are too numerous to cite here. As for Susan Gubernat, a former editor of Zephyr Press: Had she not proposed our embrace of this project, we would have spent the past six years very differently!

We would also like to express our gratitude to the following people for their assistance: David Applefield, Sarah Bliumis, Susan Britt, Barbara Clancy, Sam Driver, Monique Fasel, Boris Filipoff, Mark Fischer, Philip Gerstein, George Gibson, Sheelagh Graham, Daphne Herron, Inna Johnson, Jim Kates, Irena C. Katz, Wassily and Estelle Leontief, Bruce McPherson, David McDuff, Richard McKane, Jennifer Moyer, Alan Myers, Wendy Rosslyn, Fernand Rude, Peter Dale Scott, Yuri Stark, Harvey Steiner, Nikita Struve, Andreas Teuber, Robert Tracy, Michael Van Walleghen, and John Witte.

Finally, we owe a singular debt of gratitude to our loved ones, who have borne with us, encouraged us, and abided the changes brought about in their lives for the sake of this landmark endeavor.

Ed Hogan and Leora Zeitlin
December 12, 1989

Translator's Preface

I

Anna Akhmatova (born Anna Andreevna Gorenko) was one of the four major lyric poets of Twentieth-century Russia. The other three, Boris Pasternak, Osip Mandelstam and Marina Tsvetaeva, all died before her; Tsvetaeva was a suicide and Mandelstam was hunted down and hounded to death by Stalin. Pasternak died in 1960 and Akhmatova, who died in 1966, had a career that spanned more than 60 years.

Enormously resilient, intensely obsinate, she refused to emigrate, though she had many opportunities to do so. To her, being a Russian meant living in Russia no matter what its government did to her and her loved ones, and being a lyric poet meant writing the truth. Obviously, these two principles were destined to collide and they did, tragically, but it was Akhmatova's strength to be able to suffer tragedy, survive and, somehow, write about it, over and over again.

By the time she was eleven years old, Anna Gorenko knew she would be a poet, even though the only poetry book in the house was a large volume of Nekrasov. By the age of 13, she was reading the poems of Verlaine, Baudelaire and other French poets. When she started writing poetry, in her teens, her father told her he did not want his name associated with that trade, so she obliged by changing her surname to Akhmatova, the Tatar name of a maternal ancestor.

In 1903, when she was only 14, the young poet Nikolay Gumilyov began to court her desperately and she finally married him in 1910. Gumilyov introduced her to the literary society of Petersburg, which met in the fifth-floor apartment, called "The Tower," of Vyacheslav Ivanov, the reigning Symbolist poet.

In 1912, partly because he was exceedingly strong-willed, a born leader himself, and partly because he resented Ivanov's critique of one of his poems, Gumilyov, along with Sergey Gorodetsky, formed the Poets' Guild, a group of 15 young poets. At one of the Guild's early meetings, Gumilyov proposed that the members refute Symbolism and call themselves Adamists or Acmeists. Not all of the Guild members agreed, so the Acmeists, finally, numbered six: Gumilyov, Gorodetsky, Mandelstam, Narbut, Zenkevich and Akhmatova.

What united them was a rejection of the vague, the vatic, the ethereal and otherworldly aspects of Symbolism. Gorodetsky, Gumilyov and Mandelstam all wrote manifestos defining Acmeism, proclaiming the need for a poetry of real experience and tangible objects. As Mandelstam said in his essay, "The Morning of Acmeism": "We do not wish to divert ourselves with a stroll in a 'forest of symbols,' because we have a more virgin, a denser forest—divine physiology, the infinite complexity of our dark organism." Since Mandelstam and Akhmatova were already writing and publishing poems based on the conviction that life on earth is a gift and the duty of the poet is to write about what Mandelstam called "the skin of the earth," it is probable, as Akhmatova conjectured later in her life, that the critical theory evolved from an already existing body of work.

Gumilyov's poems, mostly long, heroic-romantic narratives, were set in the wilds of Africa, where he had visited, or in imaginary lands. As he said in a letter to Akhmatova in 1913: "I never would have been able to guess that hearts can decay hopelessly from joy and fame, but then you would never have been able to concern yourself with research into the country of Gaul or understand, seeing the moon, that it is the diamond shield of the goddess of the warriors of Pallas."*

That astute comment defines the essence of Akhmatova. She was a poet of encounters; her strength was in observing her own actions and emotions, reporting as accurately as she could what she was feeling, what she had done and said, what had been done and said to her. Of the Russian novelists, her favorite was Dostoevsky.

Unlike Pasternak and Tsvetaeva, who could write lyrically with only one consciousness, that of the poet, in the poem, Akhmatova almost always needed a "you." Because she was a beautiful, passionate woman, this "you" was most often the man who longed for her, the man she longed for, or someone who had betrayed or rejected her.

Akhmatova's early books, *Evening* (1912) and *Rosary* (1914) were instantly and wildly successful in pre-revolutionary Russia, especially with women. People flocked to the bohemian cabaret, the Stray Dog,

---

*Quoted in *Anna Akhmatova, A Poetic Pilgrimage,* by Amanda Haight (Oxford University Press, 1976), p. 26.

to hear her recite her poetry, and her fans, who had memorized her books, used to "say the *Rosary*," one starting an Akhmatova poem and the others finishing it.

But Akhmatova's early lyrics had more than the refreshing frankness of her treatment of love to recommend them. Each one takes place in a real setting and contains real objects minutely observed, from the dilapidated well in the fields at her mother-in-law's estate to the high, ornamental balconies of the buildings of her beloved Petersburg. Like Colette, Akhmatova was passionately fond of nature and very good at using it in her art; nature observed almost always and with seeming unconscious ease carries emotional weight. Into these settings Akhmatova places her personae: sometimes the long-suffering peasant woman, sometimes the naive, betrayed peasant girl, but most often the Petersburg sophisticate hurting others and being hurt.

Akhmatova refused to glamorize love. In poem after poem, she insisted on looking her lover, her fellow-sufferer, straight in the eye. As she says in a poem of 1912:

. . .
Don't look like that, that angry frown.
I'm your beloved, I'm yours.
Neither shepherdess nor queen
And no longer a nun, I—

In this everyday gray dress,
On rundown heels. . .
But, as before, the burning embrace,
The same fear in enormous eyes.
. . .

(Zh. 92)

It is ironic that Akhmatova's poetry, which rejected the image, so familiar in so-called love poetry, of woman as either virgin on a pedestal or whore, should be criticized according to these same tired, clichéd misconceptions of womanhood. It is equally ironic that Akhmatova, a psychological pioneer in the writing of lyric poetry, should, from the Twenties on, have been considered hopelessly old-fashioned by Soviet critics.

But that is exactly what happened. In September 1921, in a lecture entitled "Two Russias," Korney Chukovsky described Akhmatova as "a nun who crosses herself as she kisses her beloved" (Haight, p. 69). Although he went on to say that he envisioned a Russia enriched both by Akhmatova's poetry of "pre-revolutionary culture" and Mayakovsky's poetry of the "present revolutionary age," other critics pounced on this phrase. Eikhenbaum, a Formalist critic, said that Akhmatova's heroine, "half harlot burning with passion, half mendicant nun able to pray to God for forgiveness, was paradoxical, or more correctly, contradictory" (Haight, 72). The Marxist critic Lelevich, using the same phrase, pronounced her poetry as unworthy of consideration in a revolutionary Communist society.

By the time of Chukovsky's speech in 1921, Gumilyov, from whom Akhmatova was already divorced, had been accused of taking part in a counter-revolutionary plot and executed. For Akhmatova, the Terror had begun.

In a country where the government could, and increasingly did, imprison and murder millions of its citizens, where everyone was in danger all the time, the ordinary bonds between people—love, friendship, kinship, trust, shared cultural assumptions and interests—broke down and dissolved and the only shared emotion was fear. In one of her early lyrics, Akhmatova had compared love to a hangman. Now the government was the hangman and the "you" she addressed her poems to might at any moment be liquidated or had perhaps already perished.

Nadezhda Mandelstam, in her two-volume memoir, *Hope Against Hope* and *Hope Abandoned* (Athenaeum, 1970 amd 1974), details this tragic period from 1921 to the death of Stalin in 1953. She said that at one time in the Thirties, she was reduced to trusting only two people on earth, her husband and Akhmatova.

From 1925 until 1940, there was an unofficial ban on the publication of Akhmatova's poetry. Akhmatova concentrated on scholarship, immersing herself in her critical studies of Pushkin. But in 1935, following the arrest of Nikolay Punin, the man she was living with, and Lev Gumilyov, her son, she began to compose the 15-part poetry and prose cycle *Requiem*. Not daring to write it down, she recited various parts to friends, including Lidiya Chukovskaya (Korney Chukovsky's daughter), who memorized and reassembled them. *Requiem*, a tribute to the ordeal of the victims of the Terror and the women who waited in the prison lines hoping to get word of them, is based on her own experience in Leningrad, where Lev was imprisoned for 17 months. In this great cycle, the "you" becomes all Russians imprisoned and tortured by their own government. *Requiem* was finally published in the

Soviet Union in April 1987, in the journal *Novy mir* and has since been included in a book of her poems, *Anna Akhmatova, Ya—golos vash. . . (Anna Akhmatova, I—am your voice. . .*; Moscow, 1989).

Akhmatova wrote other, publishable, poems during the war, including "Courage," which was recited everywhere in Russia. She became a symbol of stoic endurance and, during the siege of Leningrad, was called on by the government to give a radio speech to the heroic women of that city. Then, in November 1941, she was evacuated to Moscow and from there to the Central Asian city of Tashkent.

While in Tashkent she wrote a play about a nightmare-like show trial; it was performed once, then burnt, as were some poems she feared might be used against her son, whose whereabouts she didn't know. She also finished the first two parts of *Poem Without a Hero*, a long poem set at a masked ball in 1913 Petersburg on the eve of World War I. *Poem Without a Hero* obsessed her for 22 years. She wrote poems to it begging it to stop tormenting her, she changed it again and again, adding sections, eliminating others, deliberately using ellipses the way Pushkin, whose works were also censored, had had to do. One thing is constant, however, the tone of guilt and the premonition of the disasters that befell Petersburg and Akhmatova's whole generation.

In 1945, Akhmatova returned to Leningrad from Tashkent, giving a reading at the Moscow Polytechnic Museum on her way. By now, thanks to her wartime poems as well as her early books, she was the most popular poet in Russia and was applauded so enthusiastically that it frightened her. She knew that to draw attention to herself in any way was dangerous. Her fears were borne out.

In 1946, as a result of this tumultuous reception and because of a visit paid to her by Isaiah Berlin, she was expelled from the Union of Soviet Writers and viciously denounced by Andrey Zhdanov, who accused her of poisoning the minds of Soviet youth. Zhdanov, Stalin's cultural watchdog, used the criticism of the Twenties against Akhmatova, calling her "half nun, half harlot." However, Akhmatova was accustomed to disaster and she bore Zhdanov's scurrilous attack with equanimity.

Then, in 1949, Lev Gumilyov was arrested again. Akhmatova tried to help him by writing a cycle of poems praising Stalin and the regime. Lev was finally released in 1956 and the last decade of Akhmatova's life, on the surface at least, became somewhat easier. She was given the use of a tiny summer house and some translating work and allowed to travel abroad twice to receive literary awards. And she wrote; right up to the end of her life she was writing fresh, powerful poems. She had, in spite of the repressions, the deaths and the betrayals, found a "you" again. Often now, the "you" was dead and the encounter was a non-meeting instead of a meeting, but the power of Akhmatova's memory for physical details and gestures never failed her. One of her last dated poems, February 1965, written when she was 75, is a tender poem about innocent love:

> *So we lowered our eyes,*
> *Tossing the flowers on the bed,*
> *We didn't know until the end,*
> *What to call one another.*
> *We didn't dare until the end*
> *To utter first names,*
> *As if, nearing the goal, we slowed our steps*
> *On the enchanted way.*
>
> *(Zh. 598)*

II

In 1973 I read a few of Akhmatova's poems in translation in the *American Poetry Review* and was so struck by one of them that I decided to learn Russian in order to read them all. Here is the poem, from *White Flock*, Akhmatova's third book:

> *The sky's dark blue lacquer has dimmed,*
> *And louder the song of the ocarina.*
> *It's only a little pipe of clay,*
> *There's no reason for it to complain.*
> *Who told it all my sins,*
> *And why is it absolving me?. . .*
> *Or is this a voice repeating*
> *Your latest poems to me?*
>
> *(Zh. 119)*

Three years later, when I could read the Russian and compare the existing, "selected Akhmatova" translations with the originals, I became convinced that Akhmatova's poems should be translated in their entirety, and by a woman poet, and that I was that person. Using literals provided by Ann Wilkinson for the first 300 poems and by Natasha Gurfinkel and Roberta Reeder for the rest, I translated the poems in the order established by the Formalist critic Victor Zhirmunsky in the Biblioteka Poeta edition of Akhmatova's works, published in Leningrad in 1976.

Zhirmunsky reproduced Akhmatova's five early, uncensored books—*Evening* (1912), *Rosary* (1914), *White Flock* (1917), *Plantain* (1921) and *Anno Domini MCMXXI* (1922)—in the order in which they were published. Just as important, he retained the poet's ordering of the poems within each volume; this allows us to participate in Akhmatova's life and loves as she orchestrated them.

She announces her main subject in the first poem of her first volume: it is titled "Love." The third poem, in which she (at 22!) compares her future fame to Pushkin's, introduces an important leitmotif—her concern for her place among the Russian poets. Another poem in *Evening* is addressed to the Muse—Akhmatova, whose poetic gift came early and very strongly, seemed to suffer intensely when she couldn't write—and the last poem, #56, is a childhood memory; but the rest of the poems in this first book are addressed to the beloved. The beloved is usually absent, because he has tired of her or betrayed her (as in the case of the peasant girl) and departed. Sometimes, as in poem #7, "Under her dark veil she wrung her hands...," the lovers have quarreled. This poem presents the quarrel not as a wistful narrative after the fact but as a dramatic vignette complete with violent physical gestures, uncontrollable facial expressions and dialogue that is both vicious and pathetic, and is a leap forward in style, subject matter and point of view. Love poetry, or rather the poetry of emotional encounters, which Akhmatova called "meetings," would never be the same. Poem after poem in *Evening* shows us two people bound together, grappling with their own and the beloved's emotions, struggling to get free, and once free, bewildered and empty.

Rosary, too, contains mostly encounter poems, and often the protagonist is ill (as Akhmatova was) with tuberculosis and (as Akhmatova also was) a Russian Orthodox Christian. Probably the poems in *Rosary* fueled Chukovsky's characterization of Akhmatova as "a nun who crosses herself as she kisses her beloved," though Akhmatova, of course, never claimed to be a nun, only a sinner longing for peace. The theme of social criticism is introduced in *Rosary*; indeed, poems 62, 76, 77 and 79 present the cast of characters and the suicide that form the story line of *Poem Without a Hero*, that indictment of the frivolous, cynical pre-World War I Petersburg society to which Akhmatova belonged.

Poem 83, which shows us a bored woman wandering the fields of an estate under the condemning eyes of the "quiet, sunburnt peasant women" indicates Akhmatova's uneasiness with the status quo.

Akhmatova's third book, *White Flock*, opens up both thematically and geographically. Although love poems predominate, the volume, written from 1912 to 1917, includes war poems—premonitory poems about World War I, poems confessing the betrayal of the soldier by the woman back home, anguished poems about the death of young men—poems celebrating Kiev, Novgorod and other cities besides her beloved Petersburg, poems about the guilt she felt as an absentee mother and, for the first time, a number of poems recognizing the spiritual isolation of the artist. By now Akhmatova has acknowledged that the role of poet is the major one in her life. As she says in poem 125:

. . .
Let him not desire my eyes,
Prophetic and fixed.
He will get a whole lifetime of poems,
The prayer of my arrogant lips.

Plantain, the shortest of Akhmatova's books, appeared in 1917, the year of the Revolution, and contains poems that refer directly to that event as well as poems that refer to it indirectly by admonishing her friends who had emigrated. The last poem in *Plantain*, written in autumn 1917, is the first of her poems to be censored. Zhirmunsky could present only 12 of its original 20 lines, but the complete poem appeared in Volume 1 of the Struve-Filipoff edition of Akhmatova's *Works*. This three-volume edition, published in Russian in Munich and Paris, does not present Akhmatova's poems as the author arranged them but contains nearly all of her poems as well as her prose writings—essays on Modigliani, Mandelstam, her own life, her critical writings, letters— and critical articles about her work.

The theme of remorse enters Akhmatova's fifth book, *Anno Domini MCMXXI*, in the many poems written to her estranged first husband, Nikolay Gumilyov, who was already dead by the end of August 1921. For the first time, there is a note of fear. A poem written a few days after Gumilyov was executed begins:

Terror, fingering things in the dark,
Leads the moonbeam to an ax.

There is an elegiac poem to Alexander Blok, who died the same month as Gumilyov, an elegiac poem describing the saints departing from the church, literally abandoning their icon frames, and a host of other poems reflecting the general confusion and suffering of the early Twenties.

There is a love story as well. From 1918 to 1921, Akhmatova was married to Vladimir Shileiko, an Assyriologist, and the story of her obsessive love-hate relationship with this man is told in a series of bitter, brilliant poems.

Akhmatova's poetry was subjected to increasing critical attack after 1924, when Stalin came to power, and it wasn't until 1940 that she prepared another book for print. This was *Reed*, poems written from 1924 to 1940; but *Reed* was never published as a separate volume. Some of the *Reed* poems were included in a 1940 collection called *From Six Books*, some were included in a 1961 collection called *Poems 1909–1960* and most, but not all of them, were included in the less heavily censored collection called *The Flight of Time* (1965). Zhirmunsky printed them according to the text of *The Flight of Time* and added five poems that were in a manuscript version, but not the final text of the book.

In the case of *Requiem*, only four of its 15 sections appeared in the Biblioteka Poeta edition. The full text of this poem appeared in Munich in 1963 and I have used the Struve-Filipoff text, from Volume I of *Works* and placed it in *Reed*, where it belongs both chronologically and emotionally.

In Poem IV of *Requiem*, Akhmatova looks back at herself as the heroine of her early books and comments, too harshly I think:

You should have been shown, you mocker,
Minion of all your friends,
Gay little sinner of Tsarskoye Selo,
What would happen in your life—
How three-hundredth in line, with a parcel,
You would stand by the Kresty prison,
Your tempestuous tears
Burning through the New Year's ice.
Over there the prison poplar bends,
And there's no sound—and over there how many
Innocent lives are ending now...

Yet that "gay little sinner" had the tenacity to stay in Russia and the capacity to move from her private anguish to the ubiquitous suffering of her nation in the Thirties.

Reed also contains the poem "Voronezh," which Akhmatova wrote after a visit to the exiled Osip Mandelstam and his wife, a generous poem to Mayakovsky, a joyous poem to Pasternak written in Pasternak's swooping, ebullient style, poems to Gumilyov, who was always present in her life even after his death, a trilogy to Nikolay Punin, the man from whom she was trying to part, poems about madness, about the burden and the poetic power of the artist and two poems, "Dante" and "Cleopatra," in which the plight of these historical figures, Dante's exile and Cleopatra's situation, her "children in chains," resembles the fate of Mandelstam and Akhmatova herself. This technique, using the past to speak about the politically dangerous present, is a standard one in Russian literature and Akhmatova used it in other poems of the Thirties, notably in the poem "Imitation from the Armenian," in which Stalin is cast as an Oriental potentate, a "Padishah" and Akhmatova appears in his dreams as an old black ewe whose lamb has been devoured.

Like *Reed, Seventh Book* (1936–1964) was never published as a separate book. In 1946, a large collection of Akhmatova's poems (*Poems 1909–1945*) was printed and, because she was expelled from the Union of Soviet Writers that September, destroyed. Some of the poems appeared 12 years later, in the severely censored *Poems* (Moscow, 1958) and some in a likewise severely censored edition, *Poems 1909–1960* (Moscow, 1961). It wasn't until the publication of *The Flight of Time* (Moscow-Leningrad, 1965) that the bulk of the poems, 146 in all, were published, under the heading *Seventh Book*. In the Biblioteka Poeta edition, Zhirmunsky follows the text of *The Flight of Time,* with the addition of eight more poems from Akhmatova's manuscript copy. Because Zhirmunsky worked closely with Akhmatova during her last years at Komarovo, he was able, he says in his notes, "to establish her last book in the order she would have liked and with the title, *Seventh Book,* chosen by herself."

Akhmatova's description of her struggle to publish *Seventh Book* appears in Part Two of *Poem Without a Hero,* in stanza 9, one of the four stanzas censored in the Biblioteka Poeta edition:

And with me is my Seventh,
Half dead and mute,
Its mouth is numb and open,
Like the mouth of a tragic mask,

But it is daubed with black paint
And stuffed with dry earth.

The English-speaking reader would have trouble finding any objectionable poems in *Seventh Book*. The main problem for us is that because *Seventh Book* consists of more than 150 poems written over 28 years, it does not have the organic unity of her other books. It begins with a marvelous section of craft poems that includes tributes to Pushkin, Mandelstam and, in a poem called "Teacher," to Annensky. Next are poems bemoaning the fate of occupied Paris and London under bombardment, then a 17-poem segment of civic poems, called "The Wind of War," written in Leningrad and in Tashkent, where she was from 1941 to 1944.

"The Moon at Zenith" follows, a section of poems about Tashkent; then, a poem about the inception of *Poem Without a Hero,* which she had already started to compose; two poems about her brush with death (from typhus); eight more poems about Tashkent, including the famous "Those lynx eyes of yours, Asia...."; twelve quatrains on diverse subjects from as early as 1910 and as late as 1962; mourning poems from 1921; poems celebrating her joyous return to Moscow after the war and elegies for the little town of Tsarskoye Selo, where she grew up, and for her long-suffering, beloved Leningrad.

Starting with poem 415 there are three cycles, "Cinque," "Sweetbrier in Bloom" and "Midnight Verses" that were inspired by the unexpected visit of Isaiah Berlin in autumn 1945. She thought—and she was probably right—that his visit had something to do with her dismissal from the Union of Soviet Writers in 1946. She even thought, in her loneliness and isolation in postwar Leningrad, that the visit had something to do with the onset of the Cold War. One of her poems, "The Burnt Notebook," refers to poems that she had to burn in what proved to be a futile attempt to keep her son from being arrested in 1949.

There are poems mourning Vladimir Garshin, who had been a close friend of hers from 1938 to 1941, Nikolay Punin, who died in a prison camp in 1953, Mikhail Zoshchenko, the satirist who had also been expelled from the Union of Soviet Writers in 1946, Alexander Blok, the Symbolist poet she most admired and Valeriya Sreznevskaya, her lifelong friend. A seven-poem sequence written in the Sixties refers to meetings and "nonmeetings" with friends and lovers. After World War II, when Akhmatova returned to Leningrad, nonmeetings occurred more often than meetings in her life and her poetry because of the absence of the friends who had emigrated and the detention and death of those who had remained in Russia.

Amidst all these elegies there are poems like the two written when Pasternak died in 1960 and others — "The Death of Sophocles" and "Alexander at Thebes" for example—that emphasize the importance and dignity of the artist and some, like "Native Land," that reaffirm Akhmatova's belief in the strength of the Russian people. The last poem in *Seventh Book* was written when Akhmatova was 74, in Italy for the first time since her youth. She had been invited to receive an Italian literary prize, Etna-Taormina, and she wrote, referring to Komarovo, the place in Finnish Russia where she had been given the use of dacha:

> *This land, although not my native land,*
> *Will be remembered forever,*
> *And the sea's lightly iced,*
> *Unsalty water.*
>
> *The sand on the bottom is whiter than chalk,*
> *The air is heady, like wine,*
> *And the rosy body of the pines*
> *Is naked in the sunset hour,*
>
> *And the sunset itself on such waves of ether*
> *That I just can't comprehend*
> *Whether it is the end of the day, the end of the world,*
> *Or the mystery of mysteries in me again.*

Like most lyric poets, Akhmatova wrote some long poems. They are collected in this edition in the section of Epic and Dramatic Fragments and Long Poems. They include "Epic Motifs" (1913–1916), a three-part blank-verse poem about Akhmatova's discovery of her poetic gift; fragments of historical poems; *Prologue,* a reconstructed fragment, in verse, of the second act of a play that she wrote, produced, acted in and then destroyed for political reasons during the war years; *At the Edge of the Sea* (1914), a three-part blank-verse poem about the awakening of love in a young girl and her relationship with an invalid sister; *The Way of All the Earth,* a rhymed, six-part poem that Akhmatova described as "a requiem for oneself," and the superb *Northern Elegies,* six poems and a fragment in which Akhmatova mingled personal, historical and political motifs.

Poem Without a Hero, the huge triptych that Akhmatova wrote and rewrote from 1940 to 1962, was described by Zhirmunsky as "the fulfillment of the Symbolists' dream—what they had preached in theory, but had never been able to realize in their creative work." (Haight, 185) Apparently, it sprang from the same impulse as *The Way of All the Earth* but it refused to stop growing.

Poem Without a Hero is a tour de force that uses personal memory to describe and indict a whole generation on the brink of 1914, the year that marked the beginning of "the real—not the calendar—Twentieth Century." Because *Poem Without a Hero* contains so many allusions to Russian poets living (in 1913) and dead and to Akhmatova's contemporaries, the actresses, composers and artists who frequented the Stray Dog cabaret, full appreciation of it—in spite of the extensive annotation—depends upon familiarity with Russian literature and a rather particularized knowledge of the Petersburg cultural milieu in 1913. Akhmatova recognized this fact and never apologized for it; indeed, she introduced, in Part Two, a grumbling editor who is baffled by the "story line" of Part One.

Part Two also contains whole stanzas of ellipses, those well-known (to Russian writers and readers) dots that indicate real or implied omissions. The Struve-Filipoff text of *Poem Without a Hero* supplies these missing stanzas, and twenty additional lines in Part Three that refer to "the camps" come from Lidiya Chukovskaya's *Zapiski ob Anne Akhmatovoi, Memoirs About Anna Akhmatova* (Paris: YMCA Press, 1980). This book, which I read in the French translation, *Entretiens avec Anna Akhmatova,** was an extremely valuable source, not only for poems hitherto unobtainable, but also, since Chukovskaya saw Akhmatova frequently from 1938 to 1941 and from 1952 to 1962, for information about the daily struggles of the poet to live with dignity under a regime that was determined to humiliate and discredit her.

In addition to the Akhmatova canon of poems that she published or intended to publish, there are more than 200 poems and fragments not included in any of the books or in any of the tables of contents she projected in the Forties, Fifties and Sixties. Most of these poems and fragments were discovered by Zhirmunsky in the Lenin Library, the Saltikov-Shchedrin Manuscript Library, the central Government Archives of Literature and Art and in the possession of Akhmatova's

---

* Volume 1, 1938–1941 of *Conversations with Akhmatova,* translated by Barry Rubin, is to be published in 1990 by Farrar, Straus & Giroux.

friends and literary acquaintances. Zhirmunsky included them in a separate, chronological section of the Biblioteka Poeta edition.

I have grouped them in five chronological sections: 1904–1917, 1919–1941, 1941–May 1945, September 1945–1956 and 1957–1965. In order to collect all of Akhmatova's poems—poems that have appeared in the Soviet Union in various journals since the compilation of the Biblioteka Poeta edition, poems discovered in archival material (letters, memoirs, etc.) and some poems that have until this year (1989) appeared in print only outside the Soviet Union—we used three recently published books. These are Volume III of *Anna Akhmatova, Sochineniya (Anna Akhmatova, Works*; Paris: YMCA Press, 1983), edited by Nikita Struve; *Anna Akhmatova, Sochineniya (Anna Akhmatova, Works*; Moscow: Khudozhestvennaya literatura, 1987), edited by V.A. Chernykh and *Anna Akhmatova, Ya—golos vash... (Anna Akhmatova, I—Am Your Voice...*; Moscow: Knizhnaya palata, 1989), also edited by V.A. Chernykh. The source for each poem in these chronological sections is indicated.

These uncollected poems are by no means weak or inferior; they are often more daring doubles of poems included or projected for inclusion in her books or, especially in the Struve volume, poems expressing criticism of the regime.

They range in date of composition from 1904 to 1965. Some of the earliest are frankly sensual—the young Akhmatova delighting in her sexual attractiveness. Two of them imply a hitherto unknown love affair with Sergey Sudeikin, the husband of Olga Glebova-Sudeikina, Akhmatova's "double" in *Poem Without a Hero*. Other poems of the 1910's are unhappy love lyrics, poems of renunciation and personal and collective guilt. One poem is atypical; it describes a domestic crisis, a sick child, from the point of view of another child and was probably related to the death of Akhmatova's sister Irina at the age of four from tuberculosis. Anna was five at the time. According to Haight (6), "Her death was kept a secret—she had been taken away to stay with an aunt—but her sister guessed what had happened in that strange unformulated way of children and said later that because of this a shadow lay across the whole of her childhood."

Some of the poems of the Twenties, Thirties and Forties are outspoken protests against the regimes of Lenin and Stalin. A poem of stark fear, "The Glass Doorbell" (S-F. 109, III, 72), indicates the hysteria people felt during the mass purges and deportations:

The glass doorbell
Rings urgently.
Is today really the date?
Stop at the door,
Wait a little longer,
Don't touch me,
             For God's sake!

There is a poem that lists the specific offenses committed by the re-
gime against Akhmatova—the imprisonment of her son, the torturing
of her friends, the fact that she was kept under surveillance by the secret
police. She even protests that she was evacuated to Tashkent during the
siege of Leningrad:

And taking me to the edge of the country,
For some reason they left me there.
I would rather, as one of the city's "crazies,"
Be wandering through the dying squares.

                    (S-F. 110, III, 72–73)

But Akhmatova does more than sing her own sorrows in these
poems of protest. She manages to convey that her sorrows were typi-
cal. Her special anguish was that for her the Terror had begun in 1921,
when Gumilyov was shot, and as a poet she was committed to telling
and writing the truth. She didn't know how to lie. Censorship seemed
to produce an almost physical sensation of suffocation in her, as
described in the poem called "The North" (S-F. 180, III, 105).

There is also a long, five-part poem in blank verse, *Grand Confession*
(S-F. 226, III, 503–506). Thematically, it belongs with the *Northern Ele-*
gies; it is less a confession than an elegy for Gumilyov and a puzzled at-
tempt to ascertain what became of their first, tender love.

One of the poems, written in 1910 and first published in the Soviet
Union in 1982, begins

In my room lives a beautiful
Slow black snake,
It is like me, just as lazy,
Just as cold,
   . . .
                    (S-F. 227, III, 506–507)

then goes on to describe an intense, physical, but troubled love. It seems
like a companion to the opening poem in Akhmatova's first book, *Eve-*

ning. That poem, written in 1911 and entitled "Love," also starts with a serpent:

Now, like a little snake, it curls into a ball,
Bewitching your heart,
Then for days it will coo like a dove
On the little white windowsill.

Or it will flash as bright frost,
Drowse like a gillyflower...
But surely and stealthily it will lead you away
From joy and from tranquillity.

It knows how to sob so sweetly
In the prayer of a yearning violin,
And how fearful to divine it
In a still unfamiliar smile.

Akhmatova, the poet of encounters, the diagnostician of love. If, in her poetic careeer of 61 years she had written of no other subject, she would still be immortal.

But the circumstances of her birth, the collision of time and geography struck another kind of poetry from her genius—the poetry of witness—and it is this poetry that cannot be ignored. Here, in the opening section of *Requiem*, is how she conceived of her mission:

INSTEAD OF A PREFACE

In the terrible years of the Yezhov terror, I spent seventeen months in the prison lines of Leningrad. Once, someone "recognized" me. Then a woman with bluish lips standing behind me, who, of course, had never heard me called by name before, woke up from the stupor to which everyone had succumbed and whispered in my ear (everyone spoke in whispers there):

"Can you describe this?"

And I answered: "Yes, I can."

Then something that looked like a smile passed over what had once been her face.

III

The act of translating, as anyone who has tried it will attest, entails sacrifices. For the music and the delicious web of connotations of the original one substitutes, if one is lucky and patient, a verbal equivalent that conveys the tone and the meaning and some kind of music of its own. The music of a translation is not the original music, of course. My suggestion is that the English-speaking reader find a Russian friend to read aloud (or recite, as many Russians will be able to do) some of the poems and thus gain some idea of the rich texture of sounds and the driving rhythms that Akhmatova achieves.

My first goal was to understand the poem; only then, I felt, could I present the poem to others. This took time—more than ten years—and at least several versions of each poem.

Because the Russian language has six cases, it is extremely rich in full rhymes, while English is extremely poor. To illustrate: how many words in English rhyme with father? The word father in Russian is, depending on its case, pronounced *ot-yets, ot-sa, ot-su, ot-se* or *ot-som*. The plural endings present another set of rhyming possibilities. Thus in Russian almost any noun can be made to rhyme with any other noun. Adjectives, too are declined—even the numbers—and verbs are conjugated; this enriches the chance for rhyming as well. Word order in the English sentence is fairly rigid, but the case endings in Russian allow for all sorts of flexibility, hence still more rhyming possibilities.

A typical lyric of Akhmatova's was 12 or 16 lines, three or four stanzas, rhymed a-b-a-b, c-d-c-d, etc. To reproduce this as full rhyme in English, one would have to skew the sense of the poem by reaching for a rhyming word at the expense of the meaning. And the result would be a trite-sounding series of jingles whose rhymes are boringly anticipated by the reader, a sort of doggerel.

I chose instead to utilize the occasional full rhyme that occurred, but to rely mainly on slant rhyme, internal rhyme, assonance and alliteration to construct the poem in English. What I found myself producing as the work went on was often an x-a-y-a rhyme scheme, one that satisfies but doesn't cloy the ear.

As for rhythm—the Russian language has a wealth of magnificent polysyllabic words and since each word gets only one accent, the good poet can command a healthy variation of metrical feet in the line. Akhmatova was a master of prosody. She used an exceptionally high number of amphibrachs—an unaccented syllable, an accented syllable, then another unaccented syllable—with the effect of suggesting rising and falling, tension and release. It was, of course, impossible to adhere to Akhmatova's exact meters and say in English what has to be said. But I repeated the poem over and over to myself in Russian to get the rhythm. Then, using the literal translation as a base, I would invite felicitous English words to alight in some kind of regular line.

I was very careful to retain Akhmatova's verbs and Akhmatova's images and I found, I think, an equivalent for her diction, which is direct but not slangy, precise but never precious. I did not add lines of explication in the body of the poem; end notes take care of that. I also tried, as far as possible, to keep Akhmatova's line breaks and the look of the poem on the page.

Here is a sonnet Akhmatova wrote in 1962, remembering the visit Isaiah Berlin paid to her. Her sonnet rhymes a-b-a-b, c-d-c-d, e-e-f, g-g-f and has lines of 10 and 9 syllables. My translation rhymes a-b-b-a, c-d-d-c, b-e-e, f-g-g. Some of my rhymes are direct, some are slant rhymes.

> I abandoned your shores, Empress,
> against my will.
> —*Aeneid*, Book 6

Don't be afraid—I can still portray
What we resemble now.
You are a ghost—or a man passing through,
And for some reason I cherish your shade.

For awhile you were my Aeneas—
It was then I escaped by fire.
We know how to keep quiet about one another.
And you forgot my cursed house.

You forgot those hands stretched out to you
In horror and torment, through flame,
And the report of blasted dreams.

You don't know for what you were forgiven...
Rome was created, flocks of flotillas sail on the sea,
And adulation sings the praises of victory.

(Zh.431)

Although I aimed for a basic decasyllabic line, I also wanted to have the meaning of each line in English match its Russian counterpart. Consequently, line 2 has only 6 syllables and there are other lines of 13 or 14 syllables. Still, it is a recognizable sonnet and it says, as gracefully as I found possible, what Akhmatova's sonnet says.

Each poem presented a new puzzle; many defied the rough formula I had devised of rhyming the second and fourth line of Akhmatova's quatrain. In this poem, for example, the end rhymes are a-b-a-b, c-d-c-d, e-f-e-f in Russian.

THE LAST ONE

I delighted in deliriums,
In singing about tombs.
I distributed misfortunes
Beyond anyone's strength.
The curtain not raised,
The circle dance of shades—
Because of that, all my loved ones
Were taken away.
All this is disclosed
In the depths of the roses.
But I am not allowed to forget
The taste of the tears of yesterday.

                    (Zh. 462)

What I have managed to devise and still stay faithful to the meaning and the line breaks is the consonance of "deliriums" and "tombs," the assonance of "deliriums" and "misfortunes," the alliteration of "delighted," "deliriums" and "distributed," the rhyming of "disclosed" and "rose" and the five long *a* sounds that, because they are so strong in English, provide the poem's dominant musical chord: "raised," "shades," "away," "taste," and "yesterday."

Because of the high achievement of Akhmatova's poetry, I never begrudged the hours and years of labor it took to solve these puzzles, these poems, one after the other. What emerges from my efforts are, I hope, translations that will give the reader of English some idea of the intensity with which Akhmatova lived and wrote. As time elapsed, I learned about her not only through her poems, but through the writings of her contemporaries, and the more I learned, the more I admired her courage, her moral integrity, her wit and, yes, her sense of humor under the direst of circumstances. Nadezhda Mandelstam has this to say about Akhmatova's character in *Hope Abandoned*:

> One way or another I expect I shall now live out my life to the end, spurred on by the memory of Akhmatova's Russian powers of endurance; it was her boast to have so exasperated the accusers who had denounced her and her poetry that they all died before her of heart attacks.

Judith Hemschemeyer
August 7, 1989
Highland Park, N.J.

Mirrors and Masks:
The Life and Poetic Works
of Anna Akhmatova

—————— Roberta Reeder ——————

To Ivan
They said he would be a musician

A poet's life can be reflected in many mirrors. The life of Anna
Akhmatova has been reflected in autobiographical notes, recorded
conversations and interviews, letters and diaries of contemporaries,
and criticism of her works.

Yet Akhmatova remains, in many ways, a mystery. She was discreet
about the personal events in her life, and restrained in expression. Her
poems often mask more than they reveal. Though often inspired by
real events or emotions, they have a life and personality of their own.
She sometimes assumed the voice of a character out of empathy, to
convey what that figure might feel under particular personal or histor-
ical conditions. The poems do not necessarily represent her directly.
Indeed, Akhmatova warned against scrutinizing her lyrics for insight
into her thoughts and feelings. Someone once suggested to her that the
prose author's personality is reflected in everything she or he writes.
Not so with poetry, Akhmatova replied. "Lyric verse is the best armor,
the best cover. You don't give yourself away."[1]

Still, by comparing the images reflected in the many mirrors, a pic-
ture emerges of a great poet who practiced her art under extraordinar-
ily difficult conditions, and who won the respect and admiration of
the world. Akhmatova looked back at her difficult life not with regret,
but with gratitude that she had lived through one of the most complex
epochs in the history of her country, and that she was able to capture
the events in the rhythms and imagery of her poetry:

> I never stopped writing poems. In them is my link with time, with the
> new life of my people. When I wrote them, I believed in the resound-
> ing rhythms reflected in the heroic history of my country. I am happy
> that I lived in these years and saw events which cannot be equalled.[2]

I. Early Years: 1889–1912

Akhmatova was born in a time of chaos and ferment, when the wings of the Angel of Death hovered over the land. The revolution was slow in coming, but every decade saw increasingly violent and radical political solutions. The end of the Romanov dynasty was drawing near. It was the twilight of Imperial Russia,[3] as Nicholas II, a weak and indecisive ruler, made frantic efforts to preserve the foundations of a crumbling monarchy.

She was born Anna Gorenko on 23 June 1889 (11 June old style)[4] in Bolshoy Fontan on the Black Sea, near Odessa, in the Ukraine. Her father was Ukrainian[5] and her mother of Novgorod origin. In her autobiographical notes, she juxtaposes the date with other notable contemporary events: "I was born the same year as Charlie Chaplin and Tolstoy's *Kreutzer Sonata,* the Eiffel Tower and, I believe, T.S. Eliot. That summer Paris celebrated 100 years since the fall of the Bastille. On the night of my birth the famous St. John's Eve was celebrated—23 June (Midsummer's Night)."[6]

Akhmatova's family moved to Pavlovsk, a suburb of St. Petersburg, when she was eleven months old, and then to the town of Tsarskoye Selo, the royal family's summer residence. In the midst of elegant pavilions, allées of tall trees, and beautiful parks with replicas of ancient statues—which gave the young Akhmatova contact with antiquity—stood the baroque Catherine's Palace. Part of it had been turned into a lyceum that Pushkin had attended as a boy, and Akhmatova felt his presence while growing up.

Of all the houses she lived in—and she lived in many—Akhmatova said she remembered best the one where she spent most of her childhood and early adolescence. "My childhood is as unique and grand as the childhood of all children in the world. My first memories are those of Tsarskoye Selo—the green grandeur of the parks, the groves where nanny took me, the hippodrome where small, mottled ponies jumped, and the old train station."[7] Her room was Spartan—an iron bed, a desk to prepare her lessons, a stand for her books, and a candle in a brass candlestick (there was no electricity). Her close friend from childhood, Valeriya Sreznevskaya, describes what Akhmatova's life was like at this time:

> In Tsarskoye Selo she did everything a well brought-up young lady was supposed to do at the time. She knew how to fold her hands,

Inna Erazmovna Gorenko, mother of Akhmatova

Victor and Anna Gorenko, ca. 1892

curtsy, respond politely and briefly to an old lady's question in French, and prepare for Holy Week in the school chapel. Once in a while her father brought her (dressed in her lycée uniform) to the opera at the Mariinsky Theatre. She visited the Hermitage, the great art collection in the Museum of Alexander III. She attended concerts in the spring and autumn at the hall in the Pavlovsk train station.[8]

Akhmatova learned to read from the alphabet book of Lev Tolstoy and at five she began to speak French. As a child she heard the sounds of the Russian poet Nikolay Nekrasov, whose poetry was full of sympathy for the plight of the lower classes. Her mother, who had been active in politics when she was young, recited his poems to her.[9] Akhmatova was also given his work to read on holidays; a large volume of Nekrasov was virtually the only book the family owned.[10] Many of Akhmatova's poems reflect both the beauty of the Russian countryside and the expression of political consciousness Nekrasov so memorably conveyed.[11] While the aesthetic circles in which Akhmatova later moved rejected Nekrasov's verse as too politically *engagé,* it presented her early on with examples of strong female personae—Russian women of all classes who were oppressed, and who displayed a fortitude that Akhmatova herself later exhibited in both her life and work.

Akhmatova was, as the Russian poet Marina Tsvetaeva writes in a poem dedicated to her, "Anna of *all* the Russias."[12] The epithet was appropriate: every summer the family spent several months in the south, at Streletsky Bay on the Black Sea coast, near an ancient monastery at Khersones. There, as Akhmatova later wrote, she "became friends with the sea."[13] Korney Chukovsky, a critic and friend of Akhmatova's, observes her southern side—that trace of the wild child behind the austere pose of the northern woman:

> Critics who stress that Akhmatova had many features of someone brought up in Northern Russian culture have forgotten she was born by the Black Sea, and in her youth was a wild southern child. For days at a time she would find herself...on the shores of Khersones, barefoot, merry, tanned by the sun. No matter in what attire she appeared in her books and in her life, I always sensed within her that unkempt impetuous little girl who, no matter what the weather was like, was always ready to hurl herself from any cliff into the sea.[14]

Akhmatova tells of an incident reflecting this free spirit. The typical beach attire of young ladies in that era was a corset, bodice, two skirts (one starched) and a silk dress, rubber slippers, and a special cap. They "swam" by daintily tiptoeing into the water, splashing a bit, and running back to shore. "And then there appeared the monster—me, in a thin dress over my naked body, barefoot. I jumped into the sea and swam for two hours."[15]

In 1905 Akhmatova's father, a maritime engineer, retired and her parents separated. Akhmatova went with her mother, sisters, and brothers to Evpatoriya on the Black Sea, while her father moved to Petersburg. As beautiful as the south was, she longed for Tsarskoye. She began writing poetry during this period, though she says her early verses were poor. In a conversation about them with the poet Margarita Aliger right after World War II, she said: "These poems were terrible! Somehow I reread them and almost burned them from shame. Not a single one of my thoughts, not a single one of my intonations, everything alien and somehow wretched. It is totally incomprehensible how I hurled out of this shame and somehow became a poet."[16]

The year marked a major turning point in Russian history and eventually had an enormous influence on Akhmatova's life. She was only sixteen. "Vague rumors of the 1905 Revolution made their way to isolated Evpatoriya,"[17] she wrote in her autobiographical notes. She was deeply affected by the defeat in Tsushima, when the Japanese inflicted a major blow on the Russian fleet in the Russo–Japanese War. She also heard about the strikes in Odessa and the mutiny on the Battleship Potemkin.[18]

Many poets who had already achieved eminence conveyed the sense of doom hovering in the air. Their ability to describe in poetry their intense reaction to historical events is reflected in Akhmatova's poems several years later. One of those most profoundly affected by the events of 1905 was Alexander Blok, a major Symbolist poet. The novelist Georgy Chulkov describes meeting him:

> The Revolution of 1905 was like a torch illuminating the twilight of the culture of that time. And everyone for whom the revolution meant more than just an external, social and political fact, some kind of internal event, tried to meet with each other, even loners like Alexander Blok. I remember well the sleepless white Petersburg nights, our nocturnal wanderings with Blok, the nocturnal conversations behind a glass of wine somewhere in a corner of some dubious pub.[19]

Anna Gorenko. ca. 1904

Anna Gorenko. Evpatoriya, 1905

Valery Bryusov, another Symbolist, composed a poem at the begin-
ning of 1905 prophesying what soon came to pass:

> Like a giant in the nocturnal fog
> The new year arose, stern and blind
> It held in its merciless palm
> The scales of mysterious fates.
>
> . . .
>
> And in intoxication and in fear
> We, contemporaries, watch
> How the bones wander, in blood and dust
> And fall as a fatal sign.[20]

Akhmatova intended to become a student at the Kiev Upper
Courses, but tuberculosis prevented her from entering immediately. In
1905 she passed her school exam and in autumn of 1906 returned to
Kiev to complete her last year at the Funduleevskaya Gymnasium. She
once described the school to her friend Lidiya Chukovskaya. There
were rich girls whose valets brought them meals from home on silver
trays, and poor girls, daughters of tailors or orphans. Neither group
particularly liked poetry.[21] One of her schoolmates, V. Beer, recalls an
incident from those years that already distinguished Akhmatova from
her peers. At a psychology lesson devoted to associative thinking, the
teacher suggested students bring in examples from life or literature:

> Suddenly a voice rang out, calm but not languorous:
>
> > One hundred year old street lamps!
> > Oh, so many of you in the mist
> > On the firm thread of time
> > Stretched out in the mind!
>
> The solemn meter, the strange manner of recitation, the images which
> appeared so unusual forced us to pay attention. We all looked at Anya
> Gorenko, who did not stand up but spoke as if in a dream. A slight
> smile played on Shpet's face, and then it disappeared as he asked:
> "Whose verses are those?" A slightly disdainful answer rang out:
> "Valery Bryusov's." Very few of us had ever heard of Bryusov at
> that time, and certainly no one knew him as well as Anya. "Miss
> Gorenko's example is very interesting," Shpet said. And he continued
> reading and commenting on the poem she had begun. On her com-
> pressed lips played a self-satisfied smile.[22]

During 1906 and 1907 Akhmatova wrote a series of letters to her
brother-in-law, Professor Sergey von Shtein, the husband of her older

sister, Iya, who died from tuberculosis.[23] In one letter [1906], she writes of an attempted suicide: "Sergey Vladimirovich, if only you could realize how pitiful and unnecessary I feel. I'll never be necessary to anyone. To die is easy. Did Andrey tell you how I attempted to hang myself in Evpatoriya and the nail pulled out of the plaster wall? Mama cried and I was ashamed—it was awful."[24]

Akhmatova was being pursued at the time by a young student and poet, Nikolay Gumilyov. Her letters indicate she was infatuated with a university student named Vladimir Golenishchev–Kutuzov, who apparently had little interest in reciprocating her affection.[25] She begged von Shtein for a picture of him in one letter [1906]: "My dear Shtein, if you knew how stupid and naive I am. I'm even ashamed to admit it to you: I still love V. G-K. And there's nothing, absolutely nothing but this feeling in my life. . . Do you want to make me happy? Then send me his picture."[26] Akhmatova again begs for the picture in a letter written on 2 February 1907, while in the same breath announcing her intention to marry Gumilyov, although her ambivalence is apparent:

> I have decided to tell you about an event which must basically change my life, but it turned out to be so difficult that until this evening I couldn't make up my mind to send this letter. I'm marrying the friend of my youth, Nikolay Gumilyov. He has loved me for three years, and I believe it's my fate to be his wife. Whether or not I love him I really don't know, but I think I do.[27]

In this same letter she compares herself to Cassandra, an image that the poet Osip Mandelstam later used in a famous poem to her:

> I was waiting for the picture of G-K, and only after I received it did I wish to announce my marriage to you. . .I have murdered my soul, and my eyes are created for tears, as Iolanthe says. Or do you remember Schiller's prophetic Cassandra? One facet of my soul adjoins the dark image of this prophetess, so great in her suffering. But I am far from greatness. Don't say anything about our marriage to anyone. We still haven't decided where or when it will take place. . .In spite of everything, send me a picture of Vl. Vikt. [Kutuzov]. For God's sake, there is nothing else on earth I want so much.[28]

In another letter [February 1907], she seems happy about Gumilyov and their impending marriage, although it did not actually take place until 1910. She also reveals her cold relationship with her father:

I think my Kolya [Nikolay] is planning to come see me—I am so insanely happy...He loves me so much it's positively terrifying... What do you think Papa will say when he finds out about my decision? If he is against my marriage, I'll run away and marry Nikolay secretly. I cannot respect my father, I never loved him, why should I obey him?[29]

On 11 February she wrote von Shtein, thanking him for the picture of Kutuzov she finally received and revealing—despite her marriage plans—her lingering feelings for him:

I waited five months for this picture; he looks exactly the way I knew him, loved him, and madly feared him: elegant and so coldly indifferent, he looks at me with the tired, serene gaze of his myopic, light eyes. *Il est intimidant...* I can't tear my soul from him. I am maimed for my entire life, bitter is the poison of my unrequited love! Can I begin to live again? Of course not! But Gumilyov—is my fate, and I will obediently submit to him. Don't judge me if you can. I swear to you by all that's sacred to me that this unhappy man will be happy with me.[30]

In the same emotional correspondence, Akhmatova expresses her enthusiasm for the Symbolist movement in poetry. Blok's work especially interested her, particularly the poem "The Stranger," which describes a poet whose muse is a prostitute and who seeks inspiration in the drunken atmosphere of a pub: "But it's splendid, this interlacing of the vulgar commonplace with the divine, bright vision."[31] She notes she has influenced her cousin to subscribe to *Scales,* one of the leading journals of the period publishing Symbolist verse and edited by Valery Bryusov.

Akhmatova met Gumilyov in 1903 when they were attending school. He was three years older than she and had also grown up in Tsarskoye Selo. Sreznevskaya describes him at this time, noting he was not very handsome—although he had a certain elegance that was appealing—was somewhat wooden, very arrogant, and insecure. He read a great deal and loved the French Symbolists. She notes that Akhmatova, after leaving Tsarskoye Selo, never wrote about her love for Gumilyov, but often mentioned his persistent attachment to her, his frequent proposals of marriage, and her lighthearted refusals and indifference.[32]

A year before finishing at the gymnasium Gumilyov came out with his first collection of poems, *The Path of the Conquistadors,* which was imitative and largely influenced by Symbolism.[33] He left Russia in 1907 to spend a year in Paris studying French literature at the Sorbonne,[34] where he published a second collection of poems, *Romantic Flowers*. Gumilyov's poetry differed significantly from Akhmatova's early work, and had little influence on her. Only after he began writ-

Nikolay Gumilyov, ca. 1910

ing critical commentary on her works did his style become more typical of Acmeism, the movement he and Akhmatova would help to establish a few years later.

According to Amanda Haight, Gumilyov returned to Kiev to see Akhmatova at the end of April 1907, and visited her again that summer in Sebastopol, when he asked her to come away with him. She rejected his request.[35] He described this incident in his poem "Rejection" from *Romantic Flowers*:[36]

A princess—or maybe nothing but a sad child—
She leant out over the sleepy, sighing sea
And her figure so graceful and lithe seemed so terribly slight
As it secretly strained out to meet the silver of dawn.

*Anna Gorenko with brothers Andrey, Victor and sister Iya.
In center, mother Inna. Kiev, 1909*

. . .
But the crystal voice seemed to ring so clearly when
It stubbornly pronounced the fatal "No, I cannot. . ."
A princess—or maybe just a capricious child,
A tired child with a look of helpless sorrow.[37]

In December of that year Gumilyov attempted suicide by poison
—one of several attempts between 1905 and 1908—and was found
lying unconscious in the Bois de Boulogne.[38]

Gumilyov made frequent trips to Africa, the first in 1907.[39] Yury
Aikhenvald describes Gumilyov and his journeys abroad in quest of
adventure and the unknown:

> Last of the conquistadors, poet-knight, seeker and finder of the
> exotic. He continues the discoveries, conquests, and wanderings of his
> spiritual ancestors—Sinbad, Columbus, the Flying Dutchman. . .He
> is romantic, but he is a worshipper of the moon, not the sun. His soul
> is not singed by passion, not excited by emotion, and that is why with
> his moonlike love he not only totally despises sensuality but will also
> never pay the price for deep feeling. There is little in his poems of
> "spiritual warmth." He honors his homeland and identifies with the
> prodigal son in his longing for his native land.[40]

Akhmatova joined the Law Faculty at the Kiev College for Women
in the autumn of 1907, but soon grew bored. Gumilyov saw her in
April 1908, on his return from Paris, and again that summer while she
was visiting Tsarskoye Selo. In the autumn, he stopped briefly in Kiev
on his way to Egypt. She did not hear from him after his return until
January 1909.

Akhmatova married Gumilyov on 25 April 1910, near Kiev at the
Nikolaevsky Church in Nikolska Slobodka, in the Chernihov prov-
ince by the Dnieper in the Ukraine.[41] Valeriya Sreznevskaya, one of
Akhmatova's closest friends, saw the marriage as a power struggle
between two independent, creative people: "Their relationship was
more like a secret duelling—from her side, for her own affirmation of
her status as a free woman; from his, because of a desire not to submit
to any bewitchment and himself to remain independent and power-
ful. . .Alas without power over this eternally elusive, many-sided
woman who refused to submit to anyone!"[42]

Shortly after they married, they went to Paris for a month. It
was a magical time for her. Other Russians were also there. In her
memoirs she mentions that Marc Chagall had brought "his magic

Vitebsk to Paris." Some friends showed her two tables in the Taverne de Panthéon and said: "Here are your Social Democrats. Over here are the Bolsheviks and over there—the Mensheviks." She believed verse was neglected in Paris at the time and had been swallowed up by painting.[43]

While in Paris she became friends with Amedeo Modigliani, who was still unknown, poor, and lonely, and who was attracted to this young, enigmatic Russian. Akhmatova describes them in her memoirs visiting the Louvre together, strolling through the Luxembourg Garden and the Latin Quarter, roaming the old section of Paris behind the Panthéon in the moonlight. Inspired by Egypt at the time, Modigliani drew Akhmatova's head with the coiffure of queens and dancers of the Nile. One of these drawings remained with Akhmatova, no matter where she moved. On rainy days she and Modigliani often sat on a

Akhmatova by Modigliani

bench under an enormous umbrella in the Luxembourg Garden reciting verses by Verlaine. "It was Modigliani who acquainted me with the true Paris," she wrote. She also realized the significance of this time for both of them.

> We probably did not understand one important thing: everything that had happened to us up until that point was the prehistory of our life. The spirit of art had not yet transformed these two beings; it was the

hour just before dawn. But the future, as we know, throws its shadow long before it arrives, knocks at the window, hides behind street lamps, breaks into dreams and frightens you with the grotesque Paris of Baudelaire, which is hiding somewhere nearby.[44]

Akhmatova and Gumilyov returned to Tsarskoye Selo in June 1910, where they lived in a house on the Bulvarnaya, and later moved to the home of Gumilyov's mother on Malaya 63. A.I. Tynyakov, in a letter to a friend in 1912, describes their rooms as decorated with the trophies of Gumilyov's Abyssinian hunts: black panther, leopard, baboon.[45] They spent summers in Slepnyovo on the estate of Gumilyov's mother in the Bezhetsk district in the province of Tver. "I spent every summer in the former Tver province, fifteen versts from Bezhetsk," she writes in her memoirs. "This is not a picturesque spot: there are fields ploughed in even squares on a hilly spot, mills, bogs, dried-out swamps, wheat."[46] Akhmatova describes her strange reception when she arrived there in 1911, straight from a second trip to Paris.

> A hunchbacked servant in the waiting room at the Bezhetsk station, who had known everyone in Slepnyovo for ages, refused to recognize me as a Russian lady [*barinya*] and said to someone: "A French lady has come to visit the Slepnyovo gentleman." The steward Ivan Derin . . . a bearded country bumpkin, happened to be sitting next to me at lunch, and dying of embarrassment because he could not think of anything to ask, said: "You're probably very cold after Egypt?" It turned out that he had heard of my legendary slenderness so typical of young women of that time, and so I was mysteriously called the "London mummy" that brought misfortune. I didn't ride horseback and didn't play tennis, I just collected mushrooms, and over my shoulder Paris seemed to still blaze in a last sunset.[47]

One of the neighbors, V. Nevedomskaya, who lived on an estate seven miles away, recounts one of these summers in Slepnyovo:

> Gumilyov would make up games. Once he thought up a circus, stood on his saddle and jumped the barriers. Akhmatova, the "snake-woman," had the amazing facility to put her leg behind her neck. Gumilyov was the master-of-ceremonies and wore a frock coat and top hat.[48]

In September 1910 Gumilyov made another trip to Africa for six months. His constant desire to leave the domestic hearth to seek adventure dominated their marriage and helped destroy it. While

Anna Akhmatova, ca. 1910. Collection of Mikhail Baltsvinik (1931–1980)

he was away, Akhmatova studied at the Upper Historical Literary Courses of Raev.[49] She was already beginning to impress notable members of the artistic circles. Georgy Chulkov describes meeting Akhmatova at a World of Art exhibition in March 1911, after a literary and musical evening devoted to the poet Fyodor Sologub. She read him her poems, and he found joy in predicting her place in Russian poetry before she had yet appeared in print. This episode became the material for a passage in his novel *Snowstorm*:

> Slowly the famous poetess passed by, tall, slender, stepping insecurely along the parquet floor as if having forgotten how to walk on the ground. Behind her flowed a wave of young men in tuxedos trying in vain to turn the attention of the distracted poetess toward them.[50]

Akhmatova describes the year 1911 in her memoirs as marked by the Chinese revolution, which changed the face of Asia, and the year of Blok's notebooks, full of forebodings.[51] After Gumilyov returned, they journeyed again to Paris, where she witnessed the first triumphs of Diaghilev's Ballets Russes. They stayed until the summer. Chulkov's wife describes how her husband had written to her about Akhmatova, whom she was eager to meet and befriend when she arrived:

We took walks and visited small cafés in the evening, and then usually went to shows featuring comedy acts, popular singers, and dancers. Akhmatova was very young then—not more than twenty. She was very beautiful, and everyone on the street would turn around to look at her... She was tall, elegant, and wore a white dress and a wide brimmed straw hat with a large ostrich feather which her husband, the poet Gumilyov, had brought her. He had recently returned from Abyssinia... Once we visited a restaurant in Montmartre, a gilded palace, and left at dawn, admiring Paris awakening from its sleep and preparing for the approaching day... We stopped at a milk shop and drank hot, steaming milk. It was so nice to refresh ourselves from the night's drunken trance in the noisy gatherings in Montmartre.[52]

Akhmatova and Gumilyov returned to Tsarskoye Selo in the fall of 1911. The Symbolists still dominated the literary scene in Petersburg when Akhmatova was introduced into it. It was Russia's Silver Age,[53] which produced some of the country's greatest works in art, music, and literature. Valery Bryusov, who led the first generation of Symbolists, advocated the aesthetic autonomy of art in reaction to previous decades of Russian literature devoted to social and political thought. The poets prescribed cryptic meanings, musical combinations of sounds and nuance rather than direct narration. They also turned to specific periods of history, such as the Age of Byzantium and the eighteenth century—ages devoted to turning life into works of art. Much later in her career, Akhmatova still paid homage to the importance of Symbolism: "The modernists did a great thing for Russia. Don't forget this. They gave to the country a very different form of poetry than they took. They taught people to love verse again."[54] While many acclaimed the elegance of their verse, social critics such as Georgy Plekhanov, called Symbolism "the pallid disease of an anemic social class in decline."[55]

At the beginning of the 1900s a new mystical style was introduced to the movement's younger generation under the influence of the Russian philosopher, Vladimir Solovyov. The critic Marc Slonim describes the change in the movement—toward creating myths with universal meanings. The poet was viewed not as a social reformer or solipsistic individualist, but as the bearer of a spiritual message. "In his theurgic activity, like the priest he was the bridge between Man and Divinity. His own age had to die before a new life could rise from the tomb."[56]

Symbolism's mystical aspect took on a further dimension when it

Alexander Blok, 1907. Photo by D.S. Zdobnova

began to interpret the impending revolution as an apocalyptic event that would purge Russia of all corruption and sin and replace it with a world based on love and spirituality. Blok participated in this trend. In a work that served as one of the precedents for Akhmatova's *Poem Without a Hero*, Blok's unfinished *Retribution* (1911), a long poem or *poema*, associates the downfall of his ancestral home with the fate of his country. An excerpt provides the sense of doom, a feeling expressed by Akhmatova after she was enveloped by the First World War.

> *Already the bloody dawn*
> *Has spread across the boundless horizon,*
> *Warning of Port Arthur and Tsushima,*
> *Warning of January 9th.*
> *The son pays for the sins of the fathers,*
> *Born to be destroyed*
> *The son a homeless wanderer.*[57]

The artistic life of the capital persisted, nonetheless, much of it centered in the apartment of Vyacheslav Ivanov, called the "Tower." Ivanov had begun his famous artistic salon, which met every Wednesday, in 1905. Slonim says he officiated like a high priest and was listened to as an oracle.[58] Poets from many different movements participated. Along with the Symbolists of both generations appeared Velimir Khlebnikov, who became one of the greatest representatives of Futurism. Several poets who were soon to form the Acmeist movement also appeared in the Tower. Akhmatova first met Osip Mandelstam, who became one of her closest friends, at Ivanov's Tower in the spring of 1911. "At that time he was a thin boy with a lily-of-the-valley in his buttonhole, and long eyelashes," she observed.[59] Mandelstam seemed to recognize that Akhmatova had been marked as someone special, with a great gift but who would be made to suffer for it. He expressed this in his poem of 1910:

> *TO ANNA AKHMATOVA*
>
> *Today you seemed to me*
> *a Black Angel in the snow,*
> *and I can't keep this secret to myself:*
>
> *God's seal is upon you.*
> *So strange a seal—*
> *Heaven-granted—*
> *that you seemed supposed to stand*

in a church, in a niche.
May it be that love not of this earth
and love of this earth will mix,
may it be that storm-blood
will not run into your cheeks,
and magnificent marble will set off
all the deceptions of these rages,
all the nakedness of your softest flesh,
but not your blushing cheeks.[60]

Akhmatova made her first public appearance at the Tower in 1910, on Sunday, 13 June. Ivanov's secretary, M.M. Zamyatina noted this in a letter to V.K. Shvarsalon on 16 June, observing that Akhmatova came with Gumilyov, and that they had just returned from Paris. "Vyacheslav listened closely to her poems, approved of several, criticized one and kept silent about the rest."[61] Akhmatova did not have pleasant memories of this occasion: "After our return from Paris (summer 1910) Gumilyov brought me to Vyacheslav Ivanov's. He asked me whether I wrote poetry, and I read 'And when...' [Zh. #52, written in 1909, appears in the Kiev notebook, and in Akhmatova's first book, *Evening*] and one other piece—and Ivanov said ironically, 'What pure romanticism.'"[62]

Akhmatova soon became so identified with the artistic society of Petersburg that in the memoirs of B. Temiryazev, she appears as one of the details typifying the capital in the 1910s: "Fog, streets, bronze horses, triumphal arches over the gates, Akhmatova, sailors and academics, the Neva, railings, murmuring lines at the bread shops, stray bullets of light without street lamps—have been deposited in my memory...of the past, like love, like a disease, like the years."[63]

She developed, as Chukovsky notes, from a shy young girl to a self-assured, regal woman in only a few years. He recalls the words of Nekrasov:

There are women in Russian villages
With a calm importance on their face
With beautiful power in their movements
With the walk, the gaze of a tsarina.

He credits her upbringing in Tsarskoye Selo as the source of her unique refinement:

At times, especially among guests, among strangers, she behaved with an intentional regal air, like an elegant woman of the world. That's when you sensed within her that polish by which we native Petersburgians unmistakably recognize people raised in Tsarskoye Selo. I always felt that imprint in her voice, manner and gestures... The signs of this rare type of person are a strong sensitivity to music, poetry and art, refined taste, reproachless correctness of carefully polished speech, extreme (slightly cold) politeness regarding strangers, and a total absence of passionate, strong, unrestrained gestures typical of a vulgar lack of control. Akhmatova had absorbed all these Tsarskoye Selo qualities.[64]

By the time Akhmatova published her first collection, *Evening*, in 1912, Symbolism was in a state of crisis. Slonim notes, "hundreds of minor writers and intellectual snobs who had swelled its ranks contributed to the vulgarization and disintegration of the school."[65] By 1915, in an important article called "Overcoming Symbolism," the critic Viktor Zhirmunsky asserted that poets like Akhmatova, Gumilyov and Mandelstam had left behind much of the Symbolist aesthetic:

Poets became tired of going to the Golgotha of mysticism; they wanted to be simpler, more direct, more human in their experiences. They were tired of so much lyricism, spiritual excitement... They did not feel a sacred obligation to proclaim divine truths, but wanted to speak about objects from external life simply and clearly, stories about intimate ordinary life. They continue the Symbolist's focus on artistic technique, but produce not so much melodious lines, a musical effect, as the pictorial, graphic clarity of visual images.[66]

One of the great inspirations for the new turn to simplicity and clarity of image and language was Innokenty Annensky, an outstanding scholar, professor of ancient literature and head of the gymnasium where Gumilyov attended school in Tsarskoye Selo. He linked objects from the everyday world to a psychic state rather than imbuing them, as the Symbolists might have, with transcendental meaning.[67] A deflated child's balloon, a worn-out barrel organ, or a spoiled watch corresponded to internal psychological states such as fear, disillusionment, or creative joy. While the Symbolists turned mainly to the city, Annensky also wrote about the countryside and landed estates. His innovations, including the presenting of images with emotional rather than logical relationships, and sudden transitions from one subject to the next, influenced Akhmatova.[68] In his use of conversational language, the concreteness of his poetic world, and subjects more typical of psychological prose than contemporary poetry, Annensky also no doubt impressed Akhmatova.

Around the time of their marriage in the spring of 1910, Gumilyov had shown Akhmatova a book by Annensky, *The Cypress Box,* published posthumously, which touched her deeply. Akhmatova may have known Annensky and his work before this book was put in her hands. Georgy Adamovich mentions in his memoirs an evening he spent at Annensky's home at Tsarskoye Selo, with Akhmatova present: "We arrived at Tsarskoye Selo on one of the late trains. The snow was falling and melting; everything was black and white. As always, at the first moment of being in Tsarskoye Selo the silence was amazing, and the sweet, moist air seemed particularly pure." When Adamovich entered, Annensky had just finished reading a new poem and the room was silent. In response, Gumilyov delivered an intellectual discourse on the relationship between the audience and the poet. Annensky then suddenly became lively and turned to Akhmatova, sitting far off in an armchair and slowly leafing through some old album. He asked her what she thought of his work. "She shuddered, as if frightened by something. A sad, mocking smile played over her face. She became paler than before, helplessly raised her brows, fixed her broad silk shawl falling off her shoulder, and said, 'I don't know.' Annensky shook his head. 'Yes, yes, there is wisdom in silence, as they say. But it would be better in words. And so it will be.'"[69]

In that same year Mikhail Kuzmin wrote an article advocating clarity in style. As a number of critics have pointed out, "On Beautiful Clarity" is about prose, not poetry. Several poets, however, including Akhmatova, took his advice to heart to see the ordinary world in a new way—in all its beauty rather than as a collection of symbols. Through simple everyday objects, the poet gives a concrete sense of the world the poem encompasses, including the poet's subjective experience.[70]

Akhmatova published forty-six poems in *Evening.* The 300 copies sold out quickly. In his preface to the book, Mikhail Kuzmin grasped the dramatic turn Russian poetry had taken with the appearance of these poems. He compared Akhmatova to members of an ancient Alexandrian society, who each day pretended they were condemned to death, in order to make their everyday impressions more poignant. Images appeared in their memory as vivid fragments: "Their memories do not proceed in sequence but run after one another in a jolting wave, a stream of images—once forgotten eyes, someone's light blue dress, the voice of a passing stranger." Because these concrete fragments carried the perception of imminent death, readers would associate them with important moments in their own lives. Kuzmin believed Akhmatova's work reflected this same heightened sensitivity as well as the thought processes exhibited in this Alexandrian society.[71]

The response to the book was generally positive, yet Akhmatova was insecure about the publication: "These are the poor poems of a very vapid little girl which for some reason were reprinted thirteen times... The little girl herself did not foresee such a fate for them and hid a number of journals under the sofa pillow. Because of the anxiety caused by their appearance, she went to Italy (the spring of 1912) and sitting in a tram, thought, looking at her neighbors: 'How happy they are—they haven't had a little book published.'"[72] Nevertheless, as Chukovsky points out, the youth of two or three generations fell in love to the accompaniment of Akhmatova's poems, finding in them the embodiment of their own feelings.[73]

How did Akhmatova's husband respond to her writing poetry? He was the first to publish her poems, in his journal *Sirius* in 1907. In her autobiographical notes, Akhmatova says many writers distorted the influence Gumilyov had on her poetry. Some wrote that after marrying her, Gumilyov began to teach her how to write poetry, and soon the pupil surpassed the teacher. "This is all nonsense! I'd been writing poetry since I was eleven years old, totally independently of Gumilyov. While the work was not very good, Gumilyov, being straightforward, told me so." Akhmatova claimed that only after she read Annensky's book of poems in 1910 did she begin to understand the essence of poetry. In September, when Gumilyov left for Africa, she began writing the poems that became her book, *Evening*. "When he returned on 25 March and asked me whether I had written any verse, I read him what I had done," and, she noted, he responded with praise. But their styles differed significantly. "I did not marry the head of Acmeism, but a young poet-symbolist, author of the book *Pearls* and some reviews on poetry collections."[74] In his letters from abroad, Gumilyov continually asked about the progress of her poems, provided useful commentary, and told her his favorite ones. "Why don't you send me some new poems?" he wrote in July 1915, when he was away during the war. "Except for Homer I don't have a single book of poetry, and your new poems would be a great joy to me. For whole days at a time I repeat, 'Where is she, where is the merry light of her gray eyes.' I'm not writing anything at all."[75]

She published under the name of Anna Akhmatova, rather than Gorenko. When her friend Lidiya Chukovskaya asked her about the name, Akhmatova replied she had thought of it herself. It was the name of her grandmother, and of the last Tatar princes from the Horde.[76] But the immediate impetus for the name change, she said, was her father. When he found out she was writing poetry, he said: "Don't bring shame upon my name."[77]

Evening

Evening concentrates on the many facets of love, from awakening hope to joyful fulfillment, from disillusionment to the last embers of a dying relationship. The themes and language are, as Mandelstam points out, not "ladylike" as with many of Akhmatova's imitators, but more comparable to Russian women's folk songs, where feminine emotion is generally human, just as in the "male" poems of Pushkin or Goethe.[78] Her verse becomes typified by its sparseness, by the absence of singing mellifluousness and myriads of mystical, mythological, and erudite images so typical of Symbolist verse. Her contemporaries were struck not only by what was actually present, but what had been left out, as in the works of Pushkin. The spareness itself was a form of experimentation. Chulkov comments: "Schopenhauer, annoyed by feminine chattiness, suggested they be shut up. What would he have said if he had read Akhmatova's poems? She is one of the most silent of poets, her words are sparse, restrained, severe. Strained and concentrated emotions are couched in simple, precise and harmonic form." He notes the lack of metaphors, strict selection of words, daring use of rhyme, unique rhythm, juxtaposition of images, and touching irony in her verse.[79]

Although Akhmatova describes concrete settings and landscapes, she shifts perspective, choosing what at first may seem a chance detail, and rearranging reality through the use of her highly selective eye. Kees Verheul has devoted an entire book to exploring the role of time in Akhmatova's work. Objects and events appear not in causal or chronological sequence, but through the personal associations which she attaches to them.[80] Akhmatova had studied this psychological mode of thought in her lycée[81]; it was also a favorite technique developed in poetry by Annensky.

The Russian psychological novel also played an important role in Akhmatova's development, as Mandelstam notes: "Akhmatova brought into the Russian lyric the enormous complexity and richness of the Russian novel of the nineteenth century. There never would have been an Akhmatova without Tolstoy and *Anna Karenina*, Turgenev with *Nest of Gentry* and all of Dostoevsky. The genesis of Akhmatova lies in Russian prose and not in poetry. Her poetic form, strong and unique, she developed with a glance at psychological prose."[82]

Russian folk songs, usually sung by women, influenced her as well, both through their concise way of conveying emotion and through specific techniques, such as parallelism—the juxtaposition of events from nature and the outside world with events relating to the human condition. One typical folk poem not only uses parallelism but also conveys a young girl's feeling through one simple detail, the blush:

Along the meadow, along the little meadow water flows
Along the little green meadow runs a golden stream,
And on stream after stream, a white swan is floating,
The white swan is a lovely, beautiful maiden;
And the gray drake is a fine young man.
When the maid sees the young man, she will be filled with joy,
A blush will spread over her white face.[83]

Akhmatova often alludes to Russian culture and folklore in the poems in *Evening*. In "High in the sky..." (Zh. 9), for example, the speaker's lover refers to the famous Russian tale of the Snow Maiden, who falls in love with a mortal. Before the Snow Maiden can experience ultimate happiness, the sun's rays melt her on her wedding day, as she is caught up in the divine plan of revenge of Yarilo the sun god. Akhmatova implies her heroine will experience the same grief in love as this poetic figure. At the end, Akhmatova refers to another Russian custom: on Epiphany Eve, young girls tell their fortunes and guess who their bridegrooms will be. The heroine also partakes in this hopeful ritual, even though she seems to believe subconsciously that her love, like that of the Snow Maiden, will bring grief in the spring.

In another poem, "My husband whipped me..." (Zh. 21), Akhmatova takes on the persona of a peasant woman. Like many of her poems, this work relates to the peasant milieu without reflecting folk styles in any way. Akhmatova's main interest in Russian folk poetry, in fact, was not to imitate devices of oral literature, but to present the peasant's point of view.[84] Even the device of parallelism, though perhaps originally derived from folk lyrics, is used throughout Akhmatova's poetry, and becomes an integral part of her own technique. In this poem, Akhmatova picks up a theme that permeates the Russian women's folk lyric—an unhappy young wife, beaten and held psychological prisoner by her unloved husband, sits by the window waiting for her lover. In one famous folk song, for example, the young girl compares herself to a piece of wood used to light the house. It no longer burns brightly, for her mother-in-law has poured water on it, just as her husband's family has made her own life miserable. But she looks forward to a temporary respite in the arms of her lover:

> . . . *I must make the bed*
> *Make the bed and wait for my sweetheart!*
> *The first dream I dreamt—my sweetheart's not here;*
> *The second dream I dreamt—my darling's not here;*
> *The third dream I dreamt—the white light of dawn!*
> *My sweetheart's walking in the white dawn:*
> *His boots squeak*
> *His sable coat rustles,*
> *And on his fur coat the buttons jingle.*[85]

In Akhmatova's poem, the heroine's lack of sleep is revealed through a metonymic detail—the sheets on her bed are unrumpled.

Viktor Vinogradov discusses how Akhmatova's descriptions of the external world form a central core of "nests," which juxtaposed with other "nests" result in even more associations. The image "song," for example, is related to "voice," which in turn may be the voice of the wind, an organ, a bird's voice. The bird, in turn, is a symbol of the poet's childhood, a white bird recalls sweet memories of a happy past, the dove symbolizes love. When love is betrayed it becomes a crow, friends are in the form of birds, and swans are associated with Tsarskoye Selo. Particular combinations of concrete images lead to abstract meanings: a crane by a wretched well evokes pining. Conversely, Akhmatova transforms an abstract word into a concrete image, such as "From my heart I drew out *black shame*" [italics mine].

Vinogradov also examines Akhmatova's use of dialogue. While most poems are in monologue form, some consist of dialogue with narration. She alternates laconic remarks, interrupted conversation, monologue and dialogue, intercrossing on several psychological planes. The poet acts as narrator and participant. Some poems contain or consist of an aphorism structured in the form of contrast: "To me, praise from others is— ashes,/ From you even a reproach is—high praise" (Zh. 306).[86]

Akhmatova joins ordinary adjectives and nouns into unusual combinations to produce a metaphoric effect—"broad sound," "trembling February"—as T. V. Tsivyan points out.[87] The same adjective may be either positive or negative, depending on context: white may be the color of a bridal veil or shroud, a yellow ray or yellow roses may signify joy, but a yellow sky evokes anxiety.[88] She devises oxymorons such as "bitter fame" and "joyful grief."

Akhmatova is cited for her extensive use of the *dolnik,* a poem with a fixed number of accents but not a fixed number of syllables. About a quarter of her poems—including most of her long poems—are *dolniks.* Rarely do strictly accentual or folk meters appear in her works, and there is no free verse. However, as Anthony Hartman observes, the *dolnik* had already become a popular form among the Symbolists, especially Bryusov and Blok.[89] Akhmatova's fondness for it contributed to the development of the metrical typology of narrative verse.[90] But, as he points out, "A detailed investigation of Akhmatova's metrical typology to a large extent confirms the commonly held view that Akhmatova is not a metrical innovator... Although the frequent use of *dolnik* in her lyric verse prior to 1915 was one of the features which impressed contemporaries, in fact the use of the *dolnik* represents a continuation of one of the main developments associated with Symbolist verse, rather than a new direction. Stress-meters other than the *dolnik* never play a significant role in her metrical typology, as they do in that of the more innovative Futurists and Constructivists."[91]

Critics frequently mention the influence of Alexander Pushkin's laconic style on Akhmatova without making specific comparisons. Certainly, her lifelong interest in Pushkin influenced her work. Pushkin wrote in an age of romanticism, when poetic style was typically rhetorical. Unlike his contemporaries, he chose one telling gesture, facial expression, or metonymic detail of clothing or environment that revealed the state of mind or character of the protagonist. In his poem "Dorida," the shyness, careless dress and speech, and endearing names are enough to reveal to the speaker that he is loved:

I believe: I am loved; my heart must believe this,
No, my sweetheart is not hypocritical.
Nothing is feigned: the languorous head of desire,
Shy embarrassment, the invaluable gift of the Graces,
The lovely carelessness of dress and speech
And the young tenderness of endearing names.[92]

The inner feelings are not described directly, but indirectly, through simple outward signs.

Another lovely poem by Pushkin, "The Storm," compares a maid to a stormy sea. Certain verses of Akhmatova's *poema* entitled *At the Edge of the Sea* (Zh. 646) recall this poem:

Have you seen the maid on the cliff
In a white garment over the waves
When, raging in a stormy mist,
The sea was playing with the shore,
When a ray of lightning illuminated her again and again
With a crimson gleam
And the wind beat hard and flew off
With her flying blanket?
The lovely sea in a stormy mist
And the sky in flashes without blue;
But believe me: the maid on the cliff
Is lovelier than the waves, and the storm, and the sky.[93]

In her early poem "On his hand are lots of shining rings..." (Zh. 485), published by Gumilyov in *Sirius,* Akhmatova already uses psychological associations with objects to characterize the true state of a relationship. Each of the rings worn by the speaker's lover was given to him by a different woman, and thus represents her. But the poet has another gift—the gift of poetry—which she will never bestow upon him, even if it means the loss of love.[94]

Some of Akhmatova's poems show traces of Symbolism, with its love of fantasy, costume, and the eighteenth century. Her poem "Masquerade in the Park" (Zh. 32), with its moonlit cornices, a marquise, and French phrases is reminiscent of Andrey Bely's poem, "Declaration of Love." In Bely's poem, an ornate cornice serves as the backdrop to a tryst between a lady and her cousin, who slips French phrases into his wooing.

Two of Akhmatova's early poems, "Reading *Hamlet*" (Zh. 50–51), illustrate how soon in her career she alluded to great literature to illuminate the subject of her own work. Like Ophelia, the speaker defends herself against her beloved's cruel words. The image of the falling ermine mantle suggests that power is slipping not only from Hamlet but also from the poem's speaker. In the second work, "forty tender sisters" refers to a line in Hamlet: "I loved Ophelia. Forty thousand brothers/ Could not with all their quantity of love/ Make up my sum."[95]

"The Gray-Eyed King" (Zh. 34), one of Akhmatova's most popular poems, was set to music by Sergey Prokofiev. According to some critics, the apparent fairy tale, written in couplets, reflects Akhmatova's own dilemma: they suggest she married Gumilyov thinking he was the fairy prince, and he turned out to be an ordinary human being. Another interpretation suggests she had waited for her prince, her ideal love, to come along before she married, and never saw Gumilyov as someone with whom she could ever be passionately involved. The poem conveys that she has given up any hope of meeting this ideal: the gray-eyed king is dead.

Throughout her career Akhmatova wrote poems exploring her relationship with the Muse. One of the first such poems, "To the Muse" (Zh. 29) appears in *Evening*. In it, the muse becomes the poet's sister.

The cycle of poems in *Evening* devoted to Tsarskoye Selo initiates a motif that develops over time, as Akhmatova faced increasingly difficult experiences. Her life in Tsarskoye Selo eventually became symbolic of calm before the storm of revolution and war. In 1911, however, although she has complaints, life was still relatively peaceful. In the first poem of the cycle, "In Tsarskoye Selo" (Zh. 2), she emphasizes the refined cultivation of nature so typical of the atmosphere of the time—the combed-out manes of the horses, the allée with its planted trees. In this toy town it is difficult to take relationships or people seriously, and she, too, has been reduced to a toy like her rosy friend the cockatoo. In the last two lines Akhmatova provides images from nature to reflect the speaker's state of mind: the hour before sunset means the end of day, and the wind from the sea signifies departures. Both are reinforced by the last word, "Leave!"—the word she is expecting from her lover, suggesting the end of their relationship.

The last poem in this cycle refers to Pushkin.[96] The subject remains unnamed, however, since the poet assumes a reader familiar with Pushkin and his biography. The "dark-skinned youth" refers to

Pushkin's African heritage.[97] While attending the lyceum in Tsarskoye Selo, he wandered along these same allées and wrote beautiful verses describing the landscape so dear to him:

In mute silence slumber the vale and the groves,
In the gray mist, a distant forest.
Barely heard is the brook, rushing into a canopy of oaks.
Barely breathes the zephyr, falling asleep in the leaves.
And the quiet moon, like a magnificent swan,
Floats in the silver clouds.

. . .

There, in the quiet lake, water sprites splash.

. . .

Didn't earthly gods spend peaceful days here?[98]

The poem "He Loved . . . [three things in life]" (Zh. 36) illustrates the danger of using Akhmatova's poetry as evidence of events in her life. The poem is often seen as describing Akhmatova's role as wife to the poet Gumilyov. In the first half, "he" is depicted with three images—evensong, white peacocks, and old maps of America, none of which would relate to everyday life except in the world of an aesthete. The last lines convey three more images, which might indeed reflect the daily life of an ordinary family: crying children, sticky raspberry jam, and women's hysterics. The pause in the last line leads up to the revelation of the psychological relationship—the speaker is his wife. She must deal with the difficulties of everyday life while he remains in his aesthetic dream world. But Akhmatova was no more equipped to be an ordinary housewife than Gumilyov was to be an ordinary bread-winner and *paterfamilias*. She wrote this poem before she even had a child, but soon after the birth of her son, she took him to her mother-in-law's in Slepnyovo because she felt she could not take the responsibility of raising him. Numerous friends recount how helpless Akhmatova was in matters of housekeeping. Layers of dust lay over books and belongings, and furniture and clothes remained in disrepair after the revolution, when Akhmatova had to make do without servants. The poem brilliantly conveys in a few simple lines the plight of the ordinary woman married to the aesthete, but not the real life situation and character of the poet herself.

II. St. Petersburg: 1912–1914

The marriage between Akhmatova and Gumilyov soon began to show signs of disillusionment. In *Alien Skies* (1910–1912), Gumilyov published a poem, "From a serpent's nest," which may reflect his feelings for his wife at the time.

From a serpent's nest,
From the city of Kiev,
I took not a wife but a witch.
I thought her amusing
Guessed she might be capricious,
A gay and happy song bird.

You call out and she frowns
You hug her and she bristles
When the moon comes out she starts pining.
She stares and groans
As if she were burying
Someone and wanted to drown herself.[1]

The Gumilyovs left for Switzerland and Italy in April 1912. It was the last time until the end of her life that Akhmatova visited Western Europe. When they returned, Akhmatova spent the summer with her mother at the estate of her cousin Nanichka Zmunchilla, near the Austrian border. She was expecting a child. Gumilyov spent the summer at Slepnyovo trying to read Dante in Italian and Byron in English, riding, playing tennis, and writing poetry. A son, Lev Gumilyov, was born in October.[2]

Accounts about Akhmatova's initial desire to raise her child differ. Sreznevskaya says that at first the birth tied Akhmatova down. She nursed the child herself and stayed home in Tsarskoye Selo, but "little by little she liberated herself from the role of mother in the sense of really taking care of the infant—for this there was a grandmother and a nurse—and she began to lead her usual life of a literary bohemian."[3] However, Pavel Luknitsky, who kept a diary of his conversations with Akhmatova in the 1920s, claims she told him that when Lev was born, the grandmother and aunt took him, saying "You, Anechka, are young and pretty. What do you need a baby for?" According to Akhmatova, she protested strongly, but in vain; her husband was on the side of his family, and allowed them to take Lev to Bezhetsk. Luknitsky also notes in his diary on 24 March 1925 that Alexandra

Sverchkova, Gumilyov's step-sister, angered Akhmatova when she reported having asked Lev what he was doing one day, and he answered, "I am calculating what percentage of the time mama thinks about me."[4]

Gumilyov departed in the spring of 1913 for Africa as director of an expedition to Abyssinia and Somaliland commissioned by the Academy of Science. Beforehand, he had played a leading role in forming the Poets' Guild in 1911. As various scholars have noted, there was little that held the group together other than their rejection of Symbolism. Sergey Gorodetsky, one of the theoreticians of the group, said: "When Gumilyov and I decided to found the Poets' Guild, Gumilyov was a convinced Parnassian, putting mastery of form above all. For me the goal was fusion of folk poetry with literary form using revealing symbols, which is mythmaking."[5] The group founded the journal, *Hyperborean* (1912–1914), which published not only their own members but also poets such as Blok and Kuzmin.

Six of the members—Gumilyov, Akhmatova, Gorodetsky, Mandelstam, Vladimir Narbut, and Mikhail Zenkevich—soon developed a new movement called Acmeism, or Adamism. Gumilyov defined the movement in his article "Acmeism and the Heritage of Symbolism," which appeared in the January 1912 issue of *Apollon*: "Acme in Greek means the point of highest achievement, the time of blossoming; Adamism—virile, firm and clear outlook on life."[6] Gorodetsky emphasized the difference between the Acmeists and the Symbolists. "For the Acmeists," he wrote, "a rose is more beautiful for itself, its petals, fragrance, and color, than because of its abstract resemblance to mystic love or anything else."[7] Like the Poets' Guild, the Acmeists were drawn together more by their rejection of the mysticism and ornate style of Symbolism than by what they actually wrote. Gorodetsky wrote: "Acmeism was not created or invented; it appears as a result of the collective work of a group of young poets developing under intercrossing influences."[8]

The first meeting of the Poets' Guild took place in the autumn of 1911 at Gorodetsky's, and subsequent meetings were hosted by the Gumilyovs in Tsarskoye Selo, and Lozinsky. Kuzmin and Blok attended a meeting, but soon found they had little interest in the group and left. There were readings and then discussion. Adamovich writes: "I only attended five or six meetings. Gumilyov had an amazing ear for poetry, an exceptional feeling for the verbal texture of poems. But he was better at judging other people's verses than his own. Akhmatova spoke little and became animated only when Mandelstam read his works."[9] The criticism was insightful and useful for the development of the poets involved, including Akhmatova. It provided her an opportunity to test her work against the opinions of friends, who were also good critics and sensitive poets. The Guild published Akhmatova's first collection, *Evening*.

Some critics welcomed this new group on the scene. Others, like Bryusov, responded harshly. In an article published in 1913, he wrote: "Acmeism, which has been such a great topic of discussion recently, is a hothouse plant cultivated under the glass hood of a literary circle by several young poets who certainly wish to say something new... Acmeism is an invention, a whim. It is possible to take it seriously only because under its transparent banner there are several poets who are definitely talented."[10]

While the Acmeists were attracting attention in Petersburg, another group, the Futurists, focused mainly in Moscow, was beginning to make an impact in Petersburg circles. They rejected all art of the past and embraced the age of modernism and technology, speed, and energy. They not only used ordinary words—as the Acmeists did—but vulgar ones as well, often breaking all grammatical rules. Like the Symbolists and the Acmeists, the works of the members varied. Some, like Velimir Khlebnikov, created a new transrational language called *zaum*, made up of pure sounds or neologisms formed from Slavic roots—a transrational language that was supposed to communicate directly without reflection of logic or the real world. Khlebnikov was also interested in number theory and Slavic paganism. Vladimir Mayakovsky, on the other hand, was an urban poet more concerned with politics and revolution. What they did share was a focus on the future and rejection of the past. Their manifesto of 1912, "A Slap in the Face of Public Taste," declared: "Throw Pushkin...Tolstoy and all others overboard from the ship of modernity." Their dress and behavior were consciously shocking. They painted their faces, wore wooden spoons in their lapels and put on outrageous scenes, interrupting solemn banquets or meetings. Mayakovsky frequently appeared on the rostrum wearing a bright yellow jacket, silk top hat, and no necktie. He was big and burly and looked more like a boxer than an aesthete; certainly he did not fit the idealized image of the poet that Blok fit so well. The poet Benedikt Livshits describes him: "His bass

Vladimir Mayakovsky, 1918

voice, traditionally associated with operatic villains, his protruding lower jaw, which gave his mouth a look of strong will—all this made Mayakovsky look even more like a member of a gang of bandits, or an anarchist bomb thrower... It was enough, however, to look into the wise, mocking eyes, to discern that the outward appearance was distinct from the inner man, that all this was 'theater for its own sake' which Mayakovsky was somewhat tired of already."[11]

In one of his greatest poems before the revolution, "Cloud in Trousers," Mayakovsky combines personal themes of rejected love with public themes of revolution and motifs of metapoetry, discussing the rejection of traditional literature in the name of the new. Before, "a poet came,/ lightly opened his lips,/ and the inspired fool burst into song"; now, poets must tramp for days with calloused feet, pick up the themes and sounds of the street, write hymns to the street folk: students, prostitutes, salesmen. The poet identifies with them. He spits on the fact that neither Homer nor Ovid invented characters like them. The poet calls himself the precursor of the revolution, which he predicts will be in 1916:

> *Where men's eyes stop short,*
> *there, at the head of hungry hordes,*
> *the year 1916 cometh*
> *in the thorny crown of revolutions.*[12]

He finds religion useless and God impotent for the goals he wishes to achieve. He challenges God to help humanity, but receives no reply, just as he receives no answer from his mistress, who will not let him in.

The Acmeists, while rebels in the poetic world, never attempted to appear as outrageous in their behavior. One critic ascribes this to their being "Petersburgians." In contrast to the Futurists, the Acmeists "were dandies with a certain defiance rather than 'hooligans' with a vengeance."[13]

Ivan Bunin, a poet and writer who refused to join any of these movements, sums up the chaotic kaleidoscope of the Russian literary world at the time:

> What haven't we done with our literature in recent years, what haven't we mimicked, what haven't we imitated, from what styles and epochs haven't we borrowed, to what gods have we not bowed down! Literally every winter has brought us a new idol. We have experienced decadence, symbolism, neo-naturalism, pornography...godfight-

ing, mythmaking, a kind of mystical anarchism, Dionysius and Apollo, "stages to eternity," sadism, snobism, "acceptance of the world" and "non-acceptance of the world," cheap imitations of the Russian style, Adamism, acmeism—and now we have sunk to the tritest type of hooliganism, named by the ridiculous word "futurism." Is this not a Walpurgis night![14]

During this time, Akhmatova became the center of the artistic world in Petersburg. Zhirmunsky notes she was adored not only as a poet but also as a beautiful woman. Many portraits were made of her, and her characteristic hairstyle with bangs, and classical shawl were preserved in the memory of her contemporaries.[15] It was the fashion to turn poets into cult figures, the precedent having been set with Blok. Often readers did not distinguish between the persona portrayed in the poetry and the poet. "The private person had been totally absorbed into the poetic mask; the distance between life and work had been eliminated."[16]

The place where these different currents converged, met and clashed was the famous artistic cabaret, the Stray Dog, on Mikhailovsky Square. Its very name, Stray Dog, ironically symbolized the lack of refuge in the lives of the cabaret patrons. They could realize their dream of turning life into art.[17] One patron said that in the Stray Dog, more than anywhere else, one found the atmosphere of doom typical of the epoch, "which you didn't feel consciously at the time, but which pursued everyone everywhere, whether it was in the bosom of their family, in a festively lit hall, comfortable theaters, or stuffy, smoky wine cellars like this cabaret."[18] In her novel *Above Love,* Tatyana Krasnopolskaya describes the walls of the "Wandering Sheep" (the novel's cabaret based on the Stray Dog) as painted with Baudelairean "'flowers of evil'—bright to the point of poison."[19]

The cabaret was opened on 31 December 1911 by Boris Pronin, a former associate of the avant-garde director Vsevolod Meyerhold. It had two narrow rooms painted brightly, a buffet to the side, a small stage, little tables, benches, a fireplace, and colored lanterns.[20] Benedikt Livshits described the audience as "divided into two unequal categories: the representatives of art and the 'pharmacists,' a term used to describe all others, no matter what their occupation. The program varied, from . . . Pyast's 'On the Theater of the Word and the Theater of Movement' to 'musical Mondays,' Karsavina's dancing or a banquet in honor of the Moscow Art Theater . . . The main substance, however, was not the planned part of the program but the unscheduled happenings which lasted all night."[21] The evenings devoted to music included contemporary works by composers such as Debussy, Ravel, Frank, Schoenberg, Richard Strauss, Reger, and Scriabin. Sergey Sudeikin, who designed many sets for performances at the cabaret, made special decorative panels as backdrops for these evenings.[22]

The great ballerina of the Ballets Russes, Tamara Karsavina,[23] describes her performance at the Stray Dog in her memoirs:

> I had been brought there for the first time by a friend, a painter, in the year before the war. Sudeikin had decorated it—Tartaglia and Pantalone, Smeraldina and Brigella and Carlo Gozzi himself smiled and grimaced from the walls... Actors would declaim, poets recite poetry, the host take a guitar and sing. I danced for them one night to the music of Couperin... not on the stage, but in the midst of them, within a small space encircled by garlands of fresh flowers.[24]

Poets who read at the cabaret included Akhmatova, Kuzmin, Mandelstam, Adamovich, and Vladimir Shileiko. Works of the Symbolists were often read by Olga Glebova-Sudeikina or Blok's wife, Lyubov. Mikhail Kuzmin spent many nights accompanying himself on the piano to poems he had composed.

Livshits describes one of Akhmatova's "entrances" into the Stray

Osip Mandelstam, Korney Chukovsky, Benedikt Livshits,
Yury Annenkov. 1914

Akhmatova. Painting by Natan Altman, ca. 1914
Reproduced in Apollon, *1916*

Dog: "When Akhmatova sailed in, in a tight-fitting black silk dress, with a large oval cameo on her belt, she had to pause by the entrance in order to write her latest poems in the pigskin-bound book handed her by the insistent Pronin."[25] Adamovich recalls admiring Akhmatova when he visited the cabaret in 1912:

> They now sometimes refer to her in memoirs as a great beauty. No, that she wasn't. She was more than beautiful, something better. I have never seen another woman so expressive, her ability to capture attention. Later something of the tragic appeared in her. Rachel in "Phaedra" as Mandelstam said in his famous poem after one of her readings in the Stray Dog when . . . she seemed to ennoble and exalt everything around her . . . but my first impression was different. She smiled, laughed, was merry, slyly whispering to her neighbor. But then they asked her to read something, and she suddenly changed, as if turning pale, and in the "mocker," and "gay little sinner of Tsarskoye Selo" (as Akhmatova later characterized herself at the end of her life in *Requiem*) flashed the future Phaedra. But only for a moment. After that I frequently met her at the Stray Dog.[26]

Adamovich was referring to Mandelstam's poem written in 1914, when he compares Akhmatova reading her verse in the Stray Dog to the great actress Rachel playing Phaedra:

> *With a half-turn, oh sorrow,*
> *you note the indifferent.*
> *The imitation classical shawl turned to stone*
> *falling off a shoulder.*
>
> *Ominous voice—bitter rhapsody*
> *soul unchanging the womb:*
> *like Rachel, once, standing*
> *an indignant Phaedra.*[27]

Mayakovsky became a frequent visitor at the Stray Dog. Livshits describes a typical pose: "Mayakovsky was half-lying in the position of a wounded gladiator, on a Turkish drum which he banged every time the figure of a stray Futurist showed itself in the doorway."[28] Akhmatova relates that Mandelstam introduced her to Mayakovsky in the cabaret, and she recounts an amusing incident between the frail Mandelstam and the stalwart Mayakovsky: "Once when everyone was eating and dishes rattling, Mayakovsky decided to read his poetry. Mandelstam went up to him and said: 'Mayakovsky, stop reading poetry. You're not a Roumanian orchestra!'"[29]

Adamovich describes another encounter at the cabaret, this one between Akhmatova and Mayakovsky: "Once Mayakovsky, holding Akhmatova's slender, refined hand in his big paw, said with mocking enthusiasm: '*Palchiki-to, palchiki-to, Bozhe ty moi*' [These fingers, oh, these fingers, My God, you are mine!] She frowned and turned away."[30] Lily Brik, Mayakovsky's mistress for many years, said that whenever Mayakovsky was in love he read Akhmatova, quoting her poetry from morning until night while he suffered. She said he read Akhmatova constantly, every day.[31]

One of the members of the bohemian crowd that frequented the Stray Dog was Vladimir Shileiko, a noted Assyriologist and poet who married Akhmatova after the revolution. On 23 December 1913, after a lecture by Shklovsky on the place of Futurism in the history of language, Shileiko attacked the young orator, accusing him of complete ignorance and comparing Futurism to black magic. In the cabaret Shileiko's name was associated with a form of satirical improvisation he invented called "Zhora." Every line had to include a combination of the syllables *zho-ra*; the rest was up to the taste of the author. Akhmatova included a poem written to him at this time in her cycle devoted to him in *Anno Domini* (Zh. 246).

The central figure of the cabaret was the famous actress, dancer and singer, Olga Glebova-Sudeikina, who for many years was Akhmatova's closest friend, and later, the prototype for the female protagonist of her famous work recalling this period, *Poem Without a Hero*. Andrey Bely describes Sudeikina as "a fragile, youthful, charming blond, twittering pleasantly like a bird, reminding one of a Ceylonese butterfly with a swash of silks in a cloud of muslin."[32] Chukovsky notes that beginning in December 1909, her performances were mentioned in newspapers and magazines. She had, he said, infallible aesthetic taste and was close to the literary circles. He had met her at the home of the Symbolist poet, Fyodor Sologub, and at Ivanov's with Blok. "Elegant, charmingly feminine, always surrounded by hordes of admirers, she was the living embodiment of her desperate and piquant epoch." [33]

According to Elaine Moch-Bickert's excellent biography of the actress, Sudeikina was born on 27 May 1886 in Petersburg.[34] After leaving school, she played small roles in the Theatre Dramatique directed by Vera Kommisarzhevskaya, danced in "Swan Lake" at the Maly Theater and acted in Yury Belyaev's play "Psyche." Her repertoire in-

Akhmatova and Olga Sudeikina, 1924

cluded Rostand, Schiller, and the Commedia dell'Arte, and she had played the role of Columbine in Meyerhold's "Scarf of Columbine" at his experimental studio, the House of Intermediaries. One of Sudeikina's most popular theatrical roles was Confusion in Yury Belyaev's play of that name. It was a Christmas farce taking place in the middle of the nineteenth century. Kuzmin reviewed it in the 4 January 1910 issue of *Apollon.* "There is no production more graceful, more touching, more captivating." Her husband painted a full length portrait of her in the role, with cape, bonnet, and muff. Some of these works are associated with the heroine of Akhmatova's *Poem Without A Hero.* Sudeikina was also known for her sensitive interpretations of great poetry—not only Russians but also Baudelaire, Verlaine, Rimbaud, and Mallarmé—which she read at the Stray Dog.

On Twelfth Night, 6 January 1913, Sudeikina played the Madonna in a nativity play by Kuzmin, with sets and costumes by Sudeikin. The cellar was lit by candles and the public sat at long tables among which angel-children walked in silver garments with gold wings, carrying tall candles in their hands and singing in thin voices.[35] The ballet historian V. Krasovskaya describes another episode, which took place on 1 April 1913, one of the musical Mondays. The walls and windows were decorated with huge panels sewn from pieces of cloth based on Sudeikin's drawings. That night Sudeikina appeared as a bacchante in a nightmarish scene from a piece called *The Goat-legged Nymph,* with grotesque piano music by I.A. Stas. The gorgeous costumes of Sudeikina, her frenzied dance, and her unconsciously expressive movements all added to the effect. The choreography was by Boris Romanov and the music avant-garde and dissonant.[36] Akhmatova alludes to both the mystery play and the bacchanalian dance in *Poem Without a Hero.*

Rosary

In March 1914 Akhmatova's second volume of poetry, *Rosary,* was published. New religious motifs appear in this collection. At times these images function as sincere quests by Akhmatova to achieve comfort and solace through God. Elsewhere, she uses religion as an aesthetic device, part of her cultural heritage with its inbuilt associations, to express the many nuances of her relationships with a lover. Several critics emphasize her use of religious motifs as only a particular treatment of the love theme, and A. Gizetti goes so far as to see it only as a decadent pose: "She tries to...seek salvation in religion, but

Akhmatova's religiosity is merely externally clothed (though with complete sincerity) in simple, almost traditional forms; in essence it is the true religiosity of the 'fin-de-siècle'. . . an illusion of simplicity and beauty."[37] Sam Driver believes the subthemes of old Russia, Russian Orthodoxy, the Russian folk, ancient cities, and the Russian countryside all reflect Akhmatova's normal cultural heritage. She does not use mystical words, but ordinary ones any Russian Orthodox would know: *epitrakhil* (the long stole of the Orthodox priest), or *emalevy obrazok* (an enamel icon). These religious artifacts, Driver notes, "are as much a part of the tradition in which Akhmatova was nurtured as were the literary soirées and prerevolutionary intelligentsia society of St. Petersburg."[38] Yet this combination of religious themes with the dominant motif of passionate, earthly love led the critic Boris Eikhenbaum to call Akhmatova, "half-nun, half-harlot," a phrase that was picked up and used maliciously by the authorities much later in her career.

Other critics argue that the religion in these poems adds a dimension to the feelings depicted in earlier works, and shows her suffering to be not merely egocentric and personal but part of the Christian experience on earth. Chukovsky goes further: not just Christianity, but Russian Orthodoxy in particular informs Akhmatova's world view. "The immemorial Russian temptation: self-abnegation, resignation, martyrdom, meekness, poverty—recalling Tyutchev, Tolstoy, and Dostoevsky—fascinates [Akhmatova] as well."[39] Mandelstam says her "hieratic dignity, religious simplicity and solemnity" help distinguish her from the typical woman depicted in verse. "Her heroine is a strong personality who does not correspond with the conventional stereotype of a weak, sentimental woman."[40] Nadezhda Mandelstam says that Mandelstam spoke to her of Akhmatova in these terms before the revolution: "In Akhmatova's recent verse there has been a turn toward hieratic stateliness, a religious simplicity and solemnity. . . The voice of renunciation grows stronger all the time in her verse, and at the moment her poetry bids fair to become a symbol of Russian grandeur."[41]

Another prominent motif in *Rosary* is the city of St. Petersburg, which Akhmatova, unlike her Symbolist and Futurist contemporaries, portrays in all its historic beauty. As Driver notes, "it is the Petersburg of history which captures the imagination of the poet, not the modernity of the contemporary metropolis which so intrigued the Symbolists and Futurists."[42] They were drawn more to its ugliness and depravity. Akhmatova also used the city figuratively to reveal emotional states, as she used other aspects of her environment in her earlier poetry. Her appreciation of the solid, enduring nature of architecture has been contrasted with her observations about the frail human condition:

> It is as if the poet is saying to us: how much elegance, self-assurance, beauty, and strength in these towers, arches, cupolas erected by the human hand—and what vacillation, ephemeralness, bitterness, and sorrow in these flashing human shadows with their eternal mutual misunderstandings, fatal disagreements, and fleeting change of feeling. How heavy and sad is this fatal contrast between the world and life: the imperious charm of human construction and the insulting imperfection of its vacillating feelings and shy passions.[43]

Her poems also beautifully portray other Russian cities and towns —Tsarskoye Selo, Novgorod, Kiev, and golden Bakhchisarai.

One series of poems in *Rosary* depicts the male as victim, and the pity of the woman who hurt him as coming too late. Akhmatova may be assuming the persona of a woman who rejects her young admirer, or she may be portraying an actual affair she had with a young man whom she hurt. She may also be writing of her friend the cabaret actress, Olga Glebova-Sudeikina, who rejected a young poet-officer, Vsevolod Knyazev. Knyazev then committed suicide in March 1913, an event that became the main plot of Akhmatova's *Poem Without a Hero*. In the last two lines of "The boy said to me..." (Zh. 76), Akhmatova typically selects a few details to reveal the relationship between the two: the young man's passion is reflected in how he ardently strokes the woman's cold hands, which in turn reflect her feelings toward him. His dimming eyes suggest his grief. The poem is reminiscent of Pushkin's poetic narrative, "Cleopatra," in which the last lover to pay with death for his night of love with the priestess of Aphrodite is a young boy, and he will feel the most pain.[44] In "The Voice of Memory" (Zh. 79), the epigraph devoted to Sudeikina indicates that the speaker is alluding to the suicide and perhaps condemning Sudeikina for her apparent indifference. The motif of memory serves a moral function, as it does in much of Akhmatova's work, especially *Poem Without a Hero:* forgetting one's past sins is self-deceit, but consciously remembering and atoning for them leads to salvation.

Other motifs in *Rosary,* or in poems written during this period, became allusions in *Poem Without a Hero.* Akhmatova makes several references to the Stray Dog and to those who frequented and entertained there. In "To Tamara Platonova Karsavina" (Zh. 512), she recalls the evening devoted to the prima ballerina of the Ballets Russes. Her poem on the artistic cabaret (Zh. 62), dated 1 January 1913, exemplifies the vast difference between her work and that of Alexander Blok, whose poem "The Stranger" is set in a similar environment. While the Symbolist found revelation in the eyes of the celebrants and creative intuition in wine (*in vino veritas*), Akhmatova sees unhappy carousers shut up in a cellar, making merry, hiding from the storm outside—which may signify the increasing political chaos leading to the revolution. The same cast of characters, including the poet, shows up later in *Poem Without a Hero.* The poem is reminiscent of Pushkin's "small tragedy," *The Feast During the Time of the Plague,* in which the aristocracy revels when death is near instead of helping those in dire need around them.[45]

Over the course of her life, Akhmatova wrote several poems to Blok. One of the most famous, "I visited the poet..." (Zh. 106), was written in January 1914. Although rumors hinted of an affair, Akhmatova insisted she did not meet Blok more than ten times in her life, and with one exception, the visits were always in the company of other people.[46] The exception was at the end of December 1913, when she went to get a book inscribed by Blok and stayed forty minutes.[47] In spite of their brief acquaintance, Blok had a profound influence on her work. Rather than a continuation of his work, however, hers was a conscious reaction against it. Her poem "I visited the poet," for example, is a deliberate answer to Blok's poem written about her on 16 December 1913.

"Beauty is terrible," they'll tell you—
You'll lazily throw
The Spanish shawl over your shoulders
A red rose—in your hair.

"Beauty is simple," they'll tell you—
Awkwardly with your colorful shawl
You'll cover the baby,
The red rose—on the floor.

But, distracted, listening
To every word around you,
You'll muse sadly
And say to yourself:

"Not terrible nor simple am I;
I'm not so terrible simply
to kill; not so simple am I,
Not to know how terrifying life is."[48]

A few months earlier, in the autumn of 1913, Blok and Akhmatova gave a poetry reading on a day honoring the poet Verhaeren, then visiting Russia. Akhmatova describes in her memoirs an incident revealing the awe she felt toward Blok. A student came to tell Akhmatova she would be reading after Blok, and she was afraid. When Blok heard this he said, "We are not tenors," meaning they need not act like prima donnas. Akhmatova says: "By this time Blok was very famous. I had been reciting my poems quite frequently at the Poets' Guild, the Society of Admirers of the Artistic Word, and in Ivanov's Tower, but this was something different."[49]

Blok noted in his diary the first time he met Akhmatova in 1911, and says he found her work exciting. She describes in her memoirs her visit to him at home on Ofitserskaya Street.

> I brought Blok his books so he could inscribe them... In the third volume he wrote a madrigal devoted to me... I never had a Spanish shawl...but at this time Blok was raving about Carmen and Spanishized me. I also, of course, never wore a red rose in my hair. It makes sense that he wrote in the Spanish form of a *romancero.* At our last meeting behind the wings of the Bolshoy Theater in the spring of 1921 Blok came up to me and asked: "And where is your Spanish shawl?" Those were the last words I heard from his lips.[50]

The incident, according to Zhirmunsky, was more complicated than Akhmatova's version. Blok had been notified in advance about Akhmatova's visit as well as her intention to ask him for an inscription to the books. As his notebooks show, he had written the "madrigal" the evening before, experimenting with various forms before settling on the Spanish form.[51] Akhmatova deliberately contrasts her portrait of him with his romanticized portrayal of her in his own poem. In her work she replaces the Spanish exotica with a realistic picture of the Russian winter and the poet himself. After writing it, Akhmatova sent the poem to Blok. It was published along with his poem to her in the March 1914 issue of the journal *Love for Three Oranges,* of which he was poetry editor. She also sent him a copy of *Rosary* in March 1914, and inscribed the title page with the lines:

"From you came uneasiness
And the ability to write verse"   (S-F. 27, III, 31)

Many beautiful poems in *Rosary* further explore the theme of unre-
quited love that appeared in *Evening*. Here, too, Akhmatova selects a
gesture to reveal the true nature of a relationship, as in one of her most
often quoted verses, "One would not mistake true tenderness..."
(Zh. 68). Actions, without sincere feeling behind them, cannot fool a
woman who loves: the suitor, to whom she addresses the poem, wraps
her in furs and utters respectful words about first love, but this means
nothing; his eyes reveal his indifference.

Several poems continue another theme established earlier: the price
a poet must pay for her gift of poetry—disappointment in love. In
"How many demands the beloved can make..." (Zh. 71), fame has be-
come bitter because the speaker can find neither love nor peace. In "We
met for the last time..." (Zh. 72), a woman's creativity is ridiculed by
the lover who is about to leave her forever. Instead of despairing, she
becomes inspired by the beauty of Petersburg, by the famous fortress
and the tsar's palace, and arrives at her latest song.[52] Gumilyov,
reviewing *Rosary* in *Apollon 5* of 1914, had nothing but praise for his
wife's work: "As with most young poets, in Anna Akhmatova one fre-
quently finds the words pain, sorrow, death. This youthful pessimism,
so natural and therefore so beautiful, has been the property of 'pen
testers' until now but in her verse it has attained a place in poetry for
the first time. Women in love, sly, dreamy, and rapturous, at last speak
their own genuine and at the same time artistically convincing lan-
guage."[53] In his letters during these years, Gumilyov continually
asked her for poems and frequently praised those he received.

In 1915 Akhmatova wrote her first great *poema,* entitled *At the Edge
of the Sea* (S-F. I, 349-357; Zh. 646). Haight interprets it to be about
childhood brought to an end by contact with death.[54] Akhmatova
borrowed the title from the beginning of Pushkin's "Tale of the
Fisherman and Fisherman's Wife": "There lives an old man with his
old woman/ By the shore of the blue sea." In her notes, Akhmatova as-
sociates the first lines of *At the Edge of the Sea* with her recollection of
Blok's poem, "Venice," from his cycle "Italian Verses":[55]

With her I went out to sea,
With her I abandoned the shore
With her I was off afar
With her I forgot those nearby...[56]

The work, as Zhirmunsky shows, is not a departure from her lyric poetry, but reflects "the maturation of the youthful poetic consciousness, the awakening of love and grief."[57]

The poet Marietta Shaginyan wrote in 1922 what this poem meant to her generation and what it would mean to the one following the revolution:

> Now when the old editions have disappeared, many (especially the contemporary adolescent readers) have not read this poem. For them it will be a discovery; for us it was a revelation. Can it be the real *aesthetic* charm which at first was hidden from us now suddenly has become a classical work? The rhythm, which seems broken, reflected a very profound similarity to Russian folk song. The images which at that time seemed mannered, now have become truly, simply, a drawing true and eternal in its absolute truth... The entire poem seems like a marvelous seashell full of the sound of the sea and the wind, just like when you put a shell to your ear. The mannered Petersburg lady, foster child of the once fashionable Acmeism, as fashionable as the poet herself, is concealed by her behind this personal and most wonderful simple lyric.[58]

III. The "True Twentieth Century" Begins: 1914–1917

In the summer of 1914 the war that would move Russia ever closer to revolution finally arrived. The Germans attacked in June, and the Emperor assumed the role of commander-in-chief, leaving the capital in the hands of the reactionary Empress, and, through her, to Rasputin. The Russians suffered greater casualties than the armed forces of any other country involved in the struggle. Russian weapons were inferior, ammunition was in short supply, transportation often broke down, there were food and fuel shortages among the urban population, inflation ran rampant. Richard Charques sums up the effect of the war: "For none of the belligerents was the First World War so catastrophic or so costly as it was for Russia."[1]

For Akhmatova, the twentieth century really began in 1914 with the war, just as the nineteenth century had begun in 1814 with the international Congress of Vienna, after Napoleon's banishment to Elba. "Calendrical dates have no meaning. In essence no one knows what epoch he lives in. We also did not know at the beginning of the 1910s that we lived on the eve of the first European war and the October

Revolution,"[2] she wrote in her memoirs.

She spent that summer at Slepnyovo, one of the last peaceful periods she would have in her life. "I wore a green malachite necklace and cap of fine lace. In my room was a hard, narrow couch, and in the cupboard the remains of an old library. It was there that I greeted the war of 1914 and spent the last summer of 1917... Peasant women went out into the fields to work in homespun sarafans and at that time the old women and uncouth young wenches seemed more elegant than ancient statues."[3]

Gumilyov enlisted immediately. In war he could prove his love for his homeland, and also realize the role of the conquistador heroes of his own works. Other poets were affected differently. Blok at the time was helping families of the mobilized. Akhmatova tells how Blok lunched at the Tsarskoye Selo train station with her and Gumilyov, who was already in uniform, on 5 April 1914. When Blok left, Gumilyov turned to Akhmatova and said: "Are they really sending him to the front? That's like roasting nightingales."[4]

Mayakovsky read a poem in the Stray Dog ridiculing the bourgeoisie for failing to show up at the front, but he had no more desire to fight than they did. The army decided to use his artistic talents in the draftsman's office of an automobile school for the duration of the war.

White Flock

Akhmatova's third collection of poetry, *White Flock,* appeared in 1917, with many of the poems written during the war. In a few poems she uses parallelism typical of folk poetry, depicting a human or philosophical condition in a scene from nature. In "May Snow" (Zh. 153), for example, the spring snow that kills the swelling buds, bringing death during the ritual time of youth, rebirth, and renewal, evokes the young soldiers dying before their time. She dates the poem "Prayer" (Zh. 162) on a holy day, Pentecost, and offers to suffer—to give up child and lover, and even her gift of song—if only Russia may be saved. Her most famous war poems appear under the general title "July 1914." As in the *Igor Tale,* Russia's great epic,[5] nature reflects the doom hovering over the Russian land: "The birds have not even sung today,/ And the aspen has stopped quaking." At the end, Akhmatova invokes her Orthodox culture, predicting that the Mother of God will spread her mantle in protection. The gesture refers to the Russian Orthodox holiday of Pokrov, which commemorates the legend of the

Gumilyov and Akhmatova with their son Lev. 1915 or 1916

Madonna appearing to Andrew, a saint in a church in Constantinople. By extending her veil over the congregation, the Madonna conveyed that she would forever be protector and intercessor for her people.

Even before the war, during the winter of 1913, in "Oh, it was a cold day..." (Zh. 125), Akhmatova began to portray the poet as prophet. The role was part Cassandra, part Russian *klikusha* (screamer), the female counterpart of the "holy fool," who, though considered mad, is treated with great respect since she is believed to be endowed by God with the gift of prophecy.[6] As Blok had been doing for so many years, Akhmatova was beginning to express in her poetry the impending doom over Russia. In "This was my prayer..." (Zh. 126), written that same year, she echoes motifs from Pushkin's famous poem "The Prophet." The poet in Pushkin's poem passively receives the gift of the Lord through a visit from an angel:

> Tormented by spiritual thirst I dragged myself through a sombre desert. And a six-winged seraph appeared to me at the crossing of the ways. He touched my eyes with fingers as light as a dream: and my prophetic eyes opened like those of a frightened eagle... He bent

down to my mouth and tore out my tongue, sinful, deceitful, and given to idle talk; and with his right hand steeped in blood he inserted the forked tongue of a wise serpent into my benumbed mouth... And the voice of God called out to me: "Arise, O prophet, see and hear, be filled with My will, go forth over land and sea, and set the hearts of men on fire with your Word."[7]

In Akhmatova's poem, the speaker actively prays for the Lord to open her sealed eyes and make her mute tongue speak again.

The city of Petersburg functions figuratively in a poem in *White Flock* that, once again, concerns the poet's relationship to the Muse (Zh. 145). The city symbolizes the alienation fame brings, the price paid by the poet and those who share the major events taking place in the capital. Those who live there cannot live "somewhere [where] there is a simple life." Yet those cursed to live in this city also achieve fame and would not choose to live otherwise:

> *But not for anything would we exchange this splendid*
> *Granite city of fame and calamity,*
> *The wide rivers of glistening ice,*
> *The sunless, gloomy gardens,*
> *And, barely audible, the Muse's voice.*

In "No, tsarevitch..." (Zh. 182) Akhmatova combines the motifs of the prophet and the price of fame. Fame is a trap with neither joy nor light, and hers are the lips that no longer kiss but prophesy.

Her poems, like those of Gumilyov at this time, also reveal the disintegration of a marriage. Gumilyov expresses his inability to display passionate emotion or give his wife the attention she needs in "Iambic Pentameter"(1913), written on his last trip to Africa:

> *I know that life has not worked out...and you,*
>
> *You for whom I searched through the Levant*
> *For royal mantles of unfading purple,*
> *I've gambled you away as crazy Nalla*
> *Did Damayanti that time long ago.*
> *The dice fell with a ring like steel,*
> *The dice fell—and there sorrow lay.*
>
> *You said in a thoughtful and strict tone:*
> *"I have believed and loved too much, I go*
> *No longer holding any trust or love*
> *And maybe before God's all-seeing face*

I am wrecking my life as I cut off
Myself from you for ever."

I was not brave enough to kiss your hair
Or even press your cold, thin hands in mine,
Was hateful like a spider to myself
And every sound frightened and tortured me
And in a plain dark dress you walked away
Like an ancient crucifix.[8]

In "Ah! It's you again..." (Zh. 121), the speaker confesses adultery, realizing that the enamored youth who fell in love with her has now turned into a stern, inflexible, and unforgiving husband. She admits her guilt and asks for forgiveness, but knows it will not come easily. As in Akhmatova's earlier poetry, a sudden switch to a scene from nature is prompted by its emotional associations: the speaker conjures up an autumnal landscape, with the eerie cries of cranes and the leafless garden, a time of dying and sorrow.

Another poem, "Under an oaken slab..." (Zh. 170), may reveal the guilt Akhmatova felt as a mother. The poem projects into the future, with a mother dreaming of her child who comes to the place where she is buried. From beyond the grave, she asks forgiveness for ignoring him. The mother did not act in a typical maternal way—she did not scold him, did not hold him, and did not take him to Communion. She is a "non-mother." It is one of Akhmatova's first poems to use the motif of the "non-event," where something that should happen or is hoped for never takes place—a motif that becomes stronger in later works.

The critic Nikolay Nedobrovo was a close friend of Akhmatova's during this time, and above all others remained perceptive of the true nature of her poetry. Nedobrovo was noted for his handsome features and refined manners. He was slender, with narrow, expressive hands and skin that resembled porcelain. "People who had only seen him for a moment remembered him forever," Yu. L. Sazonovaya wrote. "He seemed to be from the nineteenth century, so refined and fragile."[9] Nedobrovo's article, "Anna Akhmatova" (1915) predicted Akhmatova's great future and set her off from sentimental female poets of the time.[10] The poem written to him in May 1915, "There is a sacred boundary..." (Zh. 127), reveals a restraint on the part of the speaker, who explains how they always keep a part of themselves away from the other: "There is a sacred boundary between those who are close." She met Nedobrovo in 1913, and that summer he spent more than a

Nikolay Nedobrovo

month in Pavlovsk where they frequently saw each other. In a letter to
his friend, the artist Boris Anrep, dated 27 April 1914, he writes that
it is impossible to call her beautiful, but she looks so unique that a
Leonardo drawing or Gainsborough portrait should be made of her.
In another letter to Anrep dated 12 May of that year, he says he is writ-
ing material to amuse Akhmatova in her "Tver solitude."[11]

    Akhmatova's relationship to Anrep was revealed in a memoir in-
cluded in a letter to Gleb Struve, which he asked Struve not to publish
until after his death.[12] Anrep explains the story of the famous poem,
"The Tale of the Black Ring" (Zh. 266), which appears in *Anno Domini*.
He says the ring was gold, with black enamel in the center and a small
diamond. Akhmatova always wore this ring and ascribed mysterious
powers to it. After receiving numerous enthusiastic letters from his
friend Nedobrovo, praising the beauty and poetic gift of Akhmatova,

Anrep finally met her in 1914 on his return from Paris before leaving for the front. He was charmed by her exciting personality and witty remarks, but even more by "the lovely, tormentedly touching poetry." Anrep soon became a central figure in Akhmatova's life, winning her affection in a way Nedobrovo had been unable to do.[13]

Struve reports that a woman named V. A. Znamenskaya, who was an admirer of Nedobrovo when she was a young student at the time, wrote to Anrep on 20 October 1967 saying Nedobrovo's wife had been upset about her husband's relationship with Akhmatova. Nedobrovo wrote Znamenskaya from the Crimea in the summer of 1915, reporting his unexpected grief because of the change in Akhmatova's relationship to him.[14] During that year, Anrep frequently saw Akhmatova when on leave from the front. He gave her a copy of his poem "Fiza," which she sewed into a silken purse and said she would keep as a sacred relic. They would go sleighing, eat supper at restaurants, and she would recite her poems to him, smiling and singing them in a quiet voice. "Often we were silent and listened to the sounds around us."[15] During one of their meetings in 1915 he spoke about his lack of faith, and she scolded him, pointing to faith as a pledge of happiness. Later, she wrote a poem relating to this conversation, "I will root out this day from your memory..." (Zh. 183).

Early in 1916 Anrep was assigned to England on a mission and came to Petersburg for an extended period to prepare for his departure to London. Nedobrovo and his wife were living in Tsarskoye Selo. He invited Anrep to visit on 13 February to listen to him read his just-completed tragedy, *Judith*. "Anna Akhmatova will be there," he added. Anrep describes the incident:

> For me to come from the front and find myself in the refined atmosphere of Nedobrovo's Tsarskoye Selo home, hear *Judith*... and see Anna Akhmatova was very attractive. I entered and saw Akhmatova sitting on a small divan, and as I went up to her a secret anxiety came over me, an incomprehensible sick feeling which I always felt whenever I met her or even thought about her. I sat down beside her and Nedobrovo opened the manuscript, sitting behind a lovely Italian Renaissance desk and began to read... In spite of his impeccable verse, I listened without hearing and tried to concentrate... I closed my eyes and put my hand on the seat of the couch. Suddenly something fell into my hand; it was the black ring. "Take it," whispered Akhmatova, "It's for you." I wanted to say something. My heart was

beating. I looked questioningly at her face, but she looked silently ahead. I compressed my hand into a fist and Nedobrovo continued reading. Finally it was over... Tea was poured and Akhmatova spoke with his wife. I rushed to leave and Akhmatova stayed on. In a few days I had to leave for England.[16]

The day before his departure he received Akhmatova's book *Evening* with the inscription: "To Boris Anrep—One hope less has become one song more. 13 February 1916. Tsarskoye Selo." Earlier he had given Akhmatova a wooden cross he had taken from a half-ruined, abandoned church in the Carpathian mountains of Galicia and had written a four-line poem:

I forgot the words and didn't say a vow.
Idiot, I put my hands on the helpless maiden
To guard her from the goblet and torment of crucifixion
Which I myself, as a sign of friendship, had given her.[17]

Anrep left for London and planned to return in six weeks, but the war prevented his doing so. He came back at the end of 1916 for a short time, and then left Russia forever. His crucifix did not guard Akhmatova from the torment she felt because of his departure, which she expressed in several poems at various points in her life. They saw each other in Paris at the end of Akhmatova's life, when she went there after receiving an honorary degree at Oxford, but the meeting was awkward for both of them. How different her life might have been had she left Russia, as Anrep did.[18]

IV. The Revolution: 1917–1922

In 1917 power was rapidly slipping out of the tsar's hands. Many thought the legislative body, the Duma, should assume power, carry the war to a victorious conclusion, and create a republic or constitutional monarchy. In February the tsar was deposed and a new government born; but another authority arose at the same time—the soviets, or councils of workers and soldiers. "By March Russia had in fact two governments, the Provisional headed by Prince Lvov and liberal noblemen, the other the Soviet of Workers' and Soldiers' Deputies."[1] Each issued conflicting orders, compounding the chaos. In July Alexander Kerensky became Prime Minister, but his leadership grew weaker as that of the soviets increased. Finally, on 25 October 1917, the Winter Palace—where the Provisional government conferred—

was stormed, and the government handed over to the Bolsheviks. A peace treaty was signed with Germany in March 1918. The capital was moved to Moscow. But the fighting did not end. For three years the Bolsheviks waged a bloody civil war.

Akhmatova describes the winter in Slepnyovo just before the revolution:

Once I was at Slepnyovo in the winter. It was wonderful. Everything seemed to go back to the nineteenth century, to Pushkin's time. Sleighs, felt boots, bear lap rugs, huge fur coats, gaping silence, snow-drifts, diamond snow. It was there I met and welcomed 1917. After the gloomy military Sebastopol where I had been resting from asthma and was freezing in a cold rented room, it was as if I had come upon some kind of promised land. In Petersburg Rasputin had already been killed, and they were awaiting the revolution.[2]

She lived in Petersburg with her friends, the Sreznevskys, from January 1917 until the autumn of 1918 at Botkinskaya 9. Valeriya Sreznevskaya was a childhood friend, and her husband a senior doctor at a mental institution. Boris Anrep came to see her before he left for England. He describes his last visit with Akhmatova in his letter to Struve:

The streets of Petrograd were full of people. Shots were heard everywhere. I was not spending much time thinking about the revolution. I had only one thought, one desire: to see Akhmatova. At that time she was living in the apartment of Professor Sreznevsky on the other side of the Neva. I crossed the ice of the Neva in order to avoid the barricades near the bridges. I reached the house and rang the bell. The door opened and Akhmatova said, "Oh, it's you? On a day like this? They're grabbing officers on the street." She was visibly touched... For some time we spoke about the meaning of the revolution. She was excited and said we must expect more changes in our lives. "The same thing's going to happen that happened in France during the revolution, but maybe even worse." We became silent and she dropped her head. "We won't see each other any more. You're leaving." "I'll come back. Look: your ring." I unfastened my jacket and showed her the black ring on the chain around my neck. She touched the ring. "That's good, it'll save you. It's a sacred object," she whispered. Something eternally feminine clouded her eyes as she held out her arms to me. I burned in sexless ecstasy, kissed her hands and got up. Akhmatova smiled tenderly. "It's better this way," she said. I left for England on the first train.[3]

Once abroad, Anrep notes in the same letter, he soon heard of Nedobrovo's death from tuberculosis. "Just before this I had written him a wild letter from which I remember one stupid but sincere phrase: 'Dear Nikolay, please don't die, you and Anna Akhmatova are the only thing left of Russia for me!'"

After the revolution, Akhmatova worked at the Library of the Institute of Agronomy, and wrote little. Mandelstam often came to see her. "We drove in horse-drawn cabs over the incredible ruts in the roads that winter of revolution, between the famous bonfires that burnt almost until May, to the rumble of guns carried from somewhere unknown," she wrote in her memoirs. "We drove like this to poetry recitals at the Academy of Arts, where there were evenings in aid of the wounded and where we both performed several times."[4] His attention became too much for her and went beyond her sense of decorum: "I had to explain to Osip that we should not meet so frequently, that it would provide material for a negative interpretation of the nature of our relationship. After this, around March, Mandelstam disappeared."[5]

Akhmatova had difficulties adjusting to the harshness of the post-revolutionary years. A contemporary describes her at this time: "She was often sick, very thin, her dry hands folded (like the claws of a great bird). She lived in misery and dressed very modestly. One day she showed me a piece of money which she was keeping as a souvenir: an old woman had given it to her in the street, taking her for a beggar. Apparently, the old lady did not see very clearly because the carriage and demeanor of this beggar was that of a queen."[6]

In 1918 Gumilyov returned from Europe and Akhmatova asked for a divorce. While in England, he had visited Anrep, who tried to persuade him not to leave. But his homeland beckoned him. Anrep said they frequently discussed Akhmatova's poetry, and clearly remembered one thing Gumilyov said: "I highly esteem her poems but to understand all their beauty is given only to one who understands the depths of her beautiful soul."[7] Gumilyov had spent six months in Paris, from July 1917 to January 1918, and had fallen in love with a half-Russian and half-French woman, Elena Duboucher.[8] He devoted a cycle of poems to her, "To the Blue Star," which was published posthumously in 1923.

Akhmatova also found out about Gumilyov's affair with Larisa Reisner during the war. Reisner was a beautiful young woman, a poet who became a devoted Bolshevik after the revolution. Gumilyov wrote her passionate love poems. On 8 December 1916 he wrote how much he missed her: "Everything I know and love, I want to see as if through colored glass, through your soul, because it has a special color... I remember your every word, every nuance, every movement, but it's not enough. I want more."[9]

In spite of his infidelity, Gumilyov had difficulty granting Akhmatova the divorce: "I lived with Nikolay seven years. We were friendly and inwardly obligated to each other. But I told him we must divorce. He didn't object but I saw he was insulted... He had just returned from Paris after his unsuccessful love for Elena the Blue Star. He was full of her, but still my desire to leave him insulted him... We went together to Bezhetsk to see Lev. We sat on the couch, and Levushka played between us. Kolya said, 'And why are you doing this?' And that was all."[10]

That same year, 1918, Akhmatova married the Assyriologist Vladimir Shileiko. Nadezhda Mandelstam said Shileiko took Akhmatova to the house manager's office and registered her there, although the manager was not authorized to approve marriages. Nobody was quite certain in those days about the procedure for get-

Vladimir Shileiko

ting married, and Akhmatova thought this was sufficient. "Only when they parted she understood the difference between the Register's Office [at the official 'House of Marriage'] and the house manager's office."[11] Shileiko was also a poet who published in leading journals such as *Apollon* and *Hyperborean*. While most critics see him as a negative influence during the difficult years after the revolution, his daughter-in-law, Tamara Shileiko, argues otherwise. In a long article chronicling him as both an internationally-known scholar and a deeply caring individual, she notes how much affection he felt for Akhmatova, even though their marriage lasted only three years. Anatoly Naiman says that Akhmatova spoke about her marriage with Shileiko as a sad misunderstanding, but without any shade of the resentment or anger that was reflected in the poems addressed to him.[12]

Shileiko became a member of the Collegium of the Hermitage for the Preservation of Monuments in 1918 and was given lodgings in Fountain House, the former Scheremetev Palace. He had a dark, oblong room, with a bed, sofa and large round table, and at night, to the light of a kerosene lamp, he would analyze clay tablets. He continued to publish his poems in journals at this time and was on the Board of Editors of Maxim Gorky's publishing house, All World Literature, and head of the Translators' Studio.

Akhmatova expressed interest in his stories about the Near East and loved to listen to him recite Egyptian and Babylonian texts, appreciating the music of ancient speech. Shileiko told her about gods and kings, read tablets in the language of the original, and then translated them for her into Russian.[13] For some time they lived in his room in the servants' wing in Fountain House. Later they moved to the Marble Palace on Millionnaya Street (now Khalturin 5) where they had two rooms—a luxury at the time, although residents heated their own stoves and had no electricity, only kerosene lamps and candles.[14] Several memoirs reproach Shileiko for making Akhmatova stand in long lines to get rations. Yet as Tamara Shileiko points out, he had to work in the library all day, and thanks to his ration cards, the family survived. Gorky was doing everything possible for the colleagues of his publishing house to ensure they would not die of starvation.

Chukovsky records their harsh living conditions in a diary entry of 19 January 1920. "Yesterday at Anna Akhmatova's. She and Shileiko are in one large room with a bed behind a screen. It's damp in the room, cold, with books all over the floor. Her eyes seem dim, and her throat raspy. She told me with pride that Shileiko is translating verse, dictating it to her directly." On 25 January he wrote of a terrible frost, and went to see Akhmatova again. Shileiko was sick in bed. She recited Pushkin by heart. But her conversation with Chukovsky suggests she could not easily adapt to her circumstances and forget her more elegant past: "Today she's like a woman of the world, speaking about the latest fashion in Europe and how Russia was behind."[15]

When the Civil War ended in 1921, the state was in economic turmoil. Lenin realized he lacked trained managers to run the new socialist society, and introduced NEP (the New Economic Policy), with the state retaining large industrial plants, transportation, big banks and trade, while permitting private enterprise on a small scale. Although this policy helped industry and agriculture meet the basic needs of the population, it encouraged large-scale corruption and speculation among a new breed spawned by this period, the NEP-men.[16]

By 1921 Akhmatova's relationship with Shileiko had deteriorated. Zhirmunsky notes that Shileiko had been an enthusiastic admirer of Akhmatova's poetry, but a difficult and eccentric man. He cites a conversation between Akhmatova and Chukovskaya that sums up their life together: "Three years of hunger... Vladimir was sick. He could manage without anything, only not without tea and something to

Artur Lourié

smoke. We rarely cooked food—there was nothing to make. . . If I had lived with him any longer I also would have forgotten how to write poetry. He simply was a man with whom it was impossible to live."[17]

Akhmatova moved in with her friends Olga Sudeikina and composer Artur Lourié, at Fontanka 2, an 18th century hotel.[18] On 24 December 1921, Chukovsky visited her in Sudeikina's apartment. She had a small room with a large bed and a table.

> We talked for a long time. The old female servant came in and said there was no wood for tomorrow. "Never mind," said Akhmatova. "Tomorrow I'll bring a saw and we'll saw together." She put down some large pieces of paper on the table. "This is the ballet 'Snow Mask,' based on Blok. Please pay attention to the style. I don't know how to write prose," and she began to read her libretto to me, which was like a beautiful, elegant commentary to "Snow Mask." She was writing for Artur Lourié. "Perhaps Diaghilev will produce it in Paris." Then she began to read me her poems, and when she read the one about Blok (about his death in 1921) I began to sob and ran out.[19]

The artist Yury Annenkov also recounts in his memoirs visiting Akhmatova. At the beginning of the 1920s, after an evening at a poetry reading in late autumn, he accompanied Sudeikina home. It was raining, and Olga suggested he sleep on the couch, since he had no umbrella. In the morning Akhmatova knocked and came in wearing a dark dress and striped apron, and carrying a tray with cups, tea, and black bread. "I've brought the children something to eat," she smiled. Annenkov writes: "What could have been more humble or comfortable than this scene? I must admit the tea and sugar that day tasted better than the most elegant dish somewhere at the Tour d'Argent or at Maxim's."[20]

Even after she left Shileiko in 1921, Akhmatova saw him frequently. On the title page of a copy of *White Flock* that she gave him as a gift, she inscribed, "To Vladimir Shileiko with love, Anna Akhmatova, Autumn, 1922," and below, a line from a Mandelstam poem: "In Petersburg we will meet again."

Petersburg at that time was in its death throes, soon to be rebuilt and transformed into the Soviet city of Leningrad. The poet Vladislav Khodasevich describes it exhibiting a stark and almost terrifying beauty:

> The society of old Petersburg had outlived the period of its blossoming. The more life forged ahead, the more sharply members of the

Akhmatova. Drawing by Yury Annenkov, 1921

society felt the inevitable separation with the past, and this was the
reason they so much wanted to preserve a memory of it... At that
time Petersburg became more lovely than it had ever been and might
ever be again. Even the most ordinary houses took on a severity and
grandeur that only the palaces used to have. Petersburg had been
depopulated, trams had stopped running, only rarely could the sound
of hooves or cars honking be heard—but the absence of movement
was more suitable to Petersburg than motion. There are some people
who look better in their coffin—so it was with Petersburg. This was
a beauty that was ephemeral. Right after came the horrible ugliness of
the end. Right in front of our eyes decay began to touch Petersburg:
the sidewalks collapsed, plaster crumbled...hands broke off statues.
But even this barely perceptible decay was lovely. Nightingales sang
at night in Alexander Square and on the Moika.[21]

The cultural life of Petersburg, he notes, was concentrated around
three centers: the House of Scholars, the House of Literature, and the
House of Arts. During the afternoon meal at the House of Arts the in-
telligentsia came from all over the city to meet with colleagues and
friends. Adamovich describes one evening when he met Akhmatova at
the House of Arts just before he left Russia. Vodka, hors d'oeuvres,
and meat-filled tarts were served—a feast for those years. He saw
Akhmatova—the same shawl on her shoulders, the same sad and calm
glance, the same singular figure. "I went up to her and told her how
beautiful she looked. She smiled, and bending over, whispered, 'The
dog has become old' [She was about 30 at the time]. Those were the
last words I heard from Akhmatova before I left Russia."[22]

During these difficult years, Akhmatova's innate generosity did
not wane. Chukovsky mentions several times when she helped his
young daughter. On 3 February 1921 he notes in his diary that he en-
countered Akhmatova in the vestibule of the House of Scholars, and
she told him to come see her so she could give him milk for his daugh-
ter. "I ran over to see her in the evening and she gave it to me! Imagine
in February 1921 someone offering another person a bottle of milk!"[23]

The year 1921 brought the deaths of two major figures in both the
intellectual milieu and Akhmatova's life, Gumilyov and Blok, leaving
a terrible gap in many people's lives. Adamovich writes: "After the
revolution everything in our lives changed. True, not immediately. At
first it seemed the political revolution would not touch our private
lives—but this illusion did not last long. Akhmatova and Gumilyov
were divorced, the First Guild ceased, the Stray Dog closed, Blok

died, Gumilyov was arrested and shot. The times became difficult, dark, and hungry."[24]

Blok died in August 1921, exhausted and disillusioned. He was buried on 10 August. Vitaly Vilenkin, a theater historian and friend of Akhmatova, describes the last time Akhmatova saw Blok.

Akhmatova spoke about Blok's evening in the Bolshoy Drama Theatre in the spring of 1921. That evening all the Petrograd literary and artistic intelligentsia arrived. They came by foot, from everywhere— there were no trams. Everyone dressed poorly; they were hungry. Akhmatova sat with Khodasevich in a box. Everyone asked Blok to keep reading. It was obvious how tired he was. "If only they would leave him alone!"—she whispered in Khodasevich's ear. They met behind the wings. Blok raised his eyes to her and greeted her. "But where's your Spanish shawl?" They never saw each other again.[25]

Blok at this time was made to feel he was but a remnant of the past, just as critics tried to make Akhmatova feel several years later. Chukovsky describes Blok's appearance at a reading in May 1921: "I was sitting backstage with him. On stage some 'orator' or other... was cheerfully demonstrating to the crowd that as a poet Blok was already dead. 'These verses are just dead rubbish written by a corpse.' Blok leaned over to me and said, "That's true. He's telling the truth, I'm dead.'"[26] When Chukovsky asked him why he did not write poetry any more, Blok always gave the same reply: "All sounds have stopped. Can't you hear that there are no longer any sounds?"

Like Akhmatova, Blok turned to Pushkin in times of internal turmoil. In a poem called "To Pushkin House," the Institute devoted to the study of the great poet, he calls on Pushkin for guidance:

Pushkin! Following in your steps
We sang of secret freedom!
Give us your hand in these troubled times,
Help us in our silent struggle![27]

While attending Blok's funeral, Akhmatova heard Gumilyov had been arrested. After his return to Russia, Gumilyov took an active part in the literary world. He founded a new version of the Poets' Guild, although most of the members of the earlier Guild, including Akhmatova, did not participate. Blok wrote a scathing review of the new group, saying it was "without divinity and without inspiration," and he found the works of Gumilyov and other members vapid and pretentious.

In his memoirs, Khodasevich describes Gumilyov during this period, when they both stayed at the House of Arts. Gumilyov had difficulty adapting to the new conditions. Khodasevich begins by describing the reaction of the post-revolutionary intelligentsia. They were cold and hungry, trying in vain to keep up appearances under the new circumstances: "My God, how this crowd was dressed! Felt boots, sweaters, torn overcoats with which it was impossible to part even in the ballroom. Then, with befitting lateness, Gumilyov appears with a lady on his arm; she was shivering in a black dress with a deep slit. He walked upright and arrogantly in his frock coat, passing through the hall. He was trembling from the cold, but he bowed magnificently and politely to the right and left and conversed with acquaintances in a worldly tone... His entire appearance said: 'Nothing's happened. The revolution? I haven't heard anything about it.'"[28]

On 3 August 1921, Gumilyov was arrested for allegedly participating in a counterrevolutionary plot known as the Tagantsev affair.[29] Khodasevich visited him the night before, prior to leaving for a vacation in the country. Since they were not intimate friends, he was surprised by Gumilyov's great enthusiasm:

> He didn't want me to leave. I stayed until two in the morning. He was unusually cheerful and spoke a lot on various themes. I went the next day to leave something with him and knocked at the door. No one answered. In the dining room the servant Efim told me Gumilyov had been arrested during the night and had been taken away. Thus I was the last to see him free. In his exaggerated joy at my arrival there must have been a presentiment that after me he would see no one.[30]

Before he died Gumilyov wrote a famous poem, "The Streetcar Gone Astray," expressing his horror at what Russia had become after the revolution. As Sampson points out, the images are obscure and puzzling, with a continual shifting and interplay of temporal and spatial planes. This style may have served as one of the models for Akhmatova's *Poem Without a Hero*. The central image is a streetcar that has jumped the track of chronological time and passes freely between past, present, and future. The speaker presents himself to the Empress in the eighteenth century, then thinks of Mashenka, a simple girl who is his ideal love, weaving a rug, living on a side street of Petersburg. In one of the most grotesque visions, the poet talks of signboards written in letters of blood and human heads being sold at the grocery instead of cabbages.[31]

Gumilyov was executed by a firing squad three weeks after his arrest, on 25 August 1921.[32] Akhmatova learned of his death on 1 September in Tsarskoye Selo, by reading the newspaper report. On the eve of his arrest Gumilyov wrote "Starry Horror," predicting his fate: "Grief! Grief! Fear, the noose and the pit! For whomever was born on earth."[33] The funeral was on 9 September in the Kazan Cathedral. Nine years later Akhmatova learned where he was buried:

> I know about Kolya [Gumilyov]. They shot him near Berngardovka, along the Irininskaya Road . . . I found out nine years later and went there. Groves, a small curved pine; next to it another, powerful one but with torn roots. This was the wall. The earth sank down, dropped, because they had not filled in the graves. Pits. Two fraternal pits for 60 people.[34]

At the beginning of September rumors circulated about Akhmatova's death. In a letter to Akhmatova on 13 September 1921, the poet Marina Tsvetaeva wrote that one rumor said she caught cold at Blok's funeral, and another that she had been poisoned.[35]

Mandelstam survived this period. Like many of his generation, he was seriously questioning the relationship between the poet and the state, a particularly pertinent issue in Russian literature, since state censorship dated back to the beginning of the 19th century.

In a moving work entitled "Word and Culture," written in 1921, Mandelstam admits the old world is dead and the contemporary poet seems to serve the state in particular rather than humanity in general:

> Yes, the old world is "not of this world," yet it is more alive than it ever was. Culture has become the Church. A separation of Church-culture and the State has taken place . . . Today the State has a unique relationship to culture that is best expressed by the term *tolerance*. But at the same time a new type of organic intellectual is beginning to appear . . . Cultural values ornament the State . . . Inscriptions on State buildings, tombs, and gateways insure the State against the ravages of time . . . He [the modern poet] sings of ideas, systems of knowledge, and State theories just as his predecessors sang of nightingales and roses.[36]

Mandelstam further developed this idea in another essay, "On the Nature of the Word," written in 1922, in which he ascribed social and artistic aims to Acmeism. He cites Bryusov's philosophy of "beyond good and evil" as the Symbolist credo that Acmeism had to overcome: "I want my free boat to sail in every direction;/ And I shall praise the Lord and the Devil equally." Mandelstam finds this credo a form of bankrupt "nihilism," which must never be repeated in Russian poetry. Poetry's social role must not be only to educate citizens of the state, but to address all humanity: "Until now the social inspiration of Russian poetry has reached no further than the idea of 'citizen,' but there is a loftier principle than 'citizen,' there is the concept of 'Man.' As opposed to the civic poetry of the past, modern Russian poetry must educate not merely citizens, but Men."[37]

Plantain

Akhmatova had heeded this advice in her first collection of poems after the revolution, *Plantain,* published in 1921. It was a small book, three inches by six, and contained poems of both public and private nature written mainly from 1917 to 1919.

Akhmatova included in *Plantain* several poems dedicated to Anrep, which depict the range of emotions she felt for him over the course of their relationship. In the summer of 1917, in Slepnyovo, Akhmatova composed a series of bitter poems about a man leaving his homeland and his beloved. In "You are an apostate. . ." (Zh. 207), the speaker attacks the man using details with profound emotional associations for a Russian of the period—the beauty of the folk songs, the icons that are both religious and aesthetic, and Russian nature exemplified by pine trees and a quiet lake. Here, she does not use religion simply as cultural background or a convenient set of allusions. The sentiment is of a believer who warns that the "apostate" will lose his soul, has forfeited grace, and that to destroy ties with one's native land has religious consequences: it is a mortal sin. Akhmatova also includes an earlier verse from February 1916, "Like the angel. . ." (Zh. 210), which refers to her relationship with Anrep. The speaker recalls a ring given to her friend as a token of her love, and for the strength and freedom he bestowed upon her, but that love is now only a remembrance. In "When he finally hears the news. . ." (Zh. 211), written in 1917, the speaker projects her death and her lover's probable reaction to it. She refers to a cold wintry day similar to the one Anrep described many years later in his letter to Struve, when he crossed the ice of the Neva to see Akhmatova before he left forever, betraying his promise to "look after his friend from the East." She may be identifying Russia as Eastern rather than the Western Europe, where Anrep was headed, and perhaps also referring to her Tatar ancestry mixed with her Russian blood. After these poems of reproach, Akhmatova includes an earlier, happier poem, "All week I don't say a word..." (Zh. 215),[38] written in Sebastopol in the autumn of 1916. The ring the speaker's friend gives her to protect her from love evokes the crucifix Anrep gave Akhmatova to protect her from the torments of romantic involvement.

Akhmatova's most damning poem against those who deserted Russia is "When in suicidal anguish..." (S-F. I, 378). It is not divided into stanzas, but like a chant, continues in one sonorous flow of sounds, hypnotically reaching a crescendo at the end. She compares Russia to a drunken prostitute, taken by one invader after another. Though the speaker is tempted by the voice calling her to leave her suffering country, she stays, not realizing that the horrors she now faces are small in comparison to those she and her compatriots will endure in the future.

In 1917 Akhmatova wrote "And here, left alone..." (Zh. 224), another poem relating to Tsarskoye Selo. Unlike her earlier poems that portray the peaceful elegance of this place, now she is there alone, as if abandoned. The swans associated with Tsarskoye Selo become a symbol of the changes in both Tsarskoye and her life. One swan has died and another has changed into a black crow.

Several poems in this collection relate to Slepnyovo, where Akhmatova visited her son Lev at Gumilyov's mother's estate. Slepnyovo was virtually oblivious to the cataclysmic historical events that transformed the rest of Russia. In "The river flows..." (Zh. 231), the inhabitants are unaware of what is transpiring during the summer of 1917, between the February and October revolutions. They live in the past "as in Catherine's days," attending prayer service, awaiting the harvest, and carrying on their love affairs. But that same summer Akhmatova wrote another poem, "And all day..." (Zh. 234), which marks a dramatic change in her perception of these events. The poet envisions crowds churning in agonized grief, funeral banners on which sinister skulls laugh, and death patrolling the courtyard. No specific events are mentioned, just the atmosphere of horror and doom hanging over the cities and towns.

Anno Domini MCMXXI

In 1922 Akhmatova published a large collection of her works, *Anno Domini MCMXXI,* which in its first edition consisted of three parts—fourteen poems in a section called "1921," fifteen in "The Voice of Memory," and the republication of *Plantain* with the addition of one poem. Later editions included more works. She wrote many of the poems in 1921.

Two poems from December 1921 may evoke Akhmatova's relationship to Gumilyov, now dead but remembered with grief. The verses are written from the perspective of the husband, who calls back to earth to tell his wife he is sorry he left her behind to suffer. The first, "I didn't mean to trick you..." (Zh. 241), expresses a relationship in which they admire each other's poetry but have little love for one another: the wife praises his name, but it is bitter to her. In the second poem, "In that year long ago..." (Zh. 242), the male persona is the husband reproaching the guilty wife for betraying him.

A poem about the beautiful and ancient cathedral of St. Sophia in Kiev, "The gates are thrown wide open..." (Zh. 287), opens the section, "The Voice of Memory." Akhmatova wrote it on 15 September 1921, soon after she heard that Gumilyov had been executed. In Aesopic language she speaks of the tolling of the bell of Mazepa, thundering inexorably as if heretics were being executed. Mazepa was the fearless Ukrainian leader who fought, as Gumilyov allegedly did, for freedom against the state when he battled Peter the Great for Ukrainian independence. The setting recalls the location where Akhmatova and Gumilyov were married, on the shores of the Dnieper near Kiev.[39]

In a cycle of six poems, "Dark Dream," Akhmatova expresses feelings typical of those she felt toward the man closest to her at this time, Shileiko. The cycle begins with a poem written much earlier to him, in 1913, when they and their bohemian crowd attended the Stray Dog. Tamara Shileiko suggests that Akhmatova's poem "Praising me inarticulately..." (Zh. 246) was a response to a poem written by Shileiko to Akhmatova that same year:

> *You ascend again*
> *The penitential steps*
> *To unbind before the heart of God*
> *Burdens of imaginary crimes.*
>
> *Your closed eyes*
> *Are carried away beyond the earthly sphere,*
> *And on your lips burns the thunder*
> *Of words not yet found.*

And for a long time you speak slowly, dead...
But in prophetic light, in the light smoke,
Words numbed with cold
Again come alive—

But barely breathing I hear
How the trembling in your heart increases,
How the soul on soft wings
Flies into this world.[40]

The other poems in the cycle refer to the period when Akhmatova and Shileiko were married. Cold, famine, and war increased the tension which apparently developed between them as the years wore on. In "You are always novel and mysterious..." (Zh. 247), written in 1917, the speaker accuses her spouse of smothering her voice, for she can no longer pray or sing. In "Submissive to you..." (Zh. 251), she calls her husband a hangman and his home a prison. Akhmatova later included a poem in the cycle written in 1940, because it also was associated with Shileiko. "Number Three, Zachatevsky" (Zh. 250) was the side street in Moscow where they lived briefly before moving into the Fountain House in Petersburg. Details associated with death and grief—vacant lots, groans at night, a rotting lamppost—reinforce the atmosphere established with the opening simile, "A side street, a side str.../ Stretched like a noose around your neck." It is the atmosphere she felt in the apartment during that difficult period.

The short cycle labelled "Biblical Verses" comprises the first of the lyrical portraits Akhmatova created at various points in her career. The first, "Rachel" (Zh. 260), recounts the story of Jacob's hardship in winning Rachel for his bride. The second, "Lot's Wife" (Zh. 261), was added later to *Anno Domini* as part of this cycle. One of Akhmatova's most famous poems, it has been cited by critics as an example of Akhmatova's use of Aesopic language—how she expresses through allusion to myth and history what she cannot say openly. Knowing it is a sin to look back, Lot's wife perishes as she glances back at what is dear to her—simple things, really—the square where she sang, the courtyard where she spun, the tall house where she bore children. The speaker sympathizes with her, knowing how much the past meant to Lot's wife. Similarly, Akhmatova knew when she wrote the poem in 1924 how many simple things she took for granted in her past were lost forever in post-revolutionary Russia.[41]

Poems written at this time that allude to the revolution do not mention it directly. Grief and devastation have taken over the land. "Everything has been plundered. . ." (Zh. 268) is reminiscent of Blok's premonition poems before the revolution. The wing of black death is flashing, but a brightness beyond from an unknown source promises an unknown miracle:

> *And how near the miraculous draws*
> *To the dirty, tumbledown huts. . .*
> *No one, no one knows what it is,*
> *But for centuries we have longed for it.*

In another poem written a few months later in 1921, "Bezhetsk" (S-F. I, 214), the speaker turns from the memories of the past, from the old Russia represented by the peaceful life of Bezhetsk—its white churches, the beauty of the countryside, and the people celebrating a traditional Christmas. These are no more. Instead, she tries to make her peace with the present, no matter how threatening.

In the cycle "The Voice of Memory" in *Anno Domini*, Akhmatova turns to the period before the revolution, to World War I. "That August was like a yellow flame. . ." (Zh. 289) recalls how the beautiful city of Petersburg was turned into a savage camp when the new age arrived. In "Apparition" (Zh. 290), she predicts the downfall of the tsar, as his eyes, light and empty, signifying imminent death, "look around strangely."

During this period, harsh critics, including friends of her youth like Kuzmin, were beginning to claim Akhmatova had lived out her role as a poet in Russian society, and was important only as a relic of the past.[42] In a poignant poem written in 1922, "Slander" (Zh. 286), Akhmatova depicts slander as an allegorical figure pursuing the poet. The verse was written in direct reaction to some of the negative criticism beginning to appear about Akhmatova and her work. It was eerily prophetic of the events of 1946, however, when Akhmatova was accused of having a baneful influence on the new generation and expelled from the Union of Soviet Writers—especially the lines depicting the effect of the slander:

> *And her shameful raving will reach everyone,*
> *So that neighbors will avoid each other's eyes,*
> *So that my body will be abandoned in a terrible void. . .*

V. The Soviet State Takes Shape: 1922–1941

After the Civil War ended and the Soviet State was established, poets and artists had to find a place for themselves. Akhmatova remained popular among the poetry-loving public. Her poems were the subject of important works by leading scholars such as Boris Eikhenbaum and Viktor Vinogradov, as well as chapters in books by Chulkov and Aikhenvald. Editions of her poems sold out very quickly. Chukovsky gave a speech about her in 1921 at the House of Arts, which he then published as an article in 1922. In it he said that Akhmatova and Mayakovsky represented the two possible paths Russian poetry could take.[1] He saw Akhmatova's glorification of pain as a form of Christian humiliation. "She is the last poet of Orthodoxy... Never mind that Akhmatova sometimes talks about Paris, automobiles, literary cafés, this only lends stronger nuance to her real old-Russian soul."[2] He focuses on her style, what he calls the unsimple simplicity *(neprostaya prostota)* accessible only to great masters. "Next to her, other poets seem like bombastic rhetoricians." He then contrasts her to Mayakovsky, who is eternally shouting and raging. While Akhmatova speaks of angels, the Madonna, and God, Mayakovsky cannot pass God by without threatening him with a jackknife. Chukovsky ends the long essay noting that all of Russia seems divided between the Akhmatovas and Mayakovskys. Akhmatova is heiress of all that is most valuable in the richness of pre-revolutionary Russian letters, while Mayakovsky has no predecessors and focuses on the future. The future literature, he thought, should combine the best of both. "They are both equally necessary. In the future they must exist only as a synthesis, otherwise each of them will inevitably perish."[3]

Marietta Shaginyan noted in January 1922 how touched she was when she reread *At the Edge of the Sea* and advised her readers: "We know how to love those who have departed. If only we could learn to preserve and love those who are still alive!"[4] Alexandra Kollontay, one of the leading female revolutionaries, claimed Akhmatova's poetry is "the entire novel of a woman's soul, the poetic expression of the battle of a woman enslaved by bourgeois society, struggling for her human personality. She is not alien; her verses reflect the soul of a woman of a transitional epoch, an epoch marked by a break in human psychology, the mortal struggle of two cultures, two ideologies—bourgeois and proletariat. Akhmatova is not on the side of an outlived ideology but one that is creative."[5] Nikolay Osinsky, an active participant in the October Revolution who reviewed Akhmatova favorably in *Pravda,* pointed out Akhmatova's refusal to leave her country: "Although we are dealing with a person not of our way of life, this person has what is most important, most necessary to a poet—an honorable soul and civic consciousness. She refuses to leave not for revolutionary reasons, but for nationalistic ones."[6]

However, many other critics did not share these sentiments. In *Young Guard,* V. Arvatov attacks Kollontay, saying Akhmatova's poems develop the neurotic emotions of the submissive martyr in young working women.[7] He denounces Akhmatova as being too narrow, reeking of the boudoir, home, and the family. P. Vinogradskaya in *Red Virgin Soil* (1923) asserted that Akhmatova represented capricious women who serve only as toys in the hands of men and in no way reflect the contemporary working woman.[8] Another harsh article appeared in *On Guard* by G. Lelevich (1923), who wrote: "Akhmatova' s poetry is a small and beautiful fragment of aristocratic culture... The circle of emotions open to the poet is exceptionally limited. She has responded to social upheavals, basically the most important phenomenon of our time, in a feeble and hostile manner."[9]

Mayakovsky also viewed Akhmatova as a relic who had not adapted to the new age. In an evening dedicated to the "purge of contemporary poetry" on 19 January 1922, he recommends Akhmatova among the poets to be purged. D. Furmanov recorded in his diary Mayakovsky's speech, which was delivered in the Polytechnic Museum in Moscow. Mayakovsky said the Futurists could best express the rich harmony of new ideas and emotions. The real task of the artist was to convey the contemporary age in artistic images, and "participate actively in the creation of a new kingdom."

> When we approach poets of the contemporary period with this criterion, many remain overboard; they cannot be called poets in the real sense of this word: the chamber intimacy of Anna Akhmatova, the mystical verses of Vyacheslav Ivanov and his Hellenic motives— what meaning do they have for our harsh, iron age? And yet should we suddenly count Ivanov and Akhmatova as zero? Of course, as literary milestones, as the last born child of a collapsing structure, they find their place on the pages of literary history, but for us, for our epoch—these are insignificant, pathetic, and laughable anachronisms.[10]

Ironically, Mayakovsky was soon viewed as an anachronism and committed suicide, unable to endure the very purges he helped perpetrate against others.

Leon Trotsky, who was not only interested in politics but also well-read in the arts, wrote an interesting book called *Literature and Revolution*, in which he interprets the main movements before and after the revolution and their relevancy to the new Soviet State:

> One reads with dismay most of the poetic collections, especially those of the women. Here, indeed, one cannot take a step without God. The lyric circle of Akhmatova, Tsvetaeva, Radlova...is very small. He [God] is a very convenient and portable third person, quite domestic, a friend of the family who fulfills from time to time the duties of a doctor of female ailments. How this individual, no longer young, and burdened with the personal and too often bothersome errands of Akhmatova, Tsvetaeva and others, can manage in his spare time to direct the destinies of the universe, is simply incomprehensible.[11]

The attacks against Akhmatova culminated in 1925 when her poetry was banned by an unofficial Communist Party resolution that was not made public.[12] Akhmatova said: "I found out about it only in 1927 after meeting Shaginyan on Nevsky Avenue. Judging by memoirs, I was swallowed up by my 'personal life'—isn't that what you call it now?—and paid no attention. I didn't even know at that time what the Communist Party was."[13] While Akhmatova may not have remembered being particularly concerned about her publishing problems, Chukovsky describes how she felt about all this as early as 1922. On 14 February of that year he wrote: "Her fame was at its peak. Yesterday the Philosophical Association had arranged an evening of her poetry, and editors from various journals were calling her day and night: 'Please give us something.'" On 26 March he visited her and found her very upset. "We went into her narrow room, most of which was occupied by a double bed. It was very cold. 'Have you read the editorial?' She handed me the journal *Novaya Rossiya*. 'It's about me. They're making fun of me! Do you have any money now?' She said she had just received a sum of money for *White Flock*. 'I was able to sew a dress for myself, sent Levushka [her son Lev Gumilyov] something and wanted to send something to my mother in the Crimea. I'm very upset. I know they're in great need, but I can't send anything. Mama writes not to send anything by mail.'"[14]

In 1924, Olga Sudeikina and Artur Lourié departed for Paris,[15] begging Akhmatova in vain to come with them.[16] She moved to the Marble Palace, and began research on Pushkin, consulting with various leading scholars,[17] and eventually produced a number of insightful articles on Pushkin's life and work.

Shileiko was still living at the Marble Palace, but was spending seven months each year working in Moscow. At one point, Akhmatova made a short visit to Moscow, and he arranged for her to have the key to his apartment. His lingering attachment to her is apparent from a note he left, entrusting her care to a friend, Vera Andreeva: "Dear Vera, here's Anna for you. Take good care of her: I worry about her a lot. Write me if she is well. She's too lazy to write herself." Although certain sources claim Shileiko demanded she stopped writing verse,[18] Akhmatova obviously valued his opinion very much. On 26 November 1928 she wrote him a note: "Dear friend, I'm sending you my poems. If you have some time this evening, please take a look at them... Please note down on a separate piece of paper what you don't consider worth printing. I'll come by tomorrow. Please forgive me for disturbing you. Your Akhmatova."[19] In the Shileiko archive, there is a small volume of poetry by François Villon with the dedication: "To Vladimir Shileiko from his old friend Akhmatova. Carnival. Sunday 1927."

In 1925 Akhmatova stayed in Tsarskoye Selo to recover from tuberculosis and found Nadezhda Mandelstam, Osip's wife, whom she had met the previous year, staying in the same pension. Nikolay Punin, a well known art critic and supporter of the Russian avant-garde, came to visit Akhmatova frequently.

Punin knew many of the leading artists of the period.[20] Artur Lourié describes him in a memoir: "Punin was one of my best friends. He was a colleague in *Apollon,* wrote critical articles on art, especially the contemporary and most advanced. Punin had a very radical position, supporting new quests in their most daring manifestations. He supported the Futurists as innovators and was a great admirer of Tatlin. Later he became Director of the former Imperial Porcelain Factory and in this post gave commissions to young artists. Punin was a refined and noble person and extremely loyal."[21]

Haight suggests that Akhmatova went to live with Punin in 1926. Punin never formally registered their marriage, although Akhmatova and Shileiko were officially divorced in 1928. They shared a small apartment in Fountain House with his former wife Anna Arens, a doc-

Akhmatova with Nikolay Punin, 1926. Photo by Pavel Luknitsky

tor, and Punin's small daughter Irina. In 1927 Akhmatova's son Lev joined them and became a student at Leningrad University. This arrangement lasted until the late 1930s.[22]

Luknitsky notes that Akhmatova said she spent much of her time during this period translating Cézanne for Punin and helping him prepare lectures for the Institute of Art History. On 20 March 1926 Luknitsky writes of Punin's satisfaction with their collaboration on the French artist David. But Punin also expressed his displeasure that Shileiko's presence prevented Akhmatova from working regularly on the Cézanne.[23] On 22 November 1926, the diary recounts that Punin asked Akhmatova to prepare a lecture for him for the next day. She worked all night, read a book of 120 pages about Ingres, and had finished the lecture by seven in the morning.[24]

Shileiko became very sick in 1929, and Akhmatova visited him with Luknitsky on 4 August. He was pale and coughed up blood, and asked Akhmatova to take his and her belongings to Fountain House, since his apartment was being given to another department. Luknitsky and Akhmatova spent the following day packing everything from archives to Babylonian tablets. Shileiko left for Moscow on 7 August. On one of his letters to Akhmatova dated 29 July, she wrote in pencil, "last letter." He died soon after from tuberculosis at the age of 39.[24]

The terror began to infiltrate Akhmatova's life. Her poetry was suppressed from 1925 on, and in the 1930s, those close to her were arrested, including her son and Punin in 1935. They were released two weeks later. Lev was arrested again on 10 March 1937, and his sentence commuted to exile.

Mayakovsky ended his life in despair. After receiving bad reviews for the play *The Bathhouse,* in which he criticized the corruption of the regime, he was constantly mocked by students and workers at his readings in 1930. He committed suicide on 14 April 1930, and wrote his last poem in his suicide note:

As they say,
        a bungled story.
Love's boat
        smashed
                against existence.
And we are quits
        with life.
                So why should we

idly reproach each other
with pains and harms?
To those who remain—I wish happiness.

Vladimir Mayakovsky
12/4/30[26]

Mandelstam became a victim of the purges. Akhmatova spent much time with him and his wife during these years. They were among the few remaining in Russia from Akhmatova's past who shared her needs and concerns. In turn, she helped them in any way she could. As Nadezhda Mandelstam wrote, "The Akhmatova I knew was a fierce and passionate friend who stood by Mandelstam with an unshakable loyalty, his ally against the savage world in which we spent our lives, a stern, unyielding abbess ready to go to the stake for her faith."[27]

Mandelstam had written some negative criticism about Akhmatova in the early 1920s. His wife claims these critical remarks were a concession to the times: "His disavowal of Akhmatova in 1922 was a concession to all the hue and cry about Acmeism, allegations that it was outmoded...the logic of the times demanded that Mandelstam part company with Akhmatova... But he very soon came to his senses. In 1927 when he was gathering his articles together as a book, he threw out one of the pieces that had appeared in *Russian Art* and removed his attack on Akhmatova from the other."[28] In fact, in a letter written to Akhmatova on 25 August 1928, Mandelstam wrote from the Crimea: "You know I have the ability to carry on an imaginary conversation only with two people in the world: with Nikolay Stepanovich [Gumilyov] and you."[29]

The friends often shared their love of literature. In the 1930s both he and Akhmatova became engrossed in Dante and Italian literature. Akhmatova recalls in her memoirs of Mandelstam the time he came to Leningrad for two evenings devoted to his poetry. "He had just learned Italian and was mad about Dante. I began to read a piece from the XXX Canto (the appearance of Beatrice). He began to cry. I got frightened. 'What's wrong?' 'No, it's nothing, only those words and your voice.'"[30]

By 1928 Stalin had consolidated his position and launched one of the worst and most memorable periods in Soviet history, the era of collectivization, which lasted from 1928 to 1933. The peasants put up an enormous resistance against having their land taken away, burning their crops and killing their livestock. The result was famine, and millions of people were deported and resettled. Purges followed, during which millions more were sent to camps or killed for alleged crimes against the state. The secret police, headed by Henryk Yagoda and later by Nikolay Yezhov, were efficient and ruthless. Yezhov became so infamous that the period 1936–1938 has been named after him— *Yezhovshchina*—which Ulam calls a "democracy of fear: a Politburo

Georgy Chulkov, Maria Petrovykh, Akhmatova. 1934

member as well as the humblest citizen went to bed not knowing if this was the night they would come after him."[31] Nadezhda Mandelstam explains why people continued to believe all was well with the nation: their everyday needs were being met. "We think that everything is going along as it should, and that life continues—but that is only because the trams are running."[32]

But things were not well with the nation, and its greatest artists, musicians, and poets, including Mandelstam, became victims of the terror. On the basis of a satirical poem he wrote against Stalin, he was arrested on the night of 13 May 1934. Akhmatova had come that night to stay with the Mandelstams at their Moscow apartment on Furmanov Street. During her frequent visits that year, Akhmatova always stayed in their small kitchen, with its old kerosene stove in the corridor and a gas cooker—covered with oil cloth—disguised as a table. Akhmatova had little money, and to raise funds for her trip she had brought a small porcelain statue of her by Elena Danko, as well as a Charter of the Palace of the Apes given to her by Aleksey Remizov and brought to her after his escape in 1921.[33]

The arrest took place at one in the morning. Right after he was locked up in the Lubyanka prison, Akhmatova and Pasternak appealed to influential colleagues of Stalin, attempting to have him released. Haight notes that Akhmatova went to the Kremlin to see the Georgian Bolshevik, Enukidze, a member of the Central Committee, and was granted a meeting with the help of the actor Ruslanov, who knew Enukidze's secretary.[34] But it was to no avail. A few years before his

Akhmatova and Mandelstam. 1934

arrest Mandelstam dedicated a poem to Akhmatova, hinting at the foreboding he had of imminent doom:

Preserve my words for their after-taste of misery and smoke,
for the resins of circular patience, the honest tar of labor.
The way water in Novgorod wells must be honey-black
so by Christmas you can see, reflected, a star with seven fins. . .

And in payment, father, friend, rough helper,
I—unacknowledged brother, renegade in the people-family—
I promise to build such thick log-walls
that Tartars could lower princes in them like buckets.

If only those old executioners' blocks loved me!
The way they play croquet in the garden, like aiming at Death himself,
oh we'd walk the rest of my life in an iron shirt, for that, and
for executions like Peter's, I'd hunt a huge axe-handle in the woods.

(May 1931) [35]

In spite of his suffering, Mandelstam never forgot how important poetry was to the Russians: "I do not know how it is elsewhere, but here, in this country, poetry is a healing, life-giving thing, and people have not lost the gift of being able to drink of its inner strength. People can be killed for poetry here—a sign of unparalleled respect—because they are still capable of living by it." [36]

A few months before the arrest, while Akhmatova was visiting Moscow in February 1934, she and Mandelstam turned onto Gogol Boulevard and he remarked: "I am ready for death." Akhmatova said she always remembered these words whenever she passed by this place. [37] But Mandelstam was never ready for death, and prison and exile destroyed this fragile human being. Eventually he was allowed to go with his wife into exile to Voronezh, where Akhmatova visited him in February 1936. His wife reports that Akhmatova was the first person to visit. "Mandelstam paced rapidly around the room and recited to Akhmatova. He was giving her an account of what he had written in Voronezh. In return Akhmatova read him a poem she had written about him in Voronezh." [38]

The Mandelstams spent three years in Voronezh. They were finally able to have a short vacation in Zadonsk because Akhmatova and Pasternak each contributed 500 rubles. Nadezhda says they felt so rich they stayed in Zadonsk for six weeks. [39] Akhmatova visited them again in Voronezh [40] before Mandelstam was arrested a second time on 1 May 1938 and sent to a concentration camp. He died there at the age of forty-seven. He "perished in a pitifully demented condition according to one version, refusing food because he believed it poisoned."[41]

Akhmatova, despite the deprivations of those years, continued to show her generosity. In September 1936, the newspaper *Literaturnyi Leningrad* published her translation of a poem by E. Chrenets with this note: "The honorarium for the translation of this poem I wish to be conveyed to the fund for the aid of wives and children of the heroic

Vladimir Garshin

Spanish people fighting for the freedom and independence of their country."[42]

Another person soon entered Akhmatova's life who was to have an important influence on her fate—Vladimir Garshin (1887–1956), a professor, medical doctor, and member of the Academy of Medical Sciences who was the nephew of the famous Russian writer of the 19th century, Vsevelod Garshin. His interests were not confined to his professions. He was close to many writers in Leningrad, was a serious coin collector,[43] had a large collection of books on art, loved Russian poetry, and wrote verse himself. He had become acquainted with Akhmatova when she was a patient in the Kuibyshev Hospital, and he began to visit her in Fountain House. They went to museums together, and he helped her get through this very difficult period of her life. Their relationship led her to finally leave Punin. Akhmatova tried to explain to her friend Lidiya Chukovskaya why she had not left him earlier.

It's strange. I lived so long with Nikolay Nikolayevich after the end. But it was so depressing I had no strength. I hadn't written poems for 13 years. I tried to leave in 1930. Sreznevsky promised me a room. But Nikolay went to him and said my leaving was a matter of life and death . . . so I stayed. You can't believe how crude he's been with his flirtations. He always has to make it so obvious how bored he is with you.[44]

Chukovskaya, daughter of Korney Chukovsky, the eminent writer and critic who wrote so many insightful words about Akhmatova, describes the first time she heard Akhmatova recite. Even after many years of suffering Akhmatova could still strike people by her unique presence. In her diary entry of 10 November 1938, Chukovskaya records an evening at the House of Literature that was devoted to the memory of Blok. Akhmatova had recited her poem "Today is the nameday. . ." (Zh. 279) and immediately departed. "I was struck by her bearing, her azure shawl, her distracted glance, and her voice. It was impossible to believe she was just like the rest of us."[45] As the daughter of Korney Chukovsky, Chukovskaya grew up in an environment where Akhmatova and other great poets were part of everyday conversation. Chukovskaya became one of Akhmatova's best friends, memorizing poems which were too dangerous to keep in written form. Akhmatova would write a poem on a piece of paper, Chukovskaya would memorize it, and then Akhmatova would talk about the weather as she burned it in an ashtray.[46] Chukovskaya kept a remarkable diary of their conversations, which were interrupted after Akhmatova, for some reason inexplicable to Chukovskaya, turned away from her in Tashkent during World War II. The friendship was resumed in the 1950s.[47]

Chukovskaya describes the neglected and disorganized room where Akhmatova lived at the time. By the oven,[48] there was an armchair without a leg, ragged with protruding springs, and the floor was unswept. Akhmatova had pretty things—a carved stool, a mirror in a bronze frame, prints on the walls, but Chukovskaya suggests that instead of decorating the room, these objects only emphasized the wretchedness of it all.[49]

Chukovsky also visited Akhmatova in this period and recorded his impressions in his diary. "In the cursed walls of the communal apartment where the roar of the gramophone never stopped from behind the doors of polite neighbors, she took care of her neighbors' children for hours, treating them with sweets and reading them books." He cites a young woman who knew Akhmatova then: "I often noted that with a child in her arms she immediately resembled a statue of the Madonna, not only her face but her entire being, with a certain mournful and humble grandeur."[50]

In 1940 Akhmatova was spending a few days in Moscow with the Ardov family when Pasternak telephoned to say that the poet Marina Tsvetaeva was in the city and wanted to see her. Akhmatova had always expressed ambivalence toward Tsvetaeva's works, although in 1921 Tsvetaeva had written Akhmatova, saying how much she admired her, and in 1916 sent Akhmatova the manuscript of the poems dedicated to her. Akhmatova carried them in her purse until they disintegrated.[51] The two women were very different personalities, one the poet of the north, grand in her restraint and solemnity, and the other the Muscovite, boiling over with intense emotion in highly charged poetic phrases.[52] Adamovich comments that Artur Lourié once compared the relationship of Akhmatova and Tsvetaeva to Chopin and Schumann. He remarked to Akhmatova: ["You treat Tsvetaeva like Chopin treated Schumann—Schumann thanked Chopin and the latter got out of it with polite, evasive remarks. Tsvetaeva is Schumann in relation to the 'golden-mouthed Anna of All Rus.'"[53]

Marina Tsvetaeva

Victor Ardov describes the visit. The two poets went into the tiny room where Akhmatova usually stayed when visiting the Ardovs and remained there for most of the day. Akhmatova never revealed what they discussed. The next day Tsvetaeva saw Akhmatova at the home of Nikolay Khardzhiev. Haight describes this second meeting as reported by Khardzhiev. "Tsvetaeva was sparkling. She was full of Paris and talked brilliantly. Akhmatova told him later that she felt herself to be dull and cow-like in contrast. But Khardzhiev, on the contrary, seeing her with the quicksilver Tsvetaeva, was struck by what he describes as Akhmatova's complete and utter genuineness."[54]

From 1935–1940, Akhmatova wrote her great cycle *Requiem,* which several friends memorized. It contains fifteen poems and was not published until 1963 in Munich. The cycle conveys the anguish of mothers whose sons are suffering, and who helplessly look on, able only to express their yearning and grief. Joseph Brodsky writes:

> The degree of compassion with which the various voices of Requiem are rendered can be explained only by the author's Orthodox faith; the degree of understanding and forgiveness which account for this work's piercing, almost unbearable lyricism, only by the uniqueness of her heart, her self, and this self's sense of time. No creed would help to understand, much less forgive, let alone survive this double widowhood at the hands of the regime, this fate of her son, these 40 years of being silenced and ostracized.[55]

Milivoe Jovanovich notes that the cycle relates to Nekrasov's portrayals of Russian women that Akhmatova heard as a child, especially the wives of the Decembrists appealing to the tsar and following their husbands into exile. He compares the situation of the mother portrayed in *Requiem* to that of the heroines of Euripides—Andromache, Hecuba, the Trojan women—ready for death and suffering because of the loss of their children. All of them share a similar range of emotions: hope, the threat of death, madness, indifference, and a readiness to accept death.[56]

Some of the poems refer specifically to Russian culture. The speaker of "They led you away . . ." (S-F. I, 363, dated 1935), for example, is a peasant woman, and the images include an icon, icon shelf, and the *vynos,* or ceremony of "taking out" the coffin from the hut so it may be driven to the cemetery. The poem's scope broadens when the speaker's grief is compared to that of the wives of the Streltsy. These women lamented their husbands who had fought bravely against Peter the Great, believing he was destroying the great traditions and religion of Russia. This theme, popular in Russian culture, was celebrated by Modest Mussorgsky in his opera *Khovanshchina* and in a famous painting by Vasily Surikov.

Kiril Taranovsky suggests that the poem "Quietly flows the quiet Don..." (S-F. I, 363) echoes the rhyme and rhythm of a famous Russian lullaby about the cat's burning house:

Don, don, don!
Zagorelsia koshkin dom
Bezhit kuritsa s vedrom
Zalivat' koshkii dom

  Don, don, don!
  The cat's house is burning.
  The hen runs with a pail
  Pours water on the cat's house.[57]

In the next few poems the speaker progresses from numbness, to a death wish, to a feeling of impending madness. Akhmatova ends the cycle with allusions to the Bible. The archetypal relationship of the mother grieving for her suffering son is expressed through the story of Christ's passion in two poems under the title "Crucifixion."

In the second epilogue, Akhmatova uses the theme of remembrance as a moral category—as an agent of retribution—a theme that will take on even broader connotations in *Poem Without a Hero*. A day of remembrance is set aside in the Orthodox Church to remember the dead. The speaker realizes that if a monument were ever erected for her, its location would somehow be connected with an important part of her life. Alluding to biographical elements in Akhmatova's life, the speaker asks that the monument not be connected with her carefree youth by the sea, nor near the stump in the garden in Tsarskoye Selo where she grew up, but here before the prison where she stood for three hundred hours. This is the hour and place she hopes no one will forget.

With war impending, the restrictions against writers were relaxed. Akhmatova received permission to publish a collection of her poems, *From Six Books,* containing previous works as well as some new ones in the section "Willow." Boris Pasternak sent her a long letter in 1940 praising the work. Previously, Akhmatova and Pasternak had been friendly but not particularly close. Only with the appearance of this

Boris Pasternak

collection did Pasternak become an appreciative reader of her verse.[58] He exclaims in this letter that lines of people trailed over two streets waiting to buy her book. It had already sold out and second-hand copies sold for 150 rubles. He writes:

Your name is once more AKHMATOVA in the same way it was when that name stood for the best part of the Petersburg you described. It has its previous power to recall the time when I would not have dared believe that I would ever know you, or have the honour and good fortune to write you a letter. This summer it stands for all it stood for then and, as well, for something new and extremely great, which I have observed lately but have never before connected with the former.[59]

Pasternak noted certain passages he particularly liked and commented on changes he noticed in her work. While Akhmatova may have been flattered, she suspected he had not read much of her earlier poetry before. "The poems he mentions were mainly from *Rosary* and *Anno Domini,* that is, the ones everyone has known for ages by heart. I'll explain this. He's simply reading my poetry for the first time. When I began he was in Centrifuge[60] and was hostile toward me and simply hadn't read my poems. Now he's reading them for the first time and suddenly making a discovery... Dear, naive, beloved Boris Leonidovich."[61]

A few months after Akhmatova's book appeared it was withdrawn from sale and libraries. Akhmatova had no time to grieve; her life was being overwhelmed again by the forces of history—another world war. In 1940, with Hitler's shadow over Europe, she wrote a haunting *poema* called *The Way of All the Earth.* The heroine, who tells her own tale, is a woman from Kitezh, a medieval city allegedly saved by prayer from a Tatar invasion. Haight summarizes the legend: "Some say it was lifted up to the heavens and its reflection seen on a lake into which the enemy rushed to their death, others that like other legendary cities it sunk deep into the lake where its towers can be seen on days when the water is specially clear."[62] The heroine has been summoned home across a land filled with soldiers, trenches, bayonets—a Hoffmannesque world, where reality turns into the grotesque. It is a lament for old Europe, of which only "a scrap remains." The woman of Kitezh recalls other historical events that had a great impact: Tsushima, the Dreyfus affair, the Boer War. She now prays just to be allowed to reach her home, to be with her people and be laid to rest.[63]

But the author of the *poema* would not be allowed to go home and escape from historical events. Instead, Akhmatova would be forced to leave her home for several years, and external events would continue to impinge upon both her personal and creative life.

VI. The War: 1941–1945

War with Germany was imminent. Stalin watched as Hitler seized one country after another in Eastern Europe, and on 23 August 1939 signed a pact with him, temporarily keeping the Soviet Union out of the international conflict. Stalin took advantage of the momentary peace to invade Finland. The Finns maintained their independence in this brutal war, ceding some territory in 1940.[1] On 22 June 1941 the German ambassador, Count von der Schulenburg, delivered Hitler's Declaration of War to the Soviet Commissar for Foreign Affairs.[2] While the Soviet Union suffered enormous losses in lives, by the close of the war it had made tremendous gains in territory, incorporating the Baltic states and bringing many Eastern European countries into its sphere of influence. The early phases of the war were savage and will remain forever in the collective memory of the Russian people.

Akhmatova was in Leningrad at the start of the war. She had little money and lived next door to a young woman named Smirnov with two little boys. Akhmatova took care of the children while their mother was at work. At the end of September, when the German blockade of the city was beginning, she flew to Moscow. Along with other writers, artists, musicians and filmmakers in Leningrad and Moscow, Akhmatova was evacuated for the duration of the war to Tashkent, in Central Asia, where she lived until May 1944.

Before departing, Akhmatova addressed the women of Leningrad on the radio. The poet Olga Berggolts recalls this episode: "On a piece of lined paper torn out of a ledger I wrote down the script for the radio dictated to me by Akhmatova. It was addressed to the city during the difficult days of the storming of Leningrad and the attack on Moscow. . . . How I remember her near the old iron gates of the fence of Fountain House. . . With a face severe and angry, a gas mask thrown over her shoulder, she took on the fire watch like a regular soldier. She sewed bags for sand which were put on the trenches."[3]

Akhmatova told her fellow citizens—the mothers, wives, and sisters of Leningrad—that this city, the city of Lenin, Pushkin,

*Akhmatova with
"my neighbor,
the Leningrad boy,
Valya Smirnov,"
1940*

*Olga Berggolts,
Leningrad poet*

Dostoevsky, and Blok, was now being threatened and urged them to fight:

> Our descendants will honour every mother who lived at the time of the war, but their gaze will be caught and held fast particularly by the image of the Leningrad woman standing during an air-raid on the roof of a house, with boat-hook and fire tongs in her hands, protecting the city from fire; the Leningrad girl volunteer giving aid to the wounded among the still smoking ruins of a building... No, a city which has bred women like these cannot be conquered. We, the women of Leningrad, are living through difficult days, but we know that the whole of our country, all its people, are behind us. We feel their alarm for our sakes, their love and help. We thank them and we promise them that we will be ever stoic and brave.[4]

Akhmatova's friend N.G. Chulkova notes in her diary that she met Akhmatova in Moscow on 9 October 1941, after Akhmatova had been evacuated from Leningrad.

> Anna Andreevna came over and spent an hour with me. I treated her to an omelette and coffee with cream. She was amazed I could feed her like this. In Leningrad they were starving. She told me when she and her neighbors sat in a bomb shelter in the garden (with a child in her arms) she suddenly heard such roaring, shrieking and whistling as she had never heard in her life. They were hellish sounds. "I thought I was going to die."[5]

Margarita Aliger went on the train with Akhmatova from Moscow to Central Asia. Akhmatova and Pasternak sat together, talking quietly and seemingly unaffected by the stresses of the moment. "Many of us were upset, anxious about the future, worried about our luggage—which was quite natural at that point, no one could condemn us for that—but these two were outside of everything around them. They were somehow separate from the rest, calmer, freer, more independent, and their presence somehow made it easier for us."[6]

Chukovskaya was in Moscow on 10 May 1941, and left for Chistopol on 28 July. She spent time there with Marina Tsvetaeva, but on 31 August, Tsvetaeva hanged herself in the town of Yelabuga.[7] In October, Akhmatova arrived in Chistopol, and she and Chukovskaya went to Tashkent together. Chukovskaya notes in her diary:

> Akhmatova in Chistopol! This is as imaginable as the Admiralty spire or the Galernaya Arch in Chistopol. Today I went with Akhmatova along the Kama and led her across that same swampy meadow across

which I had helped Marina a month ago. "She asked me about you. And now she doesn't exist, and you're asking me about her. At this very spot!" Akhmatova didn't reply, only looked at me. I didn't tell her about our conversation. Not realizing what Akhmatova was going through in Leningrad at the time, I had expressed my joy to Marina: thank God Akhmatova was in her own home in Leningrad and not here in this weird Chistopol drowning in mud, cut off from the world, in this half Tatar village. "This life would kill her," I said. "She doesn't know how to do anything; she's completely helpless. She'd die here." "And you think I can live here," Marina interrupted me. "It's not any easier for me here than it would be for her."[8]

Tashkent, however, was exotic, and Akhmatova's sojourn there is reminiscent of the period Pushkin lived in the south of Russia.[9] Akhmatova missed Leningrad, but as she shows in her poetry, the Central Asian landscape awoke a strong feeling for the sensual beauty of the East and her Tatar heritage. She says: "It was in Tashkent that I found out for the first time what a tree's shadow meant in the scorching heat, and the sound of water. And I also discovered what human kindness was: I was very sick in Tashkent."[10] Chukovskaya describes it: steep and narrow alleys winding down from the street to the bazaar, an Eastern marketplace with vegetables and fruit piled high, sheep's carcasses hanging just out of people's reach, flat white loaves of bread offered at staggering prices by hucksters, and sun-blackened women trading in oriental sweets.[11]

Akhmatova stayed in the Hostel for Moscow Writers, which had been a hotel, at Karl Marx Street 7. Her small room under the iron roof was meant to be a temporary home, but she lived there from November 1941 until May 1943, except for a period convalescing at Dyurmen outside the town.[12] One witness living in Tashkent testified to the bareness of Akhmatova's dwelling, but Akhmatova showed endurance while others gave up hope. The radio in her room was always on. "When she listened to the regular report her face seemed like the living embodiment of tragedy. But even in the most gloomy days she reflected deep faith. It was as if she knew what none of the rest of us knew. She not only believed in final victory, but she knew victory would come and waited for it, when everyone else had exhausted their patience."[13]

Many members of the intelligentsia were in Tashkent, and they sometimes gathered during the evening. Joseph Czapski, a Polish soldier, describes one such evening when a group of translators and writers, including Akhmatova, met at the home of the writer Aleksey Tolstoy. "About 10 o'clock we gathered in a large drawing room around a table loaded with wines, some excellent dried fruits and other sweetmeats. . . It was cool, and there was a feeling of buoyancy in the air. I can still see Akhmatova, as she sat that evening, silent, with tears in her eyes, while I gave a clumsy translation of the last verse of 'Christmas in Warsaw.'"[14] Czapski tells of his difficulties conveying

Karl Marx Street, Tashkent

the beauty of Polish poetry to foreigners, but he notes he had never aroused such interest in it as on that night among this "last remaining handful of Russian intellectuals. . . . I realized what a hunger there is among Russians for poetry, genuine poetry." Akhmatova, he writes, wore a simple dress, her hair lightly touched with gray and kept in place by a colored handkerchief. She spoke little, but when he asked her to read she recited passages from *Poem Without a Hero,* which she had recently begun. He calls it "The Poem of Leningrad." "The verses which she declaimed in a strange sort of chant. . .were devoid of optimistic propaganda. . . But 'The Poem of Leningrad' is in fact, the only work of its kind that has moved me, however briefly, to under-stand as something *real* the defence of the heroic, half-starved and ruined city."[15]

Letters and memoirs during this period reveal Akhmatova's rela-tionship with Garshin, who had remained in Leningrad. On 25 May 1942 she received a postcard from him. In a letter to her friend

Khardzhiev, she says Garshin was mentally ill and had not written her for five months. Haight notes the infrequency of his letters, including one in which he described his long-estranged wife as the most important person in his life. "Akhmatova was furious and said to Chukovskaya: 'What if I wrote to him that Lourié had been the most important person in my life?'"[16]

In October 1942 Garshin's wife collapsed on the street and died.[17] Garshin found her in a morgue and identified her by her clothes; her face had been devoured by rats.[18] Aliger says that Garshin was haunted by this image, and his memories of it disturbed his relations with Akhmatova. He soon sought companionship with a young nurse working with him. Yet he continued to write Akhmatova, even proposing marriage, making it conditional that she take his name. She agreed.[19] In a letter to a friend, Professor I.D. Khlopina, who was in Samarkand he wrote: "Don't judge me. I can't live without Anna Akhmatova. I have summoned her to Leningrad. Don't judge me for wanting to be with her so soon after the death of Tatyana."[20] He had promised Akhmatova that on her return he would find them a new apartment, since she did not want to return to Fountain House. On 6 April 1943 she wrote: "I live in mortal fear for Leningrad, for Vladimir Georgeyevich [Garshin], I've been very sick and have gone totally gray."[21] Akhmatova sent a copy of *Poem Without a Hero* to Khardzhiev on 14 April of that year, asking him to give it to Garshin, who was working in a hospital: "Vladimir Georgeyevich is in Leningrad working from 7:30 in the morning to 11:00 at night with no days off. During the shooting and bombing he gives lectures and does research. He is behaving like a real hero."[22]

Punin had been evacuated from Leningrad with his first wife and daughter, her baby, and his third wife. Akhmatova met them when the train stopped in Tashkent on their way to Samarkand. Shortly thereafter, Punin, who was very ill, wrote Akhmatova from a hospital in Samarkand, telling her how much she meant to him. He was thinking about her while staying with the Golubevs in Leningrad. She seemed, he wrote, to be the highest expression of what can be called immortal.[23]

During this period Akhmatova was working on her *Selected Poems,* which was published in Tashkent in 1943. She was also writing a play, *Enuma elish,* about the relation of the poet to the state. According to Nadezhda Mandelstam, she later burned it after her son Lev was arrested and taken away in 1949. Mandelstam believed that had the authorities read Akhmatova's play, they would have been tempted to arrest her as well.[24] The title derives from the first words of the ancient Babylonian creation epic that includes the Epic of Gilgamesh, and was part of a New Year's ritual. It means "When Above."[25] The play was divided into three parts, the first and third in prose and the middle one in poetry: (1) "On the Stairs"; (2) "Prologue, or a Dream within a Dream"; and (3) "Under the Stairs." Set during the war, it enacts the trial of a poet before a writer's tribunal.

The heroine does not have the faintest idea of what she is being accused. It is a Kafkaesque trial,[26] in which her answers bear no relation to the questions she is asked. All the trite formulas typical of official ideology are reproduced in the accusations. The second act is called "Dream within a Dream" because it opens in the depths of the stage. The curtain goes up and on the stage is an audience, an orchestra, and a stage. A mysterious dream appears to the sleeping heroine.

Only "Prologue" still exists in any form, written as fragments after the original was burned. The characters are reduced to a few anonymous figures such as "She," "He" and "the blind man." "She" is the victim of a sadistic lover, and there is some allusion to an illicit affair they had.

Akhmatova started home on 15 May 1944, stopping over in Moscow where she stayed with her friends the Ardovs. She was enthusiastically received at a reading she gave at the Polytechnic Museum. In an interview with Nina Olshevskaya-Ardov—Victor Ardov's wife and a good friend of Akhmatova—Emma Gershtein says that Akhmatova told her friends in Moscow she was going to be married.[27] Margarita Aliger comments that she had never seen Akhmatova so happy: she was lively, transformed, young, and pretty. Her son was alive and well, her city had been liberated, and people there were waiting for her. Life would begin anew.[28]

When Garshin met her at the station in Leningrad, he said he had to talk to her about something. According to Haight, Garshin had married the nurse he had befriended.[29] A.G. Admoni, who had come back on the same train, said that Akhmatova and Garshin walked up and down the platform for ten minutes, and when Akhmatova returned, she said calmly: "Everything has changed. I'm going to Rybakova" [Akhmatova's friend, Lidiya Rybakova].[30]

Akhmatova lived with the Rybakovs for several months in a small room, and did not immediately let her Moscow friends know what had happened. Finally Olshevskaya received a telegram: "I send good wishes to all of you. I'm living alone. Thanks for everything. Akhmatova." Three weeks later, on 6 August, Olshevskaya received another telegram: "Garshin is mentally ill, he's left me. I'm telling this only to you. Anna." On 9 August a postcard arrived: "Did you get my news? I'm still not living on the Fontanka. There's no water, light, or glass. And no one knows when it will be fixed. I have a cold, and something's wrong with my heart." Olshevskaya says these brief telegrams reflected the strength of Akhmatova's words: in only half a phrase she communicated the trauma she was experiencing.[31]

At first Garshin visited her. He brought her food, and they would talk for a long time in her room. Then, after ten days, Olga, Rybakova's daughter, heard Akhmatova shriek in the next room. Garshin ran out and left, and they never saw each other after that. At Akhmatova's request, Rybakova went to Garshin and took Akhmatova's letters, which Akhmatova destroyed, as well as his letters to her. Akhmatova removed the dedications she had written to Garshin on her *Poem Without a Hero*. At the end of 1949 Garshin became seriously ill. Rybakova visited him, and Olga continued the visits after her mother's death. He often asked about Akhmatova, but she never asked after him, and shut him out of her life completely. He died in 1956.[32]

When Akhmatova returned to Leningrad, she was shocked by what the city had become. She tried to express her feelings in prose, though she found it more difficult than verse:

In May 1944 I flew to Moscow, which was already full of joyful hopes and expectations of an approaching victory. On 1 June, I returned to Leningrad. The horrible spectre pretending to be my city so struck me that I described my encounter with it in prose. That's when I wrote the studies "Three Lilacs" and "A Visit With Death"—the latter about reciting poetry at the front in Terioki. Prose always seemed very mysterious and tempting. I knew everything about poetry from the very beginning—I never knew anything about prose. Everyone praised my first attempts very highly. Of course, I didn't believe it. I called Zoshchenko. He suggested I rearrange a few things but basically agreed with the rest. I was very happy.[33]

Reed

On the eve of the war Akhmatova had prepared a collection of poems for print, "Reed," containing works from 1924 to 1940. The collection was never published separately, but appeared in *From Six Books* (1940) and was entitled "Willow." These poems indicate that Akhmatova never stopped writing poetry, even during the most difficult times.

The collection includes various poems to the Muse. In a poem written in 1924 (Zh. 301), the Muse, rather than bringing torment as in the past, now is a welcome guest. Nothing from the outside world—honors, youth, freedom—are as important to the speaker as the gift of creativity. Dante is mentioned, symbolizing the speaker's sense of comradeship with the great poets. Later, Dante takes on a deeper meaning in Akhmatova's work—that of the poet in exile who is not free to express his views.

Tsarskoye Selo had become a place of memories. In this Akhmatova resembled Pushkin, who fondly reminisced about Tsarskoye Selo, as in the following work, published in 1823:

> Lead, lead me under the linden canopy,
> Always kind to my free idleness.
> To the shore of the lake, the quiet slope of the hills!. .
> And again I will see the carpet of thick meadows,
> And the decrepit handful of trees, and the bright valley,
> And familiar picture of gilded shores.
> And in the quiet lake, amidst gleaming ripples,
> The proud flock of tranquil swans.[34]

But for Akhmatova, Tsarskoye Selo begins to take on symbolic overtones as a place of "non-return," representing a way of life that is over and must be condemned. Luknitsky notes in his diary on 12 April 1925 that they went to Detskoe Selo (the early Soviet name given to Tsarskoe Selo, which since 1937 has been called "Pushkin"), and describes Akhmatova's reaction to the transformed city: "AA [sic] looked sadly at the dirty, ruined sidewalks, at the broken fences, at the vacant lots where once she remembered stood clean little houses. AA: 'Just think—this city was the cleanest in all Russia. They took such care of it! It was impossible to see a single broken fence. . . It was like a semi-Versailles. . . Now there is no Tsarskoye Selo.'"[35] In 1929 she wrote "This city, beloved by me. . ." (Zh. 305), recalling when everything came easily; now death, the noseless fiddler, plays about this past that can never return. The image of "December silence" reinforces the sense of death, and only for a brief moment does happiness appear: "as if an old dear friend had just stepped onto the porch with me."

In another poem written 11 years later, "Willow" (Zh. 322), Akhmatova again turns to Tsarskoye Selo, this time in philosophical contemplation about the vagaries of fate. Something or someone that was assumed to always be in one's life has disappeared or been lost, and the places associated with it seem different than before. The willow that is now only a stump when she returns to Tsarskoye Selo represents her friends who have long disappeared. Nothing is quite the same. It is reminiscent of Chekhov's *The Cherry Orchard,* in which the sound of the ax felling the first tree represents the end of the old aristocratic way of life in Russia. The two subsequent poems, "From the cycle 'Youth'" (Zh. 323) and "The Cellar of Memory" (Zh. 324), both written in 1940, also relate to Akhmatova's memories of Tsarskoye.[36]

Several poems in the collection may allude to Gumilyov, including "Hasn't he sent a swan..." (Zh. 308) and "Thus dark souls take flight..." (Zh. 325). "Incantation" (Zh. 307) was dated 15 April 1936, which would have been his fiftieth birthday. In a cycle of poems called "Parting," Akhmatova describes a relationship similar to what she experienced with Punin. The bitter cycle includes "Not weeks, not months..." (Zh. 327), "And, as always happens..." (Zh. 328) and "The Last Toast" (Zh. 329). The middle poem depicts people about to separate who suddenly recall the beauty of the first days of blossoming love.

Her poem "Mayakovsky in 1913" (Zh. 330), written in 1940, differs from her other reminiscences about poets. It is the only verse that bears any relation to the great Futurist, with whom she was often contrasted. She was never close to him, though they saw each other frequently in the Stray Dog and she heard enough of his poetry. But it never influenced her work the way Blok's poetry did in a polemical fashion, or the way Mandelstam's works did. In this poem, she depicts a gifted man who both created and destroyed, referring to the Futurist desire to reject the heritage of the past in order to compose great works of the future. Not mentioning his years of suffering or his suicide, she portrays Mayakovsky in 1913 when his "still unheralded name/ Flew like lightning around the stuffy hall," and notes that in 1940, when she wrote the poem, his name had become "treasured throughout the land," ringing out like a battle cry.

One of the most poignant poems (Zh. 320) is dedicated to Dante, the archetypal poet in exile who plays the same role as Ovid in Pushkin's works.[37] Like Akhmatova's Petersburg, his city represents a way of life and thought that, along with the city itself, will be lost to the poet because he dared to express his strong political beliefs. The poem may also allude to Mandelstam, another poet in exile.

In another of her lyrical portraits, "Cleopatra" (Zh. 321), written in 1940, Akhmatova depicts a woman reacting to her historical destiny by ending her life. While not accepting suicide as a solution to her own grief, Akhmatova describes the state of mind of one who does. As in many of her poems, Akhmatova expects the reader to know the "pre-history" of the episode presented here. She portrays Cleopatra at the moment before death. Her love affair with Antony is long past, and the glorious Queen of Egypt is about to be paraded like a slave before Augustus, the new Roman Emperor. In a few telling details, Akhmatova reveals that rather than encounter death with hysteria, Cleopatra will greet it with dignified restraint.

Akhmatova's reaction to the purges and suffering took many forms in her unpublished work. Sonia Ketchian compares "Imitation from the Armenian" (S-F. 65, III, 48–49), for example, to the original work by H. Tumanjan. In Akhmatova's poem the speaker projects herself as a black ewe into the dream of the person she addresses, who becomes the emperor—the Padishah—and by indirect allusion, Stalin. She asks him if he found the meal of her children tasty. The original poem, translated by Ketchian, is:

> In my dream a ewe
> came near me
> up to me
> with question:
> May God preserve
> keep
> your son
> How was the taste of my child
> infant?

As Ketchian points out, Akhmatova's poem promises no retribution: "The power and good fortune of the ruler are exemplified in his undeserved preservation through the luminous will of a biased Allah as well as by the man's might manifested through the image of holding the universe like a bead."[38]

In "Stanzas" (S-F. 70, III, 52) Akhmatova addresses Stalin indirectly as the one who "lives in the Kremlin." She alludes to some of the most famous and infamous figures of Russian history: Boris Godunov, who allegedly gained the throne by having the rightful heir, Dmitry, assassinated; all the rulers named Ivan, although the one who comes to mind is Ivan the Terrible, to whom Stalin was frequently compared because of his mad reign of terror; and Grishka Otrepiev, a monk during the reign of Boris Godunov who pretended to be Dmitry, whom, he claimed, was never murdered. Otrepiev invaded Russia with the help of the Poles—who were profoundly hated by the Russians—and within a year was killed. Akhmatova uses a device employed in Russian poetry as early as Pushkin: she refers to historical figures who the reader can compare to oppressive authorities in the present.[39] Fortunately, the authorities did not discover the poem, or Akhmatova might have shared Pushkin's fate of exile, or worse, that of Mandelstam.

VII. The Post-War Years

Akhmatova soon moved into Fountain House, where she lived with her son Lev, who returned home from six years of exile in 1945. The Punin family also shared the same apartment. Punin's first wife had died in Samarkand during the war, and he had since remarried. His daughter Irina lived there as well with her second husband, and the daughter of her first marriage, Anya Kaminskaya.[1]

In September 1946, a Literary Evening was arranged at the Hall of Columns in Moscow's House of Unions, where Akhmatova and Pasternak read their works. The young people present staged an enormous ovation in honor of the two poets. Alexander Werth, who was in the audience, writes that this may have aroused the authorities against Akhmatova.[2]

Akhmatova, however, believed another incident led to her ouster from the Union of Soviet Writers: the visit of the esteemed Oxford professor, Isaiah Berlin, who was in the British diplomatic corps at the time. This meeting touched Akhmatova deeply, and she dedicated many poems in her cycles "Sweetbrier in Blossom," "Midnight Verses," and "Cinque" to Berlin. He was a kindred spirit—one of the few people with whom Akhmatova felt on equal terms, and who in different circumstances might have been a lifelong companion and friend.

Left: *Akhmatova reciting her poems, 1946*   Above: *Akhmatova and Pasternak, 1946*   Below: *Delegation of Leningrad poets: Pavel Antokolsky, Olga Berggolts, Mikhail Dudin, Akhmatova, and Nikolay Tikhonov (poet; also Secretary of the Union of Soviet Writers, 1944–1946). Moscow, 1946*

In total disregard of the patriotic poetry Akhmatova had written during the war, and despite the fact she was a model of courage to the women of her land, the Central Committee of the Communist Party passed a resolution on 14 August 1946, condemning the magazines *Zvezda* and *Leningrad* for publishing the works of Akhmatova and Zoshchenko.[3] As in the early 1920s, Akhmatova was accused of being a relic of the past, reflecting bourgeois aestheticism and decadence rather than social awareness.

Andrey Zhdanov, Secretary of the Central Committee of the Communist Party, attacked her again a week later at the Leningrad branch of the Union of Soviet Writers, where he warned that Akhmatova's works would harm the morals of the young:

What positive contribution can Akhmatova's work make to our young people? It can do nothing but harm. It can only sow despondency, spiritual depression, pessimism, and the desire to walk away from the urgent questions of public life, to leave the wide paths of public life and activity for the narrow little world of personal experience. How can we place the education of young people in her hands![4]

Akhmatova was expelled from the Union of Soviet Writers on 4 September 1946. Chukovskaya reports in her diary a conversation she had with Akhmatova about the incident. Akhmatova said she had not been told of the 14 August resolution, nor had she read the newspapers that day. She had some business to do at the Union of Soviet Writers and could not imagine why everyone was avoiding her. On her way home she bought some herring, and ran into Zoshchenko, who said in despair: "Anna Andreevna, what can we do?" She did not know what he was talking about but replied: "We must be patient, everything will be all right." Only when she unwrapped the fish from the newspaper did she read the resolution of the Central Committee and realize why Zoshchenko had been so upset.[5]

Pasternak, who was then a member of the board of the Union of Soviet Writers, refused to attend a meeting denouncing Akhmatova and Zoshchenko. He told them he was suffering from nerve inflammation and was too ill to attend. The board expelled him for this, but Pasternak went to see Akhmatova in spite of any further consequences to himself, and gave her a thousand rubles.[6] Chukovskaya described a related incident: "On my way to the Shklovskys I ran into Pasternak. We ducked into a doorway—Pasternak wondered if we could go on living if Akhmatova were killed. His next question was what we could do for her. He saw her when she came to Moscow and put 1,000 rubles under her pillow."[7]

Hostile criticism of Akhmatova appeared in the press after the Zhdanov affair, as Chukovskaya notes. On 14 September 1946, Tamara Trifonova wrote an article in *Leningradskaya pravda,* calling Akhmatova's poetry "harmful and alien to the people." She used poems written by Akhmatova before the war in 1941 and dated them 1942, making them appear as if Akhmatova strolled through Leningrad and admired the reflection of golden spires while people were perishing during the siege of the city.[8]

After the decree, Akhmatova immersed herself in her research on Pushkin, working on two articles in particular, "Pushkin and Dostoevsky" and "The Death of Pushkin." Irina Tomashevskaya said the first article was Akhmatova's best piece on Pushkin.[9]

Akhmatova's son Lev was arrested again on 6 November 1949. Emma Gershtein says that when Akhmatova learned of it, lying alone in her unheated room, she wrote verses to Stalin and sent them to Nina Olshevskaya, who turned them over to Alexander Fadeev, First Secretary of the Union of Soviet Writers.[10] She also burned her articles on Pushkin, along with her entire archive.[11] The poems to Stalin were printed in *Ogonyok* at the beginning of 1950, but without any results.[12] Every month Akhmatova sent Lev a package. Punin had been arrested shortly before this, on 30 September 1949, and perished in a Siberian prison camp in 1953.

Stalin died on 5 March 1953. The effect this event had on Akhmatova's life was gradual but significant. She worked assiduously to free her son, who by the time of his third arrest had become a respected scholar, enlisting noted scholars to write letters on his behalf. In March 1956 Fadeev wrote to the Chief Military Prosecutor asking for Lev's release and enclosed a letter from Akhmatova. This activity may have helped; even more significant, however, was Khrushchev's anti-Stalin speech at the 20th Congress that year, which led the Mikoyan Commission to speed up the return of prisoners awaiting rehabilitation. Lev was released. He returned to Moscow in May and met his mother in the Ardovs' apartment where she usually stayed when in Moscow. They tried to live together, but had trouble getting along. After many quarrels, Lev moved out, and they rarely saw each other. Yet Akhmatova, as Haight points out, was extremely proud of her son and praised him highly as a scholar.[13]

In 1952 she was told to leave her apartment in Fountain House and move to Krasnaya Konnitsa 3, Apt. 4. She lived there with Irina Punina and her family. She was able to earn some money for translations. In 1961 she moved to another apartment on Lenin Street. When she was in Moscow, she frequently stayed in a room in the apartment of her friends, the Ardovs.

Chukovsky mentions seeing Akhmatova in 1954, for the first time after her expulsion from the Union of Soviet Writers, at the home of the scholar Vyacheslav Ivanov. He writes:

> She was gray-haired, calm, corpulent, straightforward, not at all resembling that stylish, shy and at the same time arrogant slender poet to whom Gumilyov had introduced me in 1912. She spoke about her catastrophe calmly and with humor: "I was famous, then I was very infamous, and I am convinced that essentially it's one and the same thing." I again felt that excitement in her presence that I had when I was young. I felt the grandeur, nobility, the enormity of her talent and of her fate.[14]

In May of 1954 another event reminded Akhmatova of her need to be cautious when speaking in public. A group of twenty British students—none from Oxford, and definitely not sent by Isaiah Berlin —came to visit Leningrad. Max Hayward says they did not ask to see Akhmatova or Zoshchenko, but the Leningrad branch of the Union of Soviet Writers made the two authors appear before this group. Both were asked what they thought of the Zhdanov Decrees. While Zoshchenko made some critical comments, Akhmatova said only a few words.[15]

In the summer of 1954 Akhmatova spent time in the village of Golitsyno near Moscow at a vacation lodge for writers. There she met Natalya Ilina, who had recently completed studies at a literary institute. Ilina wrote that wherever the poet appeared, silence suddenly ensued. "No one dared babble just anything that came into their heads. Not only because they knew her poetry and her life. Her very presence had an amazing effect on people. Her silence, the way she held her head, the expression on her face inspired awe."[16] After overcoming her initial shyness, Ilina became friends with Akhmatova and one of her most ardent admirers. She notes how different Akhmatova was at the Ardovs, where she was not afraid to relax and laugh. As she got older, Akhmatova remained proud and hated to acknowledge her

Above: *Akhmatova, Nadezhda Mandelstam, Emma Gershstein. 1950s*
Below: *Akhmatova, end of the 1950s. Collection of L. Ya. Ginzburg*

growing dependency on others. Ilina mentions once feeling sorry for Akhmatova because she had become hard of hearing and had difficulty walking. "But I had to hide this carefully," Ilina wrote. "She didn't want people to feel sorry for her. If I would forget and tell her I would take her somewhere, she always corrected me: 'You mean we will go together.'"[17]

Akhmatova did not lack for friends at the end of her life. In 1955 she was allowed use of a small dacha in Komarovo, a writer's colony outside Leningrad. Ilina describes a typical day when she came to visit with her sister in 1964. Akhmatova was wearing a simple lilac dress with her large gray head thrown back, looking majestic sitting at a table. "We started eating and new guests arrived, poets, actors, Zhenia Chukovsky with his wife Galina Shostakovich and a tape recorder on which they played a new work by Dmitry Shostakovich."[18]

Earlier in their relationship, Ilina writes, Akhmatova wore an impenetrable armor when meeting someone new. Later, as her books began to appear, her fame returned, and she received more letters and telephone calls, she became more open. She paid little attention to material wealth, and spent most of her time staying with friends and spending summers in Komarovo. She still wore her old coat and

Akhmatova's work table at Komarovo. 1960s

worn-out shoes, but thrived on the admirers, flowers, and phone calls.[19]

Four young poets were particularly attentive—Joseph Brodsky, Dmitry Bobyshev, Anatoly Naiman, and Evgeny Rein—and became "Akhmatova's orphans," as Bobyshev called them. In his article describing their relationship, Bobyshev says he first heard Akhmatova's name in the early 1950s, when as a child under the Stalin

Joseph Brodsky and Anatoly Naiman at Komarovo

era he was forced to study Zhdanov's speech. Later, during the Khrushchev period, the poets began to form poetic circles and tried to publish their works, but they were mainly limited to reading in student dormitories, cafés and clubs where scholars met. Bobyshev describes how he first met Akhmatova. Naiman had met her first. A few weeks later, Bobyshev and Rein went on their own to her apartment to introduce themselves. Akhmatova was packing to move, and piles of books were all over the floor. Having accepted their offer to help her move, she led them to the next room and said: "Read!" She approved of their verse, saying they "would do," but advised them to write more concisely. "And how happy we were. My God! Our poems were approved by Akhmatova herself, when they were rejected by every almanac, magazine, and publisher in Moscow and Leningrad. This gave us great confidence."[20]

The four, like many young poets, waited for a "dedication"—a touch of the magic wand, a tap of the sword on the shoulder, or a symbolic "handing down of the lyre." They all devoted verses to her with the undisguised hint that she write poems to them. Bobyshev wrote a poem to her, and brought it to her in Komarovo on her birthday along with a bouquet of five beautiful roses. Akhmatova recalled them on his next visit: "Four of them soon faded, but the fifth bloomed extraordinarily well and created a miracle, almost flying around the room..." Soon they found out what this rose had "created"—Akhmatova had written poems to them: "The Last Rose" (S-F. I, 328–329) to Brodsky, "The Fifth Rose" (Zh. 590) to Bobyshev, and "Nebyvshaya" to Naiman.[21] While the four poets eventually parted, Akhmatova brought them together for the last time at her funeral. Bobyshev wrote a poem for this occasion, "All Four," one of his "Mourning Octaves":

> *Having closed my eyes, I first drained*
> *The poison to the bottom.*
> *And, nailed to the cemetery cross*
> *My soul regained its sight: in the line of the bereaved*
> *Come Osya, Tolya, Zhenya, Dima*
> *Akhmatova's orphans all in a row.*
> *Only looking straight ahead, not at each other*
> *The four poetmakers-sworn brothers.*
> *Their friendship, as life, is irretrievable.*[22]

The Flight of Time

In 1965 Akhmatova's large collection of poems, *The Flight of Time*, appeared, which included *Reed* and her previously unpublished *Seventh Book*. In the cycle "Secrets of the Craft," with verses written from 1936 to 1959, Akhmatova discusses the art of poetry. "Creation" (Zh. 333, dated 5 November 1936), the first poem, describes the transition from the poet overhearing sounds in the air—the striking of the clock, the peal of thunder—to transforming them into words. As in her earlier poems about poetry, Akhmatova describes the poetic process as a form of dictation: the poet passively copies down the words. In the second poem of the cycle (Zh. 334), written in 1940, she sounds the tenets of Acmeism. The poet does not require lofty themes or ornamental discourse; her poetry derives from the simple things of life—the fresh smell of tar, or mold on the wall. The theme of "The Muse" (Zh. 335), also in this cycle, is related to this poem. As Jerzy

Faryno points out, Akhmatova presents two opposing concepts of the Muse. One is the stereotyped version, presented through clichés such as "the divine babble," and the other the actual, concrete experiences of the poet herself. In the first, more popular and idyllic version, the poet is a partner of the Muse. But the speaker experiences the Muse quite differently: the Muse attacks her victim "more savagely than fever," and then is silent for a whole year, unable to inspire any sound at all.[23]

The satirical seventh poem in the cycle, "Epigram" (Zh. 339), written about her imitators, reflects a humorous side of Akhmatova. Chukovsky says Akhmatova had great humor and wit, though she rarely expressed it through her works. He notes that when the poem about the glove appeared in *Evening,* she said laughing: "Watch, tomorrow (and she named one of the silliest poetesses of the time) she will write in her poems: 'I will put my right galosh on my left foot.'" He added, "She was right!... Right after *Evening* and *Rosary* appeared, along came female doggerel—mannered, tasteless, hysterical, vulgar, with none of that feeling...that is one of the achievements of the Russian lyric."[24]

In one of her most famous cycles, "In the Fortieth Year" (Zh. 347–351), Akhmatova expresses her horror of the war. Another cycle, "The Wind of War" (Zh. 352–368), includes poems written from July 1941 in Leningrad to 1944 in Tashkent. One of the most effective poems in the cycle is "Grandly they said good-bye..." (Zh. 353), in which all the soldiers die. The most popular poem from this series, "Courage" (Zh. 356), which was read many times during the war, praises the power of the Russian language. The last cycle of war poems, "Victory" (Zh. 363–367), composed between 1942 and 1945, celebrates the victory that finally comes, the "long-awaited guest."

Like Pushkin when he was exiled to the south of Russia, Akhmatova was ambivalent toward the beautiful area where she spent her wartime exile. In the cycle "The Moon at Zenith" (Zh. 369–376), while missing the north, she glorifies the exotic region of Tashkent. "Those lynx eyes..." (Zh. 381) tells how the Asiatic landscape brings out the latent Tatar side lurking inside of Akhmatova—her "prememory."

In 1959 Akhmatova wrote a poem (Zh. 463) about Joseph Czapski, the Polish artist she had met in Tashkent during the war. While they had only met once, the poem denotes a strong bond between these two

Slavs—one from Leningrad, the other from Warsaw—in the midst of a beautiful but alien culture.[25] Now, only the memory of that night links them.

Akhmatova includes a number of poems in this collection about Tsarskoye Selo. Two, "All the souls..." (Zh. 405) and "Like the fifth act of a drama..." (Zh. 406), were written more than 40 years earlier, in 1921.[26] No day or month is given, but they may have been evoked by the deaths of Blok and Gumilyov in that year. In the first, she writes that the "air of Tsarskoye Selo/ Was created for the echoing of songs," and indeed the place was associated with Pushkin, Gumilyov, and Annensky. The speaker now believes her lyre has a place there as well. In the second poem, Tsarskoye Selo represents a past she is clinging to, pretending that her beloved friends did not die. She knows she must face reality: "with a frail hand it's possible to hold/ A heavily laden boat to the pier," but eventually the boat will leave and she must say farewell.

Akhmatova's later poems also conjure up Tsarskoye Selo. In "Seaside Sonnet" (Zh. 451), Akhmatova, at 69, realizes everything from the decrepit starling houses to the vernal sea breeze will outlive her. In the second stanza she turns toward eternity, which beckons her to the beyond. But she also turns back to the peaceful landscape of her youth, Tsarskoye Selo, and everything resembles that quiet moment in her life. Tsarskoye Selo figures in two other poems in a cycle devoted to the "City of Pushkin." In "Oh, woe is me..." (Zh. 457) it again symbolizes her peaceful past, but in deadly contrast to what greets the poet when she visits Tsarskoye Selo after the war in 1945. The Nazis have burned it to the ground. She sees only remembrances—the spot where the fountain was, where she walked down the lofty allée. "The leaves of this willow..." (Zh. 458), written in 1957, recalls Tsarskoye Selo as a lyceum for Pushkin and his friends, when he turned the ephemeral beauty of the palaces and the parks into eternal verse. Tsarskoye Selo is then viewed 50 years later, when Akhmatova grew up there. She knows she cannot return to the Tsarskoye of her childhood, but she will take the enduring memories of it with her beyond the grave. In 1961 Akhmatova wrote in "Tsarskoye Selo Ode" (Zh. 477) that she will immortalize the place through her art as Chagall did Vitebsk.

From 1925 to 1940 Akhmatova composed fragments of what was intended to be a long poem devoted to Tsarskoye Selo, "The Russian Trianon" (see Zh. 632). The title implicitly compares Tsarskoye Selo with Marie Antoinette's palace in France, thereby suggesting an impending revolution and, in particular, the collapse of the tsarist regime. The fragments contrast the speaker's childhood, when the granddaughters of Pushkin's beauties strolled there with their lapdogs, with the historic events now changing the face of Russia. Those immersed in the singing of the choir at services and watching the moon on the diamond white snow are unaware—until history intrudes with a machine gun placed on the White Tower. Pushkin is now only a memory, and Tsarskoye Selo has become a way of life, where people try to hide themselves in the gentle atmosphere, refusing to face the brutality of contemporary times.

The cycle "A Sweetbrier in Blossom," which refers to Isaiah Berlin, includes poems from 1946 to 1964. "First Song" (Zh. 424), written in 1956, refers to her "nonmeeting" with Isaiah Berlin in the Soviet Union, and her fear of seeing him again: she was convinced their first meeting led to her expulsion from the Union of Soviet Writers and the suffering of her son. In "Don't be afraid..." (Zh. 431) Akhmatova illuminates a moment in her own past with historical and literary allusions. The epigraph refers to the *Aeneid,* when Aeneus leaves Dido to fulfill his destiny as the founder of Rome. Unlike the poems about Lot's wife and Cleopatra, where the reader must infer contemporary relevance from the historical events, here the poet discusses her own fate directly: Dido's grief at the loss of Aeneus reflects her own, when the man leaves her behind because of overwhelming political dangers.

Another man Akhmatova recalls with pain is Vladimir Garshin, whose promise to marry her alleviated some of her suffering in the war. Soon after he left her, she wrote in 1945 "...And the man who means..." (Zh. 436). The poem begins with an ellipsis, as if the speaker has been caught in mid-thought, pondering the fate of this man who promised her so much, but now wanders madly through the streets with a wolfish grin. In spite of her pain, she asks God to allow her to feel pity through her anger to forgive him.

Akhmatova wrote two verses under the heading "A Small Page from Antiquity" (1960), about the relation of the poet to the state. One describes the death of Sophocles (Zh. 470), who, she told Chukovskaya in 1957, she was rereading after 50 years.[27] In it, the poet is so sacred that the god Dionysus appears to the king in a dream, warning him to suspend his siege until Sophocles' funeral has been celebrated. Chukovskaya notes that Akhmatova was angry at her for finding the poem cold. " 'Cold!' Akhmatova answered in rage. Red hot! You have no ear for antiquity... The childhood of Dionysus and the legend about the death of Sophocles—for you is empty noise. But it must be within, right here,' and she pointed to her chest. 'You must live with it...and my poem about the death of Sophocles is absolutely essential for an understanding of the relationship between art and power.' "[28] In the second poem, which is about Alexander the Great (Zh. 471), the warrior king remembers the lessons of his teacher Aristotle: when he orders the city attacked, he spares the house of the poet [Pindar].

Akhmatova indirectly alludes to the great figure of Antigone in "All the unburied ones..." (Zh. 566, written in 1958), recalling the Greek heroine who ensured the dead were buried with respect. In this two-line poem the speaker mentions how she has mourned for the unburied ones, and wonders if anyone will mourn for her.

Over the course of many years, Akhmatova wrote poems she included in the cycle "Northern Elegies" (Zh. 634–639). The first, "Prehistory," written in 1940 and 1943, is a marvelous description of the period immediately before Akhmatova's birth, the time of Dostoevsky; it contains many allusions to him and his work. In the third poem of the cycle, she imagines what course the river of her life might have taken—the "life that never took place"—an easy life, full of friends and visits to many cities. The poet implies, though, that she would accept the suffering over again, knowing it went along with her special destiny.

For many years Akhmatova had been at work on the poem that would crown her last years, *Poem Without a Hero*. She started it while still in Leningrad, worked on it in Tashkent, and continued writing it into the 1960s. She says that while going through her archives in 1940, she found letters and poems she had not read before concerning the tragic event of 1913, the basis for the work.[29] In her memoirs she explains: "My memory has become unbelievably sharp. The past has engulfed me and demands something. What? Dear genies of the remote past seem to speak with me. Perhaps this is their last chance, when bliss, which people call oblivion, may pass them by. Where do the words spoken half a century ago come from, and which I haven't recalled for over 50 years?"[30] Nadezhda Mandelstam, referring to Akhmatova's poem "Lot's Wife," says the *Poema* is a last, backward glance at the "red towers" of the poet's "native Sodom"—a temptation hard to resist even knowing the price she would pay.[31]

The poem alludes to many lines from other poems and incidents from other poets' works. These references serve a specific role in *Poem Without a Hero*. In Part Two, "The Other Side of the Coin," the poet says she will be accused of plagiarism. T.S. Eliot addresses this concern in "Tradition and the Individual Talent," when he cautions not to judge a poet only on aspects of his work in which he least resembles others. The best part of a poet's work may be the parts in which "the dead poets, his ancestors, assert their immortality most vigorously."[32]

Akhmatova certainly uses citation and allusion for this effect—for the associations they immediately bring to mind. But in *Poem Without a Hero* she also employs a device that in Russian is called *tainopis* or "secret writing," by which, because of censorship or discretion, lines from another poet are cited because the author cannot be mentioned directly. Akhmatova said this enforced subtlety contributed to a writer's style. She also used the device to refer to other figures who touched her life, such as Isaiah Berlin. The third and last dedication was about the man who "will not be a beloved husband," but who is destined with her to change the course of history. She sincerely believed Berlin's visit in 1945 helped incite Zhdanov's xenophobia and partially caused the purges after the war.

In *Poem Without a Hero,* the author acts like a master-of-ceremonies, introducing the protagonists and commenting on the action. As Zhirmunsky observes, "the poet is both hero and author of the poem, contemporary and guilty along with the people of her generation but at the same time a judge pronouncing a verdict over them."[33]

The poem opens with the poet sitting in Fountain House in 1940, when guests arrive from the past, from the year 1913. They are dressed in mummers' costumes, typical of a Russian New Year's Eve celebration of that time. In the Intermezzo, a scrap of conversation is overheard about going to the Stray Dog cabaret. The second part takes place in 1913, when the actual plot begins. A handsome young poet-officer is in love with the lovely actress from the Stray Dog, but she proves unfaithful. On 31 December 1913, she arrives home with another lover. When the young officer—who is waiting across the street for her arrival—witnesses her infidelity, he commits suicide. The poem ends in 1942, when the poet tells Leningrad, her beloved city now in ruins, that she is inseparable from it: her shadow is on its walls, her reflection in its canals, the sound of her footsteps in the Hermitage halls.

The plot is loosely based on reality. Vsevolod Knyazev, once the lover of the poet Kuzmin, fell in love with Olga Sudeikina and wrote many passionate verses to her, but after being coldly rejected, shot himself at the end of March 1913 and died a few days later. In the *Poema,* the incident recalls the Commedia dell'Arte, and refers to the young poet as the pathetic Pierrot, the actress as Columbine, and the demonic lover as Harlequin.

However, the plot is raised from reminiscences about a hussar boy who wrote mediocre verse[34] to a level where the guilt for his senseless death is borne by those who refused to hear the rumbling of the future, who retreated from the threatening chaos, and made merry at their "Feast During the Time of the Plague."[35] The descent into the Stray Dog is a descent into hell, an encounter with death: salvation is possible only through one's conscience, by returning in memory to the time of one's guilt to expiate and atone for one's actions. The poet curses the beauty of an art associated with death and guilt.[36]

Some conjecture that this story refers to a young man who committed suicide after being rejected by Akhmatova herself. Evidence supporting this view is mentioned by L.L. Saulenko and Roman Timenchik, both of whom refer to the archival notes in the State Public Library where Akhmatova gives the history of the origin of *Poem Without a Hero:*

> The first impulse, which for decades I hid from myself, is of course Pushkin's note: "Only the first lover produces the same impression on a woman that the first one killed in war does." Vsevolod [Knyazev] was not the first killed and he was never my lover, but his suicide was so like another catastrophe... they were always confused for me.[37]

Vilenkin reports a conversation he had with Akhmatova after reading excerpts from the poem. She told him Knyazev is not the hero, but someone else, "an analogy."[38] Timenchik writes that the "other catastrophe" was the suicide of Mikhail Lindeberg, a member of the artillery brigade of Vladikavkaz and son of the director of the Petersburg cadet corps. The event was described in a Vladikavkaz newspaper in December 1911, which reported that the suicide was committed for romantic reasons.[39]

Timenchik claims Akhmatova's *Poema* is in part a polemic against Kuzmin's works, especially his long poem published in 1929, *The Trout Breaks the Ice,* which Akhmatova was reading when she started *Poem Without a Hero.*[40] The rhythm of *Poem Without a Hero* is similar to part of Kuzmin's work. The *Poema* is also related to Kuzmin's novel of 1915, *The Swimmers,* in which several of the same figures that Akhmatova writes about appear in "The Owl," a cabaret based on the Stray Dog. The heroine Elena resembles Olga Sudeikina. In Kuzmin's *The Trout Breaks the Ice,* uninvited guests come for tea, the dead interact with the living. The poet meets a young man, the first incarnation of the lyrical hero. They swear eternal love, but the young man leaves. Later the poet receives a letter from him posted from a Scottish town, where he has fallen in love with a woman, Ellinor. His affair with a woman is based on passion alone, and will only be destructive in contrast to his more profound love for the male. Another incarnation of the protagonist, a sea captain long thought dead, returns to his fiancée from a northern land. The young man finally returns to the poet. The culminating meeting between the two occurs with a new embodiment, the poet's identical twin displayed in the curio collection of an eccentric. The corpse comes alive, and in the final episode, the lovers share a midnight dinner on New Year's Eve. Numerous details allude to the history, philosophy and personal associations of Kuzmin's own life.[41] The work is based on complex shifts of time. It may have influenced not only specific themes and motifs, but also the formal structure of Akhmatova's poem, which also relies on constant shifts in time and associative rather than sequential, logical relationships of imagery.

Akhmatova implicitly accused Kuzmin of forgetting the tragic event of Knyazev's suicide, which is alluded to in *The Trout Breaks the Ice.* For Akhmatova, to forget was to commit a mortal sin. Memory had become a moral category: one remembers one's misdeeds, atones, and achieves redemption. By forgetting or making light of this event, Kuzmin typified for Akhmatova an age of cynicism and frivolity as Russia was facing impending doom. Nadezhda Mandelstam discusses memory in these terms: "We answer for everything, but there are many ways of trying not to. First is by deliberately not recalling something (as opposed to passively 'remembering it'). The first way of evading responsibility is not to recollect at all, the second is to embellish it, deceive oneself... The operation can be performed on an individual life history or on the past of a whole nation."[42]

When she began writing the work, Akhmatova was thinking about Kuzmin and stressed his vapidness to Chukovskaya:

> We took everything seriously, but in Kuzmin's hands everything turned into a toy... Kuzmin was very nasty and malicious. He loved

saying awful things about everyone. He could not bear Blok because he envied him... His salon had a bad influence on young people—they thought it was the culmination of thought and art but it was actually corruption where everything was taken as a game, everything was mocked... He could not endure me.[43]

In 1913, however, when the poem takes place, Kuzmin and Akhmatova were friends. He wrote the preface to her first book, *Evening,* and had the insight to prophesy her greatness. In an article in 1913, he warned her, as a friend, not to fall into the trap of repeating a successful formula, and to fail to seek new paths of creativity as she matured and developed.[44] Perhaps this chiding—at a time when other critics were attacking her work on a much pettier level—made her particularly sensitive to his words. Or perhaps when she was writing *Poem Without a Hero,* Kuzmin became the scapegoat for her own sins for which she was now feeling guilty. Kuzmin was deeply hurt when his relationship with Knyazev fell apart. A careful reading of *The Trout Breaks the Ice* reveals his obsession with the image of Knyazev to the end of his life in 1936. In Akhmatova's work, he represents the evil in the past. Her reference to Cagliostro probably refers to Kuzmin, since Cagliostro was the hero of his novel *Wonderful Life* (1916). He may also be the Prince of Darkness because Akhmatova saw him as an instigator of the evil, mockery and cynicism of the age.

Knyazev (1891–1913) was serving in the military in Riga. He began his relationship with Kuzmin in 1910, and during the next few years they wrote poems to each other. In one, Kuzmin compares Knyazev to Antinous, the Roman emperor Hadrian's lover, who died as a young man in 130 A.D.:

And with every moment obedient, voiceless,
Like a slave, I bend before the sharp arrow;
He will come, the handsome Antinous will come,
But I will meet him exhausted, mute...[45]

In late 1911, however, a new theme appeared in Knyazev's poetry, the unrequited love for a woman and the poet's identification with Pierrot. In one poem in 1912 he refers to Sudeikina as "sweet, tender Columbine," an image Akhmatova also used in relation to Sudeikina and her work. In September 1912 Kuzmin went to see Knyazev in Riga, and they travelled to Mitava. That same month, Knyazev wrote a poem about receiving a letter from Sudeikina stating she no longer

Vsevolod Knyazev

Olga Sudeikina, 1922. Photo by Moses Nappelbaum

was in love with him. J. Guenther, who was living in Riga at the time, mentions that Sudeikina had spent several days in Riga with Knyazev, and Kuzmin was very upset when he found out.[46] But the relationship between Kuzmin and Knyazev had already begun to deteriorate. Knyazev came to Petersburg on Christmas Day, 1912 and apparently celebrated New Year's Eve in the Stray Dog, even writing a poem about it ("1 January 1913"). One of his last verses to Sudeikina, written in December 1912, shows he admitted there was no hope left. In despair, he shot himself in Riga on 29 March 1913. He died on 5 April and was buried at the Smolensk Cemetery in Petersburg.[47] Kuzmin was tormented by these events, and 14 years later wrote *The Trout Breaks the Ice,* commemorating this episode.[48]

Suicide was popular at the time. Zhirmunsky notes that the Symbolist poet Sologub had published an article, "Russian Decadents and Suicide," in *Den,* and Wedekind's play about suicide, "Spring-Awakening" was being performed at the Komissarzhevsky Theatre. Chukovsky comments on this topic: "In those years there were an enormous number of suicides, especially among young people. It became an epidemic, and even the fashion... This prompted Akhmatova to make one of the personages of her story about that period a suicide. On the eve of war not only the officer Pierrot but everyone lived under the sign of death... The entire narration of Akhmatova's from the first to the last line is permeated by this apocalyptic 'feeling of the end.'"[49]

Many scholarly works have noted Osip Mandelstam's role in *Poem Without a Hero.* Nadezhda Mandelstam provides evidence that Akhmatova had Osip in mind in the First Dedication, blurring his image with that of Knyazev, since both were victims of the age. Akhmatova first dated the dedication 28 December, but when Nadezhda showed her the slip of paper from the Registrar's Office declaring Mandelstam's death on 27 December, Akhmatova put that date down instead. The "dusky eyelashes of Antinous" may refer not only to Knyazev but also to Mandelstam, since his friends frequently alluded to his long lashes. A reference in the dedication also mentions Akhmatova writing on someone's rough draft. After Nadezhda first heard Akhmatova recite the *Poema* in Tashkent, she asked to whom the First Dedication was addressed. Akhmatova replied: "Whose first draft do you think I can write on?"[50] The hero, the suffering poet, was clearly Mandelstam.

Akhmatova also identified Blok as the demonic poet. There are many indirect references to him, including the very form of the poem, which in some ways resembles his *Retribution*—a work that looks to the past to explain events in the present. Its hero is also castigated for the sins of ancestors passing from generation to generation. In his preface to this work Blok emphasizes the poem's structure, a pastiche of figures and events closely interrelated not by time or causality but by emotional association. He relates the "facts" of the winter of 1911: the stern voice of Strindberg, the smell of burning, iron and blood, and the assassination of the minister Stolypin. "All these facts apparently so different have one musical meaning for me. I am used to juxtaposing facts from all areas of life accessible to my view at a given time and am sure that all together they create a single musical melody."[51] Zhirmunsky points out the influence of Blok's other poems on *Poem Without a Hero*, including the cycle "Snow Mask" (1907), in which the snow symbolizes elementary passion. In fact, in the ballet libretto of *Poem Without a Hero*, written by Akhmatova, the female protagonist—an actress—sits in a box watching a scene from Akhmatova's ballet libretto of "Snow Mask," which she wrote in the early 1920s.[52] Several references in the poem point to Blok's famous work "The Steps of the Commandatore," about the statue claiming retribution from Don Juan for his deadly crimes. A reference to Don Juan in the epigraph to the second chapter cites a line from Da Ponte's libretto for Mozart's opera on the subject, *Don Giovanni*.[53] Donna Anna, the heroine of *Don Giovanni*, is depicted in one of the portraits hanging in the bedroom of the actress.

The second dedication of the poem is to Akhmatova's friend, Olga Glebova-Sudeikina, and is dated the year of her death. The two lost touch after Sudeikina left Russia, but Akhmatova always kept a portrait of her. She did not learn of Sudeikina's death until 1946, after she had already written the dedication (25 May 1945). The actress of *Poem Without a Hero* is largely based on Sudeikina, and allusions are made to her famous roles in Belyaev's play *Confusion*, Surovin's *Psyche*, her role of the bacchante in Satz's *The Goat-legged Nymph*, and of Columbine in a Commedia dell'Arte work directed by Meyerhold. The portraits that come to life in the actress's bedroom reflect some of these roles. The idea of pictures springing to life was popular in Russia. In Nikolay Tcherepnin's ballet *Pavillion d'Armide*, produced by the Ballets Russes, a tapestry comes to life, and in skits in the Moscow cabaret, "The Bat,"

18th century portraits would come alive and have elegant conversations with each other. Figures also emerge from portraits in Kuzmin's *The Trout Breaks the Ice*—perhaps the immediate source for the idea.

The epigraph to Part Two, "My future is in my past," introduces "The Other Side of the Coin," and serves as a commentary on the poem and the poet's past. As V.N. Toporov points out, it relates to several different poems by T.S. Eliot, whom Akhmatova frequently read, most directly to the opening line of "East Coker": "In my beginning is my end." Toporov notes two other Eliot poems that discuss the role of the past in creating one's future. The first is "Burnt Norton," which contains these lines:

> *Time present and time past*
> *Are both perhaps present in time future,*
> *And time future contained in time past.*
> . . .
> *What might have been and what has been*
> *Point to one end, which is always present.*

The other is "The Dry Salvages," which includes this passage:

> *. . . I have said before*
> *That the past experience revived in the meaning*
> *Is not the experience of one life only*
> *But of many generations—not forgetting*
> *Something that is probably quite ineffable:*
> *The backward look behind the assurance*
> *Of recorded history, the backward half-look*
> *Over the shoulder, towards the primitive terror.*[54]

In "The Other Side of the Coin" the poet discusses the difficulty the editor has understanding the poem. The subtlety of allusions hinders comprehension even for those who knew Akhmatova and her past. This disappointed her. Chukovsky tells how she visited him on 10 June 1955 to discuss the work.

> I soon understood she had come. . . because of her *Poema.* Apparently in her tragic, tormented life the *Poema* was the only ray of hope, the only illusion of happiness. She had come to speak about the *Poema,* to hear praise. It was upsetting to her that its contents had slipped away from many readers. . . Akhmatova divided the world into two unequal parts: those who understood the *Poema* and those who did not.[55]

The Epilogue takes place in 1942, when the city is in ruins. Reference is made to her "double" behind the barbed wire, to death—the Noseless Slut, guarding him—and to others in the camps. Despite enormous suffering, Akhmatova remained inseparable from her city, and from Russia. Haight summarizes what Akhmatova had discovered: "In this contrast between the world of 1913 and the 'True Twentieth Century' she finds her reward, for, despite everything, the world she lost in 1914 was incredibly poorer than the one she gained and the poet and person she was then little by comparison with what she has become."[56]

VIII. Last Years

For many years Akhmatova had been earning her living translating works by major authors from Serbia, Poland, India, Korea, and Armenia. She frequently complained it was ruining her creativity and taking time from her own work. Nadezhda Mandelstam notes that Akhmatova often gave the translations to other people and shared the fees. "She managed it very shrewdly and saved needy people by getting them paid handsomely for their drudgery."[1] This may have meant that the others produced the basic translation, and like an artist with apprentices, the final work of polishing the text into a work of art was left for the real poet. In her biographic note, Akhmatova said she had been interested in artistic translation for a long time.[2]

The poet Semyon Lipkin believes Akhmatova's love and real empathy for the works of other cultures enabled her to produce these great translations. He notes that previous Russian translators made Rabindranath Tagore's verse sound stilted and cold, while in Akhmatova's translation, he speaks clearly, simply and musically without any superfluous words.

> She is present in every line of the translation, just as an original author is present in every phrase of his hero. But a translator must not stifle the author or we lose the feeling of the original. Akhmatova does not impose anything on the author; she helps him state his relationship to the world in another language, helps him express his thoughts, his feelings... If letters, diaries, biographical notes of a poem can help us enter his world and understand more profoundly this world, then the translation by a real poet will serve us as an invaluable guide to this world. Reading her translations, we again return to Akhmatova's original poems and see what we had not noticed before.[3]

Her interest in Georgian poetry led her to translate works from this national literature as well. Akhmatova had met the famous Georgian poets Paolo Yashvili and Titsian Tabidze through Boris Pasternak at the beginning of the 1930s. She said: "Once Pasternak had brought Titsian and Paolo to see me at Fontanka 34, where I was living. At my request, Titsian read me poems in Georgian; I wanted to penetrate more deeply the music of Georgian verse."[4]

In another collection of her translations, Arseny Tarkovsky comments that the collection should occupy a place on the reader's shelf next to books of Akhmatova's own poetry. Akhmatova selected the poets she translated, he notes, and so the poems reveal something about her. "Like any other art, a poetic translation begins with selection. A painter chooses the single part of the world that best answers his ideas. The poet translator finds in the literature of another language what at any given moment of historical, social, and personal life represents for him something important and expressive, and under the pen of our contemporary, something that recently seemed strange, perhaps written long ago, is reborn and answers the needs of our time, our national milieu."[5]

Like her translations, Akhmatova's articles on Pushkin also reveal something of her thoughts and feelings. In her discussion of Pushkin's tragedy, *The Stone Guest,* she explores the concept of "prehistory" in a work of art, which figures prominently in her own poems. In this "small tragedy," the reader is expected to realize that Pushkin presents these scenes as a solution to something that has already happened outside the limits of the work—Don Juan's many love affairs, and the entire biography of Donna Anna. "This small tragedy assumed an extensive prehistory which, due to the amazing ability of the author, is compressed into several lines of the text. This device was developed magnificently by Dostoevsky in his novel-tragedies. They present a solution to something that has already happened somewhere beyond the limits of a given work."[6] She learned from Pushkin the art of *tainopis,* secret writing, as a way to express oneself under the shadow of censorship and the state. "I don't know if enough has been said in the scholarship about this feature of the greatest poet of the 19th century; it is difficult for the average reader to realize this, brought up on clichés about clarity, transparency, and the simplicity of Pushkin. Through this device he was able to state things about himself he was not allowed to share with anyone his whole life."[7] Her work on Pushkin was so highly regarded that one of Russia's leading Pushkin scholars, Boris Tomashevsky, inscribed a copy of his book for Akhmatova with: "To the best connoisseur of Pushkin—A. A. Akhmatova."[8]

In the last years of her life Akhmatova was surrounded by friends and received homage from home and abroad. Foreigners, poets, and admirers of Russian poetry came to visit her. Robert Frost visited Russia in 1962 and paid a call on Akhmatova at Komarovo. He was accompanied by the noted scholar and translator of Russian literature, Franklin Reeve, and Mikhail Alekseev, a Soviet specialist on Pushkin. At lunch, the conversation turned to American and English writers, and to Greek and Latin classics. Asked to recite a poem, Akhmatova chose "The Last Rose" (S-F. I, 328–329) written only six days before, which refers to great historical female figures who suffered for their beliefs and desires. Reeve describes the emotional effect this reading had on everyone present:

> The whole group was so caught by the immediacy of the poem and by the life and understanding which it represented that for a few seconds we were silent, still. . . . Frost remembered this, and he remembered Akhmatova's expression, for he commented later how grand she was but how sad she seemed to be.[9]

Raisa Orlova and Lev Kopelev provide Akhmatova's version of this visit, which they heard several times from her. She was not allowed to receive Frost in her little cabin, so instead, went to the dacha of the academician Mikhail Alekseev, which served as a "Potemkin village."[10]

> I still don't know where they got such a tablecloth and crystal. They combed my hair elegantly and dressed me up, since everything I had was old. Then the handsome Reeve, a young American Slavicist, came for me. . . Everyone was there already, talking excitedly. And then the old man arrived. An American grandfather. . . red-faced, gray-haired, cheerful. . . We sat next to each other in wicker chairs. All kinds of food [was] served and wine was poured. We talked without rushing. And I kept thinking: "Here are you, my dear, a national poet. Every year your books are published. . . they praise you in all the newspapers and journals, they teach you in the schools, the President receives you as an honored guest. And all they've done is slander me! Into what dirt they've trampled me! I've had everything—poverty, prison lines, fear, poems remembered only by heart, and burnt poems. And humiliation and grief. And you don't know anything about this and

wouldn't be able to understand it if I told you . . . But now let's sit together, two old people, in wicker chairs. A single end awaits us. And perhaps the real difference is not actually so great?"[11]

In 1964 Akhmatova was awarded an Italian literary prize by the Comunita Europea Degli Scrittori (Community of European Writers), which she received in Catania, Sicily. Jeanne Rude mentions that Jean-Paul Sartre and Simone de Beauvoir congratulated her by telegram.[12] In a letter to Juan Carlo Vigorelli, Akhmatova wrote:

> Your letter informing me that I am to receive the Taormina prize has brought me great joy. I do not wish to shine with wit on this occasion or hide behind false modesty, but this news, coming to me from a country which I have loved tenderly all my life, has shed a ray of sunshine on my work. I beg of you, dear Juan Carlo, to convey my thanks to the friends who have chosen me.[13]

Hans Werner Richter, who was present at the session, wrote a beautiful description of this episode. He first sees Akhmatova in the garden of a Dominican cloister, sitting on a white lacquered garden chair, with her "lady-in-waiting" in the distance—her companion, Irina

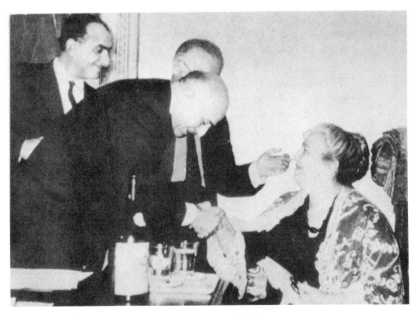

Akhmatova receives Etna-Taormina literary prize. Catania, Italy, 1964

Punina, Punin's daughter. Here at last was the Grand Duchess of poetics holding court and giving an audience.

> And before her stood poets from all countries of Europe...young and old, conservatives and liberals, communists and socialists, standing in line to kiss the hand of Anna Akhmatova, and I, too, joined them. She held her hand out as each one walked in front of her, bowed, and received a kind nod...each performed this ceremony in the manner of his country: the Italian with charm, the Spaniard with grandness, the Bulgarian with devotion, the English with restraint. Only the Russians knew the style Akhmatova expected. They stood before their tsarina, knelt down, and kissed the earth. No, they did not do this, but it seemed as if they did. It was as if when they were kissing Akhmatova's hand they were actually kissing the Russian soil, the tradition of its poetry and the magnificence of its literature.[14]

He describes the poetry recital she gave, at which 200 guests gathered in one of the halls of the cloisters in formal attire. She recited in Russian in a voice that recalled a distant tempest. Each of the other poets in turn read poems to Akhmatova.

> It was like the New Year's reception at the court of a female empress. The tsarina of poetry accepted the homage of the diplomatic corps of world literature. . . . Finally she grew weary and walked out, a grand woman, towering above all the poets, a statuesque figure, and as I watched her walk out, I suddenly understood why Russia could be ruled by a female tsarina. I saw her once more...when she received the Taormina Prize. She thanked the Minister of Culture with a few words, and in this speech there was not a single superfluous word or phrase. It was the thanks of a tsarina to her subject.[15]

The next year Akhmatova went to Oxford, where she received an honorary doctorate. Elaine Bickert, who attended the ceremony, wrote: "In silence, a heavy woman dressed in black beneath the traditional crimson robes, advanced slowly on the arm of a young companion. Thick gray hair crowned the face of an oriental empress."[16] Later Bickert was introduced to her by Yury Annenkov in a small hotel room, and they spoke about Sudeikina, about whom Bickert was writing her dissertation. Bickert saw Akhmatova again in Paris shortly thereafter, where she appeared to be more relaxed, full of humor and wit. She visited Leningrad four years after Akhmatova's death, and wrote that Akhmatova—just as she predicted in her *Poem Without a Hero*—was present in every stone, every reflection on the Neva, every

At the conferral of the Honorary Doctorate of Oxford University. Clockwise from top left: *Prof. Gianfranco Contini (University of Florence; Honorary Degree); Sir Geoffrey Keynes (Hon. Degree); Siegfried Sassoon (poet; Hon. Degree); Anna Kaminskaya (granddaughter of Nikolay Punin); Akhmatova; Sir Kenneth Wheare (Vice Chancellor of Oxford University)*

Salomea Halpern, Akhmatova, and Amanda Haight. London, 1965

leaf of a willow.[17]

At the very end of her life, Akhmatova was able to renew her acquaintance with dear friends she had not seen for years, emigrés who had left soon after the revolution. In their memoirs, many describe how moved they were to see her. Adamovich says he received a call from London. "Akhmatova speaking. Tomorrow I'll be in Paris. We'll see each other, won't we?" She was staying at the Hotel Napoléon. Adamovich describes the initial shock many friends had on first seeing Akhmatova after so many years. She was no longer the slender fashionable young Petersburg lady, but a dignified, older, portly woman. He soon recognized, however, that her brilliance and refined character had not changed.

> Tolstoy once said that the first moment you see someone after a long separation you notice all the changes. However, a moment later the changes become less clear, and it seems as if the person had always been the same. That's what happened with me. In the armchair sat a portly old woman, beautiful and grand, smiling pleasantly, but it was only by this smile that I was able to recognize Akhmatova. Yet it was exactly as Tolstoy had said, in a moment or two before me was Akhmatova, only more talkative, more sure of herself... What did we talk about? Mainly about poetry. We strolled around Paris, and she recalled Modigliani.[18]

Akhmatova said she believed that Russia was going to enter another golden age of poetry: so many young poets were now living for poetry alone, writing wonderful works. And she mentioned Joseph Brodsky. "Have you read Brodsky? I think he's a remarkable poet."[19]

She very much wanted to see Boris Anrep while in Paris, but he had many trepidations about seeing her. In his letter to Struve telling the story of the ring Akhmatova had given him, Anrep says that after he left Russia in 1917, he sent Akhmatova two packages of food, and received a brief note in reply: "Dear Boris, Thank you for feeding me. Anna Akhmatova." He wanted to write but was afraid that might get her in trouble. He wore the ring on a chain, but once when he was undressing, the chain broke, so he put it in a box where he kept other objects of sentimental value. The years passed, but he never forgot the ring. At the beginning of World War II when the Nazis invaded Paris, he was about to leave for London. Before he could leave, his studio was bombed, and when he came by the next morning, the box with the ring was gone. He met Gleb Struve in London during the war, who gave him many of Akhmatova's works that had been published in Russia and abroad. Anrep was moved by her works and felt even guiltier about the ring. When he heard Akhmatova was coming to Oxford, he says he did not want to stand in a line with her admirers. He left for Paris where he was working on a mosaic commission. He wanted to preserve the memory of the beautiful, young, fresh girl he had left in 1917. But the phone rang and it was Akhmatova. He went to see her the next day in her hotel room. They discussed contemporary poets and talked about Nedobrovo, but Anrep remained terrified she would ask about the ring. She read him some of her latest poems, and he realized he had not heard anything like this for so long. After talking about other topics, he said goodbye, rushed out of the hotel room in a trance, walked along the Champs Elysees, and sat in a café until midnight.[20]

Nikita Struve, the nephew of Gleb Struve, describes his meeting with Akhmatova in Paris as well. Like many others, he was struck by the strange, haunting quality of her recitation and presence. "She recited for me. To describe in words the magic of her recitation is impossible. The kind, mocking smile which never abandoned her during conversation disappeared. Her face became more concentrated, more serious. The poems seemed to come from within."[21]

Adamovich describes her last moments before she left Paris forever. "At our last meeting she finally spoke about herself. 'Fate did not leave anything out for me. Everything anyone could possibly experience fell to my lot.' People came with flowers, candy. It was time to get ready. There was less than an hour left before her train. She stood helpless in the middle of the room, trying to smile. 'Well, good-bye, don't forget me. Not farewell, but good-bye![22] God willing, I'll come to Paris again next year. Thank you.'"[23]

Akhmatova was never to return. After spending the summer in Komarovo, she went to Moscow in the fall and suffered a heart attack. She spent time in the hospital, stayed for awhile with the Ardovs, and then went to a convalescent home, where she died on 5 March 1966.[24] Her body was taken to a morgue in Moscow, and then flown to Leningrad. Thousands came to her funeral on 10 March at the St. Nicholas Cathedral. A ceremony also took place at the Union of Soviet Writers, where poets paid homage by reading their poems to her. Mikhail Alekseev spoke: "There has departed from us a poet of rare power, bringing fame to Russian verse far beyond the limits not only of our native city but of our entire land, because in blazing Sicily and misty

Oxford they were also able to judge the power of this poetic voice."[25] She was buried in Komarovo.

Akhmatova left behind as her gift to the world more than 700 poems—a body of work gathered together here in English translation for the first time—and made an indelible impression on many who knew her and on modern poetry itself. The "mirrors and masks" that emerge from her life and work remain behind for further study and reflection. A true modernist poet, she provides the reader with allusions to her personal life, and to Russian and world culture, but her works are accessible to readers without a scholarly background. Her ability to capture the essence of a character, event, or philosophical idea through a few carefully chosen details makes her the true heir of Pushkin. Scholars and lovers of Akhmatova's work will continue to discover more about her in the future, further illuminating this woman whom Nikita Struve appropriately called "not only a great poet but a remarkable, unusual, great human being."[26] She herself, perhaps, acknowledged the depth of what she left behind:

> *These poems have such hidden meanings*
> *It's like staring into an abyss.*
> *And the abyss is enticing and beckoning,*
> *And never will you discover the bottom of it,*
> *And never will its hollow silence*
> *Grow tired of speaking.*
>
> (Zh. 575)

Photo by Nika Glen

10 March 1966. Clockwise from lower left: *"Akhmatova's orphans":*
Anatoly Naiman, Evgeny Rein, Dmitry Bobyshev, Joseph Brodsky.
In center: *Era Korobova*

10 March 1966

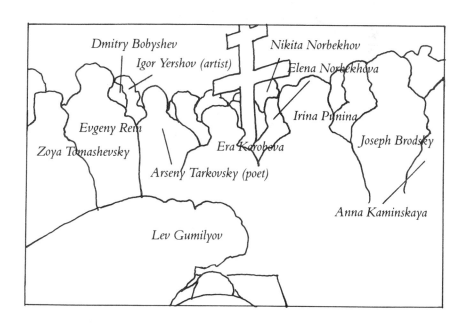

Lev Gumilyov at grave of Akhmatova

Notes

[1] Natalya Ilina, "Anna Akhmatova v poslednie gody ee zhizni," *Oktyabr,* no. 2 (February 1977), p. 123.

[2] Anna Akhmatova, "Korotko o sebe" in Anna Akhmatova, *Stikhotvoreniya i poemy,* ed. V.M. Zhirmunsky, Biblioteka poeta, Bolshaya seriya, 2nd ed. (Leningrad: Sovetskii pisatel, 1979), p. 22.

I. Early Years: 1889–1912

[3] See Richard Charques, *The Twilight of Imperial Russia* (London: Oxford University Press, 1958).

[4] Midsummer eve, 23 June, is known in Russian folklore as "The Eve of Ivan Kupala." The holiday reflects a double belief system—pagan and Christian—as it is the eve of the celebration of both St. John the Baptist and the spirit "Kupala," the "Bather." People bathed in rivers and lakes and jumped through bonfires for purification, for all of nature's forces, both good and evil, were believed strongest on this night. Satan calls his followers to a feast on Bald Mountain in the Ukraine. Akhmatova knew these customs and the significance of the date for the Russian people. For a description of the rituals and songs sung on this night, see *Down Along the Mother Volga,* trans. and ed. by Roberta Reeder (Philadelphia: University of Pennsylvania Press, 1975), pp. 84–86.

[5] In 1935 the Ukrainian writer Teren Masenko met Akhmatova in the apartment of the Russian author Boris Pilniak. Pilniak's daughter gave Akhmatova some poems by Masenko, which she began to read aloud. Masenko remarked how well she spoke Ukrainian, "with a pure pronunciation and correct accent." See Teren Masenko, "U Pilnyaka: Neopublikovannye stranitsy avtobiograficheskogo romana *Vita pochtovaya," Literaturnoe obozrenie,* no. 5 (1989), p. 74. Akhmatova's father, Andrey Gorenko, was born in Sebastopol on 13 January 1848, and served as an engineer in the Black Sea Fleet. His father had also been in the navy, and received two high awards for his service, thereby acquiring hereditary nobility. Akhmatova's father and his first wife, Maria Vasileva, daughter of a sea captain, had two sons, Nikolay and Anton. He was appointed instructor at the naval institute in Petersburg in 1875, but in 1880, some letters of his were found in the apartment of a friend that were deemed "suspicious." In September 1881, he was relieved of his position as instructor and put under surveillance. His sisters, Anna and Evgeniya, who had attended the Bestuzhev Women's Courses in Petersburg, were also under surveillance for their work in the radical "People's Will" movement. By October 1882, a lack of evidence of his wrongdoing enabled him to be returned to the military fleet on the Black Sea. He married Inna Stogova, Akhmatova's mother, in 1885, and their first daughter, Iya, was born that same year.

Gorenko retired with a pension in 1887 with the rank of captain, and he and his family settled in Odessa. He worked on the newspaper, *Odesskie novosti,* writing reviews of literature—the memoirs of Garibaldi, novels of Daudier—and published a novella, *The Philosopher Sikundus* and a short story. He frequently attended meetings of a shipping and commerce society in Petersburg, where he presented papers. His acquaintances in Odessa included people involved with the People's Will. Akhmatova's godfather, Stepan Romanenko, was imprisoned three times for his political activity at the university.

In August 1890, Gorenko and his family moved to Tsarskoye Selo. He remained a member of both the Society of Russian Commerce and Industry and the Petersburg Philosophical Society until the end of his life. In 1905 he left his family to live with E.I. Stranoliubskaya, a widow of a friend with whom he had taught at the naval institute. He died on 25 August 1915 at the age of 67. See Roman Shuvalov, "Otets poeta. K 100-letiyu so dnya rozhdeniya Anny Akhmatovoi," *Vechernyaya Odessa,* 14 June 1989, p. 3.

[6] L.A. Mandrykina, "Nenapisannaya kniga: Listki iz dnevnika A.A. Akhmatovoi," in *Knigi. Arkhivy. Avtografy.*, ed. A.S. Mylnikov et al. (Moscow: Kniga, 1973), p. 73. T.S. Eliot was born in 1888.

[7] Akhmatova, "Korotko o sebe," p. 19. In notes from her autobiography, "Dom Shukhardina," Akhmatova says the house was more than 100 years old, and belonged to the widow of a merchant, Evdokiya Shukhardina. "The house was near the train station." See Anna Akhmatova, *Ya—golos vash...,* ed. V.A. Chernykh (Moscow: Knizhnaya palata, 1989), p. 338.

[8] L.A. Mandrykina, "Iz rukopisnogo naslediya A.A. Akhmatovoi," *Neva,* no. 6 (1979), p. 198.

[9] Vitaly Vilenkin mentions that Akhmatova's mother, Inna Stogova, had become involved with one of the most radical political groups in Russia, the "People's Will." See Vilenkin, *V sto pervom zerkale* (Moscow: Sovetskii pisatel, 1987), p. 89. Akhmatova notes in a reminiscence entitled "Gorod" that when her mother visited her for the last time in 1927, she was full of memories of the People's Will and recalled the Petersburg of her youth in the 1870s. Akhmatova's mother died in 1930. See Akhmatova, *Ya—golos vash...,* p. 340. Akhmatova told her friend Lidiya Chukovskaya that her mother came from nobility but attended courses in her youth, which was unusual for women gentry of the time. See Lidiya Chukovskaya, *Zapiski ob Anne Akhmatovoi,* Vol. I, 1938–1941 (Paris: YMCA Press, 1976), p. 181. (Subsequent citations from Chukovskaya will be noted "Chukovskaya, I," with the page number.)

[10] Amanda Haight, *Anna Akhmatova: A Poetic Pilgrimage* (New York: Oxford University Press, 1976), p. 6.

[11] See *Poems by Nicholas Nekrasov,* trans. by Juliet M. Soskice (Wilmington, Del.: Scholarly Resources, 1974). R.D. Timenchik also cites A. Tinyakov's discussion of the influence of Nekrasov on Akhmatova in *Zhurnal zhurnalov,* no. 6

(1915), p. 16. See R.D. Timenchik, "Khram premudrosti boga: stikhotvorenie Anny Akhmatovoi 'Shiroko raspakhnuty vorota,'" *Slavica Hierosolymitana*, V–VI (1981), pp. 297–317. See also Milivoe Jovanovich, "K razboru 'Chuzhikh golosov' v *Rekvieme* Akhmatovoi," *Russian Literature*, XV (1984), p. 170.

[12]Tsvetaeva is alluding to the famous "Ode on the Seizure of Khotin," by the 18th century poet, Mikhail Lomonosov, in which he praises the Empress press Anna, sovereign of all of Russia.

[13]Akhmatova, "Korotko o sebe," p. 19.

[14]Korney Chukovsky, "Chukovsky ob Akhmatovoi. Po arkyivnym materialam," *Novy mir* (March 1987), p. 233.

[15]Chukovskaya, I, p. 186.

[16]Margarita Aliger, *Tropinka vo rzhi* (Moscow: Sovetskii pisatel, 1980), p. 354.

[17]Akhmatova, "Korotko o sebe," p. 19.

[18]Sergey Eisenstein immortalized the mutiny in Odessa in his famous film "Potemkin" and in an earlier film, "Strike." For further background on this period, see Michael T. Florinsky, *The End of the Russian Empire* (New York: Collier Books, 1961); Charques, *The Twilight of Imperial Russia*; and Roberta Thompson Manning, *The Crisis of the Old Order in Russia* (Princeton: Princeton University Press, 1982). The country was deeply humiliated by the events at Tsushima, where "the Russian colossus suffered defeat after defeat from the Japanese pigmy" (Nicholas V. Riasanovsky, *A History of Russia*, 2nd ed. [New York: Oxford University Press, 1969], p. 446). It marked a turning point in the downfall of the tsarist regime.

[19]Georgy Chulkov, "Anna Akhmatova," in Georgy Chulkov, *Nashi sputniki 1912–1922* (Moscow: N.V. Vasilev, 1922), p. 87.

[20]Valery Bryusov, "Na novyi 1905 god," in Valery Bryusov, *Sobranie sochinenii*, Vol. I (Moscow: Khudozhestvennaya literatura, 1973), pp. 44–45. Translated by Roberta Reeder.

[21]Chukovskaya, I, p. 158.

[22]V. Beer as cited in R.D. Timenchik and A.V. Lavrov, "Materialy A.A. Akhmatovoi v rukopisnom otdele pushkinskogo doma," *Ezhegodnik rukopisnogo otdela pushkinskogo doma na 1974* (Leningrad: Nauka, 1976), p. 66.

[23]See Anna Akhmatova, "Desyat pisem Anny Akhmatovoi (Publikatsiya, vstubpitelnaya statya E. Gershtein)" in Anna Akhmatova, *Stikhi, perepiska, vospominaniya, ikonografiya,* compiled by E. Proffer (Ann Arbor: Ardis, 1977), pp. 89–102. In her introduction to the letters, on p. 89, Emma Gershtein notes that von Shtein was already a widower by the time of this correspondence. She writes that von Shtein's second wife later married E. Gollerbakh, who inherited the von Shtein archive. In April 1935, he transferred the archive, including ten letters from Akhmatova, to the State Literary Museum, with the condition that they not be published during Akhmatova's lifetime. Gershtein

suggests that Gollerbakh's dates on the letters are inaccurate, and has proposed her own dates, which are included here in brackets. The translations are by Edith Stevens, from Anna Akhmatova, "Ten Letters of Anna Akhmatova," *Russian Literature Triquarterly* (1976), pp. 627–644.

[24] Akhmatova, *Stikhi, perepiska, vospominaniya, ikonografiya*, p. 93.

[25] Golenishchev–Kutuzov was born in 1879, and in 1907 completed studies at the Oriental Department of Petersburg University. Later, he was secretary in the Russian consulate in Serbia. See V.A. Chernykh's "Notes," in Anna Akhmatova, *Ya—golos vash...*, p. 364.

[26] Akhmatova, *Stikhi, Perepiska, Vospominaniya, Ikonografiya*, p. 92.

[27] Ibid., p. 95.

[28] Ibid., p. 96.

[29] Ibid., p. 97.

[30] Ibid., p. 98.

[31] Ibid., p. 98.

[32] V.S. Sreznevskaya, "Iz vospominanii V.S. Sreznevskoi," in N. Gumilyov, *Neizdannoe i nesobrannoe,* compiled and edited by Michael Basker and Sheelagh Duffin Graham (Paris: YMCA Press, 1986), p. 160.

[33] Earl D. Sampson, *Nikolay Gumilev* (Boston: Twayne Publishers, 1979), p. 48, states the essential themes of Gumilyov's work: the search for the ideal, the struggle of the individualist as poet, prophet, aesthete, and "conquistador."

[34] Jane G. Harris, "Nikolai Gumilyov," in *Handbook to Russian Literature,* ed. Victor Terras (New Haven: Yale University Press, 1985), pp. 188–189. For further information about Gumilyov during these years, see Sampson, *Nikolay Gumilev.*

[35] Haight, p. 13.

[36] Personal communication with Amanda Haight. Akhmatova told Haight that Gumilyov had written this poem specifically about this episode.

[37] Haight, p. 13. For the original in Russian, see Nikolay Gumilyov, *Sobranie sochinenii,* ed. G.P. Struve and B.A. Filipoff, Vol. I (Washington, D.C.: Victor Kamkin, Inc., 1962), p. 5.

[38] Haight, p.14. Haight provides no evidence or other sources concerning the suicide attempts, and they are not mentioned in the other materials consulted on Gumilyov's life and works.

[39] Gleb Struve, "N.S. Gumilyov: Zhizni i lichnost," in Gumilyov, *Sobranie sochinenii,* I, p. xii. Sampson notes the conflicting testimony regarding the number and dates of Gumilyov's trips to Africa. See Sampson, p. 24.

[40] Yury Aikhenvald, *Poety i poetessy* (Moscow: Severnye dni, 1922), p. 42.

[41] Timenchik, "Khram premudrosti...," p. 309.

[42] Haight, p. 24.

[43] Akhmatova, "Korotko o sebe," p. 20.

[44] Anna Akhmatova, "Amedeo Modigliani," in Anna Akhmatova, *Sochineniya,* ed. G.P. Struve and B.A. Filipoff, Vol. II (Munich: Inter-Language Literary Associates, 1968), pp. 157–165. All works cited henceforth from the Struve-Filipoff editions will be noted as Struve-Filipoff, with appropriate volume and pagination.

[45] A.I. Tynyakov, cited in Timenchik and Lavrov, p. 61.

[46] Cited in Mandrykina, "Iz rukopisnogo...," p. 199.

[47] Ibid., p. 199.

[48] Cited by Gleb Struve, "N.S. Gumilyov: Zhizni i lichnost," p. xviii.

[49] Akhmatova, "Korotko o sebe," p. 20.

[50] Georgy Chulkov in Timenchik and Lavrov, p. 67.

[51] Mandrykina, "Iz rukopisnogo...," p. 199.

[52] Timenchik and Lavrov, p. 67.

[53] The Golden Age was that of Pushkin in the early 19th century. The Silver Age was marked not only by great writers but also musicians such as Alexander Scriabin, Rimsky-Korsakov, and Tchaikovsky, as well as artists like Mikhail Vrubel.

[54] Chukovskaya, I, p. 158.

[55] Marc Slonim, *From Chekhov to the Revolution* (New York: Oxford University Press, 1962), p. 83.

[56] Ibid., p. 187.

[57] Aleksander Blok, *Sobranie sochinenii,* ed. V.N. Orlov, A.A. Surkov and K.I. Chukovsky, III (Moscow-Leningrad: Khudozhestvennaya literatura, 1960), p. 331. Translated by Roberta Reeder. See also Sam Driver, "Akhmatova's *Poema bez geroja* and Blok's *Vozmezdie,* in *Aleksandr Blok Centennial Conference,* ed. W. Vickery and B. Sagatov (Columbus, Ohio, 1984), pp. 89–99.

[58] Slonim, p.187.

[59] Akhmatova, "Mandelstam," Struve-Filipoff, II, p. 167.

[60] Osip Mandelstam, *Complete Poetry of Osip Emilevich Mandelstam,* trans. Burton Raffel and Alla Burago (Albany: State University of New York Press, 1973), p. 67. For the original in Russian, see Osip Mandelstam, *Sobranie sochinenii,* ed. G.P. Struve and B.A. Filipoff, Vol. I (Washington, D.C.: Inter-Language Literary Associates, 1964), p. 119. The Struve-Filipoff edition dates the poem to 1910, although Mandelstam was not introduced to Akhmatova until 1911.

[61] Cited in Gabriel Superfin and Roman Timenchik, "A Propos de Deux Lettres de A.A. Ahmatova [sic] à V. Brjusov," *Cahiers du Monde russe et soviétique* XV, 1–2 (January–June 1974), p. 190. Superfin and Timenchik also note that Mikhail Kuzmin mentions in his diary that he saw Akhmatova in Pavlovsk in

June 1910 "reading her own poems in a shy voice to her husband's friends, who had not yet become her friends," p. 191. (First cited by E. A. Znosko-Borovsky, "O Bloke," *Zapiski nablyudatelya* I [Prague, 1924], p. 125.)

[62]Ibid., p. 190.

[63]Cited by Yury Annenkov, "Anna Akhmatova," in Yury Annenkov, *Dnevnik moikh vstrech. Tsikl tragedii,* Vol. I (Munich: Inter-Language Literary Associates, 1966), p. 116.

[64]Chukovsky, "Chukovsky. . ." p. 232.

[65]Slonim, p. 211.

[66]V. Zhirmunsky, "Preodolevshie simvolizm," in V.M. Zhirmunsky, *Voprosy teorii literatury* (The Hague: Mouton & Co., 1962), p. 284.

[67]Lidiya Ginzburg, *O lyrike* (Moscow-Leningrad: Sovetskii pisatel, 1964), p. 330. See also Vsevolod Setchkarev, *Studies in the Life and Work of Innokentij Annenskij* (The Hague: Mouton & Co., 1963) and Janet G. Tucker, *Innokentij Annenskij and the Acmeist Doctrine* (Columbus, Ohio: Slavica Publishers, Inc., 1986). For an English translation of Annensky's poems, see Innokenty Annensky, *The Cypress Chest,* trans. R.H. Morrison, bilingual edition, (Ann Arbor: Ardis, 1982).

[68]See Andrey Fyodorov, "Poeticheskoe tvorchestvo Innokentiya Annenskogo" in Innokenty Annensky, *Stikhotvoreniya i tragedii,* ed. A.V. Fyodorov, Biblioteka poeta, Bolshaya seriya, 2nd ed. (Leningrad: Sovetskii pisatel, 1959), pp. 46–55, for a discussion of Annensky's poetic style.

[69]Georgy Adamovich, "Vecher u Annenskago," *Chisla,* No. 4 (1930–31), pp. 214–216. There is some controversy about whether Akhmatova knew Annensky. In a conversation with Aliger in 1946, almost 40 years after Annensky died, Akhmatova said she did not know him personally, but recognized him and frequently saw him on the street (Aliger, p. 351). She said she regarded him highly and once declared that all poetry at the beginning of the 20th century came from Annensky, at least the poetry of Mandelstam, Pasternak, and herself (Aliger, p. 352). A.V. Lavrov and R.D. Timenchik suggest that Adamovich's memoir describing the evening at Annensky's with Akhmatova, in 1909, was "pure fiction" because Akhmatova was living in Kiev at the time. See A.V. Lavrov and R.D. Timenchik, "Innokenty Annensky v neizdannykh vospomina.uyakh," *Pamyatniki kultury. Novye otkrytiya. Ezhegodnik 1981.* (Leningrad: Nauka, 1983), p. 117. However, Haight notes that Akhmatova visited Tsarskoye Selo in 1908 (Haight, p. 14). She may, therefore, have paid another visit there in 1909.

When Annensky was told that the brother of his daughter-in-law Natasha Shtein, Sergey von Shtein, had married the older Gorenko (Iya, Akhmatova's sister), he replied: "I would have married the younger." This indicates he was, at least, aware of Akhmatova. Akhmatova treasured the compliment her entire life. See Anna Akhmatova, "Avtobiograficheskaya proza," *Literaturnoe oboz-*

renie, no. 5 (1989), p. 8. (Klara Suvorova has completed typing the text of Akhmatova's numerous autobiographical notes—more than 1,000 pages. This material is being prepared for publication in a special volume of *Literaturnoe nasledstvo.*)

[70] Mikhail Kuzmin, "O preskrasnoi yasnosti (otryvki)," *Russkaya literatura XX veka,* compiled by N.A. Trifonov. (Moscow: Gos. uchebno-pedagog. izd-vo, 1962), pp. 433–434.

[71] Mikhail Kuzmin, "Predislovie M.A. Kuzmina k pervoi knige stikhov Anny Akhmatovoi" in Struve-Filipoff, III, pp. 471–473.

[72] Mandrykina, "Nenapisannaya...," p. 74.

[73] Korney Chukovsky, *Lyudi i knigi,* Vol. V (Moscow: Khudozhestvennaya literatura, 1960), p. 754.

[74] Akhmatova, "Avtobiograficheskaya proza," p. 11.

[75] Amanda Haight, "Letters from Nikolay Gumilyov to Anna Akhmatova 1912–1915," *Slavonic & East European Review,* L, no. 118 (January 1972), p. 100.

[76] Akhmatova writes in her memoir "Budka" (Akhmatova, *Ya—golos vash...,* p. 337) that she was named for her maternal grandmother, Anna Motovilov. Her great-grandmother, Praskovya, came from a family of Simbirsk gentry, the Akhmatovs. According to family legend, the Akhmatovs descended from the last of the great Tatar khans who ruled Russia, Akhmat, who died in 1481. Akhmatova says this great-grandmother was also a Genghizid—a descendent of Genghis Khan. She notes that Khan Akhmat was killed by a paid assassin, and his death symbolized the end of the Mongol yoke in Russia. Akhmatova's mother's father descended from the Stogovs, landowners from the Moscow province who moved there when Novgorod came under seige by Ivan III in the 15th century. See Charles J. Halperin, *Russia and the Golden Horde* (Bloomington: Indiana University Press, 1987) for a discussion of the Mongol invasion and the episode concerning Akhmat.

[77] Chukovskaya, I, p. 81.

[78] Osip Mandelstam, "Storm and Stress" (1923), *The Complete Critical Prose and Letters,* ed. Jane Gary Harris, trans. Jane Gary Harris and Constance Link (Ann Arbor: Ardis, 1979), p. 177.

[79] Chulkov, p. 71.

[80] Kees Verheul, *The Theme of Time in the Poetry of Anna Axmatova* (The Hague: Mouton & Co., 1971), p. 6.

[81] See p. 29 of this introduction. The works of Bergson, who wrote profusely on this subject, were known to the Russian intelligentsia of the time, as Mandelstam's article "On the Nature of the Word" makes clear (See Mandelstam, *The Complete Critical Prose and Letters,* pp. 117–132. See Elaine Rusinko, "Acmeism, Post-symbolism and Henri Bergson," *Slavic Review,* Vol. 41, no. 3 (Fall 1982), pp. 494–510. There is an earlier precedent in Russian literature as well, *Sebastopol Sketches,* by Leo Tolstoy.

[82]Osip Mandelstam, "A Letter About Russian Poetry" (1922), *The Complete Critical Prose and Letters,* p. 157.

[83]*Down Along the Mother Volga,* p. 175.

[84]See Sam Driver, *Anna Akhmatova* (New York: Twayne Publishers, 1972), p. 100.

[85]*Down Along the Mother Volga,* p. 171.

[86]V.V. Vinogradov, *Anna Akhmatova* (Munich: Wilhelm Fink Verlag, 1970), p. 153. Reprint of *O poezii Anny Akhmatovoi* (Leningrad, 1925), and "O simvolike A.A. Akhmatovoi," *Literaturnaya mysl,* Vol. I (1922).

[87]T.V. Tsivyan, "Materialy k poetike Anny Akhmatovoi," *Trudy po znakovym sistemam,* Vol. III (Tartu: Tartu State University 1967), p. 195.

[88]Ibid., p. 205.

[89]Anthony Hartman, *The Versification of the Poetry of Anna Akhmatova,* Ph.D. Dissertation (University of Wisconsin, 1978), p. 24. In the dolniki, there can be one or two syllables between accents.

[90]Ibid., p. 29.

[91]Ibid., p. 39. For more information about Akhmatova's metrics, see also M.L. Gasparov, "Stikh Akhmatovoi: chetyre ego etapa," *Literaturnoe obozrenie,* no. 5 (1989), pp. 26–28.

[92]A.S. Pushkin, *Sobranie sochinenii,* ed. D.D. Blagoi, S.M. Bondi, V.V. Vinogradov, Yu.G. Oksman, Vol. I (Moscow: Khudozhestvennaya literatura, 1959), p. 108. Translated by Roberta Reeder.

[93]Ibid., Vol. II, p. 117. Translated by Roberta Reeder.

[94]The ring image appears in several of Akhmatova's poems. Haight writes in a personal communication that she found the following passage about Akhmatova in the unfinished memoirs of Akhmatova's friend, V. Sreznevskaya: "Already as a young girl she wrote about a secret ring (later black) which she had received as a gift from the moon" (from *Dafnis and Chloe,* written 12 April 1964 in Moscow and incomplete at the time of Sreznevskaya's death that year.) Haight copied the text from a manuscript in Akhmatova's possession, Moscow 1964, Leningrad 1965.

[95]Howard Goldman, "Anna Akhmatova's Hamlet: The Immortality of Personality and the Discontinuity of Time," *Slavic East European Journal,* Vol. 22, no. 4 (1980), p. 485.

[96]Critics have suggested the influence of Annensky's poem "The Bronze Poet" on this poem. However, except for the fact the poet is not named, and the poem refers to Pushkin and Tsarskoye Selo, there is little in common with Akhmatova's work. Annensky's poem refers to the bronze statue of Pushkin sitting on a bench, which had been recently erected in Tsarkoe Selo. The poet imagines the statue coming down from his pedestal.

[97]Pushkin's great-grandfather was Avram Hannibal, the godson of Peter

the Great. He was the son of royalty in an Ethiopian tribe in Abyssinia, brought to Constantinople as a hostage and bought by a Russian envoy, who then took him to Petersburg. He became a court favorite and was sent by the tsar to France to become an engineer. See Pushkin's short story, "The Moor of Peter the Great" for his fascinating tale about his ancestor.

[98]"Reminiscences in Tsarskoye Selo" (1814) in Pushkin, Vol. I, p. 8. Translated by Roberta Reeder. See also p. 662, where Pushkin's friend V.P. Gorchakov discusses what Tsarskoye Selo meant to the poet: "Pushkin seemed to really be transported to that society where his first poetic life blossomed with all its spectres and charms. At those moments Pushkin sometimes grieved; and in the midst of this grief, reason gave way to the impressions of his young heart." This citation, reprinted in this Pushkin volume, is from M.A. Tsyavlovsky, *Kniga vospominanii o Pushkine* (Moscow, 1931), p. 170. Roman Timenchik points to a Kuzmin poem on Pushkin that was written at approximately the same time as the one by Akhmatova, and published in 1912. It is not clear which was created first:

> *With what strange force*
> *Do words reign over us...*
> *But one word "three cornered hat"*
> *Reigns over me now,*
> *For over the course of thirty years*
> *And more: Pushkin, the lyceum,*
> *But I've had enough of fashion.*

Kuzmin, cited by R.D. Timenchik, "Akhmatova i Pushkin," *Pushkinskii sbornik,* Uchenye zapiski, Vol. 106 (Riga: Latvia University, 1968), p. 130.

II. St. Petersburg: 1912–1914

[1]Haight, *Anna Akhmatova,* p. 16. For the original in Russian, see Gumilyov, Vol. I, p. 166.

[2]Haight, "Letters from Nikolay Gumilyov...," p. 101. That same year, 1912, Gumilyov had an affair with Olga Vysotskaya, who was studying in St. Petersburg with the theater directors N.N. Evreinov and Vsevolod Meyerhold. She gave birth to their son in October 1913. In his memoirs of the last years of Akhmatova's life, Anatoly Naiman writes that when Akhmatova needed to confirm some fact from the 1910s, she called Olga Vysotskaya to come over. He describes how he and Boris Ardov once brought Vysotskaya by taxi to the Ardovs, where Akhmatova was staying. Akhmatova sat with her hair carefully combed, wearing lipstick and a pretty dress, surrounded by admirers, with her one-time rival—a weak, old woman, broken by fate. She confirmed the necessary fact, and Akhmatova ordered her to be taken home. (Anatoly Naiman, *Rasskazy o Anne Akhmatovoi* (Moscow: Khudozhestvennaya literatura, 1989), p. 221) Orest Vysotsky wrote in a recent letter that his mother died in January 1966 in Tiraspol. He was on the faculty at Kishinyov University and is now retired. (This information was provided by Prof. Elaine

Rusinko, through a personal communication.) In the Appendix to Jessie Davies' biography, *Anna of all the Russias* (Liverpool: Lincoln Davies & Co., 1988), pp. 134–135, there is a translation of an interview with Orest Vysotsky that appeared in *Soviet Weekly,* 14 May 1988, p. 5, in which he says he and his mother got to know Akhmatova and Lev Gumilyov in 1936 in Leningrad, where he was studying at the Frest Engineering Academy. Orest came to see Lev in March on the evening of his arrest. Orest was also arrested at this time for "counter-revolutionary terrorist activity," and released after a year and a half.

[3]Sreznevskaya, in Gumilyov, *Neizdannoe i nesobrannoe,* p. 164.

[4]Vera Luknitskaya, *Pered toboi zemlya* (Leningrad: Lenizdat, 1988), p. 291.

[5]R.D. Timenchik, "Zametki ob akmeizme: I," *Russian Literature,* 7/8 (1974), p. 28.

[6]Cited by Slonim, p. 211.

[7]Haight, *Anna Akhmatova,* p. 19.

[8]Timenchik, "Zametki ob akmeizme: I," p. 28.

[9]Georgy Adamovich, "Moi vstrechi s Annoi Akhmatovoi," *Vozdushnye puti* (1967), p. 104.

[10]Cited by A.I. Pavlovsky, "Anna Akhmatova," in Akhmatova, *Stikhotvoreniya i poemy,* ed. N.A. Zhirmunskaya. Biblioteka poeta, Malaya seriya, 3rd ed. (Leningrad: Sovetskii pisatel, 1984), p. 22.

[11]Cited by Wiktor Woroszylski, *The Life of Mayakovsky,* trans. Boleslaw Taborski (New York: The Orion Press, 1970), p. 179.

[12]Vladimir Mayakovsky, *The Bedbug and Selected Poetry,* ed. Patricia Blake, trans. Max Hayward and George Reavey (Bloomington: Indiana University Press, 1975), p. 83. The original in Russian is on p. 82.

[13]H.W. Tjalsma, "The Petersburg Poets," in *Russian Modernism,* ed. George Gibian and H.W. Tjalsma. (Ithaca: Cornell University Press), p. 76.

[14]Valentin Katayev, *The Grass of Oblivion,* trans. by Robert Daglish (New York: McGraw-Hill Book Co., 1969) p. 56.

[15]V.M. Zhirmunsky, *Tvorchestvo Anny Akhmatovoi,* (Leningrad: Nauka, 1973), p. 38. For further information on images of Akhmatova in art, see Yury Molok, "Vokrug rannikh portretov," *Literaturnoe obozrenie,* no. 5 (1989), pp. 81–85.

[16]Jeanne van der Eng-Liedmeier, "Reception as a Theme in Akhmatova's Early Poetry," in *Dutch Contributions to the Eighth International Congress of Slavists,* ed. Jan M. Meijer (Amsterdam: John Benjamins b.V., 1979), p. 211.

[17]Dora Kogan, *Sergey Yurevich Sudeikin* (Moscow: Iskusstvo, 1974), p. 80.

[18]Yu. Sazonovaya, "Novogodnee," *Poslednie novosti* (2 January 1938), no. 6216 cited by R.D. Timenchik, V.N. Toporov, T.V. Tsivyan, "Akhmatova i Kuzmin," *Russian Literature,* VI–3 (July 1978), p. 279.

[19]Timenchik, et al., "Akhmatova i Kuzmin," p. 227. The text originally appeared in *Petrogradskie vechera*, III (1914), p. 116.

[20]Woroszylski, p. 179.

[21]Cited in Woroszylski, p. 137.

[22]Kogan, p. 90.

[23]Tamara Karsavina is often overshadowed in the West by Anna Pavlova. Yet it was she who premiered the role of the Firebird in the ballet of that name, and the Doll in *Petroushka*, both by Igor Stravinsky. She was one of Nijinsky's greatest partners.

[24]Tamara Karsavina, *Theatre Street* (New York: E.P. Dutton & Co., Inc., 1931), p. 314. Kogan describes the evening Tamara Karsavina appeared. Her dance was choreographed by V.G. Romanov to music of Couperin performed on clavesin and viola da gamba. Sudeikin created costumes for her.

[25]Livshits, as cited in Woroszylski, p. 138. For the original in Russian, see B. Livshits, *Polutoroglazyi strelets*, (Leningrad: Izdatelstvo pisatelei, 1923), p. 261.

[26]Adamovich, "Moi vstrechi...," p. 101.

[27]Osip Mandelstam, *Complete Poetry*, p. 67. For the original in Russian, see Mandelstam, *Sobranie sochinenii*, Vol. I, p. 37.

[28]Cited by Woroszylski, p. 137.

[29]Akhmatova, "Mandelstam," p. 169.

[30]Adamovich, "Moi vstrechi...," p. 102.

[31]E. Dobin, *Poeziya Anny Akhmatovoi* (Leningrad: Sovetskii pisatel, 1968), p. 16.

[32]Andrey Bely, cited by Timenchik, et al., "Akhmatova i Kuzmin," footnote #84.

[33]Chukovsky, *Lyudi i knigi*, p. 746.

[34]Elaine Moch-Bickert. *Olga Glebova-Soudeikina* (Paris: Service de reproduction des thèses université de Lille, 1972), p. 31. She says Sudeikina's papers in the Imperial Theatre of St. Petersburg indicate she entered the school in 1902, and therefore was probably born 1886, since she could not have been younger than 16 when she entered.

[35]Kogan, p. 88.

[36]V. Krasovskaya, *Russkii baletnyi teatr nachala XX veka*, I (Leningrad: Iskusstvo, 1971), p. 502.

[37]Cited by Wendy Rosslyn, *The Prince, the Fool and the Nunnery: The Religious Theme in the Early Poetry of Anna Akhmatova* (Amersham, England: Avebury Publishing Co., 1984), p. 6. For the original in Russian, see A. Gizetti, "Tri dushi (Stikhi N. Lvovoi, A. Akhmatovoi, M. Moravskoi," *Ezhemesyachnyi zhurnal*, no. 12 (1915), pp. 147–166. Sam Driver and Vinogradov agree that the use of religious imagery is a treatment of the love

theme or part of her cultural background, but not an indication of profound religious belief. See Driver, p.12.

[38]Driver, p. 114.

[39]Korney Chukovsky, "Akhmatova i Mayakovsky," *Dom isskustv,* I, p. 26. Reprinted in *Voprosy literatury,* no. 1 (1988), pp. 177–205.

[40]Mandelstam, "On Contemporary Poetry," *The Complete Critical Prose,* p. 107. First published in Petrograd, 1916.

[41]Nadezhda Mandelstam, *Hope Abandoned,* trans. Max Hayward (New York: Atheneum, 1974), p. 227.

[42]Driver, p. 77. Akhmatova's view of Petersburg is similar to that of the World of Art Group. Major articles were written for their journal about Petersburg of the 18th century and during the time of Pushkin. They called this admiration for early Petersburg "Retrospectivism," which they considered part of the Russian revival movement that began in the last part of the 19th century. Muscovites in the group mainly turned to famous medieval cities, but the Petersburg group turned to the art and architecture of their own city as equally important in reverence for Russia's past and its traditions.

[43]Leonid Grossman, *Sobranie sochinenii,* IV (Moscow: Sovremennye problemy, 1928), p. 36.

[44]Pushkin's interpretation of Cleopatra was popular at the turn of the century. Mikhail Fokine created a ballet based on it for the Ballets Russes and Valery Bryusov completed the unfinished work by Pushkin.

[45]Written in 1830, *The Feast During the Time of the Plague* is based on a play by John Wilson. It is one of Pushkin's "Small Tragedies," a collection of short plays that includes *The Stone Guest* about Don Juan, and *Mozart and Salieri.* Great power is achieved in these works through their conciseness and concentration on a climactic moment in the life of the protagonists.

[46]D. Maksimov, "Akhmatova o Bloke," *Zvezda,* no. 12 (December 1967), p. 188. Excerpts are reprinted in G. Struve's notes to Akhmatova's "Vospominaniya ob A. Bloke," Struve-Filipoff, II, pp. 411–417.

[47]V.M. Zhirmunsky, "Anna Akhmatova i Aleksandr Blok," *Russkaya literatura,* no. 3 (1970), p. 59. See also Maksimov, p. 188.

[48]Blok, Vol. III, p. 143. Translated by Roberta Reeder.

[49]Anna Akhmatova, "Vospominaniya ob A. Bloke," Struve-Filipoff, II, 1968, p. 191.

[50]Zhirmunsky, "Anna Akhmatova i Aleksandr Blok," p. 60. Cited from Maksimov, p. 187. Zhirmunsky points out that the 1914 cycle of Carmen poems was devoted to Lyubov Delmas, a famous interpreter of the Carmen role, with whom Blok was in love at the time.

[51]Ibid., p. 60.

[52]In a personal communication, Haight noted that Akhmatova told her

the poem does not refer to Gumilyov: "One doesn't meet one's husband by the river but at home, at breakfast."

[53]Nikolai Gumilev, *Nikolai Gumilev on Russian Poetry*, ed. and trans. David Lapeza (Ann Arbor: Ardis, 1977), p. 142.

[54]Haight, *Anna Akhmatova*, p. 10.

[55]See Zhirmunsky's note in Akhmatova, *Stikhotvoreniya i poemy*, ed. V.M. Zhirmunsky, p. 510.

[56]Blok, Vol. III, p. 102. Translated by Roberta Reeder.

[57]Zhirmunsky, *Tvorchestvo*, p. 126.

[58]Annenkov, "Anna Akhmatova," p. 120.

III. The "True Twentieth Century" Begins: 1914–1917

[1]Charques, p. 211. For further information, see Riasanovsky, *A History of Russia*, and Florinsky, *The End of the Russian Empire*.

[2]Mandrykina, "Nenapisannaya...", p. 70.

[3]Mandrykina, "Iz rukopisnogo...," p. 199.

[4]Anna Akhmatova, "Vospominaniya ob Al. Bloke," p. 194.

[5]When Igor begins his doomed campaign against the Polovitsians, nature looks on with horror: "Now the birds in the oak-trees lie in wait for his misfortune; the wolves stir up a storm in the ravines; the eagles by their screeching call the beasts to bones; the foxes yelp at the scarlet shields." See "The Lay of Igor's Campaign," in *The Heritage of Russian Verse*, ed. Dmitri Obolensky, Rev. ed., (Bloomington: Indiana University Press, 1965), p. 4.

[6]See the chapter "The Mad and the Klikushi" in T. Popov, *Russkaya narodno-bytovaya meditsina* (St. Petersburg, 1903), pp. 363–395. The book is based on materials from the ethnographic bureau of Prince V.N. Tenishev and contains material sent in by correspondents all over the Russian empire.

[7]*The Heritage of Russian Verse*, p. 92. The original poem in Russian appears on the same page.

[8]Haight, *Anna Akhmatova*, p. 27. For the original in Russian, see Gumilyov, *Sobranie sochinenii*, Vol. I, p. 223.

[9]Gleb Struve, "Akhmatova i Nikolay Nedobrovo" in Struve-Filipoff, III, p. 381.

[10]N. Nedobrovo, "Anna Akhmatova," *Russkaya mysl*, kn. 17 (July 1915), pp. 50–68. A translation of this article appears in *Russian Literature Triquarterly* no. 9, Spring 1974, pp. 221–236.

[11]Struve, "Akhmatova i Nikolay Nedobrovo," p. 384 (27 April letter) & p. 385 (12 May letter).

[12]Boris Anrep, "O chyornem koltse," Struve-Filipoff, III, p. 440.

[13]Haight, personal communication. Haight says Akhmatova told Anatoly Naiman that when Nedobrovo saw Anrep with her early in 1916, he realized

that his friend had been able to evoke a response in her that he had never been able to win himself. Akhmatova said she felt guilty about this.

[14]G. Struve, "Akhmatova i Nikolay Nedobrovo," p. 386.

[15]Anrep, p. 440.

[16]Ibid., p. 441.

[17]Ibid., p. 442. Translated by Roberta Reeder.

[18]For two interesting articles on Anrep in England during World War I, see Wendy Rosslyn, "A propos of Anna Akhmatova: Boris Vasilyevich Anrep (1883–1969), *New Zealand Slavonic Journal,* no. 1 (1980), pp. 25–34, and "Boris Anrep and the Poems of Anna Akhmatova," in *The Modern Language Review,* Vol. 74, pt. 4 (October 1979), pp. 884–896. In the latter article, Rosslyn cites Akhmatova's poem "I, like a river. . ." (S-F. III, 79–80) from the *Northern Elegies* in which the poet points out other directions her life might have taken. Had she gone to England, she, like Anrep, might have become part of a circle that included the writer Aldous Huxley and the art critic Roger Fry.

IV. The Revolution: 1917–1922

[1]Adam Ulam, *Stalin: The Man and His Era* (Boston: Beacon Press, 1973), p. 130.

[2]Mandrykina, "Iz rukopisnogo. . .," p. 200.

[3]Anrep, p. 446. Anrep's story about the black ring was recently published in the Soviet Union in *Literaturnoe obozrenie,* no. 5 (1989), pp. 57–63. In a preface to Anrep's story, R.D. Timenchik notes that the memoir is incomplete, since Anrep fails to mention an episode that appears in Akhmatova's autobiographical sketches—a visit by them to the general rehearsal of Vsevolod Meyerhold's famous production of Lermontov's play *Masquerade,* which coincided with the February Revolution. It was a lavish production, which marked the end of the old regime. See also Boris Anrep, "O chyornem koltse," *Literaturnoe obozrenie,* no. 5 (1989), p. 57.

[4]Haight, *Anna Akhmatova,* p. 46. See Akhmatova, "Mandelstam," p. 174, for the original in Russian.

[5]Akhmatova, "Mandelstam," p. 174.

[6]Cited in Jeanne Rude, *Anna Akhmatova. Poètes d'aujourd'hui,* no. 179 (Paris: Editions seghers, 1968), p. 45. Original appeared in W. Weidlé, *Le messenger des Etudiants Chrétiens Russes* (Paris, 1966), no. 80.

[7]Boris Anrep, letter to Gleb Struve dated 23 October 1968, cited in Struve's commentary to Anrep's "O chyornem koltse," p. 461.

[8]See Elaine Rusinko, "*K sinej zvezde:* Gumilev's Love Poems," *Russian Language Journal,* XXXI, no. 109 (1977), pp. 155–167.

[9]Nikolay Gumilyov. *Neizdannye stikhi i pisma* (Paris: YMCA Press, 1980), p. 136.

[10]Chukovskaya, I, p. 161. Gumilyov married Anna Engelhart, the daugh-

ter of a professor of Oriental Studies, and they had a daughter in 1920. In January 1921 he was elected president of the Petersburg section of the All-Russian Union of Poets, and from the spring of 1921 he lived in the House of Artists. See Nikolai Otsup, "N.S. Gumilyov," in Nikolay Gumilyov, *Izbrannoe*, ed. Nikolai Otsup, (Paris: Librarie des cinq continents, 1959), p. 16.

[11] N. Mandelstam, p. 448.

[12] Naiman, p. 79.

[13] Tamara Shileiko, "Legendy, mify i stikhi," *Novy mir*, no. 4 (April 1986), p. 208.

[14] Luknitsky provides an extensive description and diagram of the apartment. See Luknitskaya, p. 294 and p. 315. For an English translation, see Davies, pp. 43–44.

[15] Chukovsky, "Chukovsky...," p. 234.

[16] The NEP-man became a favorite target of satire. See Mayakovsky's play "The Bedbug" and his *poema, About This.*

[17] Zhirmunsky, *Tvorchestvo*, footnote 68, p. 182.

[18] Moch-Bickert, p. 56.

[19] Chukovsky, "Chukovsky...," p. 234. Akhmatova's ballet libretto is based on Blok's collection of poems, "Snow Mask" (1908), dedicated to Natalya Volokhova, an actress with whom Blok was infatuated for some time. In her ballet scenario for *Poem Without a Hero*, Akhmatova depicts in the second vignette the actress looking through her window at a vision from "Snow Mask."

[20] Annenkov, p. 124.

[21] Vladislav Khodasevich, *Literaturnye stati i vospominaniya* (New York: Chekhov, 1954), p. 399.

[22] Adamovich, "Moi vstrechi...," p. 106.

[23] Chukovsky, "Chukovsky..." p. 234.

[24] Adamovich, "Moi vstrechi...," p. 105.

[25] Vilenkin, p. 60.

[26] Korney Chukovsky, "Excerpt from 'A.A. Blok: The Man,'" from *Alexander Blok: An Anthology of Essays and Memoirs*, ed. and trans. Lucy Vogel (Ann Arbor: Ardis, 1982), p. 75.

[27] Ibid., p. 78. For the original in Russian, see "Pushkinskomu domu," in Blok, Vol. III, 1960, pp. 376–377.

[28] Vladislav Khodasevich, *Nekropol* (Paris: YMCA Press, 1976), p. 123.

[29] For a detailed account of the so-called Tagantsev Affair, see Mikhail Heller and Aleksandr M. Nekrich, *Utopia in Power: The History of the Soviet Union from 1917 to the Present,* (New York: Summit Books, 1986), pp. 139–140.

[30] Khodasevich, as cited in G. Struve, "N.S. Gumilyov: Zhizni i lichnost," p. xxxvii.

[31]Sampson, p. 134. For Russian and English versions, see *The Heritage of Russian Verse,* p. 300.

[32]G.A. Terekhov, former assistant to the Procurator General of the U.S.S.R., conducted an inquiry into Gumilyov's case and wrote about it in the 12th issue of *Novy mir.* He says that Gumilyov's complicity in a counterrevolutionary plot had not been confirmed by any documented evidence. His only guilt was a failure to report to the authorities an offer to join a clandestine organization of officers. See Appendix to Jessie Davies, *Anna of all the Russias,* p. 134. See also G.A. Terekhov, "Voz vrashchayas k delu N.S. Gumilyova," *Novy mir,* no. 12 (December 1987), pp. 257–258.

[33]Nikolay Gumilyov, "Zvezdnyi uzhas," *Sobranie sochinenii,* Vol. II, p. 63.

[34]Chukovskaya, Vol. II, 1952–62 (Paris: YMCA Press, 1980), p. 432. (Subsequent citations will be noted "Chukovskaya, II," with page number.)

[35]Timenchik, "Khram premudrosti...," note #38, p. 306.

[36]Osip Mandelstam, "The Word and Culture," *The Complete Critical Prose and Letters,* p. 112.

[37]Mandelstam, "On the Nature of the Word," p. 131.

[38]In his notes to this poem, V.A. Chernykh says the notebook version of the work included a dedication to Anrep. See Anna Akhmatova, *Sochineniya,* ed. V.A. Chernykh, Vol. I (Moscow: Khudozhestvennaya literatura, 1986), p. 403.

[39]Timenchik, in "Khram premudrosti...," suggests the subtext of this poem is Nekrasov's work "Father Frost." See p. 307.

[40]Shileiko, p. 208. Translated by Roberta Reeder.

[41]Jeanne van der Eng-Liedmeier notes that the turn to a historical or Biblical figure by a Russian poet goes back to the Decembrist poets. They obliquely referred to forbidden political masters through quasi-historical descriptions of figures from the Bible or classical antiquity. See Anna Akhmatova, *Tale Without a Hero and Twenty-Two Poems by Anna Akhmatova,* trans. and ed. by Jeanne van der Eng-Liedmeier and Kees Verheul, Dutch Studies in Russian Literature 3 (The Hague: Mouton, 1973), p. 23.

[42]Kuzmin wrote: "As soon as the suspicion of stagnation appears, the artist must plunge into the very depths of his soul and call forth a new source—or keep silent." Kuzmin, *Uslovnost. Stati ob iskusstve.* (Petrograd, 1923), p. 166, cited by Zhirmunsky, *Tvorchestvo,* p. 39.

V. The Early Years of the Soviet State: 1922–1941

[1]Chukovsky, "Akhmatova i Mayakovsky." The article was first presented by Chukovsky as a lecture on 20 September 1921 at the House of Arts in Petrograd.

[2]Ibid., p. 25.

[3]Ibid., p. 42.

[4]M. Shaginyan as cited by Annenkov, p. 120.

[5]Alexandra Kollontay, "O 'drakone' i 'beloi ptitse,'" *Molodaya gvardiya*, no. 2 (9), (Moscow, 1923), pp. 164–174. Cited in Zhirmunsky, *Tvorchestvo*, p. 41.

[6]Nikolay Osinsky (Obolensky), *Pravda*, no. 145 (4 July 1922). Cited in Zhirmunsky, *Tvorchestvo*, p. 41.

[7]V. Arvatov, "Grazhdanka Akhmatova i tovarishch Kollontay," *Molodaya gvardiya*, IV–V (Moscow, 1923), pp. 147–151. Cited in Zhirmunsky, *Tvorchestvo*, p. 40.

[8]P. Vinogradskaya, "Vorposy morali, pola, byta i t. Kollontay," *Krasnaya nov*, 1 VI (Moscow, 1923), pp. 204–14. Cited in Zhirmunsky, *Tvorchestvo*, p. 40.

[9]G. Lelevich, "Anna Akhmatova," *Na postu*, no. 2–3 (Moscow, Sept.–Oct. 1923), p. 202, in *Na postu*, Vols. 1–6, 1923–25 (Munich: Wilhelm Fink, 1971). Lelevich is the pseudonym of Labor Kalmanson (1910–1937). He was arrested at the end of 1934 and later shot.

[10]Vladimir Mayakovsky, "Vystuplenie na pervom vechere 'Chistka sovremennoi poezii,'" in Vladimir Mayakovsky, *Polnoe sobranie sochinenii*, ed. L. Yu. Brik, XII (Moscow: Khudozhestvennaya literatura, 1959), p. 460.

[11]Leon Trotsky, *Literature and Revolution*, trans. Rose Strunsky (Ann Arbor: University of Michigan Press, 1971), p. 41.

[12]Haight, *Anna Akhmatova*, p. 80.

[13]Chukovskaya, II, p. 46.

[14]Chukovsky, "Chukovsky..." p. 235.

[15]The date of Lourié's departure is disputed. Vilenkin says he left in 1922 (p. 321). The year is listed as 1924 in Giovanni Camajani's article, "Arthur Vincent Lourié," in *The New Grove Dictionary of Music and Musicians*, ed. Stanley Sadie, Vol. 11 (London: Macmillan Publishers, Ltd., 1980), p. 257. In her biography of Sudeikina, Moch-Bickert says Sudeikina left in 1924 (p. 58).

[16]Haight, in a personal communication, writes that she copied a letter written by Artur Lourié to Salomea Halpern on 21 January 1962, concerning Akhmatova's refusal to leave Russia. In the letter, Lourié says he tried to persuade Akhmatova to come to Paris, but she refused. Sudeikina came to Paris right after him. "We were living then, the three of us, on the Fontanka, and the *Poema* talks of this in a coded way. Anna is now 73. I remember her at 23."

[17]Mandrykina, "Nenapisannaya...," p. 67.

[18]Haight, *Anna Akhmatova*, p. 57.

[19]Shileiko, p. 210.

[20]Punin's reputation has now been restored in the Soviet Union. In their efforts to reflect a new enthusiasm for Russian avant-garde art, the Soviets arranged an exhibit in 1988 of art from the 1920s–1930s at the New Tretyakov Gallery in Moscow. On 24 June 1988 a "Punin Evening" in Leningrad was dedicated to his memory, emphasizing the aesthetic discoveries of this period

and his important contributions to them. The evening was sponsored by *Leningradnoe otdelenie sovetskogo funda kultury* (Leningrad section of the Soviet Cultural Fund), which also sponsored an evening devoted to Akhmatova in February, to Mikhail Zoshchenko in April, and to Osip Mandelstam in May of that same year.

[21] Artur Lourié, "Nash marsh," *Novy zhurnal,* no. 4, kn. 94 (1969), p. 140.

[22] Haight, *Anna Akhmatova,* p. 81.

[23] Luknitskaya, p. 324.

[24] Ibid., p. 323.

[25] Ibid., p. 380.

[26] Woroszylski, p. 526.

[27] N. Mandelstam, p. 247.

[28] N. Mandelstam, *Hope Against Hope,* trans. Max Hayward (New York: Atheneum, 1970), p. 173–174.

[29] Akhmatova, "Mandelstam," p. 177–178.

[30] Ibid., p. 180.

[31] Ulam, p. 393.

[32] N. Mandelstam, *Hope Against Hope,* p. 96.

[33] Timenchik and Lavrov, p. 62. See p. 64 for a copy of the actual hand-written charter. The Charter of the Apes was given to all members of the satirical society organized by Aleksey Remizov, a writer who was immersed in medieval Russian antiquity and folklore. The charter was given to Akhmatova as "a sign of raising her to the level of cavaliers of the sign of the apes of the first degree with a squirrel's paw." It was dated 5 August 1921, two days before Remizov's departure from Russia. In Gorky's memoirs he mentions this odd society: "His weird sense of humor and historical attempt to bring some laughter into what he saw as an essentially unjust and cruel world is reflected in the secret society he founded in 1908, the Grand and Free Palace of the Apes. Remizov was the clerk of the federation and issued charters signed by the tail of King Assyka I. These charters were based on medieval models done in ornate calligraphy." See Aleksey Remizov, "Gorky: A Memoir," trans. Roberta Reeder, *Yale/Theatre* (1976), p. 99.

[34] Haight, *Anna Akhmatova,* p. 90.

[35] Mandelstam, *Complete Poetry,* p. 195. For the original in Russian, see Mandelstam, *Sobranie sochinenii,* Vol. I, p. 167.

[36] N. Mandelstam, *Hope Abandoned,* p. 11.

[37] Akhmatova, "Mandelstam," p. 179.

[38] N. Mandelstam, *Hope Against Hope,* p. 217.

[39] Ibid., p. 144.

[40] Dmitry Bobyshev, in a personal communication.

[41] Ronald Hingley, *Nightingale Fever: Russian Poets in Revolution* (New York: Alfred A. Knopf, 1981), p. 220.

[42] Dmitry Khrenkov, "Ob Anne Akhmatove," in Anna Akhmatova, *Stikhi i proza* (Leningrad: Lenizdat, 1976), p. 6.

[43] Yu. I. Budyko, "Istoriya odnogo posvyashcheniya," *Russkaya literatura,* no. 1 (1984), p. 236. Budyko suggests that the association with Garshin and his coin collecting may have prompted Akhmatova to call one of the sections of *Poem Without a Hero,* "The Other Side of the Coin."

[44] Chukovskaya, I, p. 162.

[45] Ibid., p. 13.

[46] Ibid., p. 10. "This became like a ritual: [Akhmatova's] hands pointing to ceiling and walls; matches; ashtray." As early as the late 1930s, Akhmatova feared her room might be bugged.

[47] Chukovskaya, II, p. xii, notes that from 1942 to 1952 she and Akhmatova did not speak to one another. For some reason, in Tashkent, Akhmatova became irritated with Chukovskaya every time she came to see her, so Chukovskaya thought it best to avoid her. Chukovskaya left Tashkent in the autumn of 1943 for Moscow and continued to follow news of Akhmatova. In the summer of 1952 she heard Akhmatova was visiting friends in Moscow and sent a letter asking Akhmatova if she were angry. Akhmatova telegraphed her to please call and come over. From that time on they continued to be devoted friends.

[48] In Russia at this time people heated with enamel ovens. This does not refer to a kitchen stove.

[49] Chukovskaya, II, p. 14.

[50] Chukovsky, "Chukovsky...," p. 233.

[51] Haight, *Anna Akhmatova,* p. 110.

[52] For an excellent book on Tsvetaeva, see Simon Karlinsky, *Marina Tsvetaeva* (Cambridge: Cambridge University Press, 1986).

[53] Adamovich, "Moi vstrechi...," p. 110.

[54] Haight, *Anna Akhmatova,* p. 109.

[55] Joseph Brodsky, "The Keening Muse," in Joseph Brodsky, *Less Than One* (New York: Farrar, Straus & Giroux, 1986), p. 51.

[56] Jovanovich, p. 171.

[57] Ibid., p. 177. Based on private conversation with Kiril Taranovsky. In the children's lullaby, however, the "don, don, don" refers to the sound of bells and not the name of the river, the Don.

[58] See Guy de Mallac, *Boris Pasternak: His Life and Art* (Norman, Okla.: University of Oklahoma Press, 1981), p. 168.

[59] Haight, *Anna Akhmatova,* p. 111.

[60]Centrifuge was a group based in Moscow from 1913–1917, which included Boris Pasternak, Sergey Bobrov, and Nikolay Aseyev. Although its members considered themselves associated with Futurism, they were much less radical than the Futurists such as Mayakovsky and Khlebnikov.

[61]Chukovskaya, II, p. 146.

[62]Haight, *Anna Akhmatova,* p. 116.

[63]K.M. Azadovsky points out that the poet Nikolay Klyuev once called Akhmatova "Kitezhanka." Klyuev had frequently turned to the theme of Kitezh, which seemed to him to embody the most cherished ideas about ancient, mysterious, "submerged" Russia, and which he believed would rise again in all its blinding beauty. By calling Akhmatova a "Kitezhanka," he suggested their common fate and spiritual kinship. See K.M. Azadovsky, "Menya nazval 'kitezhankoi': Anna Akhmatov i Nikolay Klyuev," Literaturnoe obozrenie, no. 5 (1989), p. 69.

VI. The War: 1941–1945

[1]For more information on the winter campaign against Finland, see Georg von Rauch, *A History of Soviet Russia,* ed. and trans. by Peter and Annette Jacobsohn, 6th ed. (New York: Praeger Publishers, 1972), pp. 289–292.

[2]Ibid., p. 310.

[3]A.I. Pavlovsky, "Eto pleshchet Neva o stupeni. . .: K devyanostoletiyu Anny Akhmatovoi," *Neva,* no. 6 (1979), p. 196.

[4]Haight, *Anna Akhmatova,* p. 122.

[5]N.G. Chulkova, cited in Timenchik and Lavrov, p. 70.

[6]Aliger, p. 341.

[7]Tsvetaeva had been in Chistopol while on a visit to the poet Nikolay Aseyev.

[8]Chukovskaya, I, p. 201.

[9]Pushkin was exiled to the south of Russia in May 1820 until September 1824. It was a very creative period in his life. He wrote beautiful poems reflecting the exotic nature in the area and the cosmopolitan atmosphere, where Greeks, Serbs and Gypsies lived among the Ukrainian and Russian population. These Byronic poems depict the hero who turns against his own corrupt civilization and attempts to find happiness among native tribes he considers more noble. In spite of the attraction of the area, Pushkin longed to be back in Petersburg with his friends. His letters from this period are filled with passages begging his friends to intercede with the authorities so he may return north.

[10]Akhmatova, "Korotko o sebe," p. 21.

[11]Chukovskaya, I, p. 201.

[12]Haight, *Anna Akhmatova,* p. 124.

[13] Anna Akhmatova, *Izbrannoe*, ed. V. V. Bannikov (Moscow: Khudozhestvennaya literatura, 1974), p. 547.

[14] Joseph Czapski, *The Inhuman Land*, trans. Gerard Hopkins (London: Chatto & Windus, 1951), p. 191.

[15] Ibid., p. 191.

[16] Haight, *Anna Akhmatova*, p. 127.

[17] Budyko, p. 236. Aliger writes that Garshin's wife died in the winter of 1941 (p. 349).

[18] Aliger, p. 349.

[19] N. Mandelstam, *Hope Abandoned*, p. 449.

[20] Budyko, p. 237.

[21] Akhmatova, "Pisma," Struve-Filipoff, III, p. 347.

[22] Ibid., p. 349.

[23] Haight, *Anna Akhmatova*, p. 128–129. For Russian text, see Struve-Filipoff, III, pp. 466–468.

[24] N. Mandelstam, *Hope Abandoned*, p. 350.

[25] Zhirmunsky in Anna Akhmatova, *Stikhotvoreniya i poemy*, p. 509. Zhirmunsky notes that Akhmatova translates the title as "There Above," though the correct translation is "When Above." For a more complete synopsis, see the footnote to the poem in VOLUME II of this edition.

[26] Vilenkin says that Akhmatova knew Kafka's "The Trial" well, and once spent a whole hour telling it in her own words to the company who had been invited for the evening (p. 71).

[27] Emma Gershtein, "Nina Antonovna: Besedy ob Akhmatovoi s N. A. Olshevskoi-Ardovoi," *Literaturnoe obozrenie*, no. 5 (1989), p. 91.

[28] Aliger, p. 348.

[29] Haight, *Anna Akhmatova*, p. 136. Haight cites no evidence for this information, and it does not appear in other sources on Garshin.

[30] Budyko, p. 237–238.

[31] Gershtein, p. 91.

[32] Budyko, p. 238.

[33] Akhmatova, "Korotko o sebe," p. 21. Mikhail Zoshchenko (1895–1958) was one of Russia's leading satirists in the Soviet period. He and Akhmatova were selected as victims in the Zhdanov purge in 1946 and he was expelled along with her from the Union of Soviet Writers. He was gradually rehabilitated after Stalin's death.

[34] Pushkin, Vol. II, p. 8. Translated by Roberta Reeder. See also Pushkin, "Vospominaniya v Tsarskom Sele" (1814) and "Vospominaniya v Tsarskom Sele" (1829).

[35] Luknitskaya, p. 334.

[36]While written in 1940 and included in the original manuscript, Zh. 323, 324 and 325 were neither published in *From Six Books* in 1940, nor in *The Flight of Time* in 1965. An incomplete version of "From the Cycle 'Youth'" (Zh. 323) was published in 1945, and the complete version in 1966. The others, #324 ("The Cellar of Memory") and 325 ("Thus dark souls take flight...") were published for the first time posthumously in 1966. Zhirmunsky included them in the section "Reed" because they were part of the original manuscript.

[37]Ovid, the great Roman poet, was banished in 8 A.D. to the shores of the Black Sea, and eventually died there. It was the same general area where Pushkin spent his exile. See Pushkin's long poem, "K Ovidiyu," identifying with him as an exiled poet, in Pushkin, Vol. I, p. 165.

[38]Sonia Ketchian, "The Genre of Podrazhanie and Anna Achmatova," *Russian Literature,* XV (1984), p. 163.

[39]Pushkin did not fool the censors, and was exiled for his poems on tyrannicide.

VII. The Post-War Years

[1]Gershtein, p. 94. Fountain House was the former Sheremetev Palace, and now is the home of the Arctic Institute.

[2]Alexander Werth, "Akhmatova: The Tragic Queen Anna," *The Nation* (August 22, 1966), p. 158. See also Vilenkin, p. 20, for a description of this event.

[3]Haight, in a personal communication, notes that the resolutions against Akhmatova were published in numerous Soviet papers and journals. *Zvezda* was accused of popularizing Akhmatova's works and forced to change its editorial policy. *Leningrad* was suppressed. There was an unpleasant article on Akhmatova by I. Sergievsky ("About the Anti-National Poetry of Anna Akhmatova"), followed by another equally vile one by A. Volkov on the Acmeists ("Standard-bearers and Senselessness"), both in *Zvezda.* V. Sidelnikov accused Akhmatova of being a traitor because she suggested Pushkin had taken the story of "The Golden Cockerel" from a foreign source ("Against Perversion and Obsequiousness in Soviet Folkloristics," *Literaturnaya gazeta,* no. 26 [2431] [Moscow, 29 June 1947], p. 3.)

[4]Haight, *Anna Akhmatova,* p. 145.

[5]Chukovskaya, II, p. 25. An article in *Literaturnaya Rossiya,* no. 44 (1988), entitled "The Serpent's Head Bruised at Last," states that on 20 October 1988, the Politburo of the Central Committee of the Communist Party of the Soviet Union annulled the 14 August 1946 decree of the Central Committee of the All-Union Communist Party "Concerning the Journals *Zvezda* and *Leningrad,*" which accused Akhmatova and Zoshchenko. They called it an error that distorted Lenin's policies regarding the relationship between the state and the artistic intellentsia. "The works of Anna Akhmatova and Mikhail Zoshchenko have taken their rightful place in the enrichment of the world of

the spirit, and the shaping of man's civic position. Their personality and books are restored to us in their true greatness and significance." See the Appendix in Davies, p. 135.

[6]Mallac, p. 184.

[7]Chukovskaya, II, p. 374.

[8]Chukovskaya, II, p. vii.

[9]Akhmatova, "Avtobiograficheskaya proza," p. 14.

[10]Emma Gershtein, "Memuary i fakty" in Anna Akhmatova, *Stikhi, perepiska, vospominaniya, ikonografiya,* p. 103. Haight, in a personal communication, says Misha Ardov, the Ardovs' son, told her he took the poems to Aleksey Surkov, editor of the journal *Ogonyok* (1945–53). In 1953, Surkov took over as First Secretary of the Union of Soviet Writers, replacing Fadeev.

[11]Akhmatova, "Avtobiograficheskaya proza," p. 14.

[12]Akhmatova vigorously denounced these poems later on, and requested they not be included in her collected works.

[13]Haight, *Anna Akhmatova,* p. 175.

[14]Chukovsky, "Chukovsky...," p. 237.

[15]Note by Max Hayward in N. Mandelstam, *Hope Abandoned,* p. 357.

[16]Ilina, p. 109.

[17]Ibid., p. 122.

[18]Ibid., p. 129. Zhenia Chukovsky was the nephew of Lidiya Chukovskaya. His wife, Galina Shostakovich, was the daughter of the composer, Dmitry Shostakovich.

[19]Ibid., p. 129.

[20]Bobyshev, "Akhmatovskie siroty," *Russkaya mysl,* no. 3507 (8 March 1984), p. 8–9.

[21]"Nebyvshaya" does not have a direct translation in English. It means "non-existence" or "not having been."

[22]Ibid., p. 9. Translated by Roberta Reeder. Osya was the nickname for Joseph, Tolya for Anatoly, Zhenya for Evgeny and Dima for Dmitry. "Sworn brother" refers to a Slavic custom of good friends making a pact to be a "pobratim" or "brother for life." All eight octaves have been published in *Literaturnoe obozrenie,* no. 5 (1989), p. 111, as have poems about Akhmatova by Joseph Brodsky, Anatoly Naiman, and Evgeny Rein.

[23]See Jerzy Faryno, "Tainy remesla Akhmatovoi," *Wiener Slawistischer Almanach,* V (1980), p. 40.

[24]Chukovsky, "Chukovsky...," p. 231. An example of such a poem is provided by N.A. Bogomolova in her article "Takim ya vizhu oblik vashi vzglyad," in *Literaturnoe obozrenie,* no. 5 (1989), p. 37. The poem is by Natalya Poplavskaya:

Today we had a terrible quarrel.
Is it possible he won't come?
I ran down the stairs from the tower,
I ran after him to the gate.
I said: "My friend, it was a joke,
I love you eternally and I'll wait."
He answered directly and terribly:
"I won't come see you today."

[25]Haight writes in a personal communication that they met again in Paris in 1965.

[26]Two different manuscript versions exist of "Like the fifth act of a drama" (Zh. 406), one dated 1921 and the other 1926.

[27]Chukovskaya, II, p. 212.

[28]Ibid., p. 391.

[29]Akhmatova, "Iz pisma k N." in Struve-Filippov, II, p. 97.

[30]Mandrykina, "Nenapisannaya...," p. 62.

[31]N. Mandelstam, *Hope Abandoned,* p. 429.

[32]T.S. Eliot, "Tradition and the Individual Talent," in T.S. Eliot, *Selected Essays* (New York: Harcourt, Brace and Co., 1950), p. 4. Akhmatova's own thoughts on borrowing from the literary tradition appear in Luknitsky's diary entry from 7 June 1927 (see Luknitskaya, p. 346):

> A genius is a usurper. He collects, snatches words, similes, images from everywhere—the simplest and even those often not noticed by anyone, but—the best. He takes them, and until he does, they are not worth anything. They are in free circulation everywhere. Anyone can utter them. But when the genius takes them, he pronounces them in such a way that they become unrepeatable. He puts his own stamp on them. They become his property, and no one can repeat them; and if someone wished to repeat them, he couldn't—it is forbidden. For the stamp of genius is on them.

[33]Zhirmunsky, "Anna Akhmatova i Aleksandr Blok," p. 77.

[34]A collection of Knyazev's poetry was published posthumously in St. Petersburg in 1914. In a personal communication, Haight says Akhmatova showed her a photograph of Knyazev she had kept through the years.

[35]See note #45 of Section II (St. Petersburg: 1912–1914) of this Introduction, and the text to which it refers.

[36]See Eng-Liedmeier, "Poem Without A Hero," p. 112.

[37]L.L. Saulenko, "Pushkinskaya traditsiya v *Poeme bez geroya,* Anny Akhmatovoi," *Voprosy russkoi literatury,* vyp. 2 (36), Lvov (1980), p. 46. See also R.D. Timenchik, "Rizhskii epizod v *Poeme bez geroya* Anny Akhmatovoi," *Daugava* 2 (80), (February 1984), p. 121.

[38]Vilenkin, p. 43.

[39]Timenchik, "Rizhskii epizod...," p. 121.

[40]See "Poema bez geroya," in Struve-Filipoff, II, pp. 603–605. This article includes a summary of a talk by R.D. Timenchik published in a limited edition. The original piece is R.D. Timenchik, "K analizu *Poemy bez geroya*," *Materialy XXII nauchnoi studencheskoi konferentsii* (Tartu: Tartusskii Gosudarstvennyi Universitet, 1967), pp. 121–123.

[41]See John Malmstad and Gennady Shmakov's excellent exegesis of this difficult poem in "Kuzmin's 'The Trout Breaking Through the Ice,'" in *Russian Modernism*, ed. George Gibian and H.W. Tjalsma (Ithaca: Cornell University Press, 1976), pp. 132–165.

[42]N. Mandelstam, *Hope Abandoned*, p. 152.

[43]Chukovskaya, I, p. 149.

[44]M. Kuzmin, "Pismo v Pekin," *Uslovnosti* (Petrograd, 1923). Cited by Timenchik, et al., "Akhmatova i Kuzmin," p. 217.

[45]M. Kuzmin, *Selected Prose and Poetry*, ed. and trans. Michael Green (Ann Arbor: Ardis, 1972), p. 339.

[46]J. Guenther, cited by Timenchik, et al., "Akhmatova i Kuzmin," footnote #97.

[47]Ibid., p. 232. Akhmatova remembered that after Blok's burial in 1921, she and Sudeikina looked for Knyazev's grave by the wall in the cemetery, but could not find it.

[48]John E. Malmstad, "Mixail Kuzmin: A Chronicle of His Life and Times" in M.A. Kuzmin, *Sobranie stikhov*, ed. John E. Malmstad and Vladimir Markov, Vol. III (Munich: Wilhelm Fink, 1977), p. 185.

[49]Chukovsky, *Lyudi i knigi*, p. 746. L. Titov, in discussing the period when *Evening* was published, writes: "Figures arise, and are wiped out... 31 July 1911 in Paris, Victor Hoffman, with whom Akhmatova had recently become acquainted, shot himself. In April 1911 Kuzmin came to Tsarskoye Selo with Vsevolod Knyazev. At that time Gumilyov said that Knyazev was the handsomest man he had ever seen, and this was exactly two years before the 5th of April 1913. *Rech*, Sunday 7 (20 new style) April 1913, in the section "Obituaries," on the seventh page: "Knyazev, Vsevolod Gavrilovich." (See L. Titov, "K shestidesyatiletiyu knigi Vecher," *Pamyati Anny Akhmatovoi* (Paris: YMCA Press, 1974), pp. 213–218.

[50]N. Mandelstam, *Hope Abandoned*, p. 435. See pp. 433–443 for her discussion of *Poem Without a Hero*.

[51]Preface to *Retribution* by Blok, Vol. III, p. 297. The full preface and *poema* appear on pp. 295–344.

[52]Zhirmunsky, "Anna Akhmatova i Aleksandr Blok," p. 72. See note #19 of Section IV (The Revolution: 1917–1922) of this Introduction.

[53]Vilenkin notes that when he visited Akhmatova in the winter of 1946 she had many books in several languages from the library on Mozart, his life and work. Akhmatova told him they were related to her Pushkin studies. For

a long time she had been interested in Mozart as a personality, she said, and had thought about his fate, his creation of the *Requiem,* the mystery surrounding his death, and the place of his burial (pp. 25–26).

[54]See V.N. Toporov, "K otzvukam zapadnoevropeiskoi poezii u Akhmatovoi (T.S. Eliot)," *International Journal of Slavic Linguistics and Poetics,* XVI (1973), pp. 157–176.

[55]Chukovsky, "Chukovsky...," p. 237.

[56]Haight, *Anna Akhmatova,* p. 154.

VIII. Last Years

[1]N. Mandelstam, *Hope Abandoned,* p. 115. Mandelstam notes that Lev Gumilyov, among others, helped Akhmatova a great deal with the translations.

[2]Akhmatova, "Korotko o sebe," p. 22.

[3]S. Lipkin, "Vostochnye stroki Anny Akhmatovoi," *Klassicheskaya poeziya vostoka* (Moscow: Khudozhestvennaya literatura, 1969), p. 13.

[4]V. Baluashvili, "U Anny Akhmatovoi," Struve-Filipoff, II, p. 298.

[5]Arseny Tarkovsky, "Predislovie" in *Golosa poetov: stikhi zarubezhnykh poetov v perevode Anny Akhmatovoi,* trans. Anna Akhmatova (Moscow: Progress Publishers, 1965), p. 5. In spite of Tarkovsky's assertions, it is still uncertain how much choice Akhmatova actually had regarding which poets she translated.

[6]Anna Akhmatova, "Neizdannye zametki Anny Akhmatovoi o Pushkine," *Voprosy literatury,* no. 1 (January 1970), p. 160.

[7]Ibid., p. 191. She also uses the phrase "triple bottom" in this article, in reference to Pushkin's *Tales of Belkin.* It begins with a fictional persona, Belkin, who finds a manuscript. Each story in the manuscript is told by a different person, and takes on the coloring of that narrator's personality. Akhmatova uses the phrase "triple bottom" in relation to *Poem Without a Hero.*

[8]Evgeny Osetrov, "Gryadushchee, sozrevshee v proshedshem," *Voprosy literatury,* 4 (April 1965), p. 184.

[9]F.D. Reeve. *Robert Frost in Russia* (Boston: Little, Brown and Company, 1963), pp. 80–85.

[10]The term "Potemkin Village" derives from the period when Catherine the Great went to visit the Crimea to see the conquests of her lover Potemkin. In order to impress her from afar, whole villages were painted on flats, which she saw from a distance. It has come to mean a false facade.

[11]Raisa Orlova and Lev Kopelev, "Anna vseya Rus," *Literaturnoe obozrenie,* no. 5 (1989), p. 103. (This is a chapter from their book *My zhili v Moskve 1956–1980* [Ann Arbor: Ardis, 1988]).

[12]Rude, p. 7.

[13] Akhmatova, "Pismo k Dzhankarlo Vigorelli," Struve-Filipoff, II, p. 307.

[14] Hans Werner Richter, *Euterpe von den Ujern der Neva oder die Ehrung Anna Achmatowas in Taormina* (Berlin: Friedenauer Presse, 1965), p. 8.

[15] Ibid., p. 9.

[16] Elaine Bickert, *Anna Akhmatova: Silence à plusieurs voix* (Paris: Editions Resma, 1970), p. 107.

[17] Ibid., p. 107.

[18] Adamovich, "Moi vstrechi...," p. 107.

[19] Ibid., p. 107.

[20] Anrep, pp. 451–453.

[21] Nikita Struve, "Vosem chasov s Annoi Akhmatovoi," Struve-Filipoff, II, p. 346.

[22] *Proshchaite* is a more definitive farewell than *do svidaniya,"* which means "see you again."

[23] Adamovich, "Moi vstrechi...," p. 114.

[24] Ironically, Akhmatova died on the anniversary of Stalin's death.

[25] Timenchik and Lavrov, p. 81.

[26] Struve, "Vosem chasov...," p. 346.

A bibliography to this essay, and a Select Bibliography, will be found at the end of VOLUME II.

Chronology

1889—23 June: Anna Andreevna Gorenko is born in the Ukraine on the Black Sea at Bolshoi Fontan, near Odessa, the third of five children.

1890—July: the Gorenko family moves to Pavlovsk, then Tsarskoye Selo, near Petersburg, returning every summer to the Black Sea.

1894—Anna's sister, Irina, dies of tuberculosis, at the age of four.

1903—Anna meets Nikolay Gumilyov, a young poet; he begins his desperate courtship of her.

1905—January: The Japanese destroy the entire Russian fleet in the straits of Tsushima. Revolution of 1905.
Summer: the Gorenko marriage breaks. Andrey Gorenko, a naval engineer, moves to Petersburg; Inna Gorenko, Akhmatova's mother, takes the children to Evpatoriya on the Black Sea.
Winter: Anna Gorenko starts to write poetry, adopting the name of a maternal ancestor, Akhmatova.

1906—Autumn: Akhmatova enrolls at the Fundukleevskaya Gimnaziya in Kiev to complete her last year of schooling.
Winter: Gumilyov publishes one of her poems in *Sirius,* a small literary magazine he founded in Paris.

1907—Autumn: Akhmatova rejects Gumilyov's offer of marriage. She enrolls in the Faculty of Law at the Kiev College for Women.

1909—November: Akhmatova agrees to marry Gumilyov.

1910—Gumilyov shows Akhmatova the manuscript, "The Cypress Box," by Innokenty Annensky, a classicist and director of studies at the Tsarskoye Selo lycée. Akhmatova is deeply moved and impressed.
25 April: Akhmatova and Gumilyov are married near Kiev. No one from her family is present. The couple honeymoons in Paris.
June: The Gumilyovs settle in Tsarskoye Selo.
September: Gumilyov travels to Abyssinia on a scientific expedition.

1911—March: Gumilyov returns. They visit Paris again, where Akhmatova makes the acquaintance of Modigliani.
Summer: spent at Slepnyovo, Gumilyov's mother's country estate in the district of Tver, near the town of Bezhetsk.
Autumn: Back in Tsarskoye Selo, the Gumilyovs enjoy the literary life. Gumilyov, with other young poets, forms a Poets' Guild, whose members, originally 15, decide to break with Symbolism. In a short time, six of them—Gumilyov, Akhmatova, Mandelstam, Gorodetsky, Narbut, and

Zenkevich—decide to call themselves Acmeists, a term proposed by Gumilyov.

1912—Spring: publication of Akhmatova's first collection of poems, *Evening*.
Gumilyov and Akhmatova journey to Switzerland and Italy.
Summer: Akhmatova and her mother are at the estate of cousins near the Austrian frontier; Gumilyov is at Slepnyovo.
October 1: birth of their son, Lev Nikolayevich.

1913—Spring: Gumilyov once again in Abyssinia and Somaliland as director of an expedition financed by the Academy of Sciences.

1914—Publication of Akhmatova's second collection of poems, *Rosary*. The book is enormously popular.
August: outbreak of World War I. Gumilyov volunteers and is sent to the front.

1915—August: Akhmatova's father dies in Petersburg.
Autumn: Akhmatova, ill with tuberculosis, spends some time in a sanatorium near Helsinki.

1916—February: Akhmatova meets the artist and mosaicist Boris Anrep through Nikolay Nedobrovo, a critic and good friend. Many of the poems in her third volume, *White Flock,* are dedicated to Anrep.
Akhmatova passes the winter in the south, near Sevastopol, because of her tuberculosis.

1917—February: Akhmatova and Gumilyov separate.
The revolution breaks out and the provisional Kerensky government is established.
Akhmatova stays with her friend Valeriya Sreznevskaya and Valeriya's husband in Petersburg (called Petrograd during World War I; later renamed Leningrad).
October: Lenin and the Bolsheviks seize power.
Winter: publication of Akhmatova's third book of poems, *White Flock.*

1918—August: Akhmatova and Gumilyov divorce.
Autumn: Akhmatova marries Vladimir Shileiko, an Assyriologist. They reside first in the Marble Palace, then in a room in the Fontannyy Dom (Fountain House) on the Fontanka Canal. It is a winter of privation, cold and hunger.

1919—Nedobrovo dies of tuberculosis in Yalta.
The Civil War begins. Instigation of the Red Terror against the opponents of the new Soviet regime.

1920—Akhmatova takes a job as a librarian at the Institute of Agronomy.

1921—Akhmatova leaves Shileiko and joins Olga Glebova-Sudeikina and Artur Lourié on the Fontanka (no. 18).

Civil War ends but civil unrest continues.

7 August: death of Alexander Blok, the leading Symbolist poet.

25 August: Gumilyov is executed for allegedly taking part in the Tagantsev affair, a conspiracy against the new regime.

Publication of Akhmatova's fourth book of poems, *Plantain.*

1922—Publication of Akhmatova's fifth book of poems, *Anno Domini MCMXXI.*

January: Mayakovsky, the leading Futurist poet, publicly denounces Akhmatova's poetry.

20 September: Korney Chukovsky, in a lecture entitled "Two Russias," contrasts the Futurist poetry of Mayakovsky and the pre-revolutionary poetry of Akhmatova. Though he perceives a place for both in Russian letters, the authorities increasingly do not.

1924—Death of Lenin; emergence of Stalin, who solidifies his power by the end of the decade.

Summer: Akhmatova renews her friendship with Osip Mandelstam and meets Nadezhda Mandelstam.

1925—Spring: Nadezhda Mandelstam and Akhmatova, both ill with tuberculosis, stay together in a boarding house in Tsarskoye Selo.

Thirty-two of Akhmatova's poems appear in an anthology; they are the last to be published in the Soviet Union until 1940, though her early books continue to be reprinted by émigré presses.

1926—Akhmatova resides in the apartment of Nikolay Punin, an art historian and critic, in the Fountain House. His wife Anna Arens, a doctor, and their daughter Irina also live there.

Akhmatova begins her critical studies of Pushkin.

1928—Akhmatova and Shileiko are officially divorced.

1929 to 1933—Widespread peasant resistance to Stalin's collectivization policy is met with executions, deportations, and deliberate starvation; millions perish.

1930—Suicide of Mayakovsky.

1932—Creation of the Union of Soviet Writers under firm Communist Party control.

1934—13 May: arrest of Osip Mandelstam. The Mandelstams are exiled to Cherdyn. Akhmatova collects money for them from friends.

December: assassination of Party official Sergey Kirov. Mass arrests, among them young Lev Gumilyov, who is released. The Terror intensifies.

1935—Punin and Lev Gumilyov both arrested, then released.

1936—Publication of Akhmatova's essay, "Benjamin Constant's *Adolphe* and Pushkin's "Creation.'"

Akhmatova visits the Mandelstams in Voronezh.

1937 — The Terror in full swing. Millions are arrested, imprisoned, sent to concentration camps.

1938 — 10 March: Lev Gumilyov is rearrested, held in Leningrad and released 17 months later.
1 May: Mandelstam is arrested at Samatikha.
27 December: death of Mandelstam in a transit camp.

1935 to 1940 — Composition of the poetic cycle *Requiem*.

1939 — Marina Tsvetaeva, the Moscow poet who had emigrated to Paris, returns to the Soviet Union.

1940 — Akhmatova and Tsvetaeva meet for the first time. The ban on Akhmatova's poetry, in effect since 1925, is lifted briefly.
Summer: publication of *From Six Books,* a selection from Akhmatova's previous books and some new poems.
Autumn: *From Six Books* is withdrawn from sale and from libraries.
October: Akhmatova has her first heart attack.

1941 — 22 June: Germany invades the Soviet Union.
August: Tsvetaeva hangs herself in the town of Elabuga.
September: Akhmatova speaks to the women of besieged Leningrad on the radio, praising and encouraging them.
October: By order of the Central Committee of the Communist Party of Leningrad, Akhmatova is evacuated to Moscow; she then makes her way to Tashkent, a city in Uzbekistan. She obtains a room and somehow receives permission for Nadezhda Mandelstam and her mother to reside in the same house.

1942 to 1944 — Akhmatova gives poetry readings in hospitals. She contracts and recovers from typhus; attempts to return to Leningrad.

1943 — Publication of *Selected Poems,* a severely censored edition, in Tashkent.

1944 — May: Akhmatova flies from Tashkent to Moscow, where she gives a poetry recital in the auditorium of the Polytechnic Museum. The standing ovation frightens her because of possible political repercussions.
June: Akhmatova flies to Leningrad.

1945 — May: Victory over Germany.
Akhmatova living in two rooms in the Fountain House. Lev Gumilyov, who had been released from exile to fight in the war, joins her.
Autumn: Isaiah Berlin, First Secretary in the British Embassy in Moscow, meets Akhmatova. The visit, a long, stimulating, wide-ranging exchange of views, has repercussions. After Berlin's second visit, 5 January, 1946, Akhmatova, who has been shadowed since her return to Leningrad, observes that microphones have been installed in her room.

1946 — Publication of *Selected Poems,* also severely censored, in Moscow. 14 August: the Central Committee of the Communist Party censures the magazine *Zvezda (Star)* and closes the magazine *Leningrad* for publishing the works of Akhmatova and Mikhail Zoshchenko. The decree banning Akhmatova and Zoshchenko for "poisoning the minds of Soviet youth" is written by Andrey Zhdanov, Stalin's cultural watchdog; similar decrees on cinema and music soon follow.
Poems 1909–1945 published, then almost completely destroyed.

1949 — 30 September: Punin is arrested.
6 November: Lev Gumilyov is arrested once more, not to be freed until 1956. Akhmatova considers her 1945 meeting with Berlin to be the cause.

1950 — "In Praise of Peace," a cycle of propagandistic poems, is published by Akhmatova in hope of helping her son. She requested that they be omitted from her collected works.

1952 — Forced to leave Fountain House, Akhmatova moves to a flat on Krasnaya Konitsa with members of the Punin family.

1953 — Punin dies in a prison camp in Siberia.
5 March: Stalin dies.

1955 — May: Akhmatova is given a small dacha in Komarovo, a village near Leningrad.

1956 — February: Khrushchev's "secret speech" on Stalin at the 20th Party Congress inaugurates a general thaw and a "rehabilitation" of disgraced intellectuals. Lev Gumilyov is released.
October: the Hungarian and Polish uprisings end the liberalizing trend.

1958 — Publication of Akhmatova's heavily censored *Poems,* which also contains translations from various Oriental languages.
Boris Pasternak is forced to refuse the Nobel Prize for his novel, *Dr. Zhivago.*

1960 — Death of Pasternak.

1961 — Publication of another censored volume of Akhmatova's poems, *Poems 1909–1960.*

1963 — Publication of *Requiem* in Munich.

1964 — Awarded an Italian literary prize, Akhmatova travels to Taormina to accept it. She encourages and defends young poets, including Joseph Brodsky.

1965 — Spring: Akhmatova journeys to England to receive an honorary degree from Oxford University. She sees many old friends who had emigrated to London, Paris and the United States.
Publication of *The Flight of Time,* a less severely censored collection.

1966 — 5 March: Akhmatova dies in a convalescent home near Moscow. She is buried in Komarovo.

INDEX TO POEMS—BY SOURCE

The source used for each of Akhmatova's poems is cited in small, italic type to the left of each poem, on the Russian-language side. An abbreviation is used for each major source, as described below.

Zhirmunsky, Victor (ed.), Anna Akhmatova, *Stikhotvoreniya i poemy* (Anna Akhmatova, *Poems and Long Poems*). Biblioteka poeta, Bolshaya seriya. 2nd ed. Leningrad: Sovetskii pisatel, 1979. *Citations:* **Zh.** [poem number]; e.g., *Zh. 415.*

Gleb Struve and Boris Filipoff (eds.), Anna Akhmatova, *Sochineniya* (Anna Akhmatova, *Works*). Vol. I. 2nd ed., 1967. Vol. II, 1968. Munich: Inter-Language Literary Associates. These poems are not numbered, so the volume and page number are cited. *Citations:* *S-F. I* or *S-F. II,* [page reference]; e.g., *S-F. I, 378* or *S-F. II, 95.*

Gleb Struve, Nikita Struve and Boris Filipoff (eds.), Anna Akhmatova, *Sochineniya* (Anna Akhmatova, *Works*). Vol. III, 1983. Paris: YMCA Press. The poems in Vol. III *are* numbered; therefore, these citations include the Struve-Filipoff number, volume, and page. *Citations:* *S-F.* [poem number], III, [page reference]; e.g., *S-F. 76, III, 56–57.*

V.A. Chernykh (ed.), Anna Akhmatova, *Sochineniya* (Anna Akhmatova, *Works*). Moscow: Khudozhestvennaya literatura, 1987. *Citations:* **Ch.** [page reference]; e.g., *Ch. 302.*

V.A. Chernykh (ed.), Anna Akhmatova, *Ya—golos vash...* (Anna Akhmatova, *I—Am Your Voice...*). Moscow: Knizhnaya palata, 1989. *Citations:* **YGV,** [page reference]; e.g., *YGV, 287.*

A few poems were taken from sources other than those listed above. In these cases, a full citation of the source will be found in the endnotes.

These source-citations are of special importance, because poems are frequently cited, throughout this edition, *by source-citation* rather than by title or first line. VOLUME I consists mainly of poems taken from the Zhirmunsky edition, following the same order as in that edition. Therefore, a particular poem can generally be located with little difficulty. However, VOLUME II is a mixture of poems taken from all four of the above editions. The following *Index* is meant to assist the reader in locating poems.

Each entry in the *Index* consists of three items:

Source-citation + (**Volume** and **English Page Reference**).

Zh. 1 (I-213)

Zh. 2 (I-213)

Zh. 3 (I-215)

Zh. 4 (I-215)

Zh. 5 (I-217)

Zh. 6 (I-217)

Zh. 7 (I-219)

Zh. 8 (I-221)

Zh. 9 (I-221)

Zh. 10 (I-223)

Zh. 11 (I-225)

Zh. 12 (I-225)

Zh. 13 (I-227)

Zh. 14 (I-229)

Zh. 15 (I-229)

Zh. 16 (I-231)

Zh. 17 (I-233)

Zh. 18 (I-233)

Zh. 19 (I-235)

Zh. 20 (I-237)

Zh. 21 (I-239)

Zh. 22 (I-239)

Zh. 23 (I-241)

Zh. 24 (I-243)

Zh. 25 (I-243)

Zh. 26 (I-245)

Zh. 27 (I-245)

Zh. 28 (I-247)

Zh. 29 (I-249)

Zh. 30 (I-251)

Zh. 31 (I-253)

Zh. 32 (I-255)

Zh. 33 (I-257)

Zh. 34 (I-259)

Zh. 35 (I-259)

Zh. 36 (I-261)

Zh. 37 (I-263)

Zh. 38 (I-263)

Zh. 39 (I-265)

Zh. 40 (I-267)

Zh. 41 (I-267)

Zh. 42 (I-269)

Zh. 43 (I-269)

Zh. 44 (I-271)

Zh. 45 (I-273)

Zh. 46 (I-275)

Zh. 47 (I-277)

Zh. 48 (I-277)

Zh. 49 (I-279)

Zh. 50 (I-279)

Zh. 51 (I-281)

Zh. 52 (I-281)

Zh. 53 (I-283)

Zh. 54 (I-283)

Zh. 55 (I-285)

Zh. 56 (I-285)

Zh. 57 (I-301)

Zh. 58 (I-301)

Zh. 59 (I-301)

Zh. 60 (I-303)

Zh. 61 (I-305)

Zh. 62 (I-305)

Zh. 63. (I-307)

Zh. 64 (I-309)

Zh. 65 (I-309)

Zh. 66 (I-311)

Zh. 67 (I-313)

Zh. 68 (I-313)

Zh. 69 (I-315)

Zh. 70 (I-317)

Zh. 71 (I-317)

Zh. 72 (I-319)

Zh. 73 (I-319)

Zh. 74 (I-321)

Zh. 75 (I-323)

Zh. 76 (I-323)

Zh. 77 (I-325)

Zh. 78 (I-327)

Zh. 79 (I-327)

Zh. 80 (I-329)

Zh. 81 (I-329)

Zh. 82 (I-331)

Zh. 83 (I-333)

Zh. 84 (I-333)

Zh. 85 (I-335)

Zh. 86 (I-337)

Zh. 87 (I-337)

Zh. 88 (I-339)

Zh. 89 (I-341)

Zh. 90 (I-341)

Zh. 91 (I-343)

Zh. 92 (I-343)

Zh. 93 (I-345)

Zh. 94 (I-347)

Zh. 95 (I-347)

Zh. 96 (I-347)

Zh. 97 (I-349)

Zh. 98 (I-351)

Zh. 99 (I-351)

Zh. 100 (I-355)

Zh. 101 (I-355)

Zh. 102 (I-357)

Zh. 103 (I-359)

Zh. 104 (I-359)

Zh. 105 (I-361)

Zh. 106 (I-363)

Zh. 107 (I-365)

Zh. 108 (I-365)

Zh. 109 (I-365)

Zh. 110 (I-367)

Zh. 111 (I-369)

Zh. 112 (I-375)

Zh. 113 (I-375)

Zh. 114 (I-377)

Zh. 115 (I-377)

Zh. 116 (I-379)

Zh. 117 (I-381)

Zh. 118 (I-381)

Zh. 119 (I-383)

Zh. 120 (I-383)

Zh. 121 (I-385)

Zh. 122 (I-385)

Zh. 123 (I-387)

Zh. 124 (I-387)

Zh. 125 (I-389)

Zh. 126 (I-389)

Zh. 127 (I-391)

Zh. 128 (I-393)

Zh. 129 (I-393)

Zh. 130 (I-395)

Zh. 131 (I-395)

Zh. 132 (I-397)

Zh. 133 (I-399)

Zh. 134 (I-399)

Zh. 135 (I-399)

Zh. 136 (I-401)

Zh. 137 (I-403)

Zh. 138 (I-405)

Zh. 139 (I-405)

Zh. 140 (I-405)

Zh. 141 (I-407)

Zh. 142 (I-409)

Zh. 143 (I-409)

Zh. 144 (I-411)

Zh. 145 (I-411)

Zh. 146 (I-413)

Zh. 147 (I-413)

Zh. 148 (I-417)

Zh. 149 (I-417)

Zh. 150 (I-419)

Zh. 151 (I-421)

Zh. 152 (I-423)

Zh. 153 (I-425)

Zh. 154 (I-425)

Zh. 155 (I-427)

Zh. 156 (I-427)

Zh. 157 (I-429)

Zh. 158 (I-429)

Zh. 159 (I-431)

Zh. 160 (I-433)

Zh. 161 (I-433)

Zh. 162 (I-435)

Zh. 163 (I-435)

Zh. 164 (I-437)

Zh. 165 (I-439)

Zh. 166 (I-439)

Zh. 167 (I-441)

Zh. 168 (I-443)

Zh. 169 (I-445)

Zh. 170 (I-447)

Zh. 171 (I-447)

Zh. 172 (I-449)

Zh. 173 (I-449)

Zh. 174 (I-451)

Zh. 175 (I-453)

Zh. 176 (I-453)

Zh. 177 (I-453)

Zh. 178 (I-455)

Zh. 179 (I-457)

Zh. 180 (I-459)

Zh. 181 (I-461)

Zh. 182 (I-461)

Zh. 183 (I-463)

Zh. 184 (I-465)

Zh. 185 (I-465)

Zh. 186 (I-467)

Zh. 187 (I-467)

Zh. 188 (I-469)

Zh. 189 (I-471)

Zh. 190 (I-471)

Zh. 191 (I-473)

Zh. 192 (I-475)

Zh. 193 (I-475)

Zh. 194 (I-477)

Zh. 195 (I-479)

Zh. 196 (I-481)

Zh. 197 (I-481)

Zh. 198 (I-483)

Zh. 199 (I-483)

Zh. 200 (I-485)

Zh. 201 (I-485)

Zh. 202 (I-487)

Zh. 203 (I-489)

Zh. 204 (I-489)

Zh. 205 (I-491)

Zh. 206 (I-497)

Zh. 207 (I-497)

Zh. 208 (I-499)

Zh. 209 (I-501)

Zh. 210 (I-501)

Zh. 211 (I-501)

Zh. 212 (I-503)

Zh. 213 (I-503)
Zh. 214 (I-505)
Zh. 215 (I-505)
Zh. 216 (I-507)
Zh. 217 (I-509)
Zh. 218 (I-509)
Zh. 219 (I-511)
Zh. 220 (I-513)
Zh. 221 (I-513)
Zh. 222 (I-515)
Zh. 223 (I-515)
Zh. 224 (I-517)
Zh. 225 (I-517)
Zh. 226 (I-519)
Zh. 227 (I-519)
Zh. 228 (I-521)
Zh. 229 (I-523)
Zh. 230 (I-523)
Zh. 231 (I-525)
Zh. 232 (I-525)
Zh. 233 (I-527)
Zh. 234 (I-529)
Zh. 235 (I-529)
Zh. 236 (I-529)
Zh. 237 (I-531)
Zh. 238 (I-539)
Zh. 239 (I-541)
Zh. 240 (I-541)
Zh. 241 (I-543)
Zh. 242 (I-543)
Zh. 243 (I-545)
Zh. 244 (I-545)
Zh. 245 (I-547)
Zh. 246 (I-547)
Zh. 247 (I-549)
Zh. 248 (I-551)
Zh. 249 (I-551)
Zh. 250 (I-553)
Zh. 251 (I-553)
Zh. 252 (I-555)
Zh. 253 (I-555)
Zh. 254 (I-557)
Zh. 255 (I-559)
Zh. 256 (I-559)
Zh. 257 (I-561)
Zh. 258 (I-561)
Zh. 259 (I-563)
Zh. 260 (I-565)
Zh. 261 (I-567)
Zh. 262 (I-569)
Zh. 263 (I-571)
Zh. 264 (I-573)
Zh. 265 (I-573)

Zh. 266 (I-575)
Zh. 267 (I-579)
Zh. 268 (I-579)
Zh. 269 (I-581)
Zh. 270 (I-583)
Zh. 271 (I-583)
Zh. 272 (I-585)
Zh. 273 (I-585)
Zh. 274 (I-587)
Zh. 275 (I-589)
Zh. 276 (I-589)
Zh. 277 (I-591)
Zh. 278 (I-593)
Zh. 279 (I-593)
Zh. 280 (I-595)
Zh. 281 (I-595)
Zh. 282 (I-597)
Zh. 283 (I-599)
Zh. 284 (I-599)
Zh. 285 (I-601)
Zh. 286 (I-601)
Zh. 287 (I-603)
Zh. 288 (I-605)
Zh. 289 (I-607)
Zh. 290 (I-609)
Zh. 291 (I-611)
Zh. 292 (I-611)
Zh. 293 (I-611)
Zh. 294 (I-613)
Zh. 295 (I-613)
Zh. 296 (I-615)
Zh. 297 (I-617)
Zh. 298 (I-617)
Zh. 299 (I-619)
Zh. 300 (II-73)
Zh. 301 (II-73)
Zh. 302 (II-75)
Zh. 303 (II-77)
Zh. 304 (II-77)
Zh. 305 (II-77)
Zh. 306 (II-79)
Zh. 307 (II-81)
Zh. 308 (II-81)
Zh. 309 (II-83)
Zh. 310 (II-83)
Zh. 311 (II-85)
Zh. 312 (II-87)
Zh. 313 (II-89)
Zh. 314 (II-91)
Zh. 315 (II-93)
Zh. 316 (II-101)
Zh. 317 (II-105)
Zh. 318 (II-109)

Zh. 319 (II-109)
Zh. 320 (II-117)
Zh. 321 (II-119)
Zh. 322 (II-121)
Zh. 323 (II-121)
Zh. 324 (II-125)
Zh. 325 (II-125)
Zh. 326 (II-129)
Zh. 327 (II-129)
Zh. 328 (II-129)
Zh. 329 (II-131)
Zh. 330 (II-131)
Zh. 331 (II-133)
Zh. 332 (II-135)
Zh. 333 (II-155)
Zh. 334 (II-155)
Zh. 335 (II-157)
Zh. 336 (II-157)
Zh. 337 (II-159)
Zh. 338 (II-161)
Zh. 339 (II-163)
Zh. 340 (II-165)
Zh. 341 (II-165)
Zh. 342 (II-167)
Zh. 343 (II-167)
Zh. 344 (II-171)
Zh. 345 (II-171)
Zh. 346 (II-173)
Zh. 347 (II-173)
Zh. 348 (II-175)
Zh. 349 (II-177)
Zh. 350 (II-177)
Zh. 351 (II-179)
Zh. 352 (II-181)
Zh. 353 (II-181)
Zh. 354 (II-183)
Zh. 355 (II-183)
Zh. 356 (II-185)
Zh. 357 (II-187)
Zh. 358 (II-187)
Zh. 359 (II-189)
Zh. 360 (II-189)
Zh. 361 (II-191)
Zh. 362 (II-191)
Zh. 363 (II-193)
Zh. 364 (II-193)
Zh. 365 (II-193)
Zh. 366 (II-195)
Zh. 367 (II-195)
Zh. 368 (II-195)
Zh. 369 (II-197)
Zh. 370 (II-197)
Zh. 371 (II-199)

Zh. 372 (II-199)
Zh. 373 (II-199)
Zh. 374 (II-201)
Zh. 375 (II-201)
Zh. 376 (II-203)
Zh. 377 (II-203)
Zh. 378 (II-205)
Zh. 379 (II-207)
Zh. 380 (II-207)
Zh. 381 (II-209)
Zh. 382 (II-209)
Zh. 383 (II-209)
Zh. 384 (II-211)
Zh. 385 (II-211)
Zh. 386 (II-211)
Zh. 387 (II-213)
Zh. 388 (II-213)
Zh. 389 (II-215)
Zh. 390 (II-215)
Zh. 391 (II-217)
Zh. 392 (II-217)
Zh. 393 (II-219)
Zh. 394 (II-219)
Zh. 395 (II-219)
Zh. 396 (II-219)
Zh. 397 (II-221)
Zh. 398 (II-221)
Zh. 399 (II-221)
Zh. 400 (II-223)
Zh. 401 (II-223)
Zh. 402 (II-223)
Zh. 403 (II-225)
Zh. 404 (II-227)
Zh. 405 (II-227)
Zh. 406 (II-229)
Zh. 407 (II-231)
Zh. 408 (II-233)
Zh. 409 (II-233)
Zh. 415 (II-235)
Zh. 416 (II-237)
Zh. 417 (II-237)
Zh. 418 (II-237)
Zh. 419 (II-239)
Zh. 420 (II-241)
Zh. 421 (II-241)
Zh. 422 (II-243)
Zh. 423 (II-243)
Zh. 424 (II-245)
Zh. 425 (II-245)
Zh. 426 (II-247)
Zh. 427 (II-249)
Zh. 428 (II-249)
Zh. 429 (II-251)

Zh. 430 (II-253)   Zh. 483 (II-319)   Zh. 536 (II-579)   Zh. 590 (II-699)
Zh. 431 (II-255)   Zh. 484 (II-321)   Zh. 537 (II-587)   Zh. 591 (II-701)
Zh. 432 (II-255)   Zh. 485 (II-491)   Zh. 538 (II-587)   Zh. 592 (II-701)
Zh. 433 (II-257)   Zh. 486 (II-493)   Zh. 539 (II-595)   Zh. 593 (II-703)
Zh. 434 (II-259)   Zh. 487 (II-495)   Zh. 540 (II-595)   Zh. 594 (II-705)
Zh. 435 (II-259)   Zh. 488 (II-495)   Zh. 541 (II-597)   Zh. 595 (II-715)
Zh. 436 (II-261)   Zh. 489 (II-497)   Zh. 542 (II-599)   Zh. 596 (II-715)
Zh. 437 (II-261)   Zh. 490 (II-501)   Zh. 543 (II-599)   Zh. 597 (II-717)
Zh. 438 (II-263)   Zh. 491 (II-501)   Zh. 544 (II-601)   Zh. 598 (II-727)
Zh. 439 (II-263)   Zh. 492 (II-503)   Zh. 545 (II-601)   Zh. 599 (II-727)
Zh. 440 (II-265)   Zh. 493 (II-505)   Zh. 546 (II-603)   Zh. 600 (II-729)
Zh. 441 (II-265)   Zh. 494 (II-507)   Zh. 547 (II-603)   Zh. 601 (II-731)
Zh. 442 (II-267)   Zh. 495 (II-507)   Zh. 548 (II-605)   Zh. 602 (II-703)
Zh. 443 (II-267)   Zh. 496 (II-509)   Zh. 549 (II-605)   Zh. 603 (II-731)
Zh. 444 (II-269)   Zh. 497 (II-511)   Zh. 550 (II-607)   Zh. 604 (II-733)
Zh. 445 (II-271)   Zh. 498 (II-513)   Zh. 551 (II-609)   Zh. 605 (II-733)
Zh. 446 (II-273)   Zh. 499 (II-513)   Zh. 552 (II-615)   Zh. 606 (II-393)
Zh. 447 (II-273)   Zh. 500 (II-515)   Zh. 553 (II-613)   Zh. 607 (II-733)
Zh. 448 (II-275)   Zh. 501 (II-515)   Zh. 554 (II-617)   Zh. 608 (II-735)
Zh. 449 (II-275)   Zh. 502 (II-517)   Zh. 555 (II-625)   Zh. 609 (II-735)
Zh. 450 (II-277)   Zh. 503 (II-519)   Zh. 556 (II-625)   Zh. 610 (II-613)
Zh. 451 (II-279)   Zh. 504 (II-521)   Zh. 558 (II-635)   Zh. 611 (II-393)
Zh. 452 (II-281)   Zh. 505 (II-523)   Zh. 559 (II-639)   Zh. 612 (II-719)
Zh. 453 (II-281)   Zh. 506 (II-525)   Zh. 560 (II-639)   Zh. 613 (II-497)
Zh. 454 (II-283)   Zh. 507 (II-533)   Zh. 561 (II-647)   Zh. 614 (II-391)
Zh. 455 (II-285)   Zh. 508 (II-541)   Zh. 562 (II-649)   Zh. 615 (II-735)
Zh. 456 (II-285)   Zh. 509 (II-541)   Zh. 563 (II-651)   Zh. 616 (II-719)
Zh. 457 (II-287)   Zh. 510 (II-537)   Zh. 564 (II-651)   Zh. 617 (II-713)
Zh. 458 (II-287)   Zh. 511 (II-531)   Zh. 565 (II-653)   Zh. 618 (II-719)
Zh. 459 (II-289)   Zh. 512 (II-531)   Zh. 566 (II-653)   Zh. 619 (II-671)
Zh. 460 (II-291)   Zh. 513 (II-543)   Zh. 567 (II-683)   Zh. 620 (II-667)
Zh. 461 (II-291)   Zh. 514 (II-545)   Zh. 568 (II-655)   Zh. 621 (II-717)
Zh. 462 (II-293)   Zh. 515 (II-545)   Zh. 569 (II-657)   Zh. 623 (II-717)
Zh. 463 (II-293)   Zh. 516 (II-545)   Zh. 570 (II-659)   Zh. 624 (II-741)
Zh. 464 (II-295)   Zh. 517 (II-547)   Zh. 571 (II-661)   Zh. 625 (II-735)
Zh. 465 (II-297)   Zh. 518 (II-551)   Zh. 572 (II-661)   Zh. 626 (II-741)
Zh. 466 (II-299)   Zh. 519 (II-551)   Zh. 573 (II-663)   Zh. 627 (II-741)
Zh. 467 (II-299)   Zh. 520 (II-561)   Zh. 574 (II-667)   Zh. 628 (II-327)
Zh. 468 (II-301)   Zh. 521 (II-525)   Zh. 575 (II-669)   Zh. 629 (II-327)
Zh. 469 (II-301)   Zh. 522 (II-529)   Zh. 576 (II-669)   Zh. 630 (II-331)
Zh. 470 (II-303)   Zh. 523 (II-527)   Zh. 577 (II-671)   Zh. 631 (II-333)
Zh. 471 (II-303)   Zh. 524 (II-527)   Zh. 578 (II-671)   Zh. 632 (II-335)
Zh. 472 (II-305)   Zh. 525 (II-527)   Zh. 579 (II-673)   Zh. 633 (II-339)
Zh. 473 (II-307)   Zh. 526 (II-529)   Zh. 580 (II-679)   Zh. 634 (II-341)
Zh. 474 (II-307)   Zh. 527 (II-563)   Zh. 581 (II-681)   Zh. 635 (II-345)
Zh. 475 (II-309)   Zh. 528 (II-563)   Zh. 582 (II-683)   Zh. 636 (II-347)
Zh. 476 (II-309)   Zh. 529 (II-565)   Zh. 583 (II-685)   Zh. 637 (II-349)
Zh. 477 (II-311)   Zh. 530 (II-567)   Zh. 584 (II-689)   Zh. 638 (II-353)
Zh. 478 (II-313)   Zh. 531 (II-569)   Zh. 585 (II-691)   Zh. 639 (II-355)
Zh. 479 (II-315)   Zh. 532 (II-571)   Zh. 586 (II-693)   Zh. 640 (II-385)
Zh. 480 (II-317)   Zh. 533 (II-571)   Zh. 587 (II-695)   Zh. 641 (II-387)
Zh. 481 (II-317)   Zh. 534 (II-577)   Zh. 588 (II-697)   Zh. 642 (II-391)
Zh. 482 (II-319)   Zh. 535 (II-579)   Zh. 589 (II-697)   Zh. 643 (II-393)

Zh. 644 (II-393)
Zh. 645 (II-389)
Zh. 646 (II-357)

Zh. 647 (II-375)
Zh. 648 (II-397)
Zh. 649 (II-687)

Zh. 650 (II-643)
Zh. 651 (II-591)

S-F. I, 205–206 (I-591)
S-F. I, 214 (I-541)
S-F. I, 242–246 (II-375)
S-F. I, 299 (II-265)
S-F. I, 301–302 (II-389)
S-F. I, 302b (II-391)
S-F. I, 328–329 (II-317)
S-F. I, 349–357 (II-357)
S-F. I, 378 (I-529)
S-F. I, 361 (II-95)
S-F. I, 362 (II-97)
S-F. I, 363 (II-99)
S-F. I, 364 (II-101)
S-F. I, 364–365 (II-103)
S-F. I, 365 (II-103)
S-F. I, 365–366 (II-105)
S-F. I, 366 (II-107)
S-F. I, 367 (II-107)
S-F. I, 368 (II-109)
S-F. I, 368–369 (II-111)
S-F. I, 369–370) (II-111)
S-F. I, 376 (II-165)

S-F. II, 95–102 (II-397)

S-F. 1, III, 19 (II-487)
S-F. 2, III, 19–20 (II-489)
S-F. 4, III, 20 (II-491)
S-F. 8, III, 23 (II-499)
S-F. 18, III, 28 (II-529)
S-F. 22, III, 29 (II-537)
S-F. 23, III, 30 (II-539)
S-F. 26, III, 31 (II-539)

S-F. 27, III, 31 (II-535)
S-F. 33, III, 34 (II-543)
S-F. 34, III, 35 (II-549)
S-F. 42, III, 39 (II-547)
S-F. 47, III, 41 (II-561)
S-F. 49, III, 41–42 (II-563)
S-F. 53, III, 43 (II-569)
S-F. 55, III, 44 (II-569)
S-F. 57, III, 45 (II-571)
S-F. 61, III, 47 (II-573)
S-F. 62, III, 47–48 (II-573)
S-F. 63, III, 48 (II-575)
S-F. 64, III, 48 (II-575)
S-F. 65, III, 48–49 (II-575)
S-F. 68, III, 51 (II-577)
S-F. 70, III, 52 (II-583)
S-F. 76, III, 56–57 (II-585)
S-F. 79, III, 58 (II-595)
S-F. 81, III, 59–60 (II-597)
S-F. 94, III, 65 (II-607)
S-F. 99, III, 67 (II-619)
S-F. 103, III, 69 (II-627)
S-F. 108, III, 71 (II-637)
S-F. 109, III, 72 (II-629)
S-F. 110, III, 72–73 (II-631)
S-F. 111–115, III, 73–74 (II-633)
S-F. 116, III, 75 (II-637)
S-F. 117, III, 75 (II-627)
S-F. 119, III, 75–76 (II-641)
S-F. 120, III, 76–77 (II-643)
S-F. III, 78–79 (II-355)

S-F. III, 79–80 (II-347)
S-F. 128, III, 82 (II-647)
S-F. 130, III, 83 (II-649)
S-F. 143, III, 89 (II-667)
S-F. 151, III, 92 (II-675)
S-F. 155, III, 94–95 (II-681)
S-F. 163, III, 99 (II-685)
S-F. 164, III, 99 (II-689)
S-F. 172, III, 103 (II-695)
S-F. 180, III, 105 (II-713)
S-F. 181, III, 106 (II-603)
S-F. 195, III, 110 (II-719)
S-F. 198, III, 111 (II-725)
S-F. 199, III, 111 (II-725)
S-F. 200, III, 111 (II-725)
S-F. 213, III, 117 (II-515)
S-F. 214, III, 117 (II-503)
S-F. 216, III, 118 (II-553)
S-F. 217, III, 119 (II-553)
S-F. 218, III, 499 (II-511)
S-F. 219, III, 499 (II-517)
S-F. 220, III, 500 (II-561)
S-F. 221, III, 500 (II-567)
S-F. 222, III, 500–501 (II-583)
S-F. 223, III, 501–502 (II-589)
S-F. 224, III, 502 (II-655)
S-F. 226, III, 503–506 (II-705)
S-F. 227, III, 506–507 (II-499)

Ch. 302 (II-487)
Ch. 303 (II-489)
Ch. 306 (II-503)
Ch. 326–327 (II-611)
Ch. 327 (II-609)
Ch. 328 (II-613)
Ch. 336 (II-675)
Ch. 336 (II-678)
Ch. 337 (II-699)

Ch. 342 (II-719)
Ch. 346 (II-533)
Ch. 350 (II-555)
Ch. 351 (II-553)
Ch. 353 (II-567)
Ch. 354 (II-623)
Ch. 355 (II-625)
Ch. 358 (II-663)
Ch. 360 (II-659)

Ch. 360 (II-665)
Ch. 361 (II-677)
Ch. 362 (II-657)
Ch. 362 (II-671)
Ch. 364 (II-693)
Ch. 369 (II-725)
Ch. 373 (II-683)
Ch. 374 (II-385)
Ch. 375 (II-389

YGV, 266–267 (II-589)
YGV, 282 (II-737)
YGV, 287 (II-737)
YGV, 290 (II-555)

YGV, 290 (II-591)
YGV, 294 (II-673)
YGV, 297–298 (II-721)
YGV, 300 (II-737)

YGV, 301 (II-739)
YGV, 301 (II-741)
YGV, 302 (II-741)

Notes on the Text

Many poems were organized by Akhmatova into thematic cycles. Short rules (——) mark the beginning and end of such cycles; for example, Zh. 2–4, three poems grouped under the title "In Tsarskoye Selo," near the beginning of *Evening*. These rules also set off all *discrete* poems. Occasionally, when space at the bottom of a page was short, these rule-dividers were not used. If a new poem begins at the top of the following page, this can be determined by the presence of a source-citation at the top of that page.

An asterisk (*) always appears at the bottom of a page when the page break does *not* come at a stanza break.

Please consult the *Index to Poems—By Source* for a key to the italic *source-citations* in small type which appear to the left of each poem on the Russian-language side.

TSARSKOYE SELO

———

A dark-skinned youth wandered along
    these allées,
By the shores of this lake he yearned,
And a hundred years later we cherish
The rustle of steps, faintly heard.

1

2

3

4

5

7

1. *The Catherine Palace, facing the "Old Park," the formal gardens portion of the Catherine Park*

2. *The Hermitage, in the Old Park*

3. *A linden allée in the Old Park*

4. *"Maid with a Vase" fountain. See note to Zh. 149.*

5. *The Grand Caprice, or Chinese Pavilion. See notes to Zh. 141, 189, 309.*

6. *Allée by the Vittolovsky Canal*

7. *The Alexander Park. "And everything resembles the allée/ Along the pond at Tsarskoye Selo." (Zh. 451)*

8. *Concert Hall in the Catherine Park*

ALL PHOTOGRAPHS BY M.A. VELICHKO

АННА АХМАТОВА

ВЕЧЕРЪ

стихи

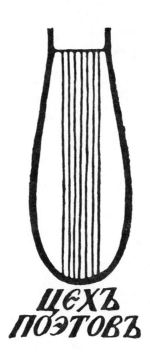

ЦЕХЪ ПОЭТОВЪ

EVENING

(1912)

La fleur des vignes pousse,
et j'ai vingt ans ce soir.

André Theuriet

Цветок виноградных лоз растет,
и мне двадцать лет сегодня вечером.

Андре Тёрье (франц.)—*Ред.*

The vineyard is breaking into blossom,
and I am twenty years old tonight.

I

Zh. 1

ЛЮБОВЬ

То змейкой, свернувшись клубком,
У самого сердца колдует,
То целые дни голубком
На белом окошке воркует,

То в инее ярком блеснет,
Почудится в дреме левкоя...
Но верно и тайно ведет
От радости и от покоя.

Умеет так сладко рыдать
В молитве тоскующей скрипки,
И страшно ее угадать
В еще незнакомой улыбке.

24 ноября 1911
Царское Село

————

Zh. 2

В ЦАРСКОМ СЕЛЕ

1

По аллее проводят лошадок.
Длинны волны расчесанных грив.
О пленительный город загадок,
Я печальна, тебя полюбив.

I

Love

Now, like a little snake, it curls into a ball,
Bewitching your heart,
Then for days it will coo like a dove
On the little white windowsill.

Or it will flash as bright frost,
Drowse like a gillyflower...
But surely and stealthily it will lead you away
From joy and from tranquillity.

It knows how to sob so sweetly
In the prayer of a yearning violin,
And how fearful to divine it
In a still unfamiliar smile.

November 24, 1911
Tsarskoye Selo

———

IN TSARSKOYE SELO

1

They're leading the horses along the allée,
Long are the waves of combed-out manes.
Oh enchanting little town of riddles,
Though I love you, I am mournful.

Странно вспомнить: душа тосковала,
Задыхалась в предсмертном бреду.
А теперь я игрушечной стала,
Как мой розовый друг какаду.

Грудь предчувствием боли не сжата,
Если хочешь, в глаза погляди.
Не люблю только час пред закатом,
Ветер с моря и слово: «уйди».

22 февраля 1911
Царское Село

Zh. 3

2

...А там мой мраморный двойник,
Поверженный под старым кленом,
Озерным водам отдал лик,
Внимает шорохам зеленым.

И моют светлые дожди
Его запекшуюся рану...
Холодный, белый, подожди,
Я тоже мраморною стану.

1911

Zh. 4

3

Смуглый отрок бродил по аллеям
У озерных грустил берегов,
И столетие мы лелеем
Еле слышный шелест шагов.

It's strange to remember: my soul yearned,
It panted, delirious, near death.
Now I've become a plaything,
Like my rosy friend the cockatoo.

No hint of pain oppresses my breast,
If you like, look into my eyes.
But I don't like the hour before sunset,
The wind from the sea and the word: "Leave!"

February 22, 1911
Tsarskoye Selo

2

... And there's my marble double,
Lying under the ancient maple,
He has given his face to the waters of the lake,
And he's listening to the green rustling.

And bright rainwater washes
His clotted wound...
Cold one, white one, wait,
I'll become marble too.

1911

3

A dark-skinned youth wandered along these allées,
By the shores of this lake he yearned,
And a hundred years later we cherish
The rustle of steps, faintly heard.

Иглы сосен густо и колко
Устилают низкие пни...
Здесь лежала его треуголка
И растрепанный том Парни.

24 сентября 1911
Царское Село

———

Zh. 5

И мальчик, что играет на волынке,
И девочка, что свой плетет венок,
И две в лесу скрестившихся тропинки,
И в дальнем поле дальний огонек, —

Я вижу всё. Я всё запоминаю,
Любовно-кротко в сердце берегу,
Лишь одного я никогда не знаю
И даже вспомнить больше не могу.

Я не прошу ни мудрости, ни силы.
О, только дайте греться у огня!
Мне холодно... Крылатый иль бескрылый,
Веселый бог не посетит меня.

30 ноября 1911
Царское Село

———

Zh. 6

Любовь покоряет обманно
Напевом простым, неискусным.
Еще так недавно-странно
Ты не был седым и грустным.

A layer of pine needles covers
The stumps with a thick, bristly mat . . .
Here lay his tattered copy of Parny
And his three-cornered hat.

September 24, 1911
Tsarskoye Selo

———

The boy who plays the bagpipes,
And the girl who twines herself a wreath,
And two paths crossing in the forest,
And a distant fire on a distant heath—

I see everything. I remember it all.
Gently, lovingly, I preserve it in my heart.
There's only one thing I will never know,
And can no longer recall.

Neither wisdom nor strength do I desire.
Oh, just let me warm myself by the fire!
I am cold . . . Winged or wingless,
The merry god will not come to call.

November 30, 1911
Tsarskoye Selo

———

Love conquers by deception,
With a simple, artless tune.
Just recently—how strange—
You were neither sad nor gray.

И когда она улыбалась
В садах твоих, в доме, в поле,
Повсюду тебе казалось,
Что вольный ты и на воле.

Был светел ты, взятый ею
И пивший ее отравы.
Ведь звезды были крупнее,
Ведь пахли иначе травы,
Осенние травы.

Осень 1911
Царское Село

Zh. 7

Сжала руки под темной вуалью...
«Отчего ты сегодня бледна?»
— Оттого что я терпкой печалью
Напоила его допьяна.

Как забуду? Он вышел, шатаясь,
Искривился мучительно рот...
Я сбежала, перил не касаясь,
Я бежала за ним до ворот.

Задыхаясь, я крикнула: «Шутка
Всё, что было. Уйдешь, я умру».
Улыбнулся спокойно и жутко
И сказал мне: «Не стой на ветру».

8 января 1911
Киев

And when it smiled,
In your garden, in the house, in the field,
No matter where you were, it seemed to you
That you were free to come and go.

You became luminous,
And, drinking its poison, enslaved.
And how much bigger the stars became,
And even the grass smelled different,
The grass of autumn.

Autumn 1911
Tsarskoye Selo

———

Under her dark veil she wrung her hands...
"Why are you so pale today?"
"Because I made him drink of stinging grief
Until he got drunk on it.

How can I forget? He staggered out,
His mouth twisted in agony...
I ran down not touching the bannister
And caught up with him at the gate.

Panting, I cried: 'A joke!
That's all it was. If you leave, I'll die.'
He smiled calmly and grimly
And told me: 'Don't stand here in the wind.' "

January 8, 1911
Kiev

———

Zh. 8

Память о солнце в сердце слабеет.
Желтей трава.
Ветер снежинками ранними веет
Едва-едва.

В узких каналах уже не струится —
Стынет вода.
Здесь никогда ничего не случится, —
О, никогда!

Ива на небе пустом распластала
Веер сквозной.
Может быть, лучше, что я не стала
Вашей женой.

Память о солнце в сердце слабеет.
Что это? Тьма?
Может быть!.. За ночь прийти успеет
Зима.

30 января 1911
Киев

Zh. 9

Высоко в небе облачко серело,
Как беличья расстеленная шкурка.
Он мне сказал: «Не жаль, что ваше тело
Растает в марте, хрупкая Снегурка!»

В пушистой муфте руки холодели.
Мне стало страшно, стало как-то смутно.
О, как вернуть вас, быстрые недели
Его любви, воздушной и минутной!

The heart's memory of the sun grows faint.
The grass is yellower.
A few early snowflakes blow in the wind,
Barely, barely.

The narrow canals have stopped flowing—
The water is chilling.
Nothing will ever happen here—
Oh, never!

The willow spreads its transparent fan
Against the empty sky.
Perhaps I should not have become
Your wife.

The heart's memory of the sun grows faint.
What's this? Darkness?
It could be!...One night brings winter's first
Hard freeze.

January 30, 1911
Kiev

———

High in the sky a small cloud grayed,
Like a stretched squirrel pelt.
He said to me: "Too bad, frail Snow Maiden,
That in March your body will melt."

My hands grew cold in my downy muff.
It became frightening and confusing to me.
Oh, how to regain you, swift weeks
Of his love, evanescent and airy!

Я не хочу ни горечи, ни мщенья,
Пускай умру с последней белой вьюгой.
О нем гадала я в канун Крещенья.
Я в январе была его подругой.

Весна 1911
Царское Село

———

Zh. 10

Дверь полуоткрыта,
Веют липы сладко...
На столе забыты
Хлыстик и перчатка.

Круг от лампы желтый...
Шорохам внимаю.
Отчего ушел ты?
Я не понимаю...

Радостно и ясно
Завтра будет утро.
Эта жизнь прекрасна,
Сердце, будь же мудро.

Ты совсем устало,
Бьешься тише, глуше...
Знаешь, я читала,
Что бессмертны души.

17 февраля 1911
Царское Село

———

I want neither bitterness nor revenge,
Let me die with the last white storm.
On Epiphany Eve I cast fortunes about him.
In January I was his friend.

Spring 1911
Tsarskoye Selo

———

The door is half open,
The lindens smell sweet...
On the table, forgotten,
A riding crop and a glove.

The yellow circle of the lamp...
I'm listening to rustlings.
Why did you go?
I don't understand...

Tomorrow morning will be
Joyful and bright.
This life is beautiful,
Heart, just be wise.

You are completely exhausted.
Your beating is fainter, more muffled...
You know, I read somewhere
That souls are immortal.

February 17, 1911
Tsarskoye Selo

———

Zh. 11

Хочешь знать, как все это было? —
Три в столовой пробило,
И прощаясь, держась за перила,
Она словно с трудом говорила:
«Это все ... Ах, нет, я забыла,
Я люблю вас, я вас любила
Еще тогда!» —
«Да».

21 октября 1910
Киев

———

Zh. 12

ПЕСНЯ ПОСЛЕДНЕЙ ВСТРЕЧИ

Так беспомощно грудь холодела,
Но шаги мои были легки.
Я на правую руку надела
Перчатку с левой руки.

Показалось, что много ступеней,
А я знала, — их только три!
Между кленов шепот осенний
Попросил: «Со мною умри!

Я обманут моей унылой,
Переменчивой, злой судьбой».
Я ответила: «Милый, милый!
И я тоже. — Умру с тобой ... »

Do you want to know how it was?—
Three o'clock struck in the dining room,
And, saying good-bye, holding the bannister,
She finally managed these words:
"That's all...Ah, no, I forgot.
I love you. I loved you
Even then!"
—"Yes."

October 21, 1910
Kiev

———

The Song of the Last Meeting

Then helplessly my breast grew cold,
But my steps were light.
I pulled the glove for my left hand
Onto my right.

There seemed to be many steps,
But I knew—there were only three!
The whisper of autumn in the maples
Was pleading: "Die with me!

I am betrayed by my doleful,
Fickle, evil fate."
I answered: "Darling, darling!
I too. I will die with you..."

Это песня последней встречи.
Я взглянула на темный дом.
Только в спальне горели свечи
Равнодушно-желтым огнем.

29 сентября 1911
Царское Село

———

Zh. 13

Как соломинкой пьешь мою душу.
Знаю, вкус ее горек и хмелен.
Но я пытку мольбой не нарушу.
О, покой мой многонеделен.

Когда кончишь, скажи. Не печально,
Что души моей нет на свете.
Я пойду дорогой недальней
Посмотреть, как играют дети.

На кустах зацветает крыжовник,
И везут кирпичи за оградой.
Кто ты: брат мой или любовник,
Я не помню, и помнить не надо.

Как светло здесь и как бесприютно,
Отдыхает усталое тело...
А прохожие думают смутно:
Верно, только вчера овдовела.

10 февраля 1911
Царское Село

———

This is the song of the last meeting.
I glanced at the dark house.
Candles were burning only in the bedroom,
With an indifferent-yellow flame.

September 29, 1911
Tsarskoye Selo

———

As if with a straw you drink my soul.
I know, it's a heady and bitter taste.
But I won't infringe on the torture with pleas,
Oh, I've been at peace for weeks and weeks.

Let me know when you're done. It's not sad
That my soul is no longer of this world.
I'll just walk down that nearby road
To see how the children play.

The gooseberry bushes are blooming,
And they're hauling bricks beyond the fence.
Who are you: my brother or a lover,
I don't remember, and I don't need to remember.

How bright it is here and how unsheltered,
My body, exhausted, rests. . .
And passers-by are thinking vaguely:
Wasn't she widowed just yesterday?

February 10, 1911
Tsarskoye Selo

———

Zh. 14

Я сошла с ума, о мальчик странный,
В среду, в три часа!
Уколола палец безымянный
Мне звенящая оса.

Я ее нечаянно прижала,
И, казалось, умерла она,
Но конец отравленного жала
Был острей веретена.

О тебе ли я заплачу, странном,
Улыбнется ль мне твое лицо?
Посмотри! На пальце безымянном
Так красиво гладкое кольцо.

18-19 марта 1911
Царское Село

———

Zh. 15

Мне больше ног моих не надо,
Пусть превратятся в рыбий хвост!
Плыву, и радостна прохлада,
Белеет тускло дальний мост.

Не надо мне души покорной,
Пусть станет дымом, легок дым,
Взлетев над набережной черной,
Он будет нежно-голубым.

Смотри, как глубоко ныряю,
Держусь за водоросль рукой,
Ничьих я слов не повторяю
И не пленюсь ничьей тоской...

Oh, strange boy, I lost my head
On Wednesday at three o'clock!
My ring finger was stung
By a buzzing wasp.

I grasped it by accident
And it seemed to be dead,
But sharper than a spindle
Was the tip of its poisonous sting.

Oh, will I weep over you, the strange one?
Will your countenance smile at me?
Look! Now on my ring finger
There's a fine smooth ring.

March 18–19, 1911
Tsarskoye Selo

———

I don't need legs anymore,
Let them turn into a fish's tail!
I'm swimming and the coolness is delightful,
The far-off bridge grows dimly white.

I don't need a submissive soul,
Let it turn into smoke, a wisp of smoke
Of tender, light blue
Flying over the blackened quay.

See how deeply I dive,
Clutching seaweed in my hands,
No one's words will I repeat
And no one's longing will capture me...

А ты, мой дальний, неужели
Стал бледен и печально-нем?
Что слышу? Целых три недели
Всё шепчешь: «Бедная, зачем?!»

⟨*1911*⟩

———

II

ОБМАН

Zh. 16

М. А. Змунчилла

1

Весенним солнцем это утро пьяно,
И на террасе запах роз слышней,
А небо ярче синего фаянса.
Тетрадь в обложке мягкого сафьяна;
Читаю в ней элегии и стансы,
Написанные бабушке моей.

Дорогу вижу до ворот, и тумбы
Белеют четко в изумрудном дерне.
О, сердце любит сладостно и слепо!

*

But you, my distant one, is it true
That you've become sadly mute and pale?
What's this I hear? That for three whole weeks
You've been whispering: "Why, unhappy girl?"

(1911)

———

II

DECEPTION

M.A. Zmunchilla

1

This morning is drunk with spring sun,
And on the terrace the smell of roses is louder,
And the sky is brighter than blue faience.
The notebook is bound in soft Morocco leather;
In it I am reading elegies and stanzas
Written to Grandmother.

I can see the road up to the gate, and the posts
Stand out white against the emerald lawn.
Oh, the heart loves sweetly and blindly!

*

И радуют пестреющие клумбы,
И резкий крик вороны в небе черной,
И в глубине аллеи арка склепа.

2 ноября 1910
Киев

Zh. 17

2

Жарко веет ветер душный,
Солнце руки обожгло,
Надо мною свод воздушный,
Словно синее стекло;

Сухо пахнут иммортели
В разметавшейся косе.
На стволе корявой ели
Муравьиное шоссе.

Пруд лениво серебрится,
Жизнь по-новому легка...
Кто сегодня мне приснится
В пестрой сетке гамака?

Январь 1910
Киев

Zh. 18

3

Синий вечер. Ветры кротко стихли,
Яркий свет зовет меня домой.
Я гадаю. Кто там? — не жених ли,
Не жених ли это мой?..

And the gaudy flower beds rejoice,
And in the sky, the black crow's harsh cry,
And far down the allée is the arc of the crypt.

November 2, 1910
Kiev

2

The wind blows stifling hot,
The sun has burned my arms,
Over me a dome of air
Like dark blue glass;

The everlastings in my loosened braid
Smell faintly dry.
On the rough trunk of the spruce tree
There's an ant highway.

Lazily, the pond turns silver,
Life once more is light...
Who will I dream of today
In my hammock's multicolored net?

January 1910
Kiev

3

Dark blue evening. The winds have subsided meekly,
And a bright light beckons me home.
I conjecture: Who is there?—My fiancé?
Isn't it my fiancé?..

На террасе силуэт знакомый,
Еле слышен тихий разговор.
О, такой пленительной истомы
Я не знала до сих пор.

Тополя тревожно прошуршали,
Нежные их посетили сны,
Небо цвета вороненой стали,
Звезды матово-бледны.

Я несу букет левкоев белых.
Для того в них тайный скрыт огонь,
Кто, беря цветы из рук несмелых,
Тронет теплую ладонь.

Сентябрь 1910
Царское Село

Zh. 19

4

Я написала слова,
Что долго сказать не смела.
Тупо болит голова,
Странно немеет тело.

Смолк отдаленный рожок,
В сердце все те же загадки,
Легкий осенний снежок
Лег на крокетной площадке.

Листьям последним шуршать!
Мыслям последним томиться!
Я не хотела мешать
Тому, кто привык веселиться.

On the terrace a familiar silhouette,
A quiet conversation barely heard.
Oh, never before have I felt
Such captivating languor.

The poplars stir uneasily,
Visited by tender dreams.
The sky is the color of burnished steel,
The stars are dull and pale.

I'm carrying a bouquet of white gillyflowers.
In them there's a secret, latent flame for the one
Who, taking the blossoms from my timid hands,
Will touch my warm palm.

September 1910
Tsarskoye Selo

4

I finally wrote down the words
That for so long I dared not say.
I have a dull headache,
And my body is strangely numb.

The sound of the horn has receded, then ceased,
But the heart's same old riddles remain.
The first light snow of autumn
Covers the croquet lawn.

Let the last leaves rustle!
Let the last thoughts languish!
I didn't want to trouble
Someone who likes to have fun.

Милым простила губам
Я их жестокую шутку...
О, вы приедете к нам
Завтра по первопутку.

Свечи в гостиной зажгут,
Днем их мерцанье нежнее,
Целый букет принесут
Роз из оранжереи.

Август 1910
Царское Село

———

Zh. 20

Мне с тобою пьяным весело —
Смысла нет в твоих рассказах.
Осень ранняя развесила
Флаги желтые на вязах.

Оба мы в страну обманную
Забрели и горько каемся,
Но зачем улыбкой странною
И застывшей улыбаемся?

Мы хотели муки жалящей
Вместо счастья безмятежного...
Не покину я товарища
И беспутного и нежного.

1911
Париж

———

I've forgiven those dear lips
Their cruel joke...
Oh, tomorrow you'll come to visit us
Over the new-fallen snow.

They will light the drawing-room candles,
Whose shimmering is more tender by day,
And from the greenhouse they will bring
Roses, a whole bouquet.

August 1910
Tsarskoye Selo

———

When you're drunk it's so much fun—
Your stories don't make sense.
An early fall has strung
The elms with yellow flags.

We've strayed into the land of deceit
And we're repenting bitterly,
Why then are we smiling these
Strange and frozen smiles?

We wanted piercing anguish
Instead of placid happiness...
I won't abandon my comrade,
So dissolute and mild.

1911
Paris

———

Zh. 21

Муж хлестал меня узорчатым,
Вдвое сложенным ремнем.
Для тебя в окошке створчатом
Я всю ночь сижу с огнем.

Рассветает. И над кузницей
Подымается дымок.
Ах, со мной, печальной узницей,
Ты опять побыть не мог.

Для тебя я долю хмурую,
Долю-муку приняла.
Или любишь белокурую,
Или рыжая мила?

Как мне скрыть вас, стоны звонкие!
В сердце темный, душный хмель,
А лучи ложатся тонкие
На несмятую постель.

Осень 1911

Zh. 22

Сердце к сердцу не приковано,
Если хочешь — уходи.
Много счастья уготовано
Тем, кто волен на пути.

Я не плачу, я не жалуюсь,
Мне счастливой не бывать,
Не целуй меня, усталую, —
Смерть придет поцеловать.

My husband whipped me with his woven belt,
Folded in two.
All night I've been at the little window
With a taper, waiting for you.

Day breaks. And over the forge
Puffs a puff of smoke.
Ah, once more you couldn't be here
With this sad prisoner.

It's a gloomy fate, a torturous fate
I've accepted for you.
Are you in love with someone fair?
Or is your sweetheart auburn-haired?

How can I suppress you, my groans!
In my heart there is dark, stifling drunkenness,
And a few slender sunbeams lie down
On the unrumpled bed.

Autumn 1911

———

One heart isn't chained to another,
If you want to—leave!
There's lots of happiness in store
For one who's free.

I'm not weeping, I'm not complaining,
Happiness is not for me.
Don't kiss me, I am weary—
Death will kiss me.

———

Дни томлений острых прожиты
Вместе с белою зимой.
Отчего же, отчего же ты
Лучше, чем избранник мой?

Весна 1911

———

Zh. 23

ПЕСЕНКА

Я на солнечном восходе
Про любовь пою,
На коленях в огороде
Лебеду полю.

Вырываю и бросаю —
Пусть простит меня.
Вижу, девочка босая
Плачет у плетня.

Страшно мне от звонких воплей
Голоса беды,
Всё сильнее запах теплый
Мертвой лебеды.

Будет камень вместо хлеба
Мне наградой злой.
Надо мною только небо,
А со мною голос твой.

11 марта 1911
Царское Село

———

Days of gnawing tedium endured
With the winter snow.
Why, oh why should you
Be better than the one I chose?

Spring 1911

———

A Song

As the sun is rising
I'm singing about love,
In the garden on my knees
I'm weeding out the goosefoot.

I tear it out and throw it down—
May it forgive me.
I see a little barefoot girl
Crying by the fence.

Terrible to me is the loud wail
Of the voice of misery,
Stronger and stronger the warm smell
Of the dying weed.

A stone instead of bread
Will be my evil reward.
Over me only the sky,
And with me, your voice.

March 11, 1911
Tsarskoye Selo

———

Zh. 24

Я пришла сюда, бездельница,
Все равно мне, где скучать!
На пригорке дремлет мельница.
Годы можно здесь молчать.

Над засохшей повиликою
Мягко плавает пчела;
У пруда русалку кликаю,
А русалка умерла.

Затянулся ржавой тиною
Пруд широкий, обмелел,
Над трепещушей осиною
Легкий месяц заблестел.

Замечаю все, как новое.
Влажно пахнут тополя.
Я молчу. Молчу, готовая
Снова стать тобой, земля.

23 февраля 1911
Царское Село

Zh. 25

БЕЛОЙ НОЧЬЮ

Ах, дверь не запирала я,
Не зажигала свеч,
Не знаешь, как, усталая,
Я не решалась лечь.

Смотреть, как гаснут полосы
В закатном мраке хвой,
Пьянея звуком голоса,
Похожего на твой.

I came here, an idler,
It's all the same to me where I'm bored!
The mill drowses on the little knoll.
One could be silent here for years.

Over the withered morning glory
A bee gently glides;
I call to the water nymph at the pond,
But the water nymph has died.

The wide pond is shallow now,
Covered with rusty slime.
Over a quivering aspen
A slender moon begins to shine.

I marvel at everything as if it were new.
There's a gust of damp from the poplars.
I am silent. I am silent, preparing
To join you again, earth.

February 23, 1911
Tsarskoye Selo

On a White Night

Ah, I didn't lock the door,
I didn't light the candles.
You don't know that, exhausted,
I decided not to go to bed.

To watch how the streaks of sunset
Died away in the gloom of the firs,
Getting drunk on the sound of a voice
That resembles yours.

И знать, что всё потеряно,
Что жизнь — проклятый ад!
О, я была уверена,
Что ты придешь назад.

6 февраля 1911
Царское Село

Zh. 26

Под навесом темной риги жарко,
Я смеюсь, а в сердце злобно плачу.
Старый друг бормочет мне: «Не каркай!
Мы ль не встретим на пути удачу!»

Но я другу старому не верю.
Он смешной, незрячий и убогий,
Он всю жизнь свою шагами мерил
Длинные и скучные дороги.

И звенит, звенит мой голос ломкий,
Звонкий голос не узнавших счастья:
«Ах, пусты дорожные котомки,
А на завтра голод и ненастье!»

24 сентября 1911
Царское Село

Zh. 27

Хорони, хорони меня, ветер!
Родные мои не пришли,
Надо мною блуждающий вечер
И дыханье тихой земли.

And to realize that all is lost,
That life—is hell!
Oh, I was so sure
That you would return.

February 6, 1911
Tsarskoye Selo

———

Under the dark roof of the threshing shed, it's hot,
I'm laughing, but in my heart I weep with spite.
My old friend mumbles to me: "Don't squawk!
Aren't we on the way to success!"

But I don't believe my old friend.
He is ludicrous, blind and wretched.
He has measured his life with careful steps
Down long and tedious roads.

Then my thin voice rings out, rings out,
A ringing voice, to happiness a stranger:
"Ah, our knapsacks are empty,
And for tomorrow, foul weather and hunger!"

September 24, 1911
Tsarskoye Selo

———

Bury me, bury me, wind!
My relatives have not come.
Over me is the wandering evening
And the earth's quiet breathing.

Я была, как и ты, свободной,
Но я слишком хотела жить.
Видишь, ветер, мой труп холодный,
И некому руки сложить.

Закрой эту черную рану
Покровом вечерней тьмы
И вели голубому туману
Надо мною читать псалмы.

Чтобы мне легко, одинокой,
Отойти к последнему сну,
Прошуми высокой осокой
Про весну, про мою весну.

Декабрь 1909
Киев

Zh. 28

Ты поверь, не змеиное острое жало,
А тоска мою выпила кровь.
В белом поле я тихою девушкой стала,
Птичьим голосом кличу любовь.

И давно мне закрыта дорога иная,
Мой царевич в высоком кремле.
Обману ли его, обману ли? — Не знаю!
Только ложью живу на земле.

Не забыть, как пришел он со мной проститься:
Я не плакала; это судьба.
Ворожу, чтоб царевичу ночью присниться,
Но бессильна моя ворожба.

Like you I was free,
But I wanted too much to live.
Here is my cold corpse, wind, do you see?
And no one to fold my arms.

Cut out for this black wound
A shroud of evening gloom
And command the blue mist
To read psalms over me.

Make it easy for me, all alone,
To embark on my final dream,
Make the tall sedge roar
That spring, my spring, is here.

December 1909
Kiev

———

Believe me, not the serpent's sharp sting,
But longing has drunk my blood.
In the white fields I became a quiet girl,
With the voice of a bird I cry out for love.

And the other road was closed to me long ago;
My tsarevich is in the high fortress.
Will I deceive him? Will I?—I don't know!
But living on earth is a lie.

I won't forget how he came to take leave of me:
I didn't cry. It was fate.
I weave spells to make the tsarevich dream at night,
But my spells are powerless.

Оттого ль его сон безмятежен и мирен,
Что я здесь у закрытых ворот,
Иль уже светлоокая, нежная Сирин
Над царевичем песню поет?

(1912)

———

III

Zh. 29

МУЗЕ

Муза-сестра заглянула в лицо,
Взгляд ее ясен и ярок.
И отняла золотое кольцо,
Первый весенний подарок.

Муза! ты видишь, как счастливы все —
Девушки, женщины, вдовы...
Лучше погибну на колесе,
Только не эти оковы.

Знаю: гадая, и мне обрывать
Нежный цветок маргаритку.
Должен на этой земле испытать
Каждый любовную пытку.

Жгу до зари на окошке свечу
И ни о ком не тоскую,
Но не хочу, не хочу, не хочу
Знать, как целуют другую.

Is his sleep untroubled and serene
Because I'm here at the barred gates,
Or is a light-eyed, tender Sirin
Already singing a song to him?

(1912)

———

III

To the Muse

The Muse, my sister, looked into my face,
Her glance was bright and clear,
And she took away the golden ring,
The first springtime gift.

Muse! You see how happy they all are,
Girls, wives, widows...
Better to perish on the wheel,
But not these chains.

I know: yes, no, even I must tear off
The delicate daisy petals.
Everyone on earth is destined to feel
The torments of love.

I keep the candle burning in the window till dawn
And I don't long for anyone,
But I don't want, don't want, don't want
To know how they kiss each other.

Завтра мне скажут, смеясь, зеркала:
«Взор твой не ясен, не ярок...»
Тихо отвечу: «Она отняла
Божий подарок».

10 октября 1911
Царское Село

———

АЛИСА

Zh. 30

1

Все ~оскует о забытом,
О своем весеннем сне,
Как Пьеретта о разбитом
Золотистом кувшине...

Все осколочки собрала,
Не умела их сложить...
«Если б ты, Алиса, знала,
Как мне скучно, скучно жить!

«Я за ужином зеваю,
Забываю есть и пить,
Ты поверишь, забываю
Даже брови подводить.

«О, Алиса! дай мне средство,
Чтоб вернуть его опять;
Хочешь все мое наследство,
Дом и платья можешь взять.

Tomorrow the mirrors will mock me:
"Your gaze is not clear, not bright..."
Quietly I will answer: "She took away
God's gift to me."

October 10, 1911
Tsarskoye Selo

―――

ALISA

1

Everything mourns for the forgotten,
For its own springtime dream,
As Pierrette for the broken
Golden pitcher...

She gathered up all the fragments,
But couldn't make them fit...
"If you only knew, Alisa,
How boring, how boring it is for me to live!

At supper I yawn, I drowse,
I forget to eat or drink,
And you can see, I even forget
To pencil in my brows.

O Alisa! give me some way
To make him return.
Do you want everything I own?
Take my house, my gowns.

«Он приснился мне в короне,
Я боюсь моих ночей!»
У Алисы в медальоне
Темный локон — знаешь чей?!

Zh. 31

2

— «Как поздно! Устала, зеваю...»
— «Миньона, спокойно лежи,
Я рыжий парик завиваю
Для стройной моей госпожи.

«Он будет весь в лентах зеленых,
А сбоку жемчужный аграф;
Читала записку: «У клена
Я жду вас, таинственный граф!»

«Сумеет под кружевом маски
Лукавая смех заглушить,
Велела мне даже подвязки
Сегодня она надушить».

Луч утра на черное платье
Скользнул, из окошка упав...
«Он мне открывает объятья
Под кленом, таинственный граф».

(1912)

In my dream he was wearing a crown.
My nights frighten me!"
In Alisa's medallion
Is a lock of dark hair—guess whose!

2

"How late it is! I'm tired, I'm yawning..."
"Mignon, just lie down and rest.
I'm curling this red wig
For my slender mistress.

It will be all in green ribbons
With a pearl clasp on the side.
I've read her note: 'I'll wait for you
By the maple, mysterious Count!'

Under her lace mask
She will manage to stifle her sly laugh,
Why, she even ordered me
To perfume her garters today."

A morning ray falling from the little window
Slid across the black gown...
"He's opening his arms to embrace me
Under the maple, my mysterious Count."

(1912)

Zh. 32

МАСКАРАД В ПАРКЕ

Луна освещает карнизы,
Блуждает по гребням реки...
Холодные руки маркизы
Так ароматно-легки.

«О принц! улыбаясь присела,
В кадрили вы наш vis-à-vis»,
И томно под маской бледнела
От жгучих предчувствий любви.

Вход скрыл серебрящийся тополь
И низко спадающий хмель.
«Багдад или Константинополь
Я вам завоюю, ma belle!»

«Как вы улыбаетесь редко,
Вас страшно, маркиза, обнять!?»
Темно и прохладно в беседке,
«Ну, что же! пойдем танцовать?»

Выходят. На вязах, на кленах
Цветные дрожат фонари,
Две дамы в одеждах зеленых
С монахами держат пари.

И бледный, с букетом азалий,
Их смехом встречает Пьеро:
«Мой принц! О не вы ли сломали
На шляпе маркизы перо?»

⟨1912⟩

Masquerade in the Park

The moon lights up the cornices,
Wanders over the crests on the river...
The cold hands of the marquise
Are aromatic, delicate.

"O Prince!"—smiling, she curtsies—
"In the quadrille you will be our *vis-à-vis*,"
And beneath her mask she grows pale
With a burning presentiment of love.

The entrance was concealed by a silvering poplar
And a hop bush fallen low.
"Baghdad or Constantinople
I'll conquer for you, *ma belle.*

How rarely you smile,
It is frightening to embrace you, Marquise!"
It is dark and cold in the summerhouse...
"Well then, shall we go and dance?"

They leave. Colored lanterns quiver
Against the elms, the maple trunks.
Two ladies dressed in green
Are betting with the monks.

And pale, with a bouquet of azaleas,
Pierrot encounters them and laughs:
"My Prince! Was it you who broke
The feather on the marquise's hat?"

(1912)

Zh. 33

ВЕЧЕРНЯЯ КОМНАТА

Я говорю сейчас словами теми,
Что только раз рождаются в душе.
Жужжит пчела на белой хризантеме,
Так душно пахнет старое саше.

И комната, где окна слишком узки,
Хранит любовь и помнит старину,
А над кроватью надпись по-французски
Гласит: «Seigneur, ayez pitié de nous».*

Ты сказки давней горестных заметок,
Душа моя, не тронь и не ищи...
Смотрю, блестящих севрских статуэток
Померкли глянцевитые плащи.

Последний луч, и желтый, и тяжелый,
Застыл в букете ярких георгин,
И как во сне я слышу звук виолы
И редкие аккорды клавесин.

⟨1912⟩

---

* «Господь, смилуйся над нами» (франц.). — *Ред.*

Evening Room

I am speaking right now with words
That only this once will arise in my soul.
A bee is buzzing on a white chrysanthemum,
There's the musty smell of old sachet.

And the room, whose windows are too narrow,
Preserves love and remembers the olden days,
And over the bed an inscription in French
Proclaims: *"Seigneur, ayez pitié de nous."**

Don't touch, don't search, my soul,
For sorrowful hints of some bygone tale...
I watch as the lustrous cloaks
Of gleaming Sèvres statuettes grow dim.

Yellow and heavy, a last ray of sun
Congeals in a brilliant bouquet of dahlias,
And as in a dream, I hear a viol
And the thin strains of a clavecin.

(1912)

---

* *"Lord, have pity on us."* (Fr.)

Zh. 34

СЕРОГЛАЗЫЙ КОРОЛЬ

Слава тебе, безысходная боль!
Умер вчера сероглазый король.

Вечер осенний был душен и ал,
Муж мой, вернувшись, спокойно сказал:

«Знаешь, с охоты его принесли,
Тело у старого дуба нашли.

Жаль королеву. Такой молодой!..
За ночь одну она стала седой».

Трубку свою на камине нашел
И на работу ночную ушел.

Дочку мою я сейчас разбужу,
В серые глазки ее погляжу.

А за окном шелестят тополя:
«Нет на земле твоего короля...»

11 декабря 1910
Царское Село

———

Zh. 35

РЫБАК

Руки голы выше локтя,
А глаза синей, чем лед.
Едкий, душный запах дегтя,
Как загар, тебе идет.

The Gray-Eyed King

Hail to thee, everlasting pain!
The gray-eyed king died yesterday.

Scarlet and close was the autumn eve,
My husband, returning, said calmly to me:

"They brought him back from the hunt, you know,
They found his body near the old oak.

Pity the queen. So young!..
Overnight her hair has turned gray."

Then he found his pipe on the hearth
And left, as he did every night, for work.

I will wake my little daughter now,
And look into her eyes of gray.

And outside the window the poplars whisper:
"Your king is no more on this earth..."

December 11, 1910
Tsarskoye Selo

The Fisherman

Arms bare above the elbows,
And eyes bluer than ice.
The stifling, pungent scent of tar
Becomes you like your tan.

И всегда, всегда распахнут
Ворот куртки голубой,
И рыбачки только ахнут,
Закрасневшись пред тобой.

Даже девочка, что ходит
В город продавать камсу,
Как потерянная бродит
Вечерами на мысу.

Щеки бледны, руки слабы,
Истомленный взор глубок,
Ноги ей щекочут крабы,
Выползая на песок.

Но она уже не ловит
Их протянутой рукой.
Всё сильней биенье крови
В теле, раненном тоской.

23 апреля 1911

———

Zh. 36

ОН ЛЮБИЛ...

Он любил три вещи на свете:
За вечерней пенье, белых павлинов
И стертые карты Америки.
Не любил, когда плачут дети,
Не любил чая с малиной
И женской истерики.
...А я была его женой.

9 ноября 1910
Киев

And your blue jacket
Is always, always flung wide,
And the fishwives, seeing you,
Blush and sigh.

Even the little girl
Who sells flounder in the city,
Like a lost soul wanders
In the evenings, on the cape.

Her cheeks are pale, her hands are weak,
Her weary glance is deep,
Crabs crawl out along the sand,
Tickling her feet.

But she no longer
Reaches out to catch them.
The blood beats ever stronger
In a body wounded by desire.

April 23, 1911

————

He Loved...

He loved three things in life:
Evensong, white peacocks
And old maps of America.
He hated it when children cried,
He hated tea with raspberry jam
And women's hysterics.
... And I was his wife.

November 9, 1910
Kiev

Zh. 37

Сегодня мне письмá не принесли:
Забыл он написать, или уехал;
Весна как трель серебряного смеха,
Качаются в заливе корабли.
Сегодня мне письма не принесли...

Он был со мной еще совсем недавно,
Такой влюбленный, ласковый и мой,
Но это было белою зимой,
Теперь весна, и грусть весны отравна,
Он был со мной еще совсем недавно...

Я слышу: легкий трепетный смычок,
Как от предсмертной боли, бьется, бьется,
И страшно мне, что сердце разорвется,
Не допишу я этих нежных строк...

⟨*1912*⟩

———

Zh. 38

НАДПИСЬ НА НЕОКОНЧЕННОМ ПОРТРЕТЕ

О, не вздыхайте обо мне,
Печаль преступна и напрасна,
Я здесь, на сером полотне,
Возникла странно и неясно.

Взлетевших рук излом больной,
В глазах улыбка исступленья,
Я не могла бы стать иной
Пред горьким часом наслажденья.

They didn't bring me a letter today:
He forgot to write, or he went away;
Spring is like a trill of silver laughter,
Boats are rocking in the bay.
They didn't bring me a letter today...

He was still with me just recently,
So much in love, affectionate and mine,
But that was white wintertime.
Now it is spring, and spring's sadness is poisonous.
He was still with me just recently...

I listen: the light, trembling bow of a violin,
Like the pain before death, beats, beats,
How terrible that my heart will break
Before these tender lines are complete...

(1912)

———

Inscription on an
Unfinished Portrait

Oh, don't sigh over me,
That would be useless, criminal grief.
Here on this square of gray linen,
I emerged strangely and vaguely.

The painful fracture of the upraised arms,
A smile of frenzy in the eyes,
I could not be otherwise
Before the bitter hour of delight.

Он так хотел, он так велел
Словами мертвыми и злыми.
Мой рот тревожно заалел,
И щеки стали снеговыми.

И нет греха в его вине,
Ушел, глядит в глаза другие,
Но ничего не снится мне
В моей предсмертной летаргии.

⟨*1912*⟩

————

Zh. 39

Сладок запах синих виноградин...
Дразнит опьяняющая даль.
Голос твой и глух и безотраден.
Никого мне, никого не жаль.

Между ягод сети-паутинки,
Гибких лоз стволы еще тонки,
Облака плывут, как льдинки, льдинки
В ярких водах голубой реки.

Солнце в небе. Солнце ярко светит.
Уходи к волне про боль шептать.
О, она наверное ответит,
А быть может будет целовать.

⟨*1912*⟩

————

That's what he wanted, that's what he ordered
With dead, malevolent words.
My anxious lips turned crimson
And my cheeks became white as snow.

And he's not guilty of any sin,
He left, he's gazing into other eyes;
But I, I dream of nothing
In my fatal lethargy.

(1912)

———

The smell of blue grapes is sweet...
The intoxicating view tantalizes.
Your voice is hollow and cheerless,
But I'm not feeling sorry for anyone, not anyone.

There are spiderwebs among the berries,
The stems of the supple vines are still thin,
Like little ice floes, little ice floes,
In the gleaming water of the sky-blue river, clouds swim.

The sun is in the sky. The sun brightly shines.
Go whisper to the wave what's amiss.
Oh, it will certainly reply,
And perhaps it will give you a kiss.

(1912)

———

Zh. 40

ПОДРАЖАНИЕ И. Ф. АННЕНСКОМУ

И с тобой, моей первой причудой,
Я простился. Восток голубел.
Просто молвила: «Я не забуду».
Я не сразу поверил тебе.

Возникают, стираются лица,
Мил сегодня, а завтра далек.
Отчего же на этой странице
Я когда-то загнул уголок?

И всегда открывается книга
В том же месте. И странно тогда:
Всё как будто с прощального мига
Не прошли невозвратно года.

О, сказавший, что сердце из камня,
Знал наверно: оно из огня...
Никогда не пойму, ты близка мне
Или только любила меня.

1911

———

Zh. 41

Вере Ивановой-Шварсалон

Туманом легким парк наполнился,
И вспыхнул на воротах газ.
Мне только взгляд один запомнился
Незнающих, спокойных глаз.

Imitation of I. F. Annensky

And to you, my first fancy,
I said farewell. The east was turning blue.
You said simply: "I won't forget."
And right then I didn't believe you.

Faces appear, are washed away,
Dear today and tomorrow far off.
Why did I once turn down
The corner of this page?

Now the book always opens
To the same place. And then it's strange:
It's as if from the moment of farewell,
The years have not passed beyond recall.

Oh, whoever said that the heart is of stone,
Certainly knew: it is made of fire...
I'll never understand, were you close to me
Or did you only love me?

1911

———

—to Vera Ivanova-Shvarsalon

The park was filled with light mist,
And the gaslight flared at the gate.
I remember only a certain gaze
From ingenuous, tranquil eyes.

Твоя печаль, для всех неявная,
Мне сразу сделалась близка,
И поняла ты, что отравная
И душная во мне тоска.

Я этот день люблю и праздную,
Приду, как только позовешь.
Меня, и грешную и праздную,
Лишь ты одна не упрекнешь.

Апрель 1911

————

Zh. 42

Я живу, как кукушка в часах,
Не завидую птицам в лесах.
Заведут — и кукую.
Знаешь, долю такую
Лишь врагу
Пожелать я могу.

7 марта 1911
Царское Село

————

Zh. 43

ПОХОРОНЫ

Я места ищу для могилы.
Не знаешь ли, где светлей?
Так холодно в поле. Унылы
У моря груды камней.

Your sorrow, unperceived by all the rest,
Immediately drew me close,
And you understood that yearning
Was poisoning and stifling me.

I love this day and I'm celebrating,
I will come as soon as you invite me.
And sinful and idle, I know
That you alone will not indict me.

April 1911

———

I live like a cuckoo in a clock,
I'm not jealous of the forest birds.
They wind me up—and I cuckoo.
You know—such a fate
I could only wish
For someone I hate.

March 7, 1911
Tsarskoye Selo

———

Funeral

I'm looking for a place for a grave.
Do you know of somewhere brighter?
It's so cold in the fields. And dreary are
The heaps of stones along the shore.

А она привыкла к покою
И любит солнечный свет.
Я келью над ней построю,
Как дом наш на много лет.

Между окнами будет дверца,
Лампадку внутри зажжем,
Как будто темное сердце
Алым горит огнем.

Она бредила, знаешь, больная,
Про иной, про небесный край,
Но сказал монах, укоряя:
«Не для вас, не для грешных рай».

И тогда, побелев от боли,
Прошептала: «Уйду с тобой».
Вот одни мы теперь, на воле,
И у ног голубой прибой.

22 сентября 1911

Zh. 44

САД

Он весь сверкает и хрустит,
Обледенелый сад.
Ушедший от меня грустит,
Но нет пути назад.

И солнца бледный тусклый лик —
Лишь круглое окно;
Я тайно знаю, чей двойник
Приник к нему давно.

But she is accustomed to peace,
And she loves the light of the sun.
I'll build a cell over her,
To be our home for many years.

Between the windows will be a little door,
We will light an icon lamp inside,
It will be like a dark heart
Burning with a vermilion fire.

She raved, you know, when she was sick,
About another, a heavenly place,
But a monk said, reproaching her:
"Not for you; sinners don't go to Paradise."

And then, white with pain,
She whispered: "I will go with you."
Now we are all alone, and free,
With the blue surf at our feet.

September 22, 1911

———

The Garden

The whole ice-covered garden
Sparkles and cracks.
Having left me, he is mournful,
But there's no way back.

And the sun is a pale, wan face—
Only a round window;
Mysteriously, I know whose double
Pressed against it long ago.

Здесь мой покой навеки взят
Предчувствием беды,
Сквозь тонкий лед еще сквозят
Вчерашние следы.

Склонился тусклый мертвый лик
К немому сну полей,
И замирает острый крик
Отсталых журавлей.

1911
Царское Село

———

Zh. 45

НАД ВОДОЙ

Стройный мальчик пастушок,
Видишь, я в бреду.
Помню плащ и посошок
На свою беду.
Если встану — упаду,
Дудочка поет: ду-ду!

Мы прощались, как во сне,
Я сказала: «Жду».
Он, смеясь, ответил мне:
«Встретимся в аду».
Если встану — упаду,
Дудочка поет: ду-ду!

О, глубокая вода
В мельничном пруду,

*

Here a foreboding of trouble
Forever destroys my peace,
Yesterday's footprints are still visible
Through the thin ice.

The wan, dead face bows
Over the mute sleep of the fields,
And the sharp cry
Of the cranes left behind dies away.

1911
Tsarskoye Selo

———

Over the Water

Handsome shepherd boy,
See, I'm delirious.
I remember your cloak and staff
At great cost.
If I stand up—I'll fall,
The pipe sings: loo-loo!

We said good-bye as if in a dream.
I said: "I will wait."
He, laughing, answered me:
"We will meet in hell."
If I stand up—I'll fall.
The pipe sings: loo-loo!

O deep water
Of the millpond,

*

Не от горя, от стыда
Я к тебе приду.
И без крика упаду,
А вдали звучит ду-ду.

⟨1911⟩

———

Zh. 46

Три раза пытать приходила.
Я с криком тоски просыпалась
И видела тонкие руки
И темный насмешливый рот.
— «Ты с кем на заре целовалась,
Клялась, что погибнешь в разлуке,
И жгучую радость таила,
Рыдая у черных ворот?
Кого ты на смерть проводила,
Тот скоро, о, скоро умрет».
Был голос, как крик ястребиный,
Но странно на чей-то похожий.
Все тело мое изгибалось,
Почувствовав смертную дрожь,
И плотная сеть паутины
Упала, окутала ложе...
О, ты не напрасно смеялась,
Моя непрощенная ложь!

16 февраля 1911
Царское Село

———

Not from grief, but shame,
I have come to you.
And without a cry I'll fall,
And from far-off comes the sound: loo-loo.

(1911)

————

Three times it came to torment me.
I woke with an anguished cry
And saw slender hands
And a dark, mocking mouth:
"Who were you kissing at sunrise,
Swearing that you would perish at parting
And, hiding your burning joy,
Sobbing at the back entrance way?
He whom you saw to his death
Will soon, oh soon, be dead."
It was a voice like a falcon's cry,
But strangely familiar.
My whole body curved,
Having felt death's chill,
And a dense, congealed spiderweb
Fell and shrouded the bed...
Oh, you didn't laugh in vain,
My unforgiven lie!

February 16, 1911
Tsarskoye Selo

————

⟨ДОПОЛНЕНИЯ⟩

Zh. 47

Молюсь оконному лучу, —
Он бледен, тонок, прям.
Сегодня я с утра молчу,
А сердце — пополам.
На рукомойнике моем
Позеленела медь.
Но так играет луч на нем,
Что весело глядеть.
Такой невинный и простой
В вечерней тишине,
Но в этой храмине пустой
Он словно праздник золотой
И утешенье мне.

1909

ДВА СТИХОТВОРЕНИЯ

Zh. 48

1.

Подушка уже горяча
С обеих сторон.
Вот и вторая свеча
Гаснет, и крик ворон
Становится все слышней.
Я эту ночь не спала,

*

(ADDITIONS)

I pray to the sunbeam from the window —
It is pale, thin, straight.
Since morning I have been silent,
And my heart — is split.
The copper on my washstand
Has turned green,
But the sunbeam plays on it
So charmingly.
How innocent it is, and simple,
In the evening calm,
But to me in this deserted temple
It's like a golden celebration,
And a consolation.

1909

———

TWO POEMS

1

Both sides of the pillow
Are already hot.
Now even the second candle
Is going out, and the cry of the crows
Gets louder and louder.
I haven't slept all night

*

Поздно думать о сне...
Как нестерпимо бела
Штора на белом окне.
Здравствуй!..

Zh. 49

2.

Тот же голос, тот же взгляд,
Те же волосы льняные.
Все, как год тому назад.
Сквозь стекло лучи дневные
Известь белых стен пестрят...
Свежих лилий аромат
И слова твои простые.

1909

———

ЧИТАЯ «ГАМЛЕТА»

Zh. 50

1

У кладбища направо пылил пустырь,
А за ним голубела река.
Ты сказал мне: «Ну что ж, иди в монастырь
Или замуж за дурака...»
Принцы только такое всегда говорят,
Но я эту запомнила речь.
Пусть струится она сто веков подряд
Горностаевой мантией с плеч.

1909
Киев

And now it's too late to think of sleep...
How unendurably white
Is the blind on the white window.
         Hello!

2

That same voice, that same gaze,
That same flaxen hair.
Everything's just like a year ago.
Through the windowpane the afternoon rays
Splash colors on the whitewashed walls...
The scent of fresh lilies
And your simple words.

1909

READING *HAMLET*

1

Dust rose from the vacant lot to the right of the cemetery,
And behind it the river flashed blue.
You told me: "All right then, get thee to a nunnery,
Or go get married to a fool..."
Only princes make such speeches,
But I remembered those words.
May they flow like an ermine mantle from your shoulders
For hundreds and hundreds of years.

1909
Kiev

Zh. 51

2

И как будто по ошибке
Я сказала: «Ты...»
Озарила тень улыбки
Милые черты.

От подобных оговорок
Всякий вспыхнет взор...
Я люблю тебя, как сорок
Ласковых сестер.

1909

Zh. 52

И когда друг друга проклинали
В страсти, раскаленной добела,
Оба мы еще не понимали,
Как земля для двух людей мала,
И что память яростная мучит,
Пытка сильных — огненный недуг! —
И в ночи бездонной сердце учит
Спрашивать: о, где ушедший друг?
А когда сквозь волны фимиама
Хор гремит, ликуя и грозя,
Смотрят в душу строго и упрямо
Те же неизбежные глаза.

1909

2

And as if by mistake
I used the familiar: "Ty..."
And the shadow of a smile lit up
Your sweet features.

From slips such as these
Such glances can blaze...
I love you like forty
Fond sisters.

1909

———

And when we had cursed each other,
Passionate, white hot,
We still didn't understand
How small the earth can be for two people,
And that memory can torment savagely.
The anguish of the strong—a wasting disease!
And in the endless night the heart learns
To ask: Oh, where is my departed lover?
And when, through waves of incense,
The choir thunders, exulting and threatening,
Those same eyes, inescapable,
Stare sternly and stubbornly into the soul.

1909

———

Zh. 53

ПЕРВОЕ ВОЗВРАЩЕНИЕ

На землю саван тягостный возложен,
Торжественно гудят колокола,
И снова дух смятен и потревожен
Истомной скукой Царского Села.
Пять лет прошло. Здесь всё мертво и немо,
Как будто мира наступил конец.
Как навсегда исчерпанная тема,
В смертельном сне покоится дворец.

1910

Zh. 54

Я и плакала и каялась,
Хоть бы с неба грянул гром!
Сердце темное измаялось
В нежилом дому твоем.
Боль я знаю нестерпимую,
Стыд обратного пути...
Страшно, страшно к нелюбимому,
Страшно к тихому войти.
А склонюсь к нему, нарядная,
Ожерельями звеня, —
Только спросит: «Ненаглядная!
Где молилась за меня?»

1911

First Return

The heavy shroud is placed on the ground,
The solemn bells are droning,
And once again my spirit is troubled and oppressed
By the weary tedium of Tsarskoye Selo.
Five years have passed. Here everything is dead
    and dumb,
As if the end of the world had come.
Like a forever exhausted theme,
The palace comes to rest in its mortal dream.

1910

I wept and repented.
If only thunder would burst from the skies!
My heavy heart was exhausted
In your inhospitable house.
I know the unendurable pain,
The shame of the road back . . .
Terrible, terrible, to return
To the unloved one, the silent one.
If I bend over him, beautifully dressed,
Necklaces ringing—
He'll only ask: "My incomparable beauty!
Where were you praying for me?"

1911

Zh. 55

Меня покинул в новолунье
Мой друг любимый. Ну, так что ж!
Шутил: «Канатная плясунья!
Как ты до мая доживешь?»

Ему ответила, как брату,
Я, не ревнуя, не ропща,
Но не заменят мне утрату
Четыре новые плаща.

Пусть страшен путь мой, пусть опасен,
Еще страшнее путь тоски...
Как мой китайский зонтик красен,
Натерты мелом башмачки!

Оркестр веселое играет,
И улыбаются уста.
Но сердце знает, сердце знает,
Что ложа пятая пуста!

Ноябрь 1911
Царское Село

———

Zh. 56

Мурка, не ходи, там сыч
На подушке вышит,
Мурка серый, не мурлычь,
Дедушка услышит.
Няня, не горит свеча,
И скребутся мыши.
Я боюсь того сыча,
Для чего он вышит?

⟨*1911*⟩

At the new moon he abandoned me,
My beloved friend. Well, so what?
"Rope dancer!" he mocked,
"How will you live until May?"

I answered him as if he were a brother,
Without grumbling, without jealousy,
But four new cloaks
Haven't made up the loss to me.

Frightening and dangerous is the path I walk,
But the path of yearning is more terrible...
How red, my Chinese parasol,
And the soles of my slippers are chalked!

The orchestra strikes up something gay
And my lips smile.
But my heart knows, my heart knows,
The fifth loge is empty!

November 1911
Tsarskoye Selo

———

Moorka, don't go, see the owl
Embroidered on the pillow,
Moorka gray, don't purr,
Grandfather will hear.
Nanny, the candle's not burning,
And the mice are scratching.
I'm afraid of that owl,
Why did they embroider him?

(1911)

PETERSBURG

But not for anything would we exchange this splendid
Granite city of fame and calamity,
The wide rivers of glistening ice,
The sunless, gloomy gardens,
And, barely audible, the Muse's voice.

1

2

3

4

5

6

1. *The Summer Gardens*

2. *Grille of the Summer Gardens*

3. *Winter Canal*

4. *Stone Bridge over Griboyedov Canal*

5. *Railings of Griboyedov Canal*

6. *Moika Embankment*

7. *Blue Bridge over Moika River, and St. Isaac's Cathedral*

8. *Railings of the Russian Museum*

ALL PHOTOGRAPHS BY N. CHAPLIN

АННА АХМАТОВА.

ЧЕТКИ.

СТИХИ.

ROSARY

(1914)

*Прости ж навек! Но знай,
что двух виновных,
не одного, найдутся имена
в стихах моих, в преданиях
любовных.*

Баратынский

*Good-bye then, forever! But know
that the names of two guilty ones,
not just one, will be found
in my poems, in these legends
of love.*

Baratynsky

I

СМЯТЕНИЕ

Zh. 57

1

Было душно от жгучего света,
А взгляды его как лучи.
Я только вздрогнула: этот
Может меня приручить.
Наклонился — он что-то скажет...
От лица отхлынула кровь.
Пусть камнем надгробным ляжет
На жизни моей любовь.

Zh. 58

2

Не любишь, не хочешь смотреть?
О, как ты красив, проклятый!
И я не могу взлететь,
А с детства была крылатой.
Мне очи застит туман,
Сливаются вещи и лица,
И только красный тюльпан,
Тюльпан у тебя в петлице.

Zh. 59

3

Как велит простая учтивость,
Подошел ко мне, улыбнулся,
Полуласково, полулениво

*

I

CONFUSION

1

It was stifling in the burning light,
And his glances—like rays.
I merely shuddered: this one
Could tame me.
He bowed—he will say something...
The blood drained from my face.
Let love be the gravestone
Lying on my life.

2

Don't you love me, don't you want to look at me?
Oh, how handsome you are, damn you!
And I can no longer fly,
I who was winged from childhood.
A mist clouds my eyes,
Things and faces merge and flow,
And there is only the red tulip,
The tulip in your buttonhole.

3

As simple civility demands,
You approached me, you smiled,
And half tenderly, half lazily,

*

Поцелуем руки коснулся —
И загадочных, древних ликов
На меня поглядели очи.

Десять лет замираний и криков,
Все мои бессонные ночи
Я вложила в тихое слово
И сказала его напрасно.
Отошел ты, и стало снова
На душе и пусто и ясно.

1913

Zh. 60

ПРОГУЛКА

Перо задело о верх экипажа.
Я поглядела в глаза его.
Томилось сердце, не зная даже
Причины горя своего.

Безветрен вечер и грустью скован
Под сводом облачных небес,
И словно тушью нарисован
В альбоме старом Булонский лес.

Бензина запах и сирени,
Насторожившийся покой . . .
Он снова тронул мои колени
Почти не дрогнувшей рукой.

Май 1913

With a kiss you brushed my hand—
And the eyes of mysterious, ancient faces
Gazed at me...

Ten years of cries and trepidation,
All my sleepless nights,
I put into one quiet word
And I uttered it—in vain.
You left and once again my soul became
Empty and serene.

1913

_____

Outing

My feather brushed the top of the carriage.
I glanced into his eyes.
My heart ached, not really
Knowing why.

The evening was windless and fettered by sadness
Under the firmament's vault of clouds,
And the Bois de Boulogne looked as if it were drawn
In India ink in some old album.

There's an odor of petrol and lilacs,
Quiet listens expectantly...
With a hand almost not trembling
Once again he touched my knees.

May 1913

_____

ВЕЧЕРОМ

Звенела музыка в саду
Таким невыразимым горем.
Свежо и остро пахли морем
На блюде устрицы во льду.

Он мне сказал: «Я верный друг!»
И моего коснулся платья.
Как не похожи на объятья
Прикосновенья этих рук.

Так гладят кошек или птиц,
Так на наездниц смотрят стройных.
Лишь смех в глазах его спокойных
Под легким золотом ресниц.

А скорбных скрипок голоса
Поют за стелющимся дымом:
«Благослови же небеса —
Ты первый раз одна с любимым».

Март 1913

Все мы бражники здесь, блудницы,
Как невесело вместе нам!
На стенах цветы и птицы
Томятся по облакам.

Ты куришь черную трубку,
Так странен дымок над ней.
Я надела узкую юбку,
Чтоб казаться еще стройней.

In the Evening

The music rang out in the garden
With such inexpressible grief.
Oysters in ice on the plate
Smelled fresh and sharp, of the sea.

He told me: "I am your true friend!"
And he touched my dress.
How unlike a caress,
The touch of those hands.

As one might stroke a cat or a bird,
Or watch slender equestriennes ride...
Under the light gold lashes
There is only laughter in his tranquil eyes.

And the voices of mournful violins
Sing through the drifting smoke:
"Praise heaven above—for the first time
You're alone with the man you love."

March 1913

———

We are all carousers and loose women here;
How unhappy we are together!
The flowers and birds on the wall
Yearn for the clouds.

You are smoking a black pipe,
The puff of smoke has a funny shape.
I've put on my tight skirt
To make myself look still more svelte.

Навсегда забиты окошки.
Что там — изморозь или гроза?
На глаза осторожной кошки
Похожи твои глаза.

О, как сердце мое тоскует!
Не смертного ль часа жду?
А та, что сейчас танцует,
Непременно будет в аду.

1 января 1913

Zh. 63

После ветра и мороза было
Любо мне погреться у огня.
Там за сердцем я не уследила,
И его украли у меня.

Новогодний праздник длится пышно,
Влажны стебли новогодних роз,
А в груди моей уже не слышно
Трепетания стрекоз.

Ах! не трудно угадать мне вора,
Я его узнала по глазам.
Только страшно так, что скоро, скоро
Он вернет свою добычу сам.

Январь 1914

The windows are boarded up forever.
What's out there—hoarfrost or a storm?
Your eyes resemble
The eyes of a cautious cat.

Oh, I am sick at heart!
Isn't it the hour of death I await?
But that woman dancing now
Will be in hell, no doubt.

January 1, 1913

———

After the wind and the frost,
It was pleasant to toast myself at the fire.
But I didn't look after my heart
And it was stolen from me.

New Year's Day stretches out luxuriantly,
The stems of the New Year's roses are moist,
And in my breast I no longer feel
The trembling of dragonflies.

Ah, it's not hard for me to guess the thief,
I recognized him by his eyes.
But it's frightening that soon, soon,
He himself will return his prize.

January 1914

———

Zh. 64

. . . И на ступеньки встретить
Не вышли с фонарем.
В неверном лунном свете
Вошла я в тихий дом.

Под лампою зеленой,
С улыбкой неживой,
Друг шепчет: «Сандрильона,
Как странен голос твой . . .»

В камине гаснет пламя;
Томя, трещит сверчок.
Ах! кто-то взял на память
Мой белый башмачок.

И дал мне три гвоздики,
Не подымая глаз.
О милые улики,
Куда мне спрятать вас?

И сердцу горько верить,
Что близок, близок срок,
Что всем он станет мерить
Мой белый башмачок.

1913

———

Zh. 65

Безвольно пощады просят
Глаза. Что мне делать с ними,
Когда при мне произносят
Короткое, звонкое имя?

...And they didn't come out with lanterns
To meet me on the steps.
By the moon's unfaithful light
I entered the quiet house.

There under the green lamp,
Smiling lifelessly,
My friend whispers: "Cinderella!
How strange your voice is!"

The flame dies in the hearth,
A tiresome cricket chirps away.
Ah! For a souvenir someone took
My little white shoe

And he gave me three carnations,
Not raising his eyes.
O sweet declarations,
Where can I hide you?

And my heart believes bitterly
That soon, very soon,
He will measure everyone's foot
With my little white shoe.

1913

———

Helplessly, my eyes ask mercy.
What am I to do with them
When someone near me utters
His short, ringing name?

Иду по тропинке в поле
Вдоль серых сложенных бревен.
Здесь легкий ветер на воле
По-весеннему свеж, неровен.

И томное сердце слышит
Тайную весть о дальнем.
Я знаю: он жив, он дышит,
Он смеет быть не печальным.

1912
Царское Село

Zh. 66

Покорно мне воображенье
В изображеньи серых глаз.
В моем тверском уединеньи
Я горько вспоминаю вас.

Прекрасных рук счастливый пленник
На левом берегу Невы,
Мой знаменитый современник,
Случилось, как хотели вы,

Вы, приказавший мне: довольно,
Поди, убей свою любовь!
И вот я таю, я безвольна,
Но все сильней скучает кровь.

И если я умру, то кто же
Мои стихи напишет вам,
Кто стать звенящими поможет
Еще не сказанным словам?

Июль 1913
Слепнево

I follow the path through the field,
Past gray timbers piled high.
Out here, the breeze blows fitfully,
As in springtime—fresh, free.

And my suffering heart hears
Secret news of the one far away.
I know: he lives, he breathes,
He has the audacity not to grieve.

1912
Tsarskoye Selo

My imagination obeys me
By portraying your gray eyes.
In my solitude here in Tver,
I remember you bitterly.

Happy captive in somebody's beautiful arms,
There on the Neva's left bank,
My famous contemporary,
You got what you wanted,

You, who commanded me: Enough,
Come now, kill your love!
And I, weak-willed, I am wasting away,
But stronger and stronger beats my blood.

And if I die, then who
Will write my poems to you,
Who will help
My still unspoken words ring out?

July 1913
Slepnyovo

Zh. 67

ОТРЫВОК

...И кто-то, во мраке дерев незримый,
Зашуршал опавшей листвой
И крикнул: «Что сделал с тобой любимый,
Что сделал любимый твой!

Словно тронуты черной, густою тушью
Тяжелые веки твои.
Он предал тебя тоске и удушью
Отравительницы любви.

Ты давно перестала считать уколы —
Грудь мертва под острой иглой.
И напрасно стараешься быть веселой —
Легче в гроб тебе лечь живой!..»

Я сказала обидчику: «Хитрый, черный,
Верно, нет у тебя стыда.
Он тихий, он нежный, он мне покорный,
Влюбленный в меня навсегда!»

1912

Zh. 68

Настоящую нежность не спутаешь
Ни с чем, и она тиха.
Ты напрасно бережно кутаешь
Мне плечи и грудь в меха.
И напрасно слова покорные

*

Fragment

... And someone invisible in the gloom of the trees
Rustled the fallen leaves
And cried: "What has your lover done to you,
What has your lover done?

Your eyelids are heavy, as if outlined
With thick, black India ink.
He has betrayed you to the torment and suffocation
Of the poisoner love.

Long ago you stopped counting the stabs—
Your breast is dead to the needle's jabs.
And it's useless to try to be happy—
Better to lie down alive in your grave!.."

I told this tempter: "Devil, dissembler,
It's true, you have no shame.
He is silent, he is submissive, he is tender,
In love with me forever!"

1912

———

One would not mistake true tenderness
For this. It is quiet.
In vain you solicitously wrap
My shoulders and my breast with furs.
And in vain you utter respectful words

*

Говоришь о первой любви.
Как я знаю эти упорные,
Несытые взгляды твои!

Декабрь 1913
Царское Село

————

Zh. 69

Не будем пить из одного стакана
Ни воду мы, ни сладкое вино,
Не поцелуемся мы утром рано,
А ввечеру не поглядим в окно.
Ты дышишь солнцем, я дышу луною,
Но живы мы любовию одною.

Со мной всегда мой верный, нежный друг,
С тобой твоя веселая подруга,
Но мне понятен серых глаз испуг,
И ты виновник моего недуга.
Коротких мы не учащаем встреч.
Так наш покой нам суждено беречь.

Лишь голос твой поет в моих стихах,
В твоих стихах мое дыханье веет.
О, есть костер, которого не смеет
Коснуться ни забвение, ни страх...
И если б знал ты, как сейчас мне любы
Твои сухие, розовые губы!

1913

————

About the first love.
How well I know those persistent,
Unsatisfied glances of yours!

December 1913
Tsarskoye Selo

———

We will not drink, from the same glass,
Either water or sweet wine,
We will not kiss at early morning,
Nor look out, at night, from the same window.
You breathe by the sun, I breathe by the moon,
But the same love keeps us alive.

My tender, true friend is always with me,
And your merry friend is with you,
But I understand the fright in your gray eyes
And you are the cause of my pain.
We don't make our short meetings more frequent.
Thus our fate looks after our peace of mind.

At least your voice sings in my verses,
In your verses my breath beats.
Oh, there is a fire beyond the reach
Of oblivion or fear. . .
And if only you knew how dear to me now
Are your dry, rosy lips, how dear.

1913

———

У меня есть улыбка одна.
Так, движенье чуть видное губ.
Для тебя я ее берегу —
Ведь она мне любовью дана.
Все равно, что ты наглый и злой,
Все равно, что ты любишь других.
Предо мной золотой аналой,
И со мной сероглазый жених.

1913

Столько просьб у любимой всегда!
У разлюбленной просьб не бывает.
Как я рада, что нынче вода
Под бесцветным ледком замирает.

И я стану — Христос помоги! —
На покров этот светлый и ломкий,
А ты письма мои береги,
Чтобы нас рассудили потомки,

Чтоб отчетливей и ясней
Ты был виден им, мудрый и смелый.
В биографии славной твоей
Разве можно оставить пробелы?

Слишком сладко земное питье,
Слишком плотны любовные сети.
Пусть когда-нибудь имя мое
Прочитают в учебнике дети,

I have a certain smile:
Like this, a barely visible movement of the lips.
I am keeping it for you —
Love gave it to me, after all.
Never mind that you are insolent and evil,
Never mind that you love others.
Before me is the golden lectern,
And beside me is my gray-eyed bridegroom.

1913

———

How many demands the beloved can make!
The woman discarded, none.
How glad I am that today the water
Under the colorless ice is motionless.

And I stand — Christ help me! —
On this shroud that is brittle and bright,
But save my letters
So that our descendants can decide,

So that you, courageous and wise,
Will be seen by them with greater clarity.
Perhaps we may leave some gaps
In your glorious biography?

Too sweet is earthly drink,
Too tight the nets of love.
Sometime let the children read
My name in their lesson book,

И, печальную повесть узнав,
Пусть они улыбнутся лукаво . . .
Мне любви и покоя не дав,
Подари меня горькою славой.

1913

―――

Zh. 72

В последний раз мы встретились тогда
На набережной, где всегда встречались.
Была в Неве высокая вода,
И наводненья в городе боялись.

Он говорил о лете и о том,
Что быть поэтом женщине — нелепость.
Как я запомнила высокий царский дом
И Петропавловскую крепость! —

Затем, что воздух был совсем не наш,
А как подарок Божий — так чудесен.
И в этот час была мне отдана
Последняя из всех безумных песен.

Январь 1914

―――

Zh. 73

Здравствуй! Легкий шелест слышишь
Справа от стола?
Этих строчек не допишешь —
Я к тебе пришла.
Неужели ты обидишь

*

And on learning the sad story,
Let them smile slyly...
Since you've given me neither love nor peace,
Grant me bitter glory.

1913

———

We met for the last time
On the embankment, where we had always met.
The Neva was high
And they were afraid the city would flood.

He spoke of the summer, and he also said
That for a woman to be a poet was—absurd.
I can still see the tsar's tall palace
And the Peter and Paul fortress!—

Because the air was not ours at all,
But like a gift from God—so miraculous.
And at that moment was given to me
The latest of all my mad songs.

January 1914

———

Hello! Do you hear the light rustling
To the right of your desk?
You won't finish writing these lines—
I've come to you.
Are you really going to hurt my feelings

*

Так, как в прошлый раз, —
Говоришь, что рук не видишь,
Рук моих и глаз.
У тебя светло и просто.
Не гони меня туда,
Где под душным сводом моста
Стынет грязная вода.

Октябрь 1913

II

Zh. 74

Цветов и неживых вещей
Приятен запах в этом доме.
У грядок груды овощей
Лежат, пестры, на черноземе.

Еще струится холодок,
Но с парников снята рогожа.
Там есть прудок, такой прудок,
Где тина на парчу похожа.

А мальчик мне сказал, боясь,
Совсем взволнованно и тихо,
Что там живет большой карась
И с ним большая карасиха.

1913

The same way you did last time—
Saying that you don't see hands,
My hands and eyes?
Here in your room it is simple and bright.
Don't drive me there
Where under the stifling vault of the bridge
The dirty water is turning to ice.

October 1913

———

II

In this house there's a pleasant smell
Of flowers and inanimate things.
In the garden, mounds of vegetables
Lie, gaudy against the rich black soil.

The cold still streams,
But the matting has been taken off the glass frames.
There's a little pond down there, the kind of pond
Where the slime resembles brocade.

And a little boy, frightened, told me,
In a voice of such quiet distress,
That in it lives a giant carp
And with him a giant carp-ess.

1913

———

Zh. 75

Каждый день по-новому тревожен,
Всё сильнее запах спелой ржи.
Если ты к ногам моим положен,
Ласковый, лежи.

Иволги кричат в широких кленах,
Их ничем до ночи не унять.
Любо мне от глаз твоих зеленых
Ос веселых отгонять.

На дороге бубенец зазвякал —
Памятен нам этот легкий звук.
Я спою тебе, чтоб ты не плакал,
Песенку о вечере разлук.

1913

Zh. 76

Мальчик сказал мне: «Как это больно!»
И мальчика очень жаль...
Еще так недавно он был довольным
И только слыхал про печаль.

А теперь он знает всё не хуже
Мудрых и старых вас.
Потускнели и, кажется, стали у́же
Зрачки ослепительных глаз.

Я знаю: он с болью своей не сладит,
С горькой болью первой любви.
Как беспомощно, жадно и жарко гладит
Холодные руки мои.

Октябрь 1913

Each day is anxious all over again,
The smell of ripe rye ever stronger.
If you are placed at my feet,
Sweetheart, just lie there.

In the wide maples, orioles shrill,
And nothing but nighttime will make them still.
What fun to fan the merry wasps away
From your green eyes.

Coach bells are jingling on the highway—
For us this gentle sound has memories.
I'll sing to you, so you don't cry,
A little song about the evening of the last good-bye.

1913

The boy said to me: "How this hurts!"
And I pitied the boy so...
Just a short time ago he was content
And had only heard about sorrow.

But now he knows everything, the same
As you who are older and wise.
It seems as if the pupils of his dazzled eyes
Have contracted and dimmed.

I understand: he can't manage his pain,
First love's bitter pain.
How helplessly, avidly, ardently he strokes
My cold hands.

October 1913

Zh. 77

Высокие своды костела
Синей, чем небесная твердь...
Прости меня, мальчик веселый,
Что я принесла тебе смерть —

За розы с площадки круглой,
За глупые письма твои,
За то, что, дерзкий и смуглый,
Мутно бледнел от любви.

Я думала: ты нарочно —
Как взрослые хочешь быть.
Я думала: томно-порочных
Нельзя, как невест, любить.

Но всё оказалось напрасно.
Когда пришли холода,
Следил ты уже бесстрастно
За мной везде и всегда,

Как будто копил приметы
Моей нелюбви. Прости!
Зачем ты принял обеты
Страдальческого пути?

И смерть к тебе руки простерла...
Скажи, что было потом?
Я не знала, как хрупко горло
Под синим воротником.

Прости меня, мальчик веселый,
Совенок замученный мой!
Сегодня мне из костела
Так трудно уйти домой.

Ноябрь 1913

The high vaults of the Polish church
Are bluer than the firmament . . .
Forgive me, merry boy,
For bringing you death —

For the roses from the oval garden,
For your foolish letters,
For the fact that, dark and impudent,
You grew dull and pale from love.

I thought: you're doing this on purpose —
You want to be like the grownups.
I thought: it's impossible to love a loose woman
As if she were a bride.

But all this was in vain.
When the cold came,
You trailed me impassively,
Always and everywhere,

As if amassing the tokens
Of my indifference. Forgive me!
Why did you take a vow
To follow the path of suffering?

And death reached out its hands to you . . .
Tell me, what happened then?
I didn't know how fragile the throat
Under the collar's dark blue.

Forgive me, merry boy,
My tormented little owl!
Today how reluctant I am
To leave the church and go home.

November 1913

———

М. *Лозинскому*

Он длится без конца — янтарный, тяжкий день!
Как невозможна грусть, как тщетно ожиданье!
И снова голосом серебряным олень
В зверинце говорит о северном сиянье.
И я поверила, что есть прохладный снег,
И синяя купель для тех, кто нищ и болен,
И санок маленьких такой неверный бег
Под звоны древние далеких колоколен.

1913

ГОЛОС ПАМЯТИ

О. А. Глебовой-Судейкиной

Что ты видишь, тускло на стену смотря,
В час, когда на небе поздняя заря?

Чайку ли на синей скатерти воды,
Или флорентийские сады?

Или парк огромный Царского Села,
Где тебе тревога путь пересекла?

Иль того ты видишь у своих колен,
Кто для белой смерти твой покинул плен?

Нет, я вижу стену только — и на ней
Отсветы небесных гаснущих огней.

18 июня 1913
Слепнево

—to M. Lozinsky

It drags on forever—this heavy, amber day!
How insufferable is grief, how futile the wait!
And once more comes the silver voice of the deer
From the menagerie, telling of the northern lights.
And I, too, believed that somewhere there was cold snow,
And a bright blue font for the poor and the ill,
And the unsteady dash of little sleighs
Under the ancient droning of distant bells.

1913

———

The Voice of Memory

—to O.A. Glebova-Sudeikina

What are you looking at, staring dully at the wall,
In the hour when the sunset lingers in the sky?

A seagull on the blue tablecloth of the sea,
Or Florentine gardens?

Or the enormous park at Tsarskoye Selo,
Where desperation crossed your path?

Or do you see him at your knees,
The one who broke your spell for white death?

No, I see only the wall—and on it
The gleam of the guttering heavenly flame.

June 18, 1913
Slepnyovo

Zh. 80

Я научилась просто, мудро жить,
Смотреть на небо и молиться Богу,
И долго перед вечером бродить,
Чтоб утомить ненужную тревогу.

Когда шуршат в овраге лопухи
И никнет гроздь рябины желто-красной,
Слагаю я веселые стихи
О жизни тленной, тленной и прекрасной.

Я возвращаюсь. Лижет мне ладонь
Пушистый кот, мурлыкает умильней,
И яркий загорается огонь
На башенке озерной лесопильни.

Лишь изредка прорезывает тишь
Крик аиста, слетевшего на крышу.
И если в дверь мою ты постучишь,
Мне кажется, я даже не услышу.

1912

Zh. 81

Здесь всё то же, то же, что и прежде,
Здесь напрасным кажется мечтать.
В доме у дороги непроезжей
Надо рано ставни запирать.

Тихий дом мой пуст и неприветлив,
Он на лес глядит одним окном.
В нем кого-то вынули из петли
И бранили мертвого потом.

I've learned to live simply, wisely,
To look at the sky and pray to God,
And to take long walks before evening
To wear out this useless anxiety.

When the burdocks rustle in the ravine
And the yellow-red clusters of rowan nod,
I compose happy verses
About mortal life, mortal and beautiful life.

I return. The fluffy cat
Licks my palm and sweetly purrs.
And on the turret of the sawmill by the lake
A bright flame flares.

The quiet is cut, occasionally,
By the cry of a stork landing on the roof.
And if you were to knock at my door,
It seems to me I wouldn't even hear.

1912

———

Here everything is the same as before, just the same,
Here it seems useless to dream.
In a house on a seldom-traveled road,
One must close the shutters early.

My silent house is empty and unfriendly,
Through one window it peers at the woods.
In it someone was cut from a noose
And afterwards the body was cursed.

Был он грустен или тайно весел,
Только смерть — большое торжество.
На истертом красном плюше кресел
Изредка мелькает тень его.

И часы с кукушкой ночи рады,
Всё слышней их четкий разговор.
В щелочку смотрю я: конокрады
Зажигают под холмом костер.

И, пророча близкое ненастье,
Низко, низко стелется дымок.
Мне не страшно. Я ношу на счастье
Темно-синий шелковый шнурок.

Май 1912

Zh. 82

БЕССОННИЦА

Где-то кошки жалобно мяукают,
Звук шагов я издали ловлю...
Хорошо твои слова баюкают:
Третий месяц я от них не сплю.

Ты опять, опять со мной, бессонница!
Неподвижный лик твой узнаю.
Что, красавица, что, беззаконница?
Разве плохо я тебе пою?

Whether he was melancholy or secretly happy,
There remains only death—the great victory.
On the worn, red plush of the armchairs
His shadow flickers occasionally.

And the cuckoo clock is happy at night,
Its precise conversation more audible.
I watch through a chink: horse thieves
Are lighting a campfire at the foot of the hill.

And, foretelling foul weather,
The smoke creeps low along the ground.
I'm not afraid. I wear for luck
A dark blue cord of silk.

May 1912

———

Insomnia

Somewhere cats are mewing pitifully,
I catch the sound of distant steps. . . .
Your words are a wonderful lullaby:
Because of them for three months I haven't slept.

Insomnia, you are with me again, again!
I recognize your fixed countenance.
What is it, my outlaw, what is it, my pretty one,
Do I sing so badly to you?

Окна тканью белою завешены,
Полумрак струится голубой...
Или дальней вестью мы утешены?
Отчего мне так легко с тобой?

Зима 1912
Царское Село

Zh. 83

Ты знаешь, я томлюсь в неволе,
О смерти господа моля.
Но всё мне памятна до боли
Тверская скудная земля.

Журавль у ветхого колодца,
Над ним, как кипень, облака,
В полях скрипучие воротца,
И запах хлеба, и тоска.

И те неяркие просторы,
Где даже голос ветра слаб,
И осуждающие взоры
Спокойных, загорелых баб.

Осень 1913

Zh. 84

Углем наметил на левом боку
Место, куда стрелять,
Чтоб выпустить птицу, мою тоску,
В пустынную ночь опять.

White cloth curtains the windows,
Dim light streams blue...
Or are we being consoled by news from afar?
Why do I feel so at ease with you?

Winter 1912
Tsarskoye Selo

———

You know, I languish in captivity,
Praying to the Lord for death.
But I remember, to the point of pain,
Tver's barren, meager earth.

The crane on the decrepit well,
Over it, boiling, the clouds,
In the field a creaking little gate,
And the smell of wheat, and weariness.

And those pale expanses,
Where even the voice of the wind is weak,
And the condemning way
Those quiet, sunburnt peasant women look at me.

Autumn 1913

———

He made a charcoal mark on the left side,
The place he would shoot
To release the bird, my anguish,
Once more into the empty night.

Милый! не дрогнет твоя рука,
И мне недолго терпеть.
Вылетит птица — моя тоска,
Сядет на ветку и станет петь.

Чтоб тот, кто спокоен в своем дому,
Раскрывши окно, сказал:
«Голос знакомый, а слов не пойму» —
И опустил глаза.

31 января 1914
Петербург

III

Zh. 85

Помолись о нищей, о потерянной,
О моей живой душе,
Ты, в своих путях всегда уверенный,
Свет узревший в шалаше.

И тебе, печально-благодарная,
Я за это расскажу потом,
Как меня томила ночь угарная,
Как дышало утро льдом.

В этой жизни я немного видела,
Только пела и ждала.
Знаю: брата я не ненавидела
И сестры не предала.

Darling! Your hand will not falter,
And I won't suffer for long.
The bird—my anguish—will fly out,
Sit on a branch and begin to sing.

So that he, in the quiet of his home,
Opening a window, will say:
"The voice is familiar, but I can't catch the words,"—
And lower his eyes.

January 31, 1914
Petersburg

———

III

I ask you to pray for my poor, my perplexed,
For my living soul,
You, always certain of your path,
Having seen light shining from the hut.

And then, sadly grateful,
I will relate to you
How the night of ecstasy exhausted me,
How the morning breathed ice.

I saw little of this life,
I only sang and waited.
I know I didn't hate my brother
And I didn't betray my sister.

Отчего же Бог меня наказывал
Каждый день и каждый час?
Или это Ангел мне указывал
Свет, невидимый для нас?

Май 1912
Флоренция

———

Zh. 86

Вижу выцветший флаг над таможней
И над городом желтую муть.
Вот уж сердце мое осторожней
Замирает, и больно вздохнуть.

Стать бы снова приморской девчонкой,
Туфли на босу ногу надеть,
И закладывать косы коронкой,
И взволнованным голосом петь.

Все глядеть бы на смуглые главы
Херсонесского храма с крыльца
И не знать, что от счастья и славы
Безнадежно дряхлеют сердца.

Осень 1913

———

Zh. 87

Плотно сомкнуты губы сухие.
Жарко пламя трех тысяч свечей.
Так лежала княжна Евдокия
На душистой сапфирной парче.

Why then did God punish me
Every day and every hour?
Or was this an angel showing me
A world that none of us can see?

May 1912
Florence

———

I see the faded flag above the customhouse
And over the city, a yellow murk.
Now my cautious heart
Slows down, and breathing hurts.

To become that seaside girl again,
With sandals on my feet,
And to heap my braids up in a crown,
And to sing in a troubled voice.

To be gazing still from the porch
At the dark cupolas of the Khersones church,
And not to know that from happiness and fame
The spirit inevitably wears away.

Autumn 1913

———

The dry lips are tightly closed,
Three thousand candles fiercely ablaze.
Thus lay the Princess Eudoxia
On sweet–scented, sapphire brocade.

И, согнувшись, бесслезно молилась
Ей о слепеньком мальчике мать,
И кликуша без голоса билась,
Воздух силясь губами поймать.

А пришедший из южного края
Черноглазый, горбатый старик,
Словно к двери небесного рая,
К потемневшей ступеньке приник.

Осень 1913

Zh. 88

Дал Ты мне молодость трудную.
Столько печали в пути.
Как же мне душу скудную
Богатой Тебе принести?
Долгую песню, льстивая,
О славе поет судьба.
Господи! я нерадивая,
Твоя скупая раба.
Ни розою, ни былинкою
Не буду в садах Отца.
Я дрожу над каждой соринкою,
Над каждым словом глупца.

19 декабря 1912

And bowing down, the tearless mother prayed
To her for her blind son,
And a hysteric, voiceless, struggled,
Trying to seize air with her lips.

And a stranger from the south,
A hunchbacked old man with dark eyes,
Was pressed against the darkening steps,
As if against the door of Paradise.

Autumn 1913

———

You gave me a difficult youth.
So much sadness in my path.
How can such a barren soul
Bear gifts to You?
Flattering fate
Sings a long song of praise.
Lord! I am negligent,
Your stingy servant.
Neither a rose nor a blade of grass
Will I be in my Father's garden.
I tremble at every mote of dust,
Before the words of any dunce.

December 19, 1912

———

Zh. 89

8 НОЯБРЯ 1913

Солнце комнату наполнило
Пылью желтой и сквозной.
Я проснулась и припомнила:
Милый, нынче праздник твой.
Оттого и оснеженная
Даль за окнами тепла,
Оттого и я, бессонная,
Как причастница спала.

———

Zh. 90

Ты пришел меня утешить, милый,
Самый нежный, самый кроткий...
От подушки приподняться нету силы,
А на окнах частые решетки.

Мертвой, думал, ты меня застанешь,
И принес веночек неискусный.
Как улыбкой сердце больно ранишь,
Ласковый, насмешливый и грустный.

Что теперь мне смертное томленье!
Если ты еще со мной побудешь,
Я у Бога вымолю прощенье
И тебе, и всем, кого ты любишь.

Май 1913
Петербург

———

November 8, 1913

Sun filled the room
With a yellow, transparent haze.
I woke up and remembered:
Darling, it's your nameday.
Because of this even the snowy
Distances beyond the windows are warm,
Because of this even I, insomniac that I am,
Have slept like a communicant.

———

You've come to comfort me, darling,
Most tender, most gentle...
No strength to raise myself from the pillow,
And a close-worked lattice across the windows.

You thought you would find me dead,
And you brought an artless little wreath.
How painfully you wound my heart with a smile,
Affectionate, mocking and sad.

What is the weight of death to me now!
If you stay with me awhile,
I'll implore God to forgive
You, and all those you love.

May 1913
Petersburg

Zh. 91

Умирая, томлюсь о бессмертьи.
Низко облако пыльной мглы...
Пусть хоть голые красные черти,
Пусть хоть чан зловонной смолы.

Приползайте ко мне, лукавьте,
Угрозы из ветхих книг,
Только память вы мне оставьте,
Только память в последний миг.

Чтоб в томительной веренице
Не чужим показался ты,
Я готова платить сторицей
За улыбки и за мечты.

Смертный час, наклонясь, напоит
Прозрачною сулемой.
А люди придут, зароют
Мое тело и голос мой.

1912
Царское Село

Zh. 92

Ты письмо мое, милый, не комкай.
До конца его, друг, прочти.
Надоело мне быть незнакомкой,
Быть чужой на твоем пути.

Не гляди так, не хмурься гневно.
Я любимая, я твоя.
Не пастушка, не королевна
И уже не монашенка я —

Dying, I am tormented by immortality.
There's a low-hanging cloud of dusty haze...
Let there be naked red devils,
Let there be vats of stinking pitch.

Crawl up to me, play your tricks,
Your threats from antiquated books,
Only leave me my memory,
Only, at the last gasp, my memory.

So that you won't be a stranger to me
In the agonizing line,
I am ready to pay a hundredfold
For a smile and for a dream.

The hour of death, bowing, slakes my thirst
With clear, corrosive lye.
And people come and bury
My body and my voice.

1912
Tsarskoye Selo

———

Darling, don't crumple my letter,
Read it through, my friend, to the end.
I've had enough of being unknown,
The strange one on your path.

Don't look like that, that angry frown.
I'm your beloved, I'm yours.
Neither shepherdess nor queen
And no longer a nun, I—

В этом сером, будничном платье,
На стоптанных каблуках...
Но, как прежде, жгуче объятье,
Тот же страх в огромных глазах.

Ты письмо мое, милый, не комкай,
Не плачь о заветной лжи,
Ты его в твоей бедной котомке
На самое дно положи.

1912
Царское Село

———

Zh. 93

ИСПОВЕДЬ

Умолк простивший мне грехи.
Лиловый сумрак гасит свечи,
И темная епитрахиль
Накрыла голову и плечи.

Не тот ли голос: «Дева! встань».
Удары сердца чаще, чаще...
Прикосновение сквозь ткань
Руки, рассеянно крестящей.

1911
Царское Село

———

In this everyday gray dress,
On rundown heels...
But, as before, the burning embrace,
The same fear in enormous eyes.

Darling, don't crumple my letter,
Don't cry over intimate lies.
Put it in your poor old knapsack,
There, at the very bottom, let it lie.

1912
Tsarskoye Selo

———

Confession

Having forgiven me my sins, he fell silent.
In the violet dusk candles sputtered,
And a dark prayer stole
Covered my head and my shoulders.

Isn't that the voice that said: "Maiden! Arise..."
My heart beats faster, faster.
The touch, through the cloth,
Of a hand absently making the sign of the cross.

1911
Tsarskoye Selo

———

Zh. 94

В ремешках пенал и книги были,
Возвращалась я домой из школы.
Эти липы, верно, не забыли
Нашу встречу, мальчик мой веселый.

Только, ставши лебедем надменным,
Изменился серый лебеденок.
А на жизнь мою лучом нетленным
Грусть легла, и голос мой незвонок.

1912
Царское Село

Zh. 95

Со дня Купальницы-Аграфены
Малиновый платок хранит.
Молчит, а ликует, как Царь Давид.
В морозной келье белы стены,
И с ним никто не говорит.

Приду и стану на порог,
Скажу: «Отдай мне мой платок!»

Осень 1913
Царское Село

Zh. 96

Я с тобой не стану пить вино,
Оттого что ты мальчишка озорной.
Знаю я — у вас заведено
С кем попало целоваться под луной.

With my pencil case and books in a bookstrap,
I was walking home from school.
Surely these lindens haven't forgotten
Our meeting, my lighthearted lad.

But the little gray cygnet changed,
Became a haughty swan,
And an undying ray of sorrow lay
On my life, and my voice ceased to sound.

1912
Tsarskoye Selo

———

Since Agrafena-Kupalnitsa's
He has kept my raspberry kerchief.
He is silent but triumphant, like King David.
The walls of his frosty cell are white,
And nobody talks to him.

I shall go and stand in the doorway.
"Give me back my kerchief!" I shall say.

Autumn 1913
Tsarskoye Selo

———

I won't start drinking wine with you,
Because you're a naughty boy.
I know—it's a custom where you come from
To kiss anyone under the sun.

А у нас тишь да гладь,
Божья благодать.

А у нас светлых глаз
Нет приказу подымать.

Декабрь 1913

———

Zh. 97

Вечерние часы перед столом,
Непоправимо белая страница,
Мимоза пахнет Ниццей и теплом,
В луче луны летит большая птица.

И, туго косы на ночь заплетя,
Как будто завтра нужны будут косы,
В окно гляжу я, больше не грустя,
На море, на песчаные откосы.

Какую власть имеет человек,
Который даже нежности не просит!
Я не могу поднять усталых век,
Когда мое он имя произносит.

Лето 1913

———

But we have peace and quiet,
Thanks be to God.

But we have no shining eyes
That rise on command.

December 1913

———

Evening hours at the desk,
The page is completely blank,
The mimosa smells of Nice and warmth,
A large bird flies in the moonlight.

And, plaiting my braids tightly for the night,
As if I must wear them tomorrow,
I look out the window at the sea and the sandbars,
No longer feeling sorrow.

How much power has a man
Who doesn't even ask for tenderness!
I won't be able to raise my weary lids
When he pronounces my name.

Summer 1913

———

IV

Zh. 98

Как вплелась в мои темные косы
Серебристая нежная прядь, —
Только ты, соловей безголосый,
Эту муку сумеешь понять

Чутким слухом далекое слышишь
И на тонкие ветки ракит,
Весь нахохлившись, смотришь — не дышишь,
Если песня чужая звучит.

А еще так недавно, недавно
Замирали вокруг тополя,
И звенела и пела отравно
Несказанная радость твоя.

1912

Zh. 99

«Я пришла тебя сменить, сестра,
У лесного, у высокого костра.

Поседели твои волосы. Глаза
Замутила, затуманила слеза.

Ты уже не понимаешь пенья птиц,
Ты ни звезд не замечаешь, ни зарниц.

И давно удары бубна не слышны,
А я знаю, ты боишься тишины.

IV

Intertwined in my dark braids
Is a delicate, silvery strand—
Only you, voiceless nightingale,
Can understand this torment.

With your keen ear you hear distant sounds
And there on the broom bush's fronds,
All ruffled up, you stare—not breathing,
If a strange song resounds.

But just recently, recently
All the poplars hushed suddenly
And your indescribable joy
Burst out and sang poisonously.

1912

———

"I came to take your place, sister,
In the woods, by the blazing fire.

Your hair has grown gray. Your eyes
Are dulled and fogged by tears.

You no longer understand the song of the birds,
You don't notice the stars or the summer lightning.

And the tambourine's beat is no longer heard,
And I know, the silence is frightening.

Я пришла тебя сменить, сестра,
У лесного, у высокого костра».

«Ты пришла меня похоронить.
Где же заступ твой, где лопата?
Только флейта в руках твоих.
Я не буду тебя винить,
Разве жаль, что давно, когда-то,
Навсегда мой голос затих.

Мои одежды надень,
Позабудь о моей тревоге,
Дай ветру кудрями играть.
Ты пахнешь, как пахнет сирень,
А пришла по трудной дороге,
Чтобы здесь озаренной стать».

И одна ушла, уступая,
Уступая место другой.
И неверно брела, как слепая,
Незнакомой узкой тропой.
И всё чудилось ей, что пламя
Близко... бубен держит рука.

И она, как белое знамя,
И она, как свет маяка.

24 октября 1912
Царское Село

I came to take your place, sister,
In the woods, by the blazing fire."

"You came to bury me.
Where is your shovel, your spade?
There is only a flute in your hands.
I'm not going to accuse you,
It's a pity that long ago,
My voice forever died away.

Put on my clothes,
Forget about my anxiety,
Let the wind play with your curls.
You give off the fragrance of lilac,
And you traveled a long, hard road
To be illuminated here."

And she left all alone, conceding,
Conceding her place to the other,
And like a blind woman, she groped
Down a narrow, unfamiliar road,
And all the time it seemed to her a flame
Was near...a hand was holding a tambourine.

And she was like a white banner,
And she was like a lighthouse beam.

October 24, 1912
Tsarskoye Selo

СТИХИ О ПЕТЕРБУРГЕ

Zh. 100

1

Вновь Исакий в облаченьи
Из литого серебра.
Стынет в грозном нетерпеньи
Конь Великого Петра.

Ветер душный и суровый
С черных труб сметает гарь...
Ах! своей столицей новой
Недоволен государь.

Zh. 101

2

Сердце бьется ровно, мерно,
Что мне долгие года!
Ведь под аркой на Галерной
Наши тени навсегда.

Сквозь опущенные веки
Вижу, вижу, ты со мной,
И в руке твоей навеки
Нераскрытый веер мой.

Оттого, что стали рядом
Мы в блаженный миг чудес,
В миг, когда над Летним садом
Месяц розовый воскрес, —

Мне не надо ожиданий
У постылого окна
И томительных свиданий —
Вся любовь утолена.

VERSES ABOUT PETERSBURG

1

Once more St. Isaac's wears robes
Of cast silver.
And frozen in fierce impatience
Stands the horse of Peter the Great.

A harsh and stifling wind
Sweeps soot from the black chimneys...
Ah! His new capital
Displeases the sovereign.

2

My heart beats calmly, steadily,
What are the long years to me!
Under the Galernaya arch,
Our shadows, for eternity.

Through lowered eyelids
I see, I see, you with me,
And held forever in your hand,
My unopened fan.

Because we were standing side by side
In that blissful miraculous moment,
The moment of the resurrection of the rose-colored moon
Over the Summer Garden—

I don't need the waiting
At some hateful window,
Or the agonizing meetings—
All my love is satisfied.

Ты свободен, я свободна,
Завтра лучше, чем вчера, —
Над Невою темноводной,
Под улыбкою холодной
Императора Петра.

1913

Zh. 102

Знаю, знаю — снова лыжи
Сухо заскрипят.
В синем небе месяц рыжий,
Луг так сладостно-покат.

Во дворце горят окошки,
Тишиной удалены.
Ни тропинки, ни дорожки,
Только проруби темны.

Ива, дерево русалок,
Не мешай мне на пути!
В снежных ветках черных галок,
Черных галок приюти.

Октябрь 1913
Царское Село

You are free, I am free,
Tomorrow will be better than yesterday—
Over the Neva's dark waters,
Under the cold smile
Of Emperor Peter.

1913

———

I know, I know—the skis
Will crunch on snow again.
There's a ginger moon in the dark blue sky
And the meadow slopes so delightfully.

The palace's little windows glow,
Remote in the stillness.
There are neither paths nor roads,
Only dark ice holes.

Willow, tree of water nymphs,
Don't block my way!
Shelter the black daws in your snowy branches,
The black daws.

October 1913
Tsarskoye Selo

———

Zh. 103

ВЕНЕЦИЯ

Золотая голубятня у воды,
Ласковой и млеюще-зеленой;
Заметает ветерок соленый
Черных лодок узкие следы.

Столько нежных, странных лиц в толпе.
В каждой лавке яркие игрушки:
С книгой лев на вышитой подушке,
С книгой лев на мраморном столбе.

Как на древнем, выцветшем холсте,
Стынет небо тускло-голубое...
Но не тесно в этой тесноте
И не душно в сырости и зное.

Август 1912

Zh. 104

Протертый коврик под иконой,
В прохладной комнате темно,
И густо плющ темнозеленый
Завил широкое окно.

От роз струится запах сладкий,
Трещит лампадка, чуть горя.
Пестро расписаны укладки
Рукой любовной кустаря.

И у окна белеют пяльцы...
Твой профиль тонок и жесток.
Ты зацелованные пальцы
Брезгливо прячешь под платок.

Venice

A golden dovecote by the water,
Soft and stunning green;
A salty breeze obliterates
The gondolas' thin wakes.

So many tender foreign faces in the crowd,
Bright toys in every shop:
A lion with a book on an embroidered pillow,
A lion with a book atop a marble pillar.

As if on an old, faded canvas,
The sky cools, dull blue. . .
But in this crush one isn't cramped,
Not stifled in the intense heat and the damp.

August 1912

———

Under the icon, a threadbare rug,
It's dark in the chilly room,
And dark green ivy thickly
Twines around the wide window.

A sweet scent streams from the roses,
The icon lamp sputters, barely aglow.
There are chests, floridly painted
By the craftsman's loving hand.

And near the window a white lace frame. . .
Your profile is sharp and drawn.
And under your handkerchief you conceal with disgust
Fingers that have just been kissed.

А сердцу стало страшно биться,
Такая в нем теперь тоска...
И в косах спутанных таится
Чуть слышный запах табака.

1912

Zh. 105

ГОСТЬ

Всё, как раньше: в окна столовой
Бьется мелкий метельный снег,
И сама я не стала новой,
А ко мне приходил человек.

Я спросила: «Чего ты хочешь?»
Он сказал: «Быть с тобой в аду».
Я смеялась: «Ах, напророчишь
Нам обоим, пожалуй, беду».

Но, поднявши руку сухую,
Он слегка потрогал цветы:
«Расскажи, как тебя целуют,
Расскажи, как целуешь ты».

И глаза, глядевшие тускло,
Не сводил с моего кольца.
Ни один не двинулся мускул
Просветленно-злого лица.

And the heart that began to pound,
How much anguish it holds now . . .
And in the dishevelled braids lurks
The smell of tobacco smoke.

1912

———

The Guest

Everything is the same: a fine snowstorm
Beats against the windows of the dining room,
And even I haven't changed,
But a man approached me.

I asked: "What do you want?"
He said: "To be with you in hell."
I laughed: "Ah, then you prophesy,
For both of us, calamity."

But raising his dry hand,
He lightly brushed the flowers:
"Tell me how they kiss you,
Tell me how you kiss."

And he stared at my ring
With fixed, lackluster eyes.
Not a single muscle moved
On his radiant, evil face.

О, я знаю: его отрада —
Напряженно и страстно знать,
Что ему ничего не надо,
Что мне не в чем ему отказать.

1 января 1914

Zh. 106

Александру Блоку

Я пришла к поэту в гости.
Ровно полдень. Воскресенье.
Тихо в комнате просторной,
А за окнами мороз

И малиновое солнце
Над лохматым сизым дымом...
Как хозяин молчаливый
Ясно смотрит на меня!

У него глаза такие,
Что запомнить каждый должен,
Мне же лучше, осторожной,
В них и вовсе не глядеть.

Но запомнится беседа,
Дымный полдень, воскресенье
В доме сером и высоком
У морских ворот Невы.

Январь 1914

Oh, I know: his consolation—
To realize with passionate intensity
That he needs nothing,
That I have nothing to refuse him.

January 1, 1914

———

—to Alexander Blok

I visited the poet.
Precisely at noon. Sunday.
It was quiet in the spacious room,
And beyond the windows, intense cold

And a raspberry sun
Above shaggy, bluish smoke. . .
How keenly my taciturn host
Regarded me!

He had the kind of eyes
That everyone must recall,
It was better for me to be careful,
And not look at them at all.

But I will recall the conversation,
The smoky noon, Sunday
In the tall, gray house
By the sea gates of the Neva.

January 1914

———

⟨ДОПОЛНЕНИЯ⟩

Zh. 107

Проводила друга до передней.
Постояла в золотой пыли.
С колоколенки соседней
Звуки важные текли.
Брошена! Придуманное слово —
Разве я цветок или письмо?
А глаза глядят уже сурово
В потемневшее трюмо.

1913
Царское Село

Zh. 108

Простишь ли мне эти ноябрьские дни?
В каналах приневских дрожат огни.
Трагической осени скудны убранства.

Ноябрь 1913
Петербург

Zh. 109

Я не любви твоей прошу —
Она теперь в надежном месте...
Поверь, что я твоей невесте
Ревнивых писем не пишу.

*

(ADDITIONS)

I led my lover out to the hall,
I stood in a golden haze.
From a nearby bell tower
Solemn sounds flowed.
A throwaway! Invented word—
Am I really a note or a flower?
But eyes already gaze bleakly
Into the darkening mirror.

1913
Tsarskoye Selo

———

Can you forgive me these November days?
Lights splinter in the Neva's waterways.
Tragic autumn's meager decorations.

November 1913
Petersburg

———

I'm not asking for your love—
It's in a safe place now. . .
Please believe that I won't write
Jealous letters to your bride.

*

Но мудрые прими советы:
Дай ей читать мои стихи,
Дай ей хранить мои портреты —
Ведь так любезны женихи!
А этим дурочкам нужней
Сознанье полное победы,
Чем дружбы светлые беседы
И память первых нежных дней...
Когда же счастия гроши
Ты проживешь с подругой милой,
И для пресыщенной души
Все станет сразу так постыло, —
В мою торжественную ночь
Не приходи. Тебя не знаю.
И чем могла б тебе помочь?
От счастья я не исцеляю.

1914

———

Zh. 110

«Горят твои ладони,
В ушах пасхальный звон,
Ты как святой Антоний
Виденьем искушен».

«Зачем во дни святые
Ворвался день один,
Как волосы густые
Безумных Магдалин».

«Так любят только дети
И то лишь первый раз»,
«Сильней всего на свете
Лучи спокойных глаз».

But take this wise advice:
Give her my poems to read,
Give her my portraits to keep—
Really, you are such a loving pair!
And these little fools need
The sense of total victory
More than friendship's casual banter
And the memory of the first tender days...
When you have spent the pennies of delight
With your sweetheart
And your surfeited soul
Feels sudden disgust—
Don't come to me in my triumphant night.
I won't know you.
And how could I help you?
I don't cure anyone of happiness.

1914

———

"The palms of your hands are burning,
The Easter bells ring in your ears,
You are like St. Anthony
Tempted by a vision."

"Why into the holy days
Did this certain day thrust its way,
Like the bushy hair
Of the crazed Magdalenes?"

"Only children love like this,
And then only the first time."
—"Stronger than anything on earth
Is the light in those tranquil eyes."

«То дьявольские сети,
Нечистая тоска»,
«Белей всего на свете
Была ее рука».

1915
Царское Село

Zh. 111

Будешь жить, не зная лиха,
Править и судить,
Со своей подругой тихой
Сыновей растить.

И во всем тебе удача,
Ото всех почет,
Ты не знай, что я от плача
Дням теряю счет.

Много нас таких бездомных,
Сила наша в том,
Что для нас, слепых и темных,
Светел Божий дом,

И для нас, склоненных долу,
Алтари горят,
Наши к Божьему престолу
Голоса летят.

1915

"This longing is impure,
The devil's snare."
— "Whiter than anything on earth
Was her hand."

1915
Tsarskoye Selo

———

You will live without misfortune,
You will govern, you will judge.
With your quiet partner
You will raise your sons.

Success in everything you do,
From everyone respect and praise,
You won't know that I, from crying,
Lose track of the days.

There are many of us homeless ones,
And our strength is
That for us, benighted and blind,
The house of God shines.

And for us, descending into the vale,
The altars burn,
And our voices soar
To God's very throne.

1915

ca. 1916

БѢЛАЯ СТАЯ

СТИХОТВОРЕНІЯ

АННЫ АХМАТОВОЙ.

ПЕТРОГРАДЪ.
Издательство Гиперборей.
1917.

WHITE FLOCK

(1917)

Горю и ночью дорога светла,
Анненский

To grief, even at night, the road is bright.
Annensky

I

Zh. 112

Думали: нищие мы, нету у нас ничего,
А как стали одно за другим терять,
Так что сделался каждый день
Поминальным днем, —
Начали песни слагать
О великой щедрости Божьей
Да о нашем бывшем богатстве.

1915

Zh. 113

Твой белый дом и тихий сад оставлю.
Да будет жизнь пустынна и светла.
Тебя, тебя в моих стихах прославлю,
Как женщина прославить не могла.
И ты подругу помнишь дорогую
В тобою созданном для глаз ее раю,
А я товаром редкостным торгую —
Твою любовь и нежность продаю.

1913
Царское Село

I

We thought: we are beggars, we have nothing,
But as we lost one thing after another,
So that each day became
A Remembrance Day —
We began to compose songs
About God's great munificence
And about how rich we once had been.

1915

———

I will leave your white house and tranquil garden.
Let life be empty and bright.
You, and only you, I shall glorify in my poems,
As a woman has never been able to do.
And you remember the beloved
For whose eyes you created this paradise,
But I deal in rare commodities —
I sell your love and tenderness.

1913
Tsarskoye Selo

———

Zh. 114

УЕДИНЕНИЕ

Так много камней брошено в меня,
Что ни один из них уже не страшен,
И стройной башней стала западня,
Высокою среди высоких башен.
Строителей ее благодарю,
Пусть их забота и печаль минует.
Отсюда раньше вижу я зарю,
Здесь солнца луч последний торжествует.
И часто в окна комнаты моей
Влетают ветры северных морей,
И голубь ест из рук моих пшеницу...
А не дописанную мной страницу,
Божественно спокойна и легка,
Допишет Музы смуглая рука.

6 июня 1914
Слепнево

Zh. 115

ПЕСНЯ О ПЕСНЕ

Она сначала обожжет,
Как ветерок студеный,
А после в сердце упадет
Одной слезой соленой.

И злому сердцу станет жаль
Чего-то. Грустно будет.
Но эту легкую печаль
Оно не позабудет.

Solitude

So many stones have been thrown at me,
That I'm not frightened of them anymore,
And the pit has become a solid tower,
Tall among tall towers.
I thank the builders,
May care and sadness pass them by.
From here I'll see the sunrise earlier,
Here the sun's last ray rejoices.
And into the windows of my room
The northern breezes often fly.
And from my hand a dove eats grains of wheat . . .
As for my unfinished page,
The Muse's tawny hand, divinely calm
And delicate, will finish it.

June 6, 1914
Slepnyovo

Song about a Song

At first it sears,
Like a freezing wind,
And then into the heart it falls,
As a single, salty tear.

And the wicked heart starts to regret
Something. It becomes melancholy.
And it can not forget
This little grief.

Я только сею. Собирать
Придут другие. Что же!
И жниц ликующую рать
Благослови, о боже!

А чтоб тебя благодарить
Я смела совершенней,
Позволь мне миру подарить
То, что любви нетленней.

1916
Слепнево

———

Zh. 116

Слаб голос мой, но воля не слабеет,
Мне даже легче стало без любви.
Высоко небо, горный ветер веет,
И непорочны помыслы мои.

Ушла к другим бессонница-сиделка,
Я не томлюсь над серою золой,
И башенных часов кривая стрелка
Смертельной мне не кажется стрелой.

Как прошлое над сердцем власть теряет!
Освобожденье близко. Все прощу,
Следя, как луч взбегает и сбегает
По влажному весеннему плющу.

Весна 1912

———

I only sow. Others
Will come to reap. Agreed!
Bless, O God,
This exultant band of reapers!

And in order to thank You
I will be completely bold,
Let me bestow upon the world
Something more imperishable than love.

1916
Slepnyovo

———

Weak is my voice, but my will isn't weakening,
It's even become easier for me without love.
The sky is sublime, a mountain wind is blowing,
And my thoughts are pure.

Insomnia, my nightnurse, is visiting elsewhere,
I'm not brooding by a cold hearth,
And the crooked hand of the tower clock
Doesn't look like the arrow of death.

How the past loses power over the heart!
Liberation is at hand. I forgive everything.
I'm keeping track of a sunbeam running up and down
The first moist ivy of spring.

Spring 1912

———

Zh. 117

Был он ревнивым, тревожным и нежным,
Как Божье солнце меня любил,
А чтобы она не запела о прежнем,
Он белую птицу мою убил.

Промолвил, войдя на закате в светлицу:
«Люби меня, смейся, пиши стихи!»
И я закопала веселую птицу
За круглым колодцем у старой ольхи.

Ему обещала, что плакать не буду.
Но каменным сделалось сердце мое,
И кажется мне, что всегда и повсюду
Услышу я сладостный голос ее.

Осень 1914

Zh. 118

Тяжела ты, любовная память!
Мне в дыму твоем петь и гореть,
А другим — это только пламя.
Чтоб остывшую душу греть.

Чтобы греть пресыщенное тело,
Им надобны слезы мои . . .
Для того ль я, Господи, пела,
Для того ль причастилась любви!

Дай мне выпить такой отравы,
Чтобы сделалась я немой,
И мою бесславную славу
Осиянным забвением смой.

18 июля 1914
Слепнево

He was jealous, troubled and tender,
He loved me as one loves God's sun,
But to keep it from singing about the past,
He killed my white bird.

Entering the front room at sunset, he murmured:
"Love me, laugh, write poetry!"
And I buried my merry bird
Beyond the round well, near the ancient alder tree.

I promised him I wouldn't mourn,
But my heart turned to stone,
And it seems to me that always and everywhere,
I hear the sweet voice of the bird.

Autumn 1914

———

Memory of love, you are painful!
I must sing and burn in your smoke,
But for others—you're just a flame
To warm a cooling soul.

To warm a sated body,
They needed my tears...
For this, Lord, I sang,
For this I received love's communion!

Let me drink some kind of poison
That will make me mute,
And turn my infamous fame
Into radiant oblivion.

July 18, 1914
Slepnyovo

———

Zh. 119

Потускнел на небе синий лак,
И слышнее песня окарины.
Это только дудочка из глины,
Не на что ей жаловаться так.
Кто ей рассказал мои грехи,
И зачем она меня прощает?..
Или этот голос повторяет
Мне твои последние стихи?

1912

———

Zh. 120

В. С. Срезневской

Вместо мудрости — опытность, пресное,
Неутоляющее питье.
А юность была — как молитва воскресная . . .
Мне ли забыть ее?

Столько дорог пустынных исхожено
С тем, кто мне не был мил,
Столько поклонов в церквах положено
За того, кто меня любил . . .

Стала забывчивей всех забывчивых,
Тихо плывут года.
Губ нецелованных, глаз неулыбчивых
Мне не вернуть никогда.

1914

———

The sky's dark blue lacquer has dimmed,
And louder the song of the ocarina.
It's only a little pipe of clay,
There's no reason for it to complain.
Who told it all my sins,
And why is it absolving me?. .
Or is this a voice repeating
Your latest poems to me?

1912

—to V.S. Sreznevskaya

Instead of wisdom—experience, a flat,
Unsatisfying drink.
And there was youth—like the Sunday prayer. . .
Could I ever forget it?

So many deserted roads walked
With him who was not dear to me,
So many bows I made in church
For him, who loved me. . .

I've become the most forgetful of all the forgetful,
Quietly the years sail by.
Those unkissed lips, unsmiling eyes
Will never return to me.

1914

А! это снова ты. Не отроком влюбленным,
Но мужем дерзостным, суровым, непреклонным
Ты в этот дом вошел и на меня глядишь.
Страшна моей душе предгрозовая тишь.
Ты спрашиваешь, что я сделала с тобою,
Врученным мне навек любовью и судьбою.
Я предала тебя. И это повторять —
О, если бы ты мог когда-нибудь устать!
Так мертвый говорит, убийцы сон тревожа,
Так Ангел смерти ждет у рокового ложа.
Прости меня теперь. Учил прощать Господь.
В недуге горестном моя томится плоть,
А вольный дух уже почиет безмятежно.
Я помню только сад, сквозной, осенний, нежный,
И крики журавлей, и черные поля . . .
О, как была с тобой мне сладостна земля!

Июль 1916
Слепнево

Муза ушла по дороге
Осенней, узкой, крутой,
И были смуглые ноги
Обрызганы крупной росой.

Я долго ее просила
Зимы со мной подождать.
Но сказала: «Ведь здесь могила,
Как ты можешь еще дышать?»

Ah! It's you again. Not as an enamoured youth
But as a husband, daring, stern, inflexible,
You enter this house and look at me.
My soul is frightened by the lull before the storm.
You ask what I have done with you,
Entrusted to me forever by love and fate.
I have betrayed you. And to have to repeat—
Oh, if only you'd get tired of it!
This is how a dead man speaks, disturbing his
    murderer's sleep,
This is how the angel of death waits by the bed of
    the dying.
Forgive me now. The Lord has taught us to forgive.
My flesh is tormented by piteous disease,
And my free spirit already rests, serene.
I remember only the garden, tender, leafless, autumnal,
And the black fields and the cry of the cranes...
Oh, how sweet was the earth for me with you!

July 1916
Slepnyovo

———

The Muse fled down the road,
The narrow, steep, autumnal road,
And her dusky feet
Were sprinkled with drops of dew.

For a long time I pleaded with her
To wait for the winter with me,
But she said: "It's like a tomb here,
How can you still manage to breathe?"

Я голубку ей дать хотела,
Ту, что всех в голубятне белей,
Но птица сама полетела
За стройной гостьей моей.

Я, глядя ей вслед, молчала,
Я любила ее одну,
А в небе заря стояла,
Как ворота в ее страну.

15 декабря 1915
Царское Село

Zh. 123

Я улыбаться перестала,
Морозный ветер губы студит,
Одной надеждой меньше стало,
Одною песней больше будет.
И эту песню я невольно
Отдам на смех и поруганье,
Затем что нестерпимо больно
Душе любовное молчанье.

Апрель 1915
Царское Село

Zh. 124

М. Лозинскому

Они летят, они еще в дороге,
Слова освобожденья и любви,
А я уже в предпесенной тревоге,
И холоднее льда уста мои.

I wanted to give her a dove,
The whitest of all doves,
But the bird itself flew
After my slender guest.

Following her with my eyes, I fell silent,
I loved her alone,
And sunrise stood in the sky
Like a gateway to her land.

December 15, 1915
Tsarskoye Selo

———

I no longer smile,
A freezing wind chills my lips,
One less hope becomes
One more song.
And this song, against my will,
I devote to desecration and mockery,
Because it is unbearably painful
For the soul to love silently.

April 1915
Tsarskoye Selo

———

—to M. Lozinsky

They are flying, they are still on their way,
The words of love and release.
I feel that uneasiness that comes before a poem,
And my lips are cold as ice.

Но скоро там, где жидкие березы,
Прильнувши к окнам, сухо шелестят, —
Венцом червонным заплетутся розы,
И голоса незримых прозвучат.

А дальше — свет невыносимо щедрый,
Как красное горячее вино . . .
Уже душистым, раскаленным ветром
Сознание мое опалено.

Лето 1916
Слепнево

Zh. 125

О, это был прохладный день
В чудесном городе Петровом!
Лежал закат костром багровым,
И медленно густела тень.

Пусть он не хочет глаз моих,
Пророческих и неизменных.
Всю жизнь ловить он будет стих,
Молитву губ моих надменных.

Зима 1913

Zh. 126

Я так молилась: «Утоли
Глухую жажду песнопенья!»
Но нет земному от земли
И не было освобожденья.

But there, where a few scraggly birches
Cling to the windows and rustle dryly—
A dark red wreath of roses twines
And the voices of invisible speakers resound.

And farther on—a light unbearably lavish,
Like hot red wine...
Already a fragrant, burning wind
Sears my consciousness.

Summer 1916
Slepnyovo

———

Oh, it was a cold day
In Peter's miraculous city!
Like a crimson fire the sunset lay,
And slowly the shadow thickened.

Let him not desire my eyes,
Prophetic and fixed.
He will get a whole lifetime of poems,
The prayer of my arrogant lips.

Winter 1913

———

This was my prayer: "Slake
The deep thirst of poetry!"
But the earthbound cannot leave the earth
And there was no setting free.

Как дым от жертвы, что не мог
Взлететь к престолу Сил и Славы,
А только стелется у ног,
Молитвенно целуя травы, —

Так, я, Господь, простерта ниц:
Коснется ли огонь небесный
Моих сомкнувшихся ресниц
И немоты моей чудесной?

1913

———

Zh. 127

Н. В. Н.

Есть в близости людей заветная черта,
Ее не перейти влюбленности и страсти, —
Пусть в жуткой тишине сливаются уста
И сердце рвется от любви на части.

И дружба здесь бессильна, и года
Высокого и огненного счастья,
Когда душа свободна и чужда
Медлительной истоме сладострастья.

Стремящиеся к ней безумны, а ее
Достигшие — поражены тоскою...
Теперь ты понял, отчего мое
Не бьется сердце под твоей рукою.

Май 1915
Петербург

———

Like the smoke of a sacrifice that cannot
Fly up to the throne of power and glory,
But only float at its foot,
Kissing the grass beseechingly —

So I, Lord, am prostrate:
Will the heavenly flame touch
My sealed eyelashes
And my astonishing muteness?

1913

———

N. V. N.

There is a sacred boundary between those who are close,
And it cannot be crossed by passion or love—
Though lips fuse in dreadful silence
And the heart shatters to pieces with love.

Friendship is helpless here, and years
Of exalted and ardent happiness,
When the soul is free and a stranger
To the slow languor of voluptuousness.

Those who strive to reach it are mad, and those
Who reach it—stricken by grief . . .
Now you understand why my heart
Does not beat faster under your hand.

May 1915
Petersburg

———

Zh. 128

Всё отнято: и сила, и любовь.
В немилый город брошенное тело
Не радо солнцу. Чувствую, что кровь
Во мне уже совсем похолодела.

Веселой Музы нрав не узнаю:
Она глядит и слова не проронит,
А голову в веночке темном клонит,
Изнеможенная, на грудь мою.

И только совесть с каждым днем страшней
Беснуется: великой хочет дани.
Закрыв лицо, я отвечала ей...
Но больше нет ни слез, ни оправданий.

Осень 1916
Севастополь

———

Zh. 129

Нам свежесть слов и чувства простоту
Терять не то ль, что живописцу — зренье,
Или актеру — голос и движенье,
А женщине прекрасной — красоту?

Но не пытайся для себя хранить
Тебе дарованное небесами:
Осуждены — и это знаем сами —
Мы расточать, а не копить.

Иди один и исцеляй слепых,
Чтобы узнать в тяжелый час сомненья
Учеников злорадное глумленье
И равнодушие толпы.

23 июня 1915
Слепнево

Everything has been cut off: both strength and love.
The body, flung into this hated town,
Does not rejoice in the sun. I feel that my blood
Has gone completely cold.

I cannot recognize my once-happy Muse:
She stares and won't utter a word,
And her head, in a dark wreath, rests,
Exhausted, on my breast.

And only my conscience, more terrible every day,
Raves, demanding great tribute.
Covering my face, I answer her. . .
But there are no more excuses, no more tears.

Autumn 1916
Sevastopol

———

For us to lose freshness of words and simplicity of feeling,
Isn't it the same as for a painter to lose—sight,
Or an actor—his voice and movement,
Or a beautiful woman—beauty?

But don't try to save for yourself
This heaven-sent gift:
We are condemned—and we know this ourselves—
To squander it, not hoard it.

Walk alone and heal the blind,
In order to know in the heavy hour of doubt
The gloating mockery of disciples,
And the indifference of the crowd.

June 23, 1915
Slepnyovo

Zh. 130

ОТВЕТ

В. А. Комаровскому

Какие странные слова
Принес мне тихий день апреля.
Ты знал, во мне еще жива
Страстная страшная неделя.

Я не слыхала звонов тех,
Что плавали в лазури чистой.
Семь дней звучал то медный смех,
То плач струился серебристый.

А я, закрыв лицо мое,
Как перед вечною разлукой,
Лежала и ждала ее,
Еще не названную мукой.

Весна 1914
Царское Село

Zh. 131

Был блаженной моей колыбелью
Темный город у грозной реки
И торжественной брачной постелью,
Над которой держали венки
Молодые твои серафимы, —
Город, горькой любовью любимый.

The Reply

—to V.A. Komarovsky

Such strange words
That quiet April day brought me.
You knew that within me, still living,
Was that terrible week of passion.

I didn't hear the peal of those bells
Floating in the pure azure.
For seven days copper laughter chimed,
Silvery lamentation streamed.

But I, covering my face
As if for the eternal separation,
Lay and waited for it,
The still-unnamed tribulation.

Spring 1914
Tsarskoye Selo

My blissful cradle was
A dark city on a menacing river
And the triumphal marriage bed,
Over which young seraphim
Held bridal wreaths—
Was a city loved with bitter love.

Солеёю молений моих
Был ты, строгий, спокойный, туманный.
Там впервые предстал мне жених,
Указавши мой путь осиянный,
И печальная Муза моя,
Как слепую, водила меня.

1914

II

Zh. 132

9 ДЕКАБРЯ 1913 ГОДА

Самые темные дни в году
Светлыми стать должны.
Я для сравнения слов не найду —
Так твои губы нежны.

Только глаза подымать не смей,
Жизнь мою храня.
Первых фиалок они светлей,
А смертельные для меня.

Вот поняла, что не надо слов,
Оснеженные ветки легки...
Сети уже разостлал птицелов
На берегу реки.

(1915)

Solium of my prayers
You were, misty, calm, severe.
There my betrothed first appeared to me,
Pointing out my shining path,
And my melancholy Muse
Led me as one leads the blind.

1914

―――

II

December 9, 1913

Even the darkest days of the year
Must become brighter.
I can't find the simile for—
How tender your lips are.

Only don't dare raise your eyes,
They hold my life.
They are brighter than the first violets,
And fatal for me.

Now I understand that words are unnecessary,
Light snowy branches...
Nets have already been spread by the bird catcher
On the banks of the river.

(1915)

―――

Zh. 133

Как ты можешь смотреть на Неву,
Как ты можешь всходить на мосты?..
Я недаром печальной слыву
С той поры, как привиделся ты.
Черных ангелов крылья остры,
Скоро будет последний суд,
И малиновые костры,
Словно розы, в снегу цветут.

1914

Zh. 134

Под крышей промерзшей пустого жилья
Я мертвенных дней не считаю,
Читаю посланья апостолов я,
Слова псалмопевца читаю.
Но звезды синеют, но иней пушист,
И каждая встреча чудесней, —
А в Библии красный кленовый лист
Заложен на Песни Песней.

Зима 1915

Zh. 135

Н. В. Н.

Целый год ты со мной неразлучен,
А как прежде и весел и юн!
Неужели же ты не измучен
Смутной песней затравленных струн, —

How can you bear to look at the Neva?
How can you bear to cross the bridges?..
Not in vain am I known as the grieving one
Since the time you appeared to me.
The black angels' wings are sharp,
Judgment Day is coming soon,
And raspberry-colored bonfires bloom,
Like roses, in the snow.

1914

———

Under the freezing roof of the empty dwelling place
I've lost track of the deadly days,
I read the Epistles of the Apostles,
I read the Psalm Singer's words.
But the stars turn blue, but the hoarfrost is downy,
And each meeting is more of a miracle—
And a red maple leaf
Marks the Song of Songs in my Bible.

Winter 1915

———

N. V. N.

All year you've been inseparable from me,
And as joyful and youthful as before!
Can it really be that you're not exhausted
By the troubled song of the slackened strings—

Тех, что прежде, тугие, звенели,
А теперь только стонут слегка,
И моя их терзает без цели
Восковая, сухая рука . . .

Верно мало для счастия надо
Тем, кто нежен и любит светло,
Что ни ревность, ни гнев, ни досада
Молодое не тронут чело.

Тихий, тихий, и ласки не просит,
Только долго глядит на меня
И с улыбкой блаженной выносит
Страшный бред моего забытья.

Весна 1915
Слепнево

Zh. 136

КИЕВ

Древний город словно вымер,
Странен мой приезд.
Над рекой своей Владимир
Поднял черный крест.

Липы шумные и вязы
По садам темны,
Звезд иглистые алмазы
К Богу взнесены.

Which before were taut, and rang out,
But now only softly moan.
They are tormented to no end
By my dry and waxen hand...

Truly it takes so little to please
Him who is tender and loves radiantly,
Whose young brow is untouched by
Anger, spite or jealousy.

Gentle, gentle, he doesn't ask to be caressed,
Only gazes at me
And endures with a smile of bliss
The frightful ravings of my semi-consciousness.

Spring 1915
Slepnyovo

Kiev

The ancient city seems deserted,
My arrival is strange.
Over its river, Vladimir
Raised a black cross.

The rustling lindens and the elms
Along the gardens are dark,
And the diamond needles of the stars
Are lifted out toward God.

Путь мой жертвенный и славный
Здесь окончу я,
И со мной лишь ты, мне равный,
Да любовь моя.

Лето 1914

———

Zh. 137

Еще весна таинственная млела,
Блуждал прозрачный ветер по горам,
И озеро глубокое синело —
Крестителя нерукотворный храм.

Ты был испуган нашей первой встречей,
А я уже молилась о второй,
И вот сегодня снова жаркий вечер, —
Как низко солнце стало над горой. . .

Ты не со мной, но это не разлука:
Мне каждый миг — торжественная весть.
Я знаю, что в тебе такая мука,
Что ты не можешь слова произнесть.

Весна 1917
Петербург

———

My sacrificial and glorious journey
I will finish here,
And with me only you, my equal
And my lover.

Summer 1914

———

The mysterious spring still thrills,
A transparent breeze wanders the hills,
And the deep lake becomes bluer still—
The temple of the Baptist not built by human hands.

You were frightened by our first meeting,
But I was already praying for a second one.
And again today the evening is sultry—
How low the sun hangs over the hill . . .

You are not with me but there's no separation:
For me each moment is a triumphant report.
I know that you are in such torment,
That you can't utter a word.

Spring 1917
Petersburg

———

Zh. 138

РАЗЛУКА

Вечерний и наклонный
Передо мною путь.
Вчера еще, влюбленный,
Молил: «Не позабудь».
А нынче только ветры
Да крики пастухов,
Взволнованные кедры
У чистых родников.

Весна 1914
Петербург

Zh. 139

Чернеет дорога приморского сада,
Желты и свежи фонари.
Я очень спокойная. Только не надо
Со мною о нем говорить.
Ты милый и верный, мы будем друзьями...
Гулять, целоваться, стареть...
И легкие месяцы будут над нами,
Как снежные звезды, лететь.

Март 1914

Zh. 140

Не в лесу мы, довольно аукать, —
Я насмешек таких не люблю...
Что же ты не приходишь баюкать
Уязвленную совесть мою?

Separation

The sloping evening
Path lies before me.
Just yesterday, in love,
He prayed: "Don't forget me."
But today there is only the wind
The herdsmen hallooing,
And the agitated cedars
By the pure springs.

Spring 1914
Petersburg

―――

The road by the seaside garden darkens,
The lanterns are yellow and crisp.
I'm very peaceful. Only you must not
Talk to me about him.
You are dear and faithful, we will be friends...
Stroll, kiss, grow old together...
And the new moons will fly over us
Like snowy stars.

March 1914

―――

We're not in the forest, that's enough shouting—
I don't like these gibes...
Why don't you quiet my wounded conscience
With lullabies?

У тебя заботы другие,
У тебя другая жена...
И глядит мне в глаза сухие
Петербургская весна.

Трудным кашлем, вечерним жаром
Наградит по заслугам, убьет.
На Неве под млеющим паром
Начинается ледоход.

Весна 1914

Zh. 141

Господь немилостив к жнецам и садоводам.
Звеня, косые падают дожди
И прежде небо отражавшим водам
Пестрят широкие плащи.

В подводном царстве и луга, и нивы,
А струи вольные поют, поют,
На взбухших ветках лопаются сливы,
И травы легшие гниют.

И сквозь густую водяную сетку
Я вижу милое твое лицо,
Притихший парк, китайскую беседку
И дома круглое крыльцо.

Лето 1915
Царское Село

You have other cares,
You have another wife...
And into my dry eyes stares
The Petersburg spring.

It will give me what I deserve,
A heavy cough, night fevers, death.
On the Neva, under the shivering mist,
The ice is beginning to drift.

Spring 1914

———

The Lord is not merciful to reapers and gardeners.
A ringing rain slants down
And wide cloaks are going to color
The sky reflected in the water.

There's an underwater kingdom of meadows
　　and cornfields,
And undulating streams sing out, sing out,
On the swelling branches plums are bursting
And the flattened grasses rot.

And through the dense scrim of water
I see your dear face,
The hushed park, the Chinese Pavilion
And the circular porch of the house.

Summer 1915
Tsarskoye Selo

———

Все обещало мне его:
Край неба, тусклый и червонный,
И милый сон под Рождество,
И Пасхи ветер многозвонный,

И прутья красные лозы,
И парковые водопады,
И две большие стрекозы
На ржавом чугуне ограды.

И я не верить не могла,
Что будет дружен он со мною,
Когда по горным склонам шла
Горячей каменной тропою.

Осень 1916
Севастополь

———

Как невеста, получаю
Каждый вечер по письму,
Поздно ночью отвечаю
Другу моему.

«Я гощу у смерти белой
По дороге в тьму.
Зла, мой ласковый, не делай
В мире никому».

И стоит звезда большая
Между двух стволов,
Так спокойно обещая
Исполненье снов.

Октябрь 1915
Хювинкка

Everything promised him to me:
The edge of the sky, a tarnished red-gold,
And that sweet dream at Christmastime,
And the Easter wind with its many chimes,

And the red rods of the twigs,
And the park's waterfalls,
And the two big dragonflies
On the rusty iron fence.

And it was impossible to believe
That he would not be mine,
When I walked up the mountain
On a path of burning stones.

Autumn 1916
Sevastopol

———

Like a fiancée, I receive
A letter every evening,
And late at night I write
An answer to my lover.

"I am the guest of white death,
On the way to darkness.
My beloved, don't do evil
To anyone on earth."

And a huge star is standing
Between the trunks of two trees,
So tranquilly promising
The fulfillment of dreams.

October 1915
Huvinkka

Zh. 144

Божий ангел, зимним утром
Тайно обручивший нас,
С нашей жизни беспечальной
Глаз не сводит потемневших.

Оттого мы любим небо,
Тонкий воздух, свежий ветер
И чернеющие ветки
За оградою чугунной.

Оттого мы любим строгий,
Многоводный, темный город,
И разлуки наши любим,
И часы недолгих встреч.

Зима 1914

Zh. 145

Ведь где-то есть простая жизнь и свет,
Прозрачный, теплый и веселый . . .
Там с девушкой через забор сосед
Под вечер говорит, и слышат только пчелы
Нежнейшую из всех бесед.

А мы живем торжественно и трудно
И чтим обряды наших горьких встреч,
Когда, с налету, ветер безрассудный
Чуть начатую обрывает речь, —

Но ни на что не променяем пышный
Гранитный город славы и беды,
Широких рек сияющие льды,
Бессолнечные, мрачные сады
И голос Музы еле слышный.

23 июня 1915
Слепнево

The angel of God, having secretly
Betrothed us one winter day,
Watches over our carefree lives
With fixed, darkening eyes.

Because of this we love the sky,
Keen air, the fresh wind
And the blackening branches
Behind the iron fence.

Because of this we love the stern
Dark city with its many waterways.
And we love our partings,
And our brief meetings.

Winter 1914

————

Somewhere there is a simple life and a world,
Transparent, warm and joyful...
There at evening a neighbor talks with a girl
Across the fence, and only the bees can hear
This most tender murmuring of all.

But we live ceremoniously and with difficulty
And we observe the rites of our bitter meetings,
When suddenly the reckless wind
Breaks off a sentence just begun—

But not for anything would we exchange this splendid
Granite city of fame and calamity,
The wide rivers of glistening ice,
The sunless, gloomy gardens,
And, barely audible, the Muse's voice.

June 23, 1915
Slepnyovo

Zh. 146

Подошла. Я волненья не выдал,
Равнодушно глядя в окно.
Села, словно фарфоровый идол,
В позе, выбранной ею давно.

Быть веселой — привычное дело,
Быть внимательной — это трудней . . .
Или томная лень одолела
После мартовских пряных ночей?

Утомительный гул разговоров,
Желтой люстры безжизненный зной
И мельканье искусных проборов
Над приподнятой легкой рукой.

Улыбнулся опять собеседник
И с надеждой глядит на нее . . .
Мой счастливый, богатый наследник,
Ты прочти завещанье мое.

1914

———

Zh. 147

ПОБЕГ

О. А. Кузьминой-Караваевой

«Нам бы только до взморья добраться,
Дорогая моя!» — «Молчи. . .»
И по лестнице стали спускаться,
Задыхаясь, искали ключи.

She approached. I didn't betray my agitation,
Just stared serenely out the window.
She sat there, like a porcelain idol,
In a pose she had adopted long ago.

Being cheerful—becomes a habit,
Being attentive—is more difficult...
Or has languorous indolence triumphed
After those heady March nights?

The tiresome buzz of conversation,
The lifeless heat of the yellow chandelier,
And over the slightly raised, slender arm,
The glimpse of an artful coiffure.

Her companion smiles again
And watches her hopefully...
My lucky, rich inheritor,
Welcome to my legacy.

1914

———

Flight

—to O.A. Kuzmina-Karavayeva

"We have only to reach the coast,
My darling!"—"Hush..."
And we started down the staircase,
Breathlessly searching for the key.

Мимо зданий, где мы когда-то
Танцевали, пили вино,
Мимо белых колонн Сената
Туда, где темно, темно.

«Что ты делаешь, ты безумный!»
— «Нет, я только тебя люблю!
Этот ветер — широкий и шумный,
Будет весело кораблю!»

Горло тесно ужасом сжато,
Нас в потемках принял челнок...
Крепкий запах морского каната
Задрожавшие ноздри обжег.

«Скажи, ты знаешь наверно:
Я не сплю? Так бывает во сне...»
Только весла плескались мерно
По тяжелой невской волне.

А черное небо светало,
Нас окликнул кто-то с моста,
Я руками обеими сжала
На груди цепочку креста.

Обессиленную, на руках ты,
Словно девочку, внес меня,
Чтоб на палубе белой яхты
Встретить свет нетленного дня.

Июнь 1914

Past the buildings where once
We had drunk wine and danced,
Past the Senate's white columns
To where it was dark, dark.

"What are you doing? You're out of your mind!"—
"No, I love only you!
This loud sweeping wind
Will be splendid on the ship!"

My throat was tight with fear,
We boarded the rowboat in darkness...
The strong smell of tarred cables
Scorched my trembling nostrils.

"Tell me, you must know:
Am I sleeping? It seems like a dream..."
The oars just splashed on steadily
Over the Neva's heavy seas.

And the black sky brightened,
Someone hailed us from the bridge,
With both hands I clenched
The chain of the cross on my breast.

I collapsed in your arms
Like a girl and you carried me
Onto the deck of the white yacht,
To meet the light of imperishable day.

June 1914

Zh. 148

О тебе вспоминаю я редко
И твоей не пленяюсь судьбой,
Но с души не стирается метка
Незначительной встречи с тобой.

Красный дом твой нарочно миную,
Красный дом твой над мутной рекой,
Но я знаю, что горько волную
Твой пронизанный солнцем покой.

Пусть не ты над моими устами
Наклонялся, моля о любви,
Пусть не ты золотыми стихами
Обессмертил томленья мои, —

Я над будущим тайно колдую,
Если вечер совсем голубой,
И предчувствую встречу вторую,
Неизбежную встречу с тобой.

1913

Zh. 149

ЦАРСКОСЕЛЬСКАЯ СТАТУЯ

Н. В. Н.

Уже кленовые листы
На пруд слетают лебединый,
И окровавлены кусты
Неспешно зреющей рябины,

I seldom think about you now
And I'm not fascinated by your fate,
But the mark of our insignificant meeting
Has not been erased from my soul.

I deliberately avoid your red house,
Your red house on the murky river,
But I know that I sorely disturb
Your sun-flecked tranquillity.

Though you didn't hover over my lips
Imploring love,
Though you didn't immortalize my desire
In verses of gold—

I secretly peer into the future
If the evening is clear, light blue,
And I foresee a second meeting,
An inevitable meeting with you.

1913

———

Statue in Tsarskoye Selo

N. V. N.

Already the maple leaves
Are falling on the swan pond,
And on the blood-stained bushes
Of late-ripening mountain ash.

И ослепительно стройна,
Поджав незябнущие ноги,
На камне северном она
Сидит и смотрит на дороги.

Я чувствовала смутный страх
Пред этой девушкой воспетой.
Играли на ее плечах
Лучи скудеющего света.

И как могла я ей простить
Восторг твоей хвалы влюбленной...
Смотри, ей весело грустить,
Такой нарядно обнаженной.

Осень 1916

———

Zh. 150

Вновь подарен мне дремотой
Наш последний звездный рай —
Город чистых водометов,
Золотой Бахчисарай.

Там, за пестрою оградой,
У задумчивой воды,
Вспоминали мы с отрадой
Царскосельские сады,

И орла Екатерины
Вдруг узнали — это тот!
Он слетел на дно долины
С пышных бронзовых ворот.

And, dazzlingly slender,
Crossed legs impervious to cold,
She sits on the northern stone
Gazing down along the roads.

I felt uneasy
Before this celebrated maid.
On her shoulders
Beams of fading light played.

And how could I forgive her
The delight of your enamoured praise...
You see, for her, so fashionably nude,
It's fun to be sad.

Autumn 1916

———

Drowsiness takes me back again
To our last starry paradise—
City of pure fountains,
Golden Bakhchisarai.

There, beyond the gaudy fence,
By the pensive waters,
We remembered with delight
The gardens of Tsarskoye Selo.

And suddenly we recognized
Catherine's eagle—there it is!
Down it swooped into the depths of the valley
From the splendid gate of bronze.

Чтобы песнь прощальной боли
Дольше в памяти жила,
Осень смуглая в подоле
Красных листьев принесла

И посыпала ступени,
Где прощалась я с тобой
И откуда в царство тени
Ты ушел, утешный мой.

Осень 1916
Севастополь

———

Н. В. Н.

Все мне видится Павловск холмистый,
Круглый луг, неживая вода,
Самый томный и самый тенистый,
Ведь его не забыть никогда.

Как в ворота чугунные въедешь,
Тронет тело блаженная дрожь,
Не живешь, а ликуешь и бредишь,
Иль совсем по-иному живешь.

Поздней осенью свежий и колкий
Бродит ветер, безлюдию рад.
В белом инее черные елки
На подтаявшем снеге стоят.

To keep the song of the pangs of parting
Alive in memory,
Dusky autumn brought red leaves
In her hem

And strewed them on the steps,
Where I said good-bye to you
And from whence, into the realm of shadows
You, my consolation, fled.

Autumn 1916
Sevastopol

———

N. V. N.

I can still see hilly Pavlovsk,
The surrounding meadow, the motionless water,
Most languorous, most blessed with shade,
Most unforgettable place.

As you drive through the cast-iron gates,
Your body trembles with bliss,
You are not living, but exulting and delirious,
Or living, but in a completely different way.

In late autumn, the fresh and biting breeze
Wanders, rejoicing in the deserted solitude.
White-rimed black fir trees
Stand in the half-melted snow.

И, исполненный жгучего бреда,
Милый голос как песня звучит,
И на медном плече Кифареда
Красногрудая птичка сидит.

1915
Царское Село

———

Zh. 152

Бессмертник сух и розов. Облака
На свежем небе вылеплены грубо.
Единственного в этом парке дуба
Листва еще бесцветна и тонка.

Лучи зари до полночи горят.
Как хорошо в моем затворе тесном!
О самом нежном, о всегда чудесном
Со мной сегодня птицы говорят.

Я счастлива. Но мне всего милей
Лесная и пологая дорога,
Убогий мост, скривившийся немного,
И то, что ждать осталось мало дней.

Лето 1916
Слепнево

———

And, full of delirious fever,
The dear voice rings out like a song,
And on the copper shoulder of the Lyre Player
Sits a little scarlet-breasted bird.

1915
Tsarskoye Selo

———

The everlasting is rosy and dry. There are clouds
Crudely sculpted in the cooling sky.
The leaves on the solitary oak in the park
Are still colorless and thin.

The rays of sunset burn until midnight.
How good I feel in my narrow cell!
About the most tender, about the most marvelous man
The birds are conversing with me today.

I am content. But more precious than anything to me
Is the forest path, sloping gently,
The dilapidated bridge, which sags a bit,
And that there are only a few days left to wait.

Summer 1916
Slepnyovo

———

III

Zh. 153

МАЙСКИЙ СНЕГ

Прозрачная ложится пелена
На свежий дерн и незаметно тает.
Жестокая, студеная весна
Налившиеся почки убивает.
И ранней смерти так ужасен вид,
Что не могу на божий мир глядеть я.
Во мне печаль, которой царь Давид
По-царски одарил тысячелетья.

Май 1916
Слепнево

Zh. 154

Зачем притворяешься ты
То ветром, то камнем, то птицей?
Зачем улыбаешься ты
Мне с неба внезапной зарницей?

Не мучь меня больше, не тронь!
Пусти меня к вещим заботам...
Шатается пьяный огонь
По высохшим серым болотам.

И Муза в дырявом платке
Протяжно поет и уныло.
В жестокой и юной тоске
Ее чудотворная сила.

Июль 1915
Слепнево

III

May Snow

A transparent shroud lies
On the fresh sod and imperceptibly melts.
The cruel, chilling spring
Is killing the swelling buds.
And the sight of this early death is so frightful,
That I can't bear to look at God's world.
I feel the sorrow that King David bequeathed,
The kingly, thousand-year grief.

May 1916
Slepnyovo

Why do you pretend to be
Now a branch, now a stone, now a bird?
Why do you smile at me
Like sudden summer lightning from the sky?

Don't torment me anymore, don't touch me!
Leave me to my prophetic woes...
A drunken flame staggers
Across the dried up, grayish bog.

And the Muse, in a ragged dress,
Sings despondently and at length.
In hard and youthful anguish
Is her miraculous strength.

July 1915
Slepnyovo

Zh. 155

Пустых небес прозрачное стекло,
Большой тюрьмы белесое строенье
И хода крестного торжественное пенье
Над Волховом, синеющим светло.

Сентябрьский вихрь, листы с березы свеяв,
Кричит и мечется среди ветвей,
А город помнит о судьбе своей:
Здесь Марфа правила и правил Аракчеев.

Сентябрь 1914
Новгород

ИЮЛЬ 1914

Zh. 156

1

Пахнет гарью. Четыре недели
Торф сухой по болотам горит.
Даже птицы сегодня не пели,
И осина уже не дрожит.

Стало солнце немилостью божьей,
Дождик с Пасхи полей не кропил.
Приходил одноногий прохожий
И один на дворе говорил:

«Сроки страшные близятся. Скоро
Станет тесно от свежих могил.
Ждите глада, и труса, и мора,
И затменья небесных светил.

The pellucid glass of the empty heavens,
The huge white building, the prison,
And the solemn chant of the religious procession
Over the Volkhov, gleaming dark blue.

A September gale, stripping the leaves from the birches,
Shrieks and hurls itself into the branches,
And the city remembers its fate:
Here Martha governed, and Arakcheyev ruled.

September 1914
Novgorod

———

JULY 1914

1

It smells of burning. For four weeks
The dry peat bog has been burning.
The birds have not even sung today,
And the aspen has stopped quaking.

The sun has become God's displeasure,
Rain has not sprinkled the fields since Easter.
A one-legged stranger came along
And all alone in the courtyard he said:

"Fearful times are drawing near. Soon
Fresh graves will be everywhere.
There will be famine, earthquakes, widespread death,
And the eclipse of the sun and the moon.

Только нашей земли не разделит
На потеху себе супостат:
Богородица белый расстелет
Над скорбями великими плат».

Zh. 157

2

Можжевельника запах сладкий
От горящих лесов летит.
Над ребятами стонут солдатки,
Вдовий плач по деревне звенит.

Не напрасно молебны служились,
О дожде тосковала земля!
Красной влагой тепло окропились
Затоптанные поля.

Низко, низко небо пустое,
И голос молящего тих:
«Ранят тело твое пресвятое,
Мечут жребий о ризах твоих».

20 июля 1914
Слепнево

Zh. 158

Тот голос, с тишиной великой споря,
Победу одержал над тишиной.
Во мне еще, как песня или горе,
Последняя зима перед войной.

But the enemy will not divide
Our land at will, for himself:
The Mother of God will spread her white mantle
Over this enormous grief."

2

The sweet smell of juniper
Flies from the burning woods.
Soldiers' wives are wailing for the boys,
The widow's lament keens over the countryside.

The public prayers were not in vain,
The earth was yearning for rain!
Warm red liquid sprinkled
The trampled fields.

Low, low hangs the empty sky
And a praying voice quietly intones:
"They are wounding your sacred body,
They are casting lots for your robes."

July 20, 1914
Slepnyovo

———

That voice opposing total silence
Has conquered silence.
Inside me still, like a song or like grief,
Is the last winter before the war.

Белее сводов Смольного собора,
Таинственней, чем пышный Летний сад,
Она была. Не знали мы, что скоро
В тоске предельной поглядим назад.

Январь 1917

Zh. 159

Мы не умеем прощаться, —
Все бродим плечо к плечу.
Уже начинает смеркаться,
Ты задумчив, а я молчу.

В церковь войдем, увидим
Отпеванье, крестины, брак,
Не взглянув друг на друга, выйдем...
Отчего все у нас не так?

Или сядем на снег примятый
На кладбище, легко вздохнем,
И ты палкой чертишь палаты,
Где мы будем всегда вдвоем.

1917

Whiter than the vaults of the Smolny Cathedral,
More mysterious than the splendid Summer Garden
It was. We didn't know that soon
We would be looking back at it in exquisite pain.

January 1917

———

We don't know how to say good-bye—
We keep wandering arm in arm.
Twilight has begun to fall,
You are pensive and I keep still.

Let's go into a church—we will watch
A funeral, christenings, a marriage service,
Without looking at each other, we will leave...
What's wrong with us?

Or let's sit on the trampled snow
Of the graveyard, sighing lightly,
And with your walking stick you'll outline palaces
Where we will be together always.

1917

———

Zh. 160

УТЕШЕНИЕ

> *Там Михаил Архистратиг*
> *Его зачислил в ратъ свою.*
>
> Н. Гумилев

Вестей от него не получишь больше,
Не услышишь ты про него.
В объятой пожарами, скорбной Польше
Не найдешь могилы его.

Пусть дух твой станет тих и покоен,
Уже не будет потерь:
Он Божьего воинства новый воин,
О нем не грусти теперь.

И плакать грешно, и грешно томиться
В милом, родном дому.
Подумай, ты можешь теперь молиться
Заступнику своему.

Сентябрь 1914
Царское Село

Zh. 161

Лучше б мне частушки задорно выкликать,
А тебе на хриплой гармонике играть,

И, уйдя обнявшись на ночь за овсы,
Потерять бы ленту из тугой косы.

Лучше б мне ребеночка твоего качать,
А тебе полтинник в сутки выручать,

Comfort

There the Archangel Michael
Has enrolled him in his host.
N. Gumilyov

You will receive no further news of him,
You won't hear about him anymore.
Nor in sorrowing Poland engulfed by flames
Will you ever find his grave.

Let your soul become quiet and tranquil,
He's no longer one of the lost.
He's a new warrior in God's host,
Don't grieve for him now.

And it's sinful to weep, it's sinful to yearn
In the comfort of your home.
Just think, now you can pray
To an intercessor of your very own.

September 1914
Tsarskoye Selo

———

I should have raucously screeched little folk tunes,
And you on a wheezy old squeeze box played,

And hugging each other at night in the oatfield,
We'd lose the ribbon of my tight braid.

Better for me to have rocked your child,
And for you to earn 50 kopecks a day,

И ходить на кладбище в поминальный день,
Да смотреть на белую божию сирень.

1914

МОЛИТВА

Дай мне горькие годы недуга,
Задыханья, бессонницу, жар,
Отыми и ребенка, и друга,
И таинственный песенный дар —
Так молюсь за твоей литургией
После стольких томительных дней,
Чтобы туча над темной Россией
Стала облаком в славе лучей.

Май 1915. Духов день
Петербург

«Где, высокая, твой цыганенок,
Тот, что плакал под черным платком,
Где твой маленький первый ребенок,
Что ты знаешь, что помнишь о нем?»

«Доля матери — светлая пытка,
Я достойна ее не была.
В белый рай растворилась калитка,
Магдалина сыночка взяла.

And to walk in the graveyard to view God's white lilacs
On Remembrance Day.

1914

———

Prayer

Give me bitter years of sickness,
Suffocation, insomnia, fever,
Take my child and my lover,
And my mysterious gift of song—
This I pray at your liturgy
After so many tormented days,
So that the stormcloud over darkened Russia
Might become a cloud of glorious rays.

May 1915. Day of the Holy Ghost
Petersburg

———

"Tall woman, where is your little gypsy,
The one who cried under your black shawl?
Where is your first little child,
What do you know of him, what do you recall?"

"A mother's fate—glorious anguish,
I was not worthy of it.
The gates of white Paradise opened,
And the Magdalene took my little son.

Каждый день мой — веселый, хороший,
Заблудилась я в длинной весне,
Только руки тоскуют по ноше,
Только плач его слышу во сне.

Станет сердце тревожным и томным,
И не помню тогда ничего,
Всё брожу я по комнатам темным,
Всё ищу колыбельку его».

11 апреля 1914
Петербург

Zh. 164

Столько раз я проклинала
Это небо, эту землю,
Этой мельницы замшелой
Тяжко машущие руки!
А во флигеле покойник,
Прям и сед, лежит на лавке,
Как тому назад три года.
Так же мыши книги точат,
Так же влево пламя клонит
Стеариновая свечка.
И поет, поет постылый
Бубенец нижегородский
Незатейливую песню
О моем веселье горьком.
А раскрашенные ярко
Прямо стали георгины
Вдоль серебряной дорожки,
Где улитки и полынь.
Так случилось: заточенье

∗

My every day—is cheerful and fine,
I'm wandering through a long springtime,
But my hands long for their burden,
But I hear him crying in my sleep.

My heart becomes anxious and weary,
And I remember nothing at all,
I keep wandering through these dark rooms,
I keep looking for his cradle."

April 11, 1914
Petersburg

———

How many times I've cursed
This sky, this earth,
The heavily flapping arms
Of this moss-grown mill!
And in the wing of the house the deceased,
Straight and gray, lies on the bench,
As it was three years ago.
The mice gnaw the books just the same,
The tallow candle bends its flame just the same,
A little to the left.
And the hateful jingling bells
Below the town
Sing, sing, a simple song
About my bitter mirth.
And the brightly colored row
Of dahlias stood straight
Along the silver path
Of snails and wormwood.
And so it happened: imprisonment

*

Стало родиной второю,
А о первой я не смею
И в молитве вспоминать.

Июль 1915
Слепнево

Ни в лодке, ни в телеге
Нельзя попасть сюда.
Стоит на гиблом снеге
Глубокая вода,
Усадьбу осаждает
Уже со всех сторон...
Ах! близко изнывает
Такой же Робинзон.
Пойдет взглянуть на сани,
На лыжи, на коня,
А после на диване
Сидит и ждет меня,
И шпорою короткой
Рвет коврик пополам.
Теперь улыбки кроткой
Не видеть зеркалам.

Осень 1916
Слепнево

Вижу, вижу лунный лук
Сквозь листву густых ракит,
Слышу, слышу ровный стук
Неподкованных копыт.

Became my second home,
As for the first, I don't dare
To remember it, even in prayer.

July 1915
Slepnyovo

———

It's impossible to get here
By either rowboat or cart.
The water stands deep
On the rotten snow,
Besieging the estate
On all sides. . .
Ah! Nearby pines
A sort of Robinson Crusoe.
He walks around staring at sleighs,
At horses, at skis,
And then he sits on the divan
And waits for me,
Shredding the carpet
With his short spurs.
Now that meek smile
Won't appear in the mirrors.

Autumn 1916
Slepnyovo

———

I see, I see the moon's bended bow
Through the thick broom groves,
I hear, I hear the regular beat
Of unshod hooves.

Что? И ты не хочешь спать,
В год не мог меня забыть,
Не привык свою кровать
Ты пустою находить?

Не с тобой ли говорю
В остром крике хищных птиц,
Не в твои ль глаза смотрю
С белых, матовых страниц?

Что же кружишь, словно вор,
У затихшего жилья?
Или помнишь уговор
И живую ждешь меня?

Засыпаю. В душный мрак
Месяц бросил лезвие.
Снова стук. То бьется так
Сердце теплое мое.

⟨1914⟩

Zh. 167

Бесшумно ходили по дому,
Не ждали уже ничего.
Меня привели к больному,
И я не узнала его.

Он сказал: «Теперь слава Богу,» —
И еще задумчивей стал.
«Давно мне пора в дорогу,
Я только тебя поджидал.

What? You don't want to sleep either?
In a year you couldn't forget me?
You haven't become accustomed
To finding your bed empty?

Do I not talk to you
With the screech of birds of prey?
Do I not stare into your eyes
From the dull, white pages?

Why then are you circling, like a thief,
Around the suddenly silent house?
Or are you remembering what we agreed
And expecting to find me alive?

I'm falling asleep. Into the stifling gloom
The moon hurls its blade.
Another knock. Just like that beats
My warm heart.

(1914)

Noiselessly they walked about the house,
No longer expecting anything.
They led me to the sick man
And I didn't recognize him.

He said: "Now praise God—"
And sank deeper into thought.
"I should have been on my way long ago,
I was only waiting for you.

Так меня ты в бреду тревожишь,
Все слова твои берегу.
Скажи: ты простить не можешь?»
И я сказала: «Могу».

Казалось, стены сияли
От пола до потолка.
На шелковом одеяле
Сухая лежала рука.

А закинутый профиль хищный
Стал так страшно тяжел и груб,
И было дыханья не слышно
У искусанных темных губ.

Но вдруг последняя сила
В синих глазах ожила:
«Хорошо, что ты отпустила,
Не всегда ты доброй была».

И стало лицо моложе,
Я опять узнала его
И сказала: «Господи Боже,
Прими раба Твоего».

Июль 1914
Слепнево

Zh. 168

МОЕЙ СЕСТРЕ

Подошла я к сосновому лесу.
Жар велик, да и путь не короткий.
Отодвинул дверную завесу,
Вышел седенький, светлый и кроткий.

You trouble me so much in my delirium,
I cherish each one of your words.
Tell me: can you not forgive?"
And I replied: "I can."

It seemed as if the walls shone
From floor to ceiling.
On the silken counterpane
Lay his shriveled hand.

And his arched, predatory profile
Became horribly heavy and coarse,
And there was no audible breath
From his dark, gnawed mouth.

But suddenly the last strength
Lit up his blue eyes:
"It's good that you forgive,
You weren't always so kind."

And his face became younger,
I recognized him again
And I said: "Lord God,
Gather your servant in."

July 1914
Slepnyovo

To My Sister

I approached the pine forest.
The heat was great and the path not short.
Pulling aside the doorway curtain,
A radiant and meek old man stepped out.

Поглядел на меня прозорливец
И промолвил: «Христова невеста!
Не завидуй удаче счастливиц,
Там тебе уготовано место.

Позабудь о родительском доме,
Уподобься небесному крину.
Будешь, хворая, спать на соломе
И блаженную примешь кончину».

Верно, слышал святитель из кельи,
Как я пела обратной дорогой
О моем несказанном весельи,
И дивяся, и радуясь много.

Июль 1914
Дарница

Zh. 169

Так раненого журавля
Зовут другие: курлы, курлы! —
Когда осенние поля
И рыхлы, и теплы...

И я, больная, слышу зов,
Шум крыльев золотых
Из плотных, низких облаков
И зарослей густых:

«Пора лететь, пора лететь
Над полем и рекой.
Ведь ты уже не можешь петь
И слезы со щеки стереть
Ослабнувшей рукой».

Февраль 1915

He stared at me perspicaciously,
And uttered: "Bride of Christ!
Don't envy the good fortune of the lucky,
A place has been prepared for you.

Forget about your native home,
Become like the heavenly lily.
Ailing, you will sleep on straw
And finish blissfully."

The holy man probably heard from his cell
How I sang on my way back
About my indescribable joy,
Marveling, and rejoicing greatly.

July 1914
Darnitsa

———

Just as the other cranes
Call to the injured one: kurli, kurli!
When the autumn fields
Are crumbly and warm . . .

So I, the sick one, hear the cries,
The noise of golden wings
From dense, low clouds
And tangled underbrush:

"It's time to fly, time to fly
Over river and land.
You see, you can no longer sing
Or brush the tears from your cheeks
With your weakening hand."

February 1915

Буду тихо на погосте
Под доской дубовой спать,
Будешь, милый, к маме в гости
В воскресенье прибегать —
Через речку и по горке,
Так что взрослым не догнать,
Издалека, мальчик зоркий,
Будешь крест мой узнавать.
Знаю, милый, можешь мало
Обо мне припоминать:
Не бранила, не ласкала,
Не водила причащать.

1915

Высокомерьем дух твой помрачен,
И оттого ты не познаешь света.
Ты говоришь, что вера наша — сон
И марево — столица эта.

Ты говоришь — моя страна грешна,
А я скажу — твоя страна безбожна.
Пускай на нас еще лежит вина, —
Всё искупить и всё исправить можно.

Вокруг тебя — и воды, и цветы.
Зачем же к нищей грешнице стучишься?
Я знаю, чем так тяжко болен ты:
Ты смерти ищешь и конца боишься.

1 января 1917
Слепнево

Under an oaken slab in the churchyard
I will sleep quietly,
You, darling, will come running
To visit Mama on Sunday—
Across the stream and along the rise,
Leaving the grownups far behind,
From far away, my sharp-sighted boy,
You will recognize my cross.
I know you won't be able
To remember much about me, little one:
I didn't scold you, I didn't hold you,
I didn't take you to Communion.

1915

———

Your spirit is clouded by arrogance,
And that's why you can't see the light.
You say that our faith is—a dream,
And a mirage—this capital.

You say—my country is sinful,
And I say—your country is godless.
If the blame were ours—
Everything could be redeemed and repaired.

All around you—water and flowers.
Why bother with this poor sinner then?
I know why you are so terribly sick:
You are seeking death and you fear the end.

January 1, 1917
Slepnyovo

———

Zh. 172

Приду туда, и отлетит томленье.
Мне ранние приятны холода.
Таинственные, темные селенья —
Хранилища молитвы и труда.

Спокойной и уверенной любови
Не превозмочь мне к этой стороне:
Ведь капелька новогородской крови
Во мне — как льдинка в пенистом вине.

И этого никак нельзя поправить,
Не растопил ее великий зной,
И что бы я ни начинала славить —
Ты, тихая, сияешь предо мной.

1916

Zh. 173

ПАМЯТИ 19 ИЮЛЯ 1914

Мы на сто лет состарились, и это
Тогда случилось в час один:
Короткое уже кончалось лето,
Дымилось тело вспаханных равнин.

Вдруг запестрела тихая дорога,
Плач полетел, серебряно звеня.
Закрыв лицо, я умоляла Бога
До первой битвы умертвить меня.

I will go there and weariness will fly away.
The cool of early morning pleases me.
There are villages mysterious and dark—
Storehouses of prayer and work.

My tranquil and trusting love
Of this place will never be conquered:
There's a drop of Novgorod blood
In me—like a shard of ice in frothy wine.

And this can never be remedied,
Great heat will not melt it,
And no matter what I begin to praise—
You, silent, shine before me.

1916

———

In Memoriam, July 19, 1914

We aged a hundred years, and this
Happened in a single hour:
The short summer had already died,
The body of the ploughed plains smoked.

Suddenly the quiet road burst into color,
A lament flew up, ringing, silver...
Covering my face, I implored God
Before the first battle to strike me dead.

Из памяти, как груз отныне лишний,
Исчезли тени песен и страстей.
Ей — опустевшей — приказал Всевышний
Стать страшной книгой грозовых вестей.

Лето 1916
Слепнево

———

IV

Zh. 174

Н. Г. Чулковой

Перед весной бывают дни такие:
Под плотным снегом отдыхает луг,
Шумят деревья весело-сухие,
И теплый ветер нежен и упруг.
И легкости своей дивится тело,
И дома своего не узнаешь,
А песню ту, что прежде надоела,
Как новую, с волнением поешь.

Весна 1915
Слепнево

———

Like a burden henceforth unnecessary,
The shadows of passion and songs vanished from
    my memory.
The Most High ordered it—emptied—
To become a grim book of calamity.

Summer 1916
Slepnyovo

———

IV

N. G. Chulkova

Before spring there are days like these:
Under the dense snow the meadow rests,
The trees merrily, drily rustle,
And the warm wind is tender and supple.
And the body marvels at its lightness,
And you don't recognize your own house,
And that song you were tired of before,
You sing like a new one, with deep emotion.

Spring 1915
Slepnyovo

———

Zh. 175

То пятое время года,
Только его славословь.
Дыши последней свободой,
Оттого что это — любовь.
Высоко небо взлетело,
Легки очертанья вещей,
И уже не празднует тело
Годовщину грусти своей.

1913

Zh. 176

Выбрала сама я долю
Другу сердца моего:
Отпустила я на волю
В Благовещенье его.
Да вернулся голубь сизый,
Бьется крыльями в стекло.
Как от блеска дивной ризы,
Стало в горнице светло.

Весна 1915
Петербург

Zh. 177

СОН

Я знала, я снюсь тебе,
Оттого не могла заснуть.
Мутный фонарь голубел
И мне указывал путь.

This fifth season of the year
Eulogizes only itself.
Breathe your last free breath,
Because this is—love.
The sky spirals upward,
Objects are outlined sketchily,
And the body no longer commemorates
The anniversary of its grief.

1913

———

I myself chose the fate
Of the friend of my heart:
I set him free
On Annunciation Day.
But the blue-gray dove returned,
To beat its wings against the window.
How bright the room became,
As if from the luster of a miraculous icon frame.

Spring 1915
Petersburg

———

Dream

I knew I was appearing in your dream
Because I couldn't fall asleep.
The lantern flickered blue
And pointed out the path to me.

Ты видел царицын сад,
Затейливый белый дворец
И черный узор оград
У каменных гулких крылец.

Ты шел, не зная пути,
И думал: «Скорей. скорей,
О, только б ее найти,
Не проснуться до встречи с ней».

А сторож у красных ворот
Окликнул тебя: «Куда!»
Хрустел и ломался лед,
Под ногой чернела вода.

«Это озеро, — думал ты, —
На озере есть островок ...»
И вдруг из темноты
Поглядел голубой огонек.

В жестком свете скудного дня
Проснувшись, ты застонал
И в первый раз меня
По имени громко назвал.

Март 1915
Царское Село

Zh. 178

БЕЛЫЙ ДОМ

Морозное солнце. С парада
Идут и идут войска.
Я полдню январскому рада,
И тревога моя легка.

You saw the tsarina's garden,
The filigreed white palace
And the black tracery of the iron fences
Around the resonant stone porches.

You went along, not knowing the way
And you thought: "Faster, faster!
Oh, only to find her,
Not to wake up until we meet."

And the watchman at the red gate
Called out to you: "Halt!"
The ice crumbled and cracked,
Black water appeared underfoot.

"This is the lake," you thought.
"In the lake there is a little island . . ."
And suddenly from the darkness
Shone the small blue flame.

In the harsh light of a meager day,
You awoke, and you began to groan,
And for the first time
You called me loudly by my name.

March 1915
Tsarskoye Selo

The White House

A frosty sun. From the parade ground
More and more soldiers keep coming.
I am happy, this January noon,
And my troubles are few.

Здесь помню каждую ветку
И каждый силуэт.
Сквозь инея белую сетку
Малиновый каплет свет.

Здесь дом был почти что белый,
Стеклянное крыльцо.
Столько раз рукой помертвелой
Я держала звонок-кольцо.

Столько раз… Играйте, солдаты,
А я мой дом отыщу,
Узнаю по крыше покатой,
По вечному плющу.

Но кто его отодвинул,
В чужие унес города
Или из памяти вынул
Навсегда дорогу туда…

Волынки вдали замирают,
Снег летит, как вишневый цвет…
И, видно, никто не знает,
Что белого дома нет.

Лето 1914
Слепнево

———

Zh. 179

Долго шел через поля и села,
Шел и спрашивал людей:
«Где она, где свет веселый
Серых звезд — ее очей?

Here I remember each twig
And every silhouette.
Raspberry light seeps
Through the frosty white net.

There was a house here, almost white,
And a sun porch.
How many times my dead-white hand
Held the bell pull.

So many times... Soldiers, play on,
And I will look for my house,
I'll recognize it by its sloping roof,
Its everlasting ivy.

But someone has carried it off,
Taken it to another town,
Or torn from my memory forever
The road that leads there...

The sound of the bagpipes dies down,
Snow flies, like cherry blossoms...
And it's obvious nobody knows
That the white house is gone.

Summer 1914
Slepnyovo

———

For a long time he walked through fields and villages,
He walked and he asked the people he met:
"Where is she, where is the joyous light
Of those gray stars—her eyes?

Ведь настали, тускло пламенея,
Дни последние весны.
Все мне чаще снится, все нежнее
Мне о ней бывают сны!»

И пришел в наш град угрюмый
В предвечерний тихий час,
О Венеции подумал
И о Лондоне зараз.

Стал у церкви темной и высокой
На гранит блестящих ступеней
И молил о наступленьи срока
Встречи с первой радостью своей.

А над смуглым золотом престола
Разгорался Божий сад лучей:
«Здесь она, здесь свет веселый
Серых звезд — ее очей».

Май 1915

Zh. 180

Широк и желт вечерний свет,
Нежна апрельская прохлада.
Ты опоздал на много лет,
Но все-таки тебе я рада.

Сюда ко мне поближе сядь,
Гляди веселыми глазами:
Вот эта синяя тетрадь —
С моими детскими стихами.

Now, burning down,
The last days of spring have come.
More and more I dream of her,
And my dreams are always more tender."

And he arrived in our gloomy city
In the quiet, early evening hour.
He thought of Venice
And London as well.

He stood near the tall, dark church
On the gleaming steps of granite,
And he prayed for the coming time
Of the meeting with his first delight.

And over the altar's tarnished gold
Flared God's garden of rays:
"She is here, here is the joyous light
Of those gray stars—her eyes."

May 1915

———

Broad and yellow is the evening light,
Tender the April coolness.
You are so many years late,
Nevertheless I am glad you came.

Sit here closer to me
And look on joyfully:
Here is a blue composition book—
With the poems of my childhood.

Прости, что я жила скорбя
И солнцу радовалась мало.
Прости, прости, что за тебя
Я слишком многих принимала.

Весна 1915
Царское Село

Я не знаю, ты жив или умер, —
На земле тебя можно искать
Или только в вечерней думе
По усопшем светло горевать.

Всё тебе: и молитва дневная,
И бессонницы млеющий жар,
И стихов моих белая стая,
И очей моих синий пожар.

Мне никто сокровенней не был,
Так меня никто не томил,
Даже тот, кто на муку предал,
Даже тот, кто ласкал и забыл.

Лето 1915
Слепнево

Нет, царевич, я не та,
Кем меня ты видеть хочешь,
И давно мои уста
Не целуют, а пророчат.

Forgive me that I ignored the sun
And that I lived in sorrow.
Forgive, forgive, that I
Mistook too many others for you.

Spring 1915
Tsarskoye Selo

———

I don't know if you're living or dead—
Whether to look for you here on earth
Or only in evening meditation,
When we grieve serenely for the dead.

Everything is for you: my daily prayer,
And the thrilling fever of the insomniac,
And the blue fire of my eyes,
And my poems, that white flock.

No one was more intimate with me,
No one made me suffer so,
Not even the one who consigned me to torment,
Not even the one who caressed and forgot.

Summer 1915
Slepnyovo

———

No, tsarevitch, I am not the one
You want me to be.
And no longer do my lips
Kiss—they prophesy.

Не подумай, что в бреду
И замучена тоскою
Громко кличу я беду:
Ремесло мое такое.

А умею научить,
Чтоб нежданное случилось,
Как навеки приручить
Ту, что мельком полюбилась.

Славы хочешь? — у меня
Попроси тогда совета,
Только это — западня,
Где ни радости, ни света.

Ну, теперь иди домой
Да забудь про нашу встречу,
А за грех твой, милый мой,
Я пред Господом отвечу.

10 июля 1915

Zh. 183

Из памяти твоей я выну этот день,
Чтоб спрашивал твой взор беспомощно-
                                    туманный:
Где видел я персидскую сирень,
И ласточек, и домик деревянный?

О, как ты часто будешь вспоминать
Внезапную тоску неназванных желаний
И в городах задумчивых искать
Ту улицу, которой нет на плане!

Don't think that, delirious
And tormented by grief,
I shriek of calamity:
This is my trade.

I know how to teach,
How to make the unexpected real,
How to domesticate forever
The one who took your fancy for awhile.

Do you want fame?—then you
Should ask me for advice,
Only—it's a trap
Where there is neither joy nor light.

Well, go home now
And forget that we met,
And as for your sin, my darling,
I will answer to the Lord for it.

July 10, 1915

———

I will root out this day from your memory,
So that your helplessly hazy glance will ask:
Where did I see Persian lilac,
And swallows, and a little wooden house?

Oh, how often you will remember
The sudden anguish of unnamed desire,
And search, in drifting dream towns,
For the street that isn't on the map!

При виде каждого случайного письма,
При звуке голоса за приоткрытой дверью
Ты будешь думать: «Вот она сама
Пришла на помощь моему неверью».

4 апреля 1915
Царское Село

Zh. 184

Не хулил меня, не славил,
Как друзья и как враги,
Только душу мне оставил
И сказал: побереги.

И одно меня тревожит:
Если он теперь умрет,
Ведь ко мне Архангел Божий
За душой его придет.

Как тогда ее я спрячу,
Как от Бога утаю?
Та, что так поет и плачет,
Быть должна в Его раю.

Июль 1915

Zh. 185

Там тень моя осталась и тоскует,
Всё в той же синей комнате живет,
Гостей из города заполночь ждет
И образок эмалевый целует.
И в доме не совсем благополучно:

*

At the sight of every chance letter,
At the sound of a voice from a half-opened door,
You will think: "She herself
Has come to dispel my disbelief."

April 4, 1915
Tsarskoye Selo

———

He didn't mock me, he didn't praise,
As friends would have, and enemies.
He only left me his soul
And said: Look after it.

And one thing troubles me:
If he dies now,
God's archangel will come to me
For his soul.

How then will I conceal it,
Keep it a secret from God?
This soul, which sings and cries,
Ought to be in His paradise.

July 1915

———

There my shadow remained, and it grieves.
Still living in that same blue room,
It waits till midnight for guests from town
And kisses the enameled icon.
And in this house all is not well:
*

Огонь зажгут, а все-таки темно...
Не оттого ль хозяйке новой скучно,
Не оттого ль хозяин пьет вино
И слышит, как за тонкою стеною
Пришедший гость беседует со мною?

Январь 1917
Слепнево

Zh. 186

Двадцать первое. Ночь. Понедельник.
Очертанья столицы во мгле.
Сочинил же какой-то бездельник,
Что бывает любовь на земле.

И от лености или со скуки
Все поверили, так и живут:
Ждут свиданий, боятся разлуки
И любовные песни поют.

Но иным открывается тайна,
И почиет на них тишина...
Я на это наткнулась случайно
И с тех пор все как будто больна.

1917
Петербург

Zh. 187

Небо мелкий дождик сеет
На зацветшую сирень.
За окном крылами веет
Белый, белый Духов День.

They light the fire but it's dark just the same...
Isn't that why the new wife is depressed,
Isn't that why the husband drinks wine
And listens, as behind the thin partition,
The guest and I engage in conversation?

January 1917
Slepnyovo

———

The twenty-first. Night. Monday.
The outlines of the capital are in mist.
Some idler invented the idea
That there's something in the world called love.

And from laziness or boredom,
Everyone believed it and here is how they live:
They anticipate meetings, they fear partings
And they sing the songs of love.

But the secret will be revealed to the others,
And a hush will fall on them all...
I stumbled on it by accident
And since then have been somehow unwell.

1917
Petersburg

———

The sky sows a fine rain
On the lilacs in bloom.
At the window beating its wings
Is the white, white Day of the Holy Ghost.

Нынче другу возвратиться
Из-за моря — крайний срок.
Все мне дальний берег снится,
Камни, башни и песок.

На одну из этих башен
Я взойду, встречая свет . . .
Да в стране болот и пашен
И в помине башен нет.

Только сяду на пороге,
Там еще густая тень.
Помоги моей тревоге,
Белый, белый Духов День!

Май 1916
Слепнево

———

Zh. 188

Я знаю, ты моя награда
За годы боли и труда,
За то, что я земным отрадам
Не предавалась никогда,
За то, что я не говорила
Возлюбленному: «Ты любим».
За то, что всем я всё простила,
Ты будешь ангелом моим.

1916

———

By today at the latest, my love
Should have returned from across the sea.
I keep dreaming of the distant coast,
Rocks, towers and sand.

I ascend one of those towers,
Meeting the light . . .
But in this country of fens and ploughed fields,
There's no trace of a tower.

I will just sit on the threshold,
There the shadow is still dense.
White, white Day of the Holy Ghost,
Dispel my uneasiness!

May 1916
Slepnyovo

———

I know that you are my reward
For years of pain and trouble,
For never devoting myself
To earthly delights,
For not saying
To the beloved: "You are loved."
Because I forgave them all for everything,
You will be my angel.

1916

———

Zh. 189

МИЛОМУ

Голубя ко мне не присылай,
Писем беспокойных не пиши,
Ветром мартовским в лицо не вей.
Я вошла вчера в зеленый рай,
Где покой для тела и души
Под шатром тенистых тополей.

И отсюда вижу городок,
Будки и казармы у дворца,
Надо льдом китайский желтый мост.
Третий час меня ты ждешь — продрог,
А уйти не можешь от крыльца
И дивишься, сколько новых звезд.

Серой белкой прыгну на ольху,
Ласочкой пугливой пробегу,
Лебедью тебя я стану звать,
Чтоб не страшно было жениху
В голубом кружащемся снегу
Мертвую невесту поджидать.

27 февраля 1915
Царское Село

Zh. 190

Юнии Анреп

Судьба ли так моя переменилась,
Иль вправду кончена игра?
Где зимы те, когда я спать ложилась
В шестом часу утра?

To the Beloved

Don't send me a dove,
Don't write me disquieting letters,
Don't make the March wind keen in my face.
Yesterday I entered green paradise,
Where there is peace for body and soul
Under a tent of the poplars' shadow.

And from here I see the little city,
The barracks and sentry boxes at the palace,
The yellow Chinese bridge above the ice.
For three hours you've been awaiting me—you waver,
But you cannot leave the porch
And you marvel, so many new stars.

As a gray squirrel, I will leap on the alder tree,
As a weasel, shy, I'll scurry by,
As a swan, I'll call to you,
So that it won't be terrible for the groom
To wait in the whirling blue snow
For his dead bride.

February 27, 1915
Tsarskoye Selo

———

—to Yunya Anrep

Has my fate changed so much,
Or is the game really over?
Where are the winters when I went to bed
At six in the morning?

По-новому, спокойно и сурово,
Живу на диком берегу.
Ни праздного, ни ласкового слова
Уже промолвить не могу.

Не верится, что скоро будут святки.
Степь трогательно зелена.
Сияет солнце. Лижет берег гладкий
Как будто теплая волна.

Когда от счастья томной и усталой
Бывала я, то о такой тиши
С невыразимым трепетом мечтала,
И вот таким себе я представляла
Посмертное блуждание души.

Декабрь 1916
Севастополь (Бельбек)

Zh. 191

Как белый камень в глубине колодца,
Лежит во мне одно воспоминанье.
Я не могу и не хочу бороться:
Оно — веселье и оно — страданье.

Мне кажется, что тот, кто близко взглянет
В мои глаза, его увидит сразу.
Печальней и задумчивее станет
Внимающего скорбному рассказу.

Я ведаю, что боги превращали
Людей в предметы, не убив сознанья,
Чтоб вечно жили дивные печали.
Ты превращен в мое воспоминанье.

5 июня 1916
Слепнево

Once more, peaceful and severe,
I am living on the wild shore.
I am no longer able to utter
Either an idle or a tender word.

I can't believe that Christmas will soon be here.
The steppe is touchingly green.
The sun is radiant. A wave that looks warm
Laps the smooth shore.

When I became weary and languorous
From happiness, I used to dream
With inexpressible trembling of such repose,
And this is how I imagined
The posthumous wanderings of the soul.

December 1916
Sevastopol (Belbek)

―――

Like a white stone in the depths of a well,
A certain memory lies within me.
I can't and I don't want to struggle:
It is―joy and it is―agony.

I think that someone looking closely
Into my eyes will see it immediately.
He will become more sorrowful and pensive
Than someone heeding a tale of grief.

I know that the gods transformed
Humans into objects without killing their minds.
So that my amazing sorrows will live forever,
You've been transformed into this memory of mine.

June 5, 1916
Slepnyovo

Первый луч — благословенье Бога —
По лицу любимому скользнул,
И дремавший побледнел немного,
Но еще покойнее уснул.

Верно, поцелуем показалась
Теплота небесного луча...
Так давно губами я касалась
Милых губ и смуглого плеча...

А теперь, усопших бестелесней,
В неутешном странствии моем,
Я к нему влетаю только песней
И ласкаюсь утренним лучом.

14 мая 1916
Слепнево

⟨ДОПОЛНЕНИЯ⟩

И мнится — голос человека
Здесь никогда не прозвучит,
Лишь ветер каменного века
В ворота черные стучит.
И мнится мне, что уцелела

*

The first ray of light—God's blessing—
Glided over my lover's face,
And drowsing, he became a bit pale,
But fell still deeper asleep.

Truly, it seemed like a kiss,
The warmth of that heavenly ray...
Thus, long ago, my lips used to touch
His dusky shoulder and his sweet lips...

But now, more disembodied than the dead,
In my inconsolable wandering
I fly to him only as a song
And caress him as a ray of morning.

May 14, 1916
Slepnyovo

———

(ADDITIONS)

And it seems—a human voice
Is never heard here,
Only the wind from the Stone Age
Knocks at the back door.
And it seems that under this wide sky

*

Под этим небом я одна —
За то, что первая хотела
Испить смертельного вина.

Лето 1917
Слепнево

Zh. 194

Когда в мрачнейшей из столиц
Рукою твердой, но усталой,
На чистой белизне страниц
Я отречение писала,

И ветер в круглое окно
Вливался влажною струею, —
Казалось, небо сожжено
Червонно-дымною зарею.

Я не взглянула на Неву,
На озаренные граниты,
И мне казалось — наяву
Тебя увижу, незабытый.

Но неожиданная ночь
Покрыла город предосенний.
Чтоб бегству моему помочь,
Расплылись пепельные тени.

Я только крест с собой взяла,
Тобою данный в день измены, —
Чтоб степь полынная цвела,
А ветры пели, как сирены.

I alone have survived—
Because I was the first who wanted
To drink the deadly wine.

Summer 1917
Slepnyovo

———

When, in the gloomiest of capitals,
With a firm but weary hand
I wrote my renunciation
On an immaculate page

And a damp wind flowed
Through the round window—
It seemed that the sky was consumed
By the tarnished, red-gold dawn.

I did not look at the Neva,
At the illuminated granite,
And it seemed to me—I really
Saw you, the one I can't forget...

But unexpected night
Covered the late-summer city.
And ash-gray shadows spread
To aid my flight.

I took with me only the cross
You gave me on the day of betrayal—
So that the steppe wormwood might bloom
And the winds, like sirens, sing.

И вот, он на пустой стене
Хранит меня от горьких бредней,
И ничего не страшно мне
Припомнить, — даже день последний.

Август 1916
Песочная бухта

Zh. 195

Как площади эти обширны,
Как гулки и круты мосты!
Тяжелый, беззвездный и мирный
Над нами покров темноты.

И мы, словно смертные люди,
По свежему снегу идем.
Не чудо ль, что нынче пробудем
Мы час предразлучный вдвоем?

Безвольно слабеют колени,
И кажется, нечем дышать...
Ты — солнце моих песнопений,
Ты — жизни моей благодать.

Вот черные зданья качнутся,
И на землю я упаду, —
Теперь мне не страшно очнуться
В моем деревенском саду.

10 марта 1917
Петербург

And here, on the bare wall,
It protects me from bitter fantasies,
And nothing is too terrible for me
To recall—not even the final day.

August 1916
Pesochnaya Bay

———

How steep and resounding these bridges are,
How vast these squares!
Heavy, peaceful and starless
Is the shroud of darkness over us.

And we, just like ordinary mortals,
Walk on the new snow.
Isn't it a wonder that we can spend
The hour before separation together?

Helplessly my knees go weak,
It's as if there is nothing to breathe...
You are—the sun of my poetry,
You are—the blessing of my life.

The black buildings are swaying
And I'm falling to the ground—
Today it's not so terrible to awaken
In my country garden.

March 10, 1917
Petersburg

———

Для того ль тебя носила
Я когда-то на руках,
Для того ль сияла сила
В голубых твоих глазах!
Вырос стройный и высокий,
Песни пел, мадеру пил,
К Анатолии далекой
Миноносец свой водил.

На Малаховом Кургане
Офицера расстреляли.
Без недели двадцать лет
Он глядел на Божий свет.

1918
Петербург

Родилась я ни поздно, ни рано,
Это время блаженно одно,
Только сердцу прожить без обмана
Было господом не дано.

Оттого и темно в светлице,
Оттого и друзья мои,
Как вечерние грустные птицы,
О небывшей поют любви.

1913

Why then did I used to
Hold you in my arms,
Why did your strength shine
From your blue eyes!
You grew up tall and handsome,
Sang songs and drank Madeira,
Then took your torpedo boat
To far-off Anatolia.

At Malakhov Kurgan
They shot an officer.
For one week less than twenty years
He had looked upon God's world.

1918
Petersburg

———

I was born neither too early nor too late,
The time was uniquely blessed,
Only the Lord did not allow my heart
To live through it without deceit.

That's why it's dark in the front room,
That's why my friends,
Like melancholy evening birds,
Sing of a love that never was.

1913

———

Zh. 198

Мне не надо счастья малого,
Мужа к милой провожу
И, довольного, усталого,
Спать ребенка уложу.

Снова мне в прохладной горнице
Богородицу молить...
Трудно, трудно жить затворницей,
Да трудней веселой быть.

Только б сон приснился пламенный,
Как войду в нагорный храм,
Пятиглавый, белый, каменный,
По запомненным тропам.

Май 1914
Петербург

Zh. 199

Город сгинул, последнего дома
Как живое взглянуло окно...
Это место совсем незнакомо,
Пахнет гарью, и в поле темно.

Но когда грозовую завесу
Нерешительный месяц рассек,
Мы увидели: на гору, к лесу
Пробирался хромой человек.

Было страшно, что он обгоняет
Тройку сытых веселых коней,
Постоит и опять ковыляет
Под тяжелою ношей своей.

I don't need much happiness,
I'm seeing my husband off to his sweetheart
And putting my contented,
Exhausted child to bed.

And again, in my cool, airy room,
I beseech the Mother of God...
Hard, it is hard to live like a hermit,
And even harder to be cheerful.

If only I could have a vision of passion,
As I enter the five-domed, white, stone
Church on the hill
By the path I know so well.

May 1914
Petersburg

The city disappeared, from the last house
A window stared as if alive...
This place is completely unfamiliar,
It smells of burning and the fields are dark.

But when the timid moon
Cleaved its stormy curtain,
We saw on the hill near the woods
A hunchbacked man struggling along.

It was frightening that he outstripped
A troika of sleek, spirited horses,
Then stopped and hobbled again,
Bearing a heavy burden.

Мы заметить почти не успели,
Как он возле кибитки возник.
Словно звезды глаза голубели,
Освещая измученный лик.

Я к нему протянула ребенка,
Поднял руку со следом оков
И промолвил мне благостно-звонко:
«Будет сын твой и жив и здоров!»

1916
Слепнево

Zh. 200

О, есть неповторимые слова,
Кто их сказал — истратил слишком много.
Неистощима только синева
Небесная и милосердье Бога.

Зима 1916
Севастополь

Zh. 201

Стал мне реже сниться, слава Богу,
Больше не мерещится везде,
Лег туман на белую дорогу,
Тени побежали по воде.

И весь день не замолкали звоны
Над простором вспаханной земли,
Здесь всего сильнее от Ионы
Колокольни Лаврские вдали.

We barely had time to notice him
When he sprang up near the sleigh.
His eyes shone blue as stars,
Illuminating his tormented face.

I held out the child to him,
He lifted his hand with the fetters' scars
And he pronounced in solemn, ringing tones:
"May your son live and thrive."

1916
Slepnyovo

———

Oh, there are unique words,
Whoever says them—spends much too much.
Only heaven's blue is inexhaustible,
And the mercy of God.

Winter 1916
Sevastopol

———

I dream of him less often now, thank God,
He doesn't appear everywhere anymore.
Fog lies on the white road,
Shadows start to run along the water.

And the ringing goes on all day.
Over the endless expanse of ploughed fields,
Ever louder sound the bells
From Jonah's Monastery far away.

Подстригаю на кустах сирени
Ветки те, что нынче отцвели;
По валам старинных укреплений
Два монаха медленно прошли.

Мир родной понятный и телесный
Для меня незрячей оживи.
Исцелил мне душу Царь Небесный
Ледяным покоем нелюбви.

1912
Киев

Zh. 202

Не тайны и не печали,
Не мудрой воли судьбы —
Эти встречи всегда оставляли
Впечатление борьбы.

Я, с утра угадав минуту,
Когда ты ко мне войдешь,
Ощущала в руках согнутых
Слабо колющую дрожь.

И сухими пальцами мяла
Пеструю скатерть стола...
Я тогда уже понимала,
Как эта земля мала.

1914 или 1915

I am clipping today's wilted branches
From the lilac bushes;
On the ramparts of the ancient fortress,
Two monks stroll.

Revive for me, who cannot see,
The familiar, comprehensible, corporeal world.
The heavenly king has already healed my soul
With the peace of unlove, icy cold.

1912
Kiev

————

Not mystery and not grief,
Not the wise will of destiny —
Those meetings always left
The impression of strife.

From dawn I would guess at the moment
You would appear,
Feeling in my folded arms,
Faint tremors.

And with dry fingers I would crumple
The table's gaily colored cloth . . .
Already then I understood
How small is this earth.

1914 or 1915

————

Zh. 203

Будем вместе, милый, вместе,
Знают все, что мы родные,
А лукавые насмешки,
Как бубенчик отдаленный,
И обидеть нас не могут,
И не могут огорчить.

Где венчались мы — не помним,
Но сверкала эта церковь
Тем неистовым сияньем,
Что лишь ангелы умеют
В белых крыльях приносить.

А теперь пора такая,
Страшный год и страшный город.
Как же можно разлучиться
Мне с тобой, тебе со мной?

Весна 1915
Петербург

Zh. 204

Черная вилась дорога,
Дождик моросил,
Проводить меня немного
Кто-то попросил.
Согласилась, да забыла
На него взглянуть,
А потом так странно было
Вспомнить этот путь.
Плыл туман, как фимиамы
Тысячи кадил.
Спутник песенкой упрямо

*

We will be together, darling, together,
They all know that we are close,
And their sneering mockery,
Like the sound of distant sleigh bells,
Cannot wound us,
Cannot grieve us.

Where we were married—we don't remember,
But that church sparkled
With the frenzied radiance
That only angels can bring
With their white wings.

And now at such a time,
In this terrible year and terrible city,
How is it possible to part,
Me from you, you from me?

Spring 1915
Petersburg

———

The dark road twisted,
The rain was drizzling,
Someone asked
To walk with me a little way.
I agreed, but I forgot
To look at him,
And later on how strange it was
To remember that journey.
Fog drifted like incense
From a thousand censers.
With a little song my companion

*

Сердце бередил.
Помню древние ворота
И конец пути —
Там со мною шедший кто-то
Мне сказал: «Прости...»
Медный крестик дал мне в руки,
Словно брат родной...
И я всюду слышу звуки
Песенки степной.
Ах, я дома как не дома —
Плачу и грущу.
Отзовись, мой незнакомый,
Я тебя ищу!

1913 (?)

Zh. 205

Как люблю, как любила глядеть я
На закованные берега,
На балконы, куда столетья
Не ступала ничья нога.
И воистину ты, столица —
Для безумных и светлых нас;
Но когда над Невою длится
Тот особенный, чистый час
И проносится ветер майский
Мимо всех надводных колонн,
Ты — как грешник, видящий райский
Перед смертью сладчайший сон...

1916

Persistently picked at my heart.
I remember the ancient gates,
And the journey's end—
There the one who had walked with me
Said to me: "Forgive..."
He put a copper cross in my hands
Just as a brother would have done...
And everywhere I hear the sounds
Of the little steppe song.
Ah, at home it's no longer like home—
I lament and mourn.
Respond to me, my unknown,
I am searching for you!

(1913)

———

How I love, how I loved to look
At your chained shores,
At the balconies, where for hundreds of years
No one has set foot.
And verily you are the capital
For us who are mad and luminous;
But when that special, pure hour
Lingers over the Neva
And the May wind sweeps
Past all the columns lining the water,
You are like a sinner turning his eyes,
Before death, to the sweetest dream of paradise...

1916

Akhmatova and Her Muse. Painting by
Kuzma Petrov-Vodkine, 1922

PLANTAIN

(1921)

*Узнай, по крайней мере, звуки,
бывало, милые тебе.*

Пушкин

*Know, at least, the sounds
That once were dear to you.*

Pushkin

Zh. 206

Сразу стало тихо в доме,
Облетел последний мак,
Замерла я в долгой дреме
И встречаю ранний мрак.

Плотно заперты ворота,
Вечер черен, ветер тих.
Где веселье, где забота,
Где ты, ласковый жених?

Не нашелся тайный перстень,
Прождала я много дней,
Нежной пленницею песня
Умерла в груди моей.

Июль 1917
Слепнево

Zh. 207

Ты — отступник: за остров зеленый
Отдал, отдал родную страну,
Наши песни и наши иконы
И над озером тихим сосну.

Для чего ты, лихой ярославец,
Коль еще не лишился ума,
Загляделся на рыжих красавиц
И на пышные эти дома?

Так теперь и кощунствуй, и чванься,
Православную душу губи,
В королевской столице останься
И свободу свою полюби.

Suddenly it's become still in the house,
The last poppy has lost its petals;
Steeped in a long drowsiness
I encounter the early gloom.

The gates are tightly closed,
The evening is black, the wind is still.
Where is happiness, where are woes,
Where are you, my tender betrothed?

The secret ring has not been found,
I have waited a long time,
And like a delicate prisoner, the song
In my breast died.

July 1917
Slepnyovo

———

You are an apostate: for a green island
You betrayed, betrayed your native land,
Our songs and our icons
And the pine above the quiet lake.

Why, dashing man of Yaroslavl,
Unless you've been deprived of reason,
Are you lost in admiration
For red-haired beauties and those splendid houses?

So now, blaspheme and swagger,
Destroy your Orthodox soul,
Stay in the city of royalty
And rejoice that you are free.

Для чего ж ты приходишь и стонешь
Под высоким окошком моим?
Знаешь сам, ты и в море не тонешь,
И в смертельном бою невредим.

Да, не страшны ни море, ни битвы
Тем, кто сам потерял благодать.
Оттого-то во время молитвы
Попросил ты тебя поминать.

Лето 1917
Слепнево

Zh. 208

Просыпаться на рассвете
Оттого, что радость душит,
И глядеть в окно каюты
На зеленую волну,
Иль на палубе в ненастье,
В мех закутавшись пушистый,
Слушать, как стучит машина,
И не думать ни о чем,
Но предчувствуя свиданье
С тем, кто стал моей звездою,
От соленых брызг и ветра
С каждым часом молодеть.

Июль 1917
Слепнево

Why do you appear and groan
Under my high window?
You know yourself that even in the sea you won't drown,
And from mortal combat you'll emerge unharmed.

Yes, neither battles nor the sea terrify
One who has forfeited grace.
Because of that you beg to be
Remembered when we pray.

Summer 1917
Slepnyovo

———

To wake at dawn
Breathless from joy,
And look through the cabin window
At the green waves,
Or on deck in rainy weather,
Wrapped in fluffy furs,
To listen to the engine throbbing
And not think of anything,
But, anticipating a meeting
With the one who became my star,
From the wind and salty spray
To grow younger every hour.

July 1917
Slepnyovo

———

Zh. 209

И в тайную дружбу с высоким,
Как юный орел темноглазым,
Я, словно в цветник предосенний,
Походкою легкой вошла.
Там были последние розы,
И месяц прозрачный качался
На серых, густых облаках...

*Лето 1917
Петербург*

———

Zh. 210

Словно ангел, возмутивший воду,
Ты взглянул тогда в мое лицо,
Возвратил и силу, и свободу,
А на память чуда взял кольцо.
Мой румянец жаркий и недужный
Стерла богомольная печаль.
Памятным мне будет месяц вьюжный,
Северный встревоженный февраль.

**Февраль 1916
Царское Село**

———

Zh. 211

Когда о горькой гибели моей
Весть поздняя его коснется слуха,
Не станет он ни строже, ни грустней,
Но, побледневши, улыбнется сухо.
И сразу вспомнит зимний небосклон
И вдоль Невы несущуюся вьюгу,
И сразу вспомнит, как поклялся он
Беречь свою восточную подругу.

1917

And into secret friendship with someone tall,
Dark-eyed as a young eagle,
I entered with a light tread,
As if into a late-summer flower bed.
There were the last roses,
And a transparent moon rocking
In thick, gray clouds...

Summer 1917
Petersburg

———

Like the angel moving upon the water,
You looked into my face.
You gave me back both strength and freedom,
And in remembrance of the miracle you took the ring.
My flush, hot and unhealthy,
Was erased by prayerful melancholy.
I will remember this month of blizzards,
This uneasy northern February.

February 1916
Tsarskoye Selo

———

When he finally hears the news
Of my bitter death,
He won't become sadder or more severe,
But turning pale, he will smile drily.
And at once he'll remember the winter horizon
And a sweeping blizzard along the Neva,
And at once he'll remember how he swore
To look after his friend from the east.

1917

Zh. 212

А ты теперь тяжелый и унылый,
Отрекшийся от славы и мечты,
Но для меня непоправимо милый,
И чем темней, тем трогательней ты.

Ты пьешь вино, твои нечисты ночи,
Что наяву, не знаешь, что во сне,
Но зелены мучительные очи, —
Покоя, видно, не нашел в вине.

И сердце только скорой смерти просит,
Кляня медлительность судьбы.
Всё чаще ветер западный приносит
Твои упреки и твои мольбы.

Но разве я к тебе вернуться смею?
Под бледным небом родины моей
Я только петь и вспоминать умею,
А ты меня и вспоминать не смей.

Так дни идут, печали умножая.
Как за тебя мне господа молить?
Ты угадал: моя любовь такая,
Что даже ты не мог ее убить.

22 июля 1917
Слепнево

Zh. 213

Пленник чужой! Мне чужого не надо,
Я и своих-то устала считать.
Так отчего же такая отрада
Эти вишневые видеть уста?

And now you are depressed and despondent,
Renouncing fame and your dreams,
But for me you are irremediably dear,
And the darker you become, the more touching.

You drink wine, your nights are slovenly,
You don't know reality from dream,
But your green eyes are tormented—
It's clear that wine hasn't brought you peace.

And your heart asks only for a quicker death,
Cursing the sluggishness of fate,
More and more often the west wind carries
Your reproaches and your pleas.

But dare I go back to you?
Under the pale sky of my native land,
I only know how to remember and sing,
But you don't dare remember me.

So the days go by, and sorrows multiply,
How can I pray to the Lord for you?
You've guessed: my love is such
That even you can't make it die.

July 22, 1917
Slepnyovo

———

Someone else's captive? I don't need anyone else's,
I'm tired of counting my own.
Then why is it so marvelous
To see those cherry-red lips?

Пусть он меня и хулит, и бесславит,
Слышу в словах его сдавленный стон.
Нет, он меня никогда не заставит
Думать, что страстно в другую влюблен.

И никогда не поверю, что можно
После небесной и тайной любви
Снова смеяться и плакать тревожно
И проклинать поцелуи мои.

1917

Zh. 214

Я спросила у кукушки,
Сколько лет я проживу...
Сосен дрогнули верхушки,
Желтый луч упал в траву,
Но ни звука в чаще свежей...
Я иду домой,
И прохладный ветер нежит
Лоб горячий мой.

1 июня 1919
Царское Село

Zh. 215

По неделе ни слова ни с кем не скажу,
Всё на камне у моря сижу,
И мне любо, что брызги зеленой волны,
Словно слезы мои, солоны.
Были весны и зимы, да что-то одна

*

Let him censure me and speak ill of me,
I hear in his words a suppressed groan.
No! He'll never make me believe
That he loves another passionately.

And I'll never believe that it's possible,
After our secret and heavenly love,
To laugh again and to weep distractedly
And to curse my kisses.

1917

———

I asked the cuckoo
How many years I would live...
The tops of the pine trees quivered,
A yellow ray fell on the grass.
But not a sound in the cool grove...
I am going home now,
And a cooling breeze caresses
My burning brow.

June 1, 1919
Tsarskoye Selo

———

All week I don't say a word to anyone,
Just sit on a stone by the edge of the sea,
And it's pleasing that the spray of green waves
Is salty, like my tears.
There were springs and winters, but somehow

*

Мне запомнилась только весна.
Стали ночи теплее, подтаивал снег,
Вышла я поглядеть на луну,
И спросил меня тихо чужой человек,
Между сосенок встретив одну:
«Ты не та ли, кого я повсюду ищу,
О которой с младенческих лет,
Как о милой сестре, веселюсь и грущу?»
Я чужому ответила: «Нет!»
А как свет поднебесный его озарил,
Я дала ему руки мои,
И он перстень таинственный мне подарил,
Чтоб меня уберечь от любви.
И назвал мне четыре приметы страны,
Где мы встретиться снова должны:
Море, круглая бухта, высокий маяк,
А всего непременней — полынь...
И как жизнь началась, пусть и кончится так.
Я сказала, что знаю: аминь!

Осень 1916
Севастополь

———

Zh. 216

В каждых сутках есть такой
Смутный и тревожный час.
Громко говорю с тоской,
Не раскрывши сонных глаз,
И она стучит, как кровь,
Как дыхание тепла,
Как счастливая любовь,
Рассудительна и зла.

1917

———

I remember only one particular spring.
The warm nights had begun, the snow was thawing,
I had come out to look at the moon,
And in the pine grove I met a stranger
Who softly demanded of me:
"Aren't you the one I've been looking for everywhere?
About whom, since infancy,
I've rejoiced and grieved, as for a dear sister?"
I answered the stranger: "No."
And as a heavenly light illuminated him,
I gave him my hand
And he bestowed upon me a mysterious ring
To protect me from love.
And he listed four emblems of the land
Where we were destined to meet again:
The sea, a circular bay, a tall lighthouse
And most important—wormwood...
And as life began, so let it end.
I said I understood: Amen!

Autumn 1916
Sevastopol

In every twenty-four hours there is one
That is confused and anxious.
I talk out loud to this anguish
Without opening my drowsy eyes,
And it beats on, like the blood,
Like warm breath,
Like happy love,
Calculating and malicious.

1917

Zh. 217

Земная слава как дым,
Не этого я просила.
Любовникам всем моим
Я счастие приносила.
Один и сейчас живой,
В свою подругу влюбленный,
И бронзовым стал другой
На площади оснеженной.

Зима 1914

Zh. 218

Это просто, это ясно,
Это всякому понятно, —
Ты меня совсем не любишь,
Не полюбишь никогда.
Для чего же так тянуться
Мне к чужому человеку,
Для чего же каждый вечер
Мне молиться за тебя?
Для чего же, бросив друга
И кудрявого ребенка,
Бросив город мой любимый
И родную сторону,
Черной нищенкой скитаюсь
По столице иноземной?
О, как весело мне думать,
Что тебя увижу я!

Лето 1917
Слепнево

Earthly fame is like smoke,
It's not what I asked for.
I brought happiness
To all my lovers.
One of them is living now,
Enamoured of his sweetheart,
And the other turned to bronze
In the snowy square.

Winter 1914

It is simple, it is clear,
Understood by everyone,
You don't love me in the least,
You never loved me.
Why am I always drawn
To someone else's man?
Why, each evening
Do I pray for you?
Why, having left my lover
And my curly-haired child,
Having abandoned my beloved city
And my native land,
Am I wandering, a melancholy beggar
In this foreign capital?
Oh, how happy it makes me to think
I'll get a glimpse of you!

Summer 1917
Slepnyovo

О нет, я не тебя любила,
Палима сладостным огнем,
Так объясни, какая сила
В печальном имени твоем.

Передо мною на колени
Ты стал, как будто ждал венца,
И смертные коснулись тени
Спокойно-юного лица.

И ты ушел. Не за победой,
За смертью. Ночи глубоки!
О, ангел мой, не знай, не ведай
Моей теперешней тоски.

Но если белым солнцем рая
В лесу осветится тропа,
Но если птица полевая
Взлетит с колючего снопа,

Я знаю: это ты, убитый,
Мне хочешь рассказать о том,
И снова вижу холм изрытый
Над окровавленным Днестром.

Забуду дни любви и славы,
Забуду молодость мою,
Душа темна, пути лукавы,
Но образ твой, твой подвиг правый
До часа смерти сохраню.

19 июля 1917
Слепнево

Oh no, it wasn't you I loved
When I burned with a sweet flame,
So explain, what kind of power
Is there in your sad name?

You knelt before me
As if waiting to be crowned,
And deathly shadows touched
Your peaceful young brow.

And you went off. Not to victory,
To death. Endless nights!
Oh my angel, may you not know, not be aware of
My present sorrow.

But if the forest path lights up
With the white sun of paradise,
But if a meadow bird
Soars from the prickly sheaves,

I will know: it is you—killed—
Wanting to tell me about it,
And again I'll see the pockmarked hill
Over the Dniestr's bloody swirl.

I will forget days of love and fame,
I will forget my youth.
The soul is dark, the way is treacherous,
But your image, your righteous deed
I will preserve until the hour of death.

July 19, 1917
Slepnyovo

Zh. 220

Я слышу иволги всегда печальный голос
И лета пышного приветствую ущерб,
А к колосу прижатый тесно колос
С змеиным свистом срезывает серп.

И стройных жниц короткие подолы,
Как флаги в праздник, по ветру летят.
Теперь бы звон бубенчиков веселых,
Сквозь пыльные ресницы долгий взгляд.

Не ласки жду я, не любовной лести
В предчувствии неотвратимой тьмы,
Но приходи взглянуть на рай, где вместе
Блаженны и невинны были мы.

27 июля 1917
Слепнево

Zh. 221

Как страшно изменилось тело,
Как рот измученный поблек!
Я смерти не такой хотела,
Не этот назначала срок.

Казалось мне, что туча с тучей
Сшибется где-то в высоте
И молнии огонь летучий
И голос радости могучей,
Как ангелы, сойдут ко мне.

1913

I am listening to the orioles' ever mournful voice
And saluting the splendid summer's decline.
And through grain pressed tightly, ear to ear,
The sickle, with its snake's hiss, slices.

And the short skirts of the slender reapers
Fly in the wind, like flags on a holiday.
The jingling of bells would be jolly now,
And through dusty lashes, a long, slow gaze.

It's not caresses I await, nor lover's adulation,
The premonition of inevitable darkness,
But come with me to gaze at paradise, where together
We were innocent and blessed.

July 27, 1917
Slepnyovo

———

How terribly the body has changed,
How withered the tormented mouth!
I didn't want a death like this,
I didn't set this date.

It seemed to me that stormcloud with stormcloud
Collided somewhere on high,
And a flying flash of lightning
And a voice of great joy
Descended, like angels, upon me.

1913

———

Zh. 222

Я окошка не завесила,
Прямо в горницу гляди.
Оттого мне нынче весело,
Что не можешь ты уйти.
Называй же беззаконницей,
Надо мной глумись со зла:
Я была твоей бессонницей,
Я тоской твоей была.

5 марта 1916

Zh. 223

Эта встреча никем не воспета,
И без песен печаль улеглась.
Наступило прохладное лето,
Словно новая жизнь началась.

Сводом каменным кажется небо,
Уязвленное желтым огнем,
И нужнее насущного хлеба
Мне единое слово о нем.

Ты, росой окропляющий травы,
Вестью душу мою оживи, —
Не для страсти, не для забавы,
Для великой земной любви.

17 мая 1916
Слепнево

I haven't covered the little window,
Look straight into my room.
Because I am happy today
That you can't leave.
Call me a sinner,
Mock me maliciously:
I was your insomnia,
I was your grief.

March 5, 1916

_____

No one sang about that meeting,
And its sadness subsided without a song.
A cool summer has set in,
Like a new life begun.

The sky seems like a vault of stone
Wounded by a yellow flame,
And more than my daily bread
I need some word of him.

You, sprinkling the grass with dew,
Revive my soul with news—
Not for passion, not for diversion,
But for great earthly love.

May 17, 1916
Slepnyovo

_____

Zh. 224

И вот одна осталась я
Считать пустые дни.
О вольные мои друзья,
О лебеди мои!

И песней я не скличу вас,
Слезами не верну,
Но вечером в печальный час
В молитве помяну.

Настигнут смертною стрелой,
Один из вас упал,
И черным вороном другой,
Меня целуя, стал.

Но так бывает: раз в году,
Когда растает лед,
В Екатеринином саду
Стою у чистых вод

И слышу плеск широких крыл
Над гладью голубой.
Не знаю, кто окно раскрыл
В темнице гробовой.

1917

Zh. 225

Чем хуже этот век предшествующих? Разве
Тем, что в чаду печали и тревог
Он к самой черной прикоснулся язве,
Но исцелить ее не мог.

And here, left alone, I
Am counting the empty days.
Oh, my freed friends,
Oh, my swans!

And I can't summon you with songs
Nor bring you back with tears,
But in the melancholy evening hour,
I'll remember you in prayer.

Overtaken by death's arrow,
One of you fell,
And another, kissing me,
Became a black crow.

But this is what happens: once a year,
When the ice melts,
In Catherine's garden I stand
Beside the pure pond

And I listen to the splash of wide wings
Over the smooth blue.
I don't know who cut a window
Into the tomb.

1917

———

Has this century been worse
Than the ages that went before?
Perhaps in this, that in a daze of grief and anguish
It touched, but could not cure, the vilest sore.

Еще на западе земное солнце светит
И кровли городов в его лучах блестят,
А здесь уж белая дома крестами метит
И кличет воронов, и вороны летят.

Зима 1919

Zh. 226

Теперь никто не станет слушать песен.
Предсказанные наступили дни.
Моя последняя, мир больше не чудесен,
Не разрывай мне сердца, не звени.

Еще недавно ласточкой свободной
Свершала ты свой утренний полет,
А ныне станешь нищенкой голодной,
Не достучишься у чужих ворот.

1917

Zh. 227

По твердому гребню сугроба
В твой белый, таинственный дом
Такие притихшие оба
В молчании нежном идем.
И слаще всех песен пропетых
Мне этот исполненный сон,
Качание веток задетых
И шпор твоих легонький звон.

Январь 1917

In the west the earthly sun is still shining,
And the roofs of the cities gleam in its rays,
But here the white one already chalks crosses on
    the houses
And summons the crows, and the crows come flying.

Winter 1919

———

Now no one will listen to songs.
The prophesied days have begun.
Latest poem of mine, the world has lost its wonder,
Don't break my heart, don't ring out.

A while ago, free as a swallow,
You accomplished your morning flight,
But now you've become a hungry beggar,
Knocking in vain at strangers' gates.

1917

———

Over the snowdrift's hard crust
Into your white, mysterious house,
We walk in tender silence,
Both hushed.
And sweeter to me than all songs sung
Is this dream fulfilled,
The gentle clinking of your spurs
And the swaying of branches we've brushed.

January 1917

———

Zh. 228

Теперь прощай, столица,
Прощай, весна моя,
Уже по мне томится
Корельская земля.

Поля и огороды
Спокойно зелены,
Еще глубоки воды
И небеса бледны.

Болотная русалка,
Хозяйка этих мест,
Глядит, вздыхая жалко,
На колокольный крест.

А иволга, подруга
Моих безгрешных дней,
Вчера вернувшись с юга,
Кричит среди ветвей,

Что стыдно оставаться
До мая в городах,
В театре задыхаться,
Скучать на островах.

Но иволга не знает,
Русалке не понять,
Как сладко мне бывает
Его поцеловать!

И все-таки сегодня
На тихом склоне дня
Уйду. Страна господня,
Прими к себе меня!

1917

Now farewell, capital,
Farewell my spring.
Already the Karelian earth
Longs for me.

The fields and vegetable gardens
Are peacefully green,
The waters are still deep
And the heavens pale.

The water nymph of the marshes,
The mistress of those places,
Stares, sighing piteously,
At the bell-tower cross.

And the oriole, a friend
From my sinless days,
Yesterday returned from the south,
And cries among the boughs

That it's shameful to stay
In the cities till May,
Stifle in theaters,
Mope on these islands.

But the oriole doesn't know,
The nymph can't understand,
How sweet it is for me
To kiss him!

And nevertheless, today,
At the day's quiet decline
I will leave. Land of our Lord,
Take me in!

1917

Zh. 229

Ждала его напрасно много лет.
Похоже это время на дремоту.
Но воссиял неугасимый свет
Тому три года в Вербную субботу.
Мой голос оборвался и затих —
С улыбкой предо мной стоял жених.

А за окном со свечками народ
Неспешно шел. О, вечер богомольный!
Слегка хрустел апрельский тонкий лед,
И над толпою голос колокольный,
Как утешенье вещее, звучал,
И черный ветер огоньки качал.

И белые нарциссы на столе,
И красное вино в бокале плоском
Я видела как бы в рассветной мгле.
Моя рука, закапанная воском,
Дрожала, принимая поцелуй,
И пела кровь: блаженная, ликуй!

1916

Zh. 230

НОЧЬЮ

Стоит на небе месяц, чуть живой,
Средь облаков струящихся и мелких,
И у дворца угрюмый часовой
Глядит, сердясь, на башенные стрелки.

Идет домой неверная жена,
Ее лицо задумчиво и строго,
А верную в тугих объятьях сна
Сжигает негасимая тревога.

Long years I waited for him in vain.
That time seems like a drowsy dream.
But an inextinguishable light began to shine
On Palm Sunday Eve three years ago.
My voice broke off and was still—
My betrothed stood before me with a smile.

And outside the window people with candles
Slowly walked by. Oh, holy night!
April's thin ice crackled lightly,
And over the crowd the voice of the bells,
As if foretelling consolation, pealed,
And a black wind swayed the little flames.

And the white narcissus on the table,
And the red wine in the crystal glass
I saw as in a sunrise mist.
My hand, spotted with wax,
Trembled, receiving a kiss,
And my blood sang: Blessed one, rejoice!

1916

———

At Night

The moon stands in the sky, barely alive,
In the midst of small, streaming clouds,
And the sullen sentry by the palace
Glares at the hands of the tower clock.

The unfaithful wife is going home,
Her face is pensive and stern,
And the faithful wife, in a dream's tight embrace,
Burns in eternal anxiety.

Что́ мне до них? Семь дней тому назад,
Вздохнувши, я прости сказала миру,
Но душно там, и я пробралась в сад
Взглянуть на звезды и потрогать лиру.

Осень 1918
Москва

Zh. 231

Течет река неспешно по долине,
Многооконный на пригорке дом.
А мы живем как при Екатерине:
Молебны служим, урожая ждем.
Перенеся двухдневную разлуку,
К нам едет гость вдоль нивы золотой,
Целует бабушке в гостиной руку
И губы мне на лестнице крутой.

Лето 1917
Слепнево

Zh. 232

На шее мелких четок ряд,
В широкой муфте руки прячу,
Глаза рассеянно глядят
И больше никогда не плачут.

И кажется лицо бледней
От лиловеющего шелка,
Почти доходит до бровей
Моя незавитая челка.

What are they to me? Seven days ago,
Taking a deep breath, I bid farewell to the world—
It was stifling there—I stole away to the garden
To look at the stars and touch my lyre.

Autumn 1918
Moscow

———

The river flows slowly through the valley,
There's a many-windowed house upon a knoll.
And we live as in Catherine's days:
We attend prayer service, we await the harvest.
After a separation of two days,
A guest rides up along the golden grain,
He kisses Grandmother's hand in the drawing room
And my lips on the curving staircase.

Summer 1917
Slepnyovo

———

Around the neck is a string of fine beads,
In a wide muff I hide the hands,
The eyes gaze vacantly about
And will never weep again.

And the face seems paler
Against lavender silk,
My straight bangs
Reach almost to the brows.

И непохожа на полет
Походка медленная эта,
Как будто под ногами плот,
А не квадратики паркета.

А бледный рот слегка разжат.
Неровно трудное дыханье,
И на груди моей дрожат
Цветы небывшего свиданья.

1913

Zh. 233

ПЕСЕНКА

Бывало, я с утра молчу
О том, что сон мне пел.
Румяной розе и лучу
И мне — один удел.
С покатых гор ползут снега,
А я белей, чем снег,
Но сладко снятся берега
Разливных мутных рек.
Еловой рощи свежий шум
Покойнее рассветных дум.

Март 1916

And how unlike flight
Is this halting gait,
As if a raft were underfoot,
Not squares of parquetry.

And the pale mouth is slightly open.
Irregular, labored, the breathing,
And on my breast tremble
The flowers of a meeting that did not happen.

1913

———

Little Song

I have been silent since morning
About what my dream sang to me.
For the red rose and the moonbeam
And for me—a single destiny.
The snows creep down the mountain slope,
And I am whiter than snow,
But sweetly the banks
Of the murky, overflowing river break off.
The cool rustling of spruce groves
Is more restful than waking thoughts.

March 1916

———

Zh. 234

И целый день, своих пугаясь стонов,
В тоске смертельной мечется толпа,
А за рекой на траурных знаменах
Зловещие смеются черепа.
Вот для чего я пела и мечтала,
Мне сердце разорвали пополам,
Как после залпа сразу тихо стало,
Смерть выслала дозорных по дворам.

Лето 1917

———

Zh. 235

Ты мог бы мне сниться и реже,
Ведь часто встречаемся мы,
Но грустен, взволнован и нежен
Ты только в святилище тьмы.
И слаще хвалы серафима
Мне губ твоих милая лесть. . .
О, там ты не путаешь имя
Мое. Не вздыхаешь, как здесь.

1914

———

S-F. I, 378
(Zh. 236)

Когда в тоске самоубийства
Народ гостей немецких ждал,
И дух суровый византийства
От русской Церкви отлетал;
Когда приневская столица,
Забыв величие свое,
Как опьяневшая блудница,
Не знала, кто берет ее,

∗

And all day, terrified by its own moans,
The crowd churns in agonized grief,
And across the river, on funeral banners,
Sinister skulls laugh.
And this is why I sang and dreamed,
They have ripped my heart in half,
As after a burst of shots, it became still,
And in the courtyards, death patrols.

Summer 1917

You shouldn't be in my dreams so often,
Since we meet so frequently,
But you are sad, troubled and tender
Only in night's sanctuary.
And sweeter to me than the praise of seraphim
Is your lips' dear flattery. . .
Oh, in dreams you don't confuse my name,
Or sigh, as you do here.

1914

When in suicidal anguish
The nation awaited its German guests,
And the stern spirit of Byzantium
Had fled from the Russian Church,
When the capital by the Neva,
Forgetting her greatness,
Like a drunken prostitute
Did not know who would take her next,

*

Мне голос был. Он звал утешно,
Он говорил: «Иди сюда,
Оставь свой край глухой и грешный,
Оставь Россию навсегда.
Я кровь от рук твоих отмою,
Из сердца выну черный стыд,
Я новым именем покрою
Боль поражений и обид».
Но равнодушно и спокойно
Руками я замкнула слух,
Чтоб этой речью недостойной
Не осквернился скорбный дух.

Осень 1917

———

⟨ДОПОЛНЕНИЕ⟩

Zh. 237

ЗАРЕ́

(С португальского)

Тот счастлив, кто прошел среди мучений,
Среди тревог и страсти жизни шумной,
Подобно розе, что цветет бездумно,
И легче по водам бегущей тени.
Так жизнь твоя была чужда заботе,
Как тонкий сон, но сладостный и нежный:
Проснулась... улыбнулась... и небрежно
Вернулась ты к нарушенной дремоте.

Июль 1920

A voice came to me. It called out comfortingly,
It said, "Come here,
Leave your deaf and sinful land,
Leave Russia forever.
I will wash the blood from your hands,
Root out the black shame from your heart,
With a new name I will conceal
The pain of defeats and injuries."
But calmly and indifferently,
I covered my ears with my hands,
So that my sorrowing spirit
Would not be stained by those shameful words.

Autumn 1917

———

(ADDITION)

To Zara

(from the Portuguese)

Happy is the one who has passed through the torments,
Through the tempests and the passion of tumultuous life
Like the rose, which blooms unthinking,
And lighter than a shadow flitting on the water.
Thus was your life a stranger to woes,
Like a fragile dream, but sweet and tender:
You awoke...you smiled...and nonchalantly
You returned to your interrupted doze.

July 1920

1921. Portrait by Yury Annenkov. Gouache.

1920s. Collection of Mikhail Baltsvinik

1920s. Photo by Moses Nappelbaum

АННА АХМАТОВА

ANNO DOMINI MCMXXI

КНИГОИЗДАТЕЛЬСТВО
ПЕТРОПОЛИС · ПЕТЕРБУРГ
ТЫСЯЧА ДЕВЯТЬСОТ
ДВАДЦАТЬ ВТОРОЙ ГОД

ANNO DOMINI MCMXXI
(1922)

В те баснословные года...
Тютчев

In those fabulous years.
Tyutchev

I

ПОСЛЕ ВСЕГО

Zh. 238

ПЕТРОГРАД, 1919

И мы забыли навсегда,
Заключены в столице дикой,
Озера, степи, города
И зори родины великой.
В кругу кровавом день и ночь
Долит жестокая истома...
Никто нам не хотел помочь
За то, что мы остались дома,
За то, что, город свой любя,
А не крылатую свободу,
Мы сохранили для себя
Его дворцы, огонь и воду.

Иная близится пора,
Уж ветер смерти сердце студит,
Но нам священный град Петра
Невольным памятником будет.

I

AFTER EVERYTHING

Petrograd, 1919

And confined to this savage capital,
We have forgotten forever
The lakes, the steppes, the towns,
And the dawns of our great native land.
Day and night in the bloody circle
A brutal languor overcomes us . . .
No one wants to help us
Because we stayed home,
Because, loving our city
And not winged freedom,
We preserved for ourselves
Its palaces, its fire and water.

A different time is drawing near,
The wind of death already chills the heart,
But the holy city of Peter
Will be our unintended monument.

———

S-F. I, 214
(Zh. 239)

БЕЖЕЦК

Там белые церкви и звонкий, светящийся лед.
Там милого сына цветут васильковые очи.
Над городом древним алмазные русские ночи,
И серп поднебесный желтее, чем липовый мед.
Там вьюги сухие взлетают с заречных полей,
И люди, как ангелы, Божьему Празднику рады,
Прибрали светлицу, зажгли у киота лампады,
И Книга Благая лежит на дубовом столе.
Там строгая память, такая скупая теперь,
Свои терема мне открыла с глубоким поклоном;
Но я не вошла, я захлопнула страшную дверь;
И город был полон веселым рождественским звоном.

26 декабря 1921

Zh. 240

ПРЕДСКАЗАНИЕ

Видел я тот венец златокованый. . .
Не завидуй такому венцу!
Оттого, что и сам он ворованный
И тебе он совсем не к лицу.
Туго согнутой веткой терновою
Мой венец на тебе заблестит.
Ничего, что росою багровою
Он изнеженный лоб освежит.

8 мая 1922

Bezhetsk

There are white churches there, and booming,
    luminous ice.
There the cornflower blue eyes of my dear son
    are blooming.
Over the ancient town are Russia's diamond nights,
And the sickle of the skies, yellower than the
    linden's honey.
There blizzards soar from the fields beyond the river,
And the people, like angels rejoicing in God's feast day,
Put the front room in order and lit the lamps in the
    icon corner,
And on the oaken table the Good Book lay.
There stern memory, so miserly now,
Opened her tower rooms to me with a deep bow;
But I didn't enter, I slammed the terrible door,
And the town was full of merry Christmas sounds.

December 26, 1921

———

Prophecy

I saw that crown of hammered gold . . .
Don't envy such a crown!
Because it is stolen
And it wouldn't become you.
Like a twisted branch of blackthorn,
My crown will begin to glow on you.
Never mind that it refreshes
The delicate brow with crimson dew.

May 8, 1922

ДРУГОЙ ГОЛОС

Zh. 241

1

Я с тобой, мой ангел, не лукавил,
Как же вышло, что тебя оставил
За себя заложницей в неволе
Всей земной непоправимой боли?
Под мостами полыньи дымятся,
Над кострами искры золотятся,
Грузный ветер окаянно воет,
И шальная пуля за Невою
Ищет сердце бедное твое.
И, одна в дому оледенелом,
Белая лежишь в сияньи белом,
Славя имя горькое мое.

7 декабря 1921
Петербург

Zh. 242

2

В тот давний год, когда зажглась любовь,
Как крест престольный, в сердце обреченном,
Ты кроткою голубкой не прильнула
К моей груди, но коршуном когтила.
Изменой первою, вином проклятья
Ты напоила друга своего.
Но час настал в зеленые глаза
Тебе глядеться, у жестоких губ
Молить напрасно сладостного дара
И клятв таких, каких ты не слыхала,
Каких еще никто не произнес.
Так отравивший воду родника
Для вслед за ним идущего в пустыне

*

THE VOICE OF ANOTHER

1

I didn't mean to trick you, my angel,
How did it happen that I left you
Behind me, a hostage in bondage
To every earthly, irremediable pain?
Under the bridges, patches of open water steam,
Over the bonfires, golden sparks gleam,
The heavy wind howls like one of the damned,
And beyond the Neva the stray bullet
Searches for your wretched heart.
And alone in the icy house,
White, in white radiance you lie,
Praising my bitter name.

December 7, 1921
Petersburg

2

In that year long ago, when love flared
Like an altar cross in a doomed heart,
You didn't cling like a gentle dove
On my breast, but clawed like a kite.
You gave your lover to drink of
The cursed wine, the first betrayal.
But the hour came for you to stare
Into green eyes, to beg those cruel lips
In vain for the sweetest gift
And for promises such as you'd never heard,
Such as no one had ever uttered.
It's as if someone poisoning the waters of a spring
For the one who comes after him into the desert

*

Сам заблудился и, возжаждав сильно,
Источника во мраке не узнал.
Он гибель пьет, прильнув к воде прохладной,
Но гибелью ли жажду утолить?

8 декабря 1921
Петербург

———

Zh. 243

Сказал, что у меня соперниц нет.
Я для него не женщина земная,
А солнца зимнего утешный свет
И песня дикая родного края.
Когда умру, не станет он грустить,
Не крикнет, обезумевши: «Воскресни!» —
Но вдруг поймет, что невозможно жить
Без солнца телу и душе без песни.
　　　…А что теперь?

1921

———

Zh. 244

Земной отрадой сердца не томи,
Не пристращайся ни к жене, ни к дому,
У своего ребенка хлеб возьми,
Чтобы отдать его чужому.
И будь слугой смиреннейшим того,
Кто был твоим кромешным супостатом,
И назови лесного зверя братом,
И не проси у Бога ничего.

Декабрь 1921
Петербург

———

Gets lost himself and, suffering terrible thirst,
Does not recognize that same spring in the darkness.
He drinks death, clinging to the water's coolness,
But can thirst be quenched by death?

December 8, 1921
Petersburg

———

He said that I have no rivals.
To him I am not an earthly woman,
But the comforting light of the winter sun,
And the wild song of his native land.
When I die he won't mourn,
He won't shout hysterically: "Rise up again!"—
But suddenly he'll understand that the body can't live
Without the sun, nor the soul without song.
             . . . But now what?

1921

———

Don't torment your heart with earthly joys,
Don't cling to your wife or your home,
Take the bread from your child
To give to a stranger.
And be the humblest servant of the one
Who was your bitterest foe,
And call the beast of the forest brother,
And don't ask God for anything, ever.

December 1921
Petersburg

———

Zh. 245

Не с теми я, кто бросил землю
На растерзание врагам.
Их грубой лести я не внемлю,
Им песен я своих не дам.

Но вечно жалок мне изгнанник,
Как заключенный, как больной.
Темна твоя дорога, странник,
Полынью пахнет хлеб чужой.

А здесь, в глухом чаду пожара
Остаток юности губя,
Мы ни единого удара
Не отклонили от себя.

И знаем, что в оценке поздней
Оправдан будет каждый час...
Но в мире нет людей бесслезней,
Надменее и проще нас.

Июль 1922
Петербург

ЧЕРНЫЙ СОН

Zh. 246

1

Косноязычно славивший меня
Еще топтался на краю эстрады.
От дыма сизого и тусклого огня
Мы все уйти конечно были рады.

I am not with those who abandoned their land
To the lacerations of the enemy.
I am deaf to their coarse flattery,
I won't give them my songs.

But to me the exile is forever pitiful,
Like a prisoner, like someone ill.
Dark is your road, wanderer,
Like wormwood smells the bread of strangers.

But here, in the blinding smoke of the conflagration
Destroying what's left of youth,
We have not deflected from ourselves
One single stroke.

And we know that in the final accounting,
Each hour will be justified . . .
But there is no people on earth more tearless
More simple and more full of pride.

July 1922
Petersburg

———

DARK DREAM

1

Praising me inarticulately,
You marked time at the edge of the stage.
We were all glad, of course, to get away
From the grayish smoke and the dim lights.

Но в путанных словах вопрос зажжен,
Зачем не стала я звездой любовной,
И стыдной болью был преображен
Над нами лик жестокий и бескровный.

Люби меня, припоминай и плачь.
Все плачущие не равны ль пред Богом.
Прощай, прощай! меня ведет палач.
По голубым предутренним дорогам.

1913

Zh. 247

2

Ты всегда таинственный и новый.
Я тебе послушней с каждым днем,
Но любовь твоя, о друг суровый,
Испытание железом и огнем.

Запрещаешь петь и улыбаться,
А молиться запретил давно.
Только б мне с тобою не расстаться,
Остальное всё равно!

Так, земле и небесам чужая,
Я живу и больше не пою,
Словно ты у ада и у рая
Отнял душу вольную мою.

Декабрь 1917

But in the muddled words there's a burning question,
Why didn't I become your beloved star,
And why, over us, was there a cruel, bloodless face
Transfigured by shameful pain?

Love me, remember and lament!
Aren't all those who lament equal before God?
Good-bye, good-bye! The hangman is leading me
Down the pale blue early-morning road.

1913

2

You are always novel and mysterious,
I am more submissive with each day.
But your love, oh my exacting lover,
Is a trial by iron and fire.

You forbid singing and smiling,
And praying you forbade long ago.
As long as we don't separate,
Let everything else go!

Thus, a stranger to heaven and earth,
I live and no longer sing,
It's as if you cut off my wandering soul
From both paradise and hell.

December 1917

3

От любви твоей загадочной,
Как от боли, в крик кричу,
Стала желтой и припадочной,
Еле ноги волочу.

Новых песен не насвистывай,
Песней долго ль обмануть,
Но когти, когти неистовей
Мне чахоточную грудь,

Чтобы кровь из горла хлынула
Поскорее на постель,
Чтобы смерть из сердца вынула
Навсегда проклятый хмель.

Июль 1918

4

Проплывают льдины, звеня,
Небеса безнадежно бледны.
Ах, за что ты караешь меня,
Я не знаю моей вины.

Если надо — меня убей,
Но не будь со мною суров.
От меня не хочешь детей
И не любишь моих стихов.

Всё по-твоему будет: пусть!
Обету верна своему,
Отдала тебе жизнь, — но грусть
Я в могилу с собою возьму.

Апрель 1918

3

Because of your enigmatic love
I shriek, as if in pain.
I've become sallow and convulsive,
Barely able to shuffle around.

Don't try to change your tune,
Songs can be deceptive,
But claw, claw more savagely
At the breast of this consumptive,

To make the blood gush faster
From my throat onto the bed,
So that death can tear
This damned intoxication from my heart forever.

July 1918

4

Ice floes float by, resounding,
The heavens are hopelessly pale.
Ah, why are you punishing me?
I don't know how I've failed.

If necessary—kill me,
But don't be stern.
You don't want children from me,
And you don't like my poetry.

Everything your way: let it be!
I was true to my vow,
To you I gave my life—but my sadness
I will take to the grave with me.

April 1918

Zh. 250

5

ТРЕТИЙ ЗАЧАТЬЕВСКИЙ

Переулочек, переул...
Горло петелькой затянул.

Тянет свежесть с Москва-реки,
В окнах теплятся огоньки.

Как по левой руке — пустырь,
А по правой руке — монастырь,

А напротив — высокий клен
Ночью слушает долгий стон.

Покосился гнилой фонарь —
С колокольни идет звонарь...

Мне бы тот найти образок,
Оттого что мой близок срок.

Мне бы снова мой черный платок,
Мне бы невской воды глоток.

1940

Zh. 251

6

Тебе покорной? Ты сошел с ума!
Покорна я одной Господней воле.
Я не хочу ни трепета, ни боли,
Мне муж палач, а дом его — тюрьма.

5

Number Three, Zachatevsky

A side street, a side str...
Stretched like a noose around your neck.

It drags coolness from the Moscow River,
In its windows little lights glimmer.

There on the left hand—vacant lots,
And on the right hand—a monastery,

And opposite—a giant maple tree
That listens to long groans at night.

The rotting lamppost leans—
The bell ringer leaves the tower...

I wish I could find that little icon,
Because my time is near.

I'd like my black shawl again,
I'd like a drink of Neva water.

1940

6

Submissive to you? You're out of your mind!
I submit only to the will of the Lord.
I want neither thrills nor pain,
My husband—is a hangman, and his home—prison.

Но видишь ли! Ведь я пришла сама;
Декабрь рождался, ветры выли в поле,
И было так светло в твоей неволе,
А за окошком сторожила тьма.

Так птица о прозрачное стекло
Всем телом бьется в зимнее ненастье,
И кровь пятнает белое крыло.

Теперь во мне спокойствие и счастье.
Прощай, мой тихий, ты мне вечно мил
За то, что в дом свой странницу пустил.

Август 1921

———

Zh. 252

Что ты бродишь неприкаянный,
Что глядишь ты не дыша?
Верно, понял: крепко спаяна
На двоих одна душа.

Будешь, будешь мной утешенным,
Как не снилось никому,
А обидишь словом бешеным —
Станет больно самому.

Декабрь 1921
Петербург

———

Zh. 253

Веет ветер лебединый,
Небо синее в крови.
Наступают годовщины
Первых дней твоей любви.

Well, look here! I came of my own accord...
It was already December, the winds were abroad,
And it was so bright in your bondage,
But outside the window, darkness stood guard.

Thus in the wintry blast, a bird
Beats its whole body against the clear glass,
And blood stains its white wing.

Now I have peace and good fortune.
Good-bye, you are dear to me forever, gentle one,
Because you let this pilgrim into your home.

August 1921

Why do you wander restlessly?
Why do you stare breathlessly?
Surely you comprehend: our two souls
Have been firmly welded into one.

You will be, you will be comforted by me
In a way no one could dream,
And when you wound with an angry word—
You yourself will feel the pain.

December 1921
Petersburg

The wind of swans is blowing,
The sky deep blue in blood.
The anniversary is approaching
Of the first days of your love.

Ты мои разрушил чары,
Годы плыли, как вода.
Отчего же ты не старый,
А такой, как был тогда?

Даже звонче голос нежный,
Только времени крыло
Осенило славой снежной
Безмятежное чело.

1922

Zh. 254

Ангел, три года хранивший меня,
Вознесся в лучах и огне,
Но жду терпеливо сладчайшего дня,
Когда он вернется ко мне.

Как щеки запали, бескровны уста,
Лица не узнать моего;
Ведь я не прекрасная больше, не та,
Что песней смутила его.

Давно на земле ничего не боюсь,
Прощальные помня слова.
Я в ноги ему, как войдет, поклонюсь,
А прежде кивала едва.

1922

You have shattered my goblets,
The years, like water, flow.
Why didn't you get old?
Why are you as you were then?

Your tender voice is even stronger,
But the wing of time
Has overshadowed your untroubled brow
With fame, with snow.

1922

———

The angel who for three years watched over me
Ascended in fire and rays,
But I'm patiently awaiting that sweetest of days,
When he returns to me.

Sunken cheeks, bloodless lips,
He won't recognize my face;
I am no longer beautiful, no longer the one
Whose song disturbed him.

For a long time I have feared nothing on earth,
Remembering his parting words.
I'll bow down at his feet, when he comes,
And I used to barely nod to him.

1922

———

Zh. 255

Шепчет: «Я не пожалею
Даже то, что так люблю, —
Или будь совсем моею,
Или я тебя убью».
Надо мной жужжит, как овод,
Непрестанно столько дней
Этот самый скучный довод
Черной ревности твоей.
Горе душит — не задушит,
Вольный ветер слезы сушит,
А веселье, чуть погладит,
Сразу с бедным сердцем сладит.

Февраль 1922

Zh. 256

Слух чудовищный бродит по городу,
Забирается в домы, как тать.
Уж не сказку ль про Синюю Бороду
Перед тем, как засну, почитать?

Как седьмая всходила на лестницу,
Как сестру молодую звала,
Милых братьев иль страшную вестницу,
Затаивши дыханье, ждала…

Пыль взметается тучею снежною,
Скачут братья на замковый двор,
И над шеей безвинной и нежною
Не подымется скользкий топор.

He whispers: "I'm not sorry
For loving you this way—
Either be mine alone
Or I will kill you."
It buzzes around me like a gadfly,
Incessantly, day after day,
This same boring argument,
Your black jealousy.
Grief smothers—but not fatally,
The wide wind dries my tears
And cheerfulness begins to soothe,
To smooth out this troubled heart.

February 1922

A monstrous rumor roams the city,
Stealing into houses, like a thief.
Shouldn't I read the story of Bluebeard
Before I lie down to sleep?

How the seventh bride mounted the staircase,
How she called to her younger sister,
She waited—holding her breath,
For her dear brothers or the dreaded messenger...

A snowy cloud of dust flies,
The brothers dash into the castle courtyard,
And over the tender and innocent neck
The slippery ax will not rise.

Этой сказкою нынче утешена,
Я, наверно, спокойно усну.
Что же сердце колотится бешено,
Что же вовсе не клонит ко сну?

Зима 1922

———

Zh. 257

Заболеть бы как следует, в жгучем бреду
Повстречаться со всеми опять,
В полном ветра и солнца приморском саду
По широким аллеям гулять.

Даже мертвые нынче согласны прийти,
И изгнанники в доме моем.
Ты ребенка за ручку ко мне приведи,
Так давно я скучаю о нем.

Буду с милыми есть голубой виноград,
Буду пить ледяное вино
И глядеть, как струится седой водопад
На кремнистое влажное дно.

Весна 1922

———

Zh. 258

За озером луна остановилась
И кажется отворенным окном
В притихший, ярко освещенный дом,
Где что-то нехорошее случилось.

Now, comforted by this fairy tale,
I'll certainly sleep peacefully.
Why then is my heart pounding,
Why can't I close my eyes?

Winter 1922

———

Falling ill, just as expected, I rave in delirium,
Meeting up with everyone again,
Walking in the wide allée
In the seaside garden full of wind and sun.

Today even the dead have agreed to come,
And the exiles are in my home.
You are leading the child to me by the hand,
I have longed for him so.

With my dear ones I will eat blue grapes,
I will drink ice cold wine
And watch how the gray-haired waterfall drops
Into the moist, flinty depths.

Spring 1922

———

The moon stalled behind the lake
And looked like the open window
Of a hushed, brilliantly illuminated house,
Where something awful had taken place.

Хозяина ли мертвым привезли,
Хозяйка ли с любовником сбежала,
Иль маленькая девочка пропала
И башмачок у заводи нашли...

С земли не видно. Страшную беду
Почувствовав, мы сразу замолчали.
Заупокойно филины кричали,
И душный ветер буйствовал в саду.

1922

———

Zh. 259

В. К. Шилейко

Как мог ты, сильный и свободный,
Забыть у ласковых колен,
Что грех карают первородный
Уничтожение и тлен.

Зачем ты дал ей на забаву
Всю тайну чудотворных дней, —
Она твою развеет славу
Рукою хищною своей.

Стыдись, и творческой печали
Не у земной жены моли.
Таких в монастыри ссылали
И на кострах высоких жгли.

1922

———

Was the owner brought in dead?
Have the mistress and her lover fled?
Or did the little girl disappear—
And by the creek they found her slipper...

From the earth it wasn't visible.
Sensing dire misfortune, we suddenly grew still.
The eagle owls shrieked for the repose of souls,
And in the garden a stifling wind howled.

1922

———

V. K. Shileiko

How could you, strong and free,
Forget at someone's comforting knee,
That original sin is punished
By destruction and decay.

Why did you give her, for her amusement,
Every secret of those marvelous days—
She will scatter your good name
With her rapacious hand.

Be ashamed, and don't beseech
An earthly woman for creative grief.
They banish such women to the convent
And burn them at the stake.

1922

———

БИБЛЕЙСКИЕ СТИХИ

Zh. 260

1

РАХИЛЬ

> И служил Иаков за Рахиль
> семь лет; и они показались ему
> за несколько дней, потому что он
> любил ее.
>
> *Книга Бытия*

И встретил Иаков в долине Рахиль,
Он ей поклонился, как странник бездомный.
Стада подымали горячую пыль,
Источник был камнем завален огромным,
Он камень своею рукой отвалил
И чистой водою овец напоил.

Но стало в груди его сердце грустить,
Болеть, как открытая рана,
И он согласился за деву служить
Семь лет пастухом у Лавана.
Рахиль! Для того, кто во власти твоей,
Семь лет словно семь ослепительных дней.

Но много премудр сребролюбец Лаван,
И жалость ему незнакома.
Он думает: каждый простится обман
Во славу Лаванова дома.
И Лию незрячую твердой рукой
Приводит к Иакову в брачный покой.

BIBLICAL VERSES

1

Rachel

And Jacob served for Rachel seven years;
and they seemed to him like seven days,
because he loved her.
Book of Genesis

And Jacob met Rachel in the valley,
He bowed to her, like a homeless wanderer.
The flocks churned up hot dust,
The spring was blocked by a huge stone.
He removed the stone with his own hand
And gave the sheep pure water to drink.

But the heart in his breast began to grieve,
To ache, like an open wound,
And he agreed to labor for the maiden
Seven years as a shepherd to Laban.
Rachel! For him who was under your sway,
Seven years were like seven dazzling days.

But very wise was Laban, the lover of silver,
And pity was unknown to him.
He thought: Everyone will forgive deceit
For the glory of Laban's house.
And with a firm hand he led unsuspecting Leah
To Jacob's marriage bed.

Течет над пустыней высокая ночь,
Роняет прохладные росы,
И стонет Лаванова младшая дочь,
Терзая пушистые косы,
Сестру проклинает и бога хулит,
И ангелу смерти явиться велит.

И снится Иакову сладостный час:
Прозрачный источник долины,
Веселые взоры Рахилиных глаз
И голос ее голубиный:
Иаков, не ты ли меня целовал
И черной голубкой своей называл?

25 декабря 1921 (ст. ст.)

Zh. 261

2

ЛОТОВА ЖЕНА

> Жена же Лотова оглянулась
> позади его и стала соляным стол-
> пом.
>
> *Книга Бытия*

И праведник шел за посланником бога,
Огромный и светлый, по черной горе,
Но громко жене говорила тревога:
Не поздно, ты можешь еще посмотреть

На красные башни родного Содома,
На площадь, где пела, на двор, где пряла,
На окна пустые высокого дома,
Где милому мужу детей родила.

Deep night flows over the desert,
Lets fall cool dew,
And Laban's younger daughter moans,
Tearing her heavy braids.
She curses her sister and blasphemes against God
And commands the angel of death to appear.

And the sweetest time for Jacob was his dream:
The limpid spring of the valley,
The joyful gaze of Rachel's eyes
And her voice like a dove:
Jacob, wasn't it you who kissed me
And called me your black dove?

December 25, 1921

2

Lot's Wife

> *Lot's wife looked back from behind him*
> *and became a pillar of salt.*
> Book of Genesis

And the righteous man followed the envoy of God,
Huge and bright, over the black mountain.
But anguish spoke loudly to his wife:
It is not too late, you can still gaze

At the red towers of your native Sodom,
At the square where you sang, at the courtyard where
  you spun,
At the empty windows of the tall house
Where you bore children to your beloved husband.

Взглянула, и, скованы смертною болью,
Глаза ее больше смотреть не могли;
И сделалось тело прозрачною солью,
И быстрые ноги к земле приросли.

Кто женщину эту оплакивать будет,
Не меньшей ли мнится она из утрат?
Лишь сердце мое никогда не забудет
Отдавшую жизнь за единственный взгляд.

24 февраля 1924

Zh. 262

3

МЕЛХОЛА

> Но Давида полюбила...
> дочь Саула, Мелхола. Саул
> думал: отдам ее за него, и она
> будет ему сетью.
>
> *Первая книга Царств*

И отрок играет безумцу царю,
И ночь беспощадную рушит,
И властно победную кличет зарю,
И призраки ужаса душит.
И царь благосклонно ему говорит:
«Огонь в тебе, юноша, дивный горит,
И я за такое лекарство
Отдам тебе дочку и царство».
А царская дочка глядит на певца,
Ей песен не нужно, не нужно венца,
В душе ее скорбь и обида,
Но хочет Мелхола Давида.
Бледнее, чем мертвая; рот ее сжат;

*

She glanced, and, paralyzed by deadly pain,
Her eyes no longer saw anything;
And her body became transparent salt
And her quick feet were rooted to the spot.

Who will weep for this woman?
Isn't her death the least significant?
But my heart will never forget the one
Who gave her life for a single glance.

February 24, 1924

3

Michal

> *But David was loved . . . by the daughter of*
> *Saul, Michal. Saul thought: I will give her to*
> *him, and she will be a snare for him.*
> First Book of Kings

And the youth plays for the mad king,
And annihilates the merciless night,
And loudly summons triumphant dawn
And smothers the specters of fright.
And the king speaks kindly to him:
"In you, young man, burns a marvelous flame,
And for such a medicine
I will give you my daughter and my kingdom."
And the king's daughter stares at the singer,
She needs neither songs nor the marriage crown;
Her soul is full of grief and resentment,
Nevertheless, Michal wants David.
She is paler than death; her mouth is compressed,

*

В зеленых глазах исступленье;
Сияют одежды, и стройно звенят
Запястья при каждом движенье.
Как тайна, как сон, как праматерь Лилит...
Не волей своею она говорит:
«Наверно, с отравой мне дали питье,
И мой помрачается дух.
Бесстыдство мое! Униженье мое!
Бродяга! Разбойник! Пастух!
Зачем же никто из придворных вельмож,
Увы, на него непохож?
А солнца лучи... а звезды в ночи...
А эта холодная дрожь...»

1959—1961

———

Zh. 263

ПРИЧИТАНИЕ

В. А. Щеголевой

Господеви поклонитеся
Во Святем Дворе Его,
Спит юродивый на паперти,
На него глядит звезда.
И крылом задетый ангельским
Колокол заговорил,
Не набатным, грозным голосом,
А прощаясь навсегда.
И выходят из обители,
Ризы древние отдав,
Чудотворцы и святители,

*

In her green eyes, frenzy;
Her garments gleam and with each motion
Her bracelets ring harmoniously.
Like a mystery, like a dream, like the first
    mother, Lilith . . .
She speaks without volition:
"Surely they have given me drink with poison
And my spirit is clouded.
My shamelessness! My humiliation!
A vagabond! A brigand! A shepherd!
Why do none of the king's courtiers,
Alas, resemble him?
But the sun's rays . . . and the stars at night . . .
And this cold trembling . . ."

1959–1961

———

Lamentation

—to V.A. Shchegoleva

You are worshipping the Lord
In his holy courtyard.
God's fool sleeps on the church porch,
And a star looks down at him.
And touched by an angel's wing,
A bell begins to speak,
Not with alarm, with a voice of terror,
But saying farewell forever.
And the saints and miracle workers,
Leaving their ancient icon frames,
Come out of the cloister

*

Опираясь на клюки.
Серафим — в леса Саровские
Стадо сельское пасти,
Анна в Кашин, уж не княжити,
Лен колючий теребить.
Провожает Богородица,
Сына кутает в платок,
Старой нищенкой оброненный
У Господнего крыльца.

24 мая 1922
Петербург

Zh. 264

Вот и берег северного моря,
Вот граница наших бед и слав, —
Не пойму, от счастья или горя
Плачешь ты, к моим ногам припав.
Мне не надо больше обреченных —
Пленников, заложников, рабов,
Только с милым мне и непреклонным
Буду я делить и хлеб и кров.

Осень 1922

Zh. 265

Хорошо здесь: и шелест, и хруст;
С каждым утром сильнее мороз,
В белом пламени клонится куст
Ледяных ослепительных роз.
И на пышных парадных снегах

*

Leaning on crutches.
Seraphim—to the woods of Sarov,
To shepherd the rural flocks,
Anna—no longer a princess,
To Kashin, to pull the prickly flax.
With them goes the Mother of God,
Wrapping her son in a shawl
Dropped by an old beggar woman
On the front steps of the Lord.

May 24, 1922
Petersburg

———

Here is the shore of the northern sea,
Here is the border of our fame and misfortune—
I don't understand, is it from joy or grief
That you are crying, fallen at my feet.
I've had enough of the doomed—
Prisoners, hostages, slaves,
Only with someone dear to me, unyielding and hard
Will I share bed and board.

Autumn 1922

———

It is good here: rustling and crackling;
It freezes harder every day,
The bush bending in a white blaze
Of dazzling, icy roses.
And on the splendid, magnificent snow

*

Лыжный след, словно память о том,
Что в каких-то далеких веках
Здесь с тобою прошли мы вдвоем.

1922

———

Zh. 266

СКАЗКА О ЧЕРНОМ КОЛЬЦЕ

1

Мне от бабушки-татарки
Были редкостью подарки;
И зачем я крещена,
Горько гневалась она.
А пред смертью подобрела
И впервые пожалела,
И вздохнула: «Ах, года!
Вот и внучка молода».
И, простивши нрав мой вздорный,
Завещала перстень черный.
Так сказала: «Он по ней,
С ним ей будет веселей».

2

Я друзьям моим сказала:
«Горя много, счастья мало», —
И ушла, закрыв лицо;
Потеряла я кольцо.
И друзья мои сказали:
«Мы кольцо везде искали,
Возле моря на песке

*

There are ski tracks, like the memory of how,
In that somehow far-off century,
We passed this way together, you and I.

1922

———

The Tale of the Black Ring

1

My Tatar grandmother
Rarely gave me gifts;
And because I was baptized,
She was bitterly angry.
But before her death she softened,
For the first time she was sorry
And she sighed: "Ah, the years!
Here's my granddaughter a young woman."
And forgiving me my foolish ways,
She bequeathed her black ring to me,
Pronouncing: "It is for her,
With it she will be happier than I was."

2

I said to my friends:
"There's lots of sorrow, little happiness" —
And I left, hiding my face;
I had lost the ring.
And my friends said:
"We looked for the ring everywhere,
In the sand along the sea

*

И меж сосен на лужке».
И, догнав меня в аллее,
Тот, кто был других смелее,
Уговаривал меня
Подождать до склона дня.
Я совету удивилась
И на друга рассердилась,
Что глаза его нежны:
«И на что вы мне нужны?
Только можете смеяться,
Друг пред другом похваляться
Да цветы сюда носить».
Всем велела уходить.

3

И, придя в свою светлицу,
Застонала хищной птицей,
Повалилась на кровать
Сотый раз припоминать:
Как за ужином сидела,
В очи темные глядела,
Как не ела, не пила
У дубового стола,
Как под скатертью узорной
Протянула перстень черный,
Как взглянул в мое лицо,
Встал и вышел на крыльцо.

. . . .

Не придут ко мне с находкой!
Далеко над быстрой лодкой
Заалели небеса,
Забелели паруса.

1917—1936

And in the meadow among the pines."
And overtaking me in the allée,
One who was bolder than the others
Tried to persuade me
To wait until the waning of the day.
I was amazed at this advice
And I got angry at my friend
Because his eyes were tender.
"Why do I need any of you?
All you can do is laugh
And brag to each other
About bringing flowers."
I sent them all away.

3

And returning to my room,
I keened like a bird of prey,
Throwing myself on the bed
To remember for the hundredth time:
How I had sat at dinner
At the oaken table,
How I stared into his dark eyes,
How I didn't eat, didn't drink,
How under the patterned table cloth
I pulled the black ring off,
How he looked into my face,
Then rose and went out to the porch.
. . . .
They won't find a treasure to bring to me!
In the distance, above the swift boat,
The sky turns crimson,
The sail whitens.

1917–1936

Zh. 267

Небывалая осень построила купол высокий,
Был приказ облакам этот купол собой не темнить.
И дивилися люди. проходят сентябрьские сроки,
А куда провалились студеные, влажные дни?
Изумрудною стала вода замутненных каналов,
И крапива запахла, как розы, но только сильней,
Было душно от зорь, нестерпимых, бесовских
                                        и алых,
Их запомнили все мы до конца наших дней.
Было солнце таким, как вошедший в столицу
                                        мятежник,
И весенняя осень так жадно ласкалась к нему,
Что казалось — сейчас забелеет прозрачный
                                        подснежник...
Вот когда подошел ты, спокойный, к крыльцу
                                        моему.

Сентябрь 1922

II

MCMXXI

Zh. 268

Наталии Рыковой

Всё расхищено, предано, продано,
Черной смерти мелькало крыло,
Всё голодной тоскою изглодано,
Отчего же нам стало светло?

The fantastic autumn constructed a high cupola,
And the clouds were ordered not to darken it.
And people marveled: Septembertime is passing by,
And where are the cold, humid days?
The water in the muddy canals became emerald,
And the nettles began to smell, like roses, but stronger.
It was stifling from sunrise, unbearable, demonic,
    vermilion dawns,
That we would remember to the end of our days.
The sun was like a rebel entering the capital,
And the springlike autumn caressed him so greedily
That it seemed—the translucent snowdrops would
    blossom whitely any day...
That's when you, so quiet, approached me.

September 1922

———

II

MCMXXI

—to Natalya Rykova

Everything has been plundered, betrayed, sold out,
The wing of black death has flashed,
Everything has been devoured by starving anguish,
Why, then, is it so bright?

Днем дыханьями веет вишневыми
Небывалый под городом лес,
Ночью блещет созвездьями новыми
Глубь прозрачных июльских небес, –

И так близко подходит чудесное
К развалившимся грязным домам...
Никому, никому не известное,
Но от века желанное нам.

Июнь 1921

Zh. 269

Путник милый, ты далече,
Но с тобою говорю.
В небесах зажглися свечи
Провожающих зарю.

Путник мой, скорей направо
Обрати свой светлый взор:
Здесь живет дракон лукавый,
Мой властитель с давних пор.

А в пещере у дракона
Нет пощады, нет закона,
И висит на стенке плеть,
Чтобы песен мне не петь.

И дракон крылатый мучит,
Он меня смиренью учит,
Чтоб забыла дерзкий смех,
Чтобы стала лучше всех.

The fantastic woods near the town
Wafts the scent of cherry blossoms by day,
At night new constellations shine
In the transparent depths of the skies of July—

And how near the miraculous draws
To the dirty, tumbledown huts...
No one, no one knows what it is,
But for centuries we have longed for it.

June 1921

———

Dear traveler, you are far away,
But I am talking to you,
Candles have been kindled
In the sky to guide you.

My traveler, quickly, to the right
Turn your bright gaze:
Here lives an evil dragon,
My longtime sovereign.

And in the dragon's cave,
Neither mercy, nor law,
And a lash hangs on the wall
To keep me from singing my songs.

And the winged dragon tortures,
He teaches me humility,
So that I may forget my daring laughter,
So that I may attain superiority.

Путник милый, в город дальний
Унеси мои слова,
Чтобы сделался печальней
Тот, кем я еще жива.

22 июня 1921
Петербург

———

Zh. 270

Сослужу тебе верную службу, —
Ты не бойся, что горько люблю!
Я за нашу веселую дружбу
Всех святителей нынче молю.

За тебя отдала первородство
И взамен ничего не прошу,
Оттого и лохмотья сиротства
Я, как брачные ризы, ношу.

Июль 1921

———

Zh. 271

Нам встречи нет. Мы в разных станах,
Туда ль зовешь меня, наглец,
Где брат поник в кровавых ранах,
Принявши ангельский венец?

И ни молящие улыбки,
Ни клятвы дикие твои,
Ни призрак млеющий и зыбкий
Моей счастливейшей любви
Не обольстят...

Июнь 1921

Dear traveler, carry my words
To that far-off town,
So that he for whom I'm living still
Will become more sorrowful.

June 22, 1921
Petersburg

———

Certainly I'll do you a good turn—
Don't be afraid that I love you bitterly!
I'm praying to all the saints today
That we can be good friends.

For you I gave up primacy
And I ask for nothing in return,
That's why I wear these orphan's rags
As if they were a wedding gown.

July 1921

———

We won't meet. We are in different camps.
Would you summon me there, insolent one,
Where my brother suffered bloody wounds,
Accepting an angel's crown?

And neither your soulful smiles
Nor your savage vows,
Not even the thrilling, rippling ghost
Of my most ecstatic love
Will seduce...

June 1921

Zh. 272

Страх, во тьме перебирая вещи,
Лунный луч наводит на топор.
За стеною слышен стук зловещий —
Что там, крысы, призрак или вор?

В душной кухне плещется водою,
Половицам шатким счет ведет,
С глянцевитой черной бородою
За окном чердачным промелькнет —

И притихнет. Как он зол и ловок,
Спички спрятал и свечу задул.
Лучше бы поблескиванье дул
В грудь мою направленных винтовок,

Лучше бы на площади зеленой
На помост некрашеный прилечь
И под клики радости и стоны
Красной кровью до конца истечь.

Прижимаю к сердцу крестик гладкий:
Боже, мир душе моей верни!
Запах тленья обморочно сладкий
Веет от прохладной простыни.

27—28 августа 1921
Царское Село

———

Zh. 273

Ты мне не обещан ни жизнью, ни Богом,
Ни даже предчувствием тайным моим;
Зачем же в ночи перед темным порогом
Ты медлишь, как будто счастьем томим?

*

Terror, fingering things in the dark,
Leads the moonbeam to an ax.
Behind the wall there's an ominous knock—
What's there, a ghost, a thief, rats?

In the sweltering kitchen, water drips,
Counting the rickety floorboards.
Someone with a glossy black beard
Flashes by the attic window—

And becomes still. How cunning he is and evil,
He hid the matches and blew out the candle.
How much better would be the gleam of the barrels
Of rifles leveled at my breast.

Better, in the grassy square,
To be flattened on the raw wood scaffold
And, amid cries of joy and moans,
Pour out my life's blood there.

I press the smooth cross to my heart:
God, restore peace to my soul.
The odor of decay, sickeningly sweet,
Rises from the clammy sheets.

August 27–28, 1921
Tsarskoye Selo

You were promised to me neither by life nor by God,
Not even by my secret premonition.
Why then do you linger at night in the doorway,
As if in the languor of happiness?

*

Не выйду, не крикну: «О, будь единым,
До смертного часа будь со мной!»
Я только голосом лебединым
Говорю с неправедною луной.

1915

О, жизнь без завтрашнего дня!
Ловлю измену в каждом слове,
И убывающей любови
Звезда восходит для меня.

Так незаметно отлетать,
Почти не узнавать при встрече.
Но снова ночь. И снова плечи
В истоме влажной целовать.

Тебе я милой не была,
Ты мне постыл. А пытка длилась,
И, как преступница, томилась
Любовь, исполненная зла.

То словно брат. Молчишь, сердит.
Но если встретимся глазами —
Тебе клянусь я небесами,
В огне расплавится гранит.

29 августа 1921

I won't come out, I won't cry: "Oh, be mine alone!
Be with me until the hour of death!"
I only speak, with the voice of the swan,
To the inconstant moon.

1915

————

Oh, life without tomorrow's day!
I detect treason in every word,
And the star of waning love
Rises for me.

To vanish like that, imperceptibly,
Almost unaware of this encounter.
But again it's night. And once more,
To kiss those shoulders in moist languor.

I was never dear to you,
You disgust me. But the torment drags on,
And love, like a criminal,
Languishes, brimming with evil.

Just like a brother. You are silent, enraged.
But if our eyes should meet—
By the heavens I swear to you,
Granite would melt in that heat.

August 29, 1921

————

Zh. 275

Кое-как удалось разлучиться
И постылый огонь потушить.
Враг мой вечный, пора научиться
Вам кого-нибудь вправду любить.

Я-то вольная. Всё мне забава, —
Ночью Муза слетит утешать,
А наутро притащится слава
Погремушкой над ухом трещать.

Обо мне и молиться не стоит,
И, уйдя, оглянуться назад...
Черный ветер меня успокоит,
Веселит золотой листопад.

Как подарок, приму я разлуку
И забвение, как благодать.
Но, скажи мне, на крестную муку
Ты другую посмеешь послать?

Август 1921

Zh. 276

А, ты думал — я тоже такая,
Что можно забыть меня
И что брошусь, моля и рыдая,
Под копыта гнедого коня.

Или стану просить у знахарок
В наговорной воде корешок
И пришлю тебе страшный подарок —
Мой заветный душистый платок.

Somehow we've managed to part,
And to put out the hateful fire.
Eternal enemy of mine, it's time for you to learn
How to love someone properly.

I'm willing. It's all fun for me—
At night the Muse flies down to comfort me,
And in the morning, fame drags herself here
To sound her rattle in my ear.

It's not even worth praying for me,
Or, leaving, to glance back . . .
The black wind will soothe,
The golden fall of leaves will gladden me.

I accept separation as a gift,
And oblivion as a blessing.
But tell me, would you dare send someone else
On this Way of the Cross?

August 1921

———

Ah—you thought I'd be the type
You could forget,
And that praying and sobbing, I'd throw myself
Under the hooves of a bay.

Or I would beg from the witches
Some kind of root in charmed water
And send you a terrible gift—
My intimate, scented handkerchief.

Будь же проклят. Ни стоном, ни взглядом
Окаянной души не коснусь,
Но клянусь тебе ангельским садом,
Чудотворной иконой клянусь
И ночей наших пламенным чадом —
Я к тебе никогда не вернусь.

Июль 1921
Петербург

—————

S-F. I, 205–206
(Zh. 277)

Пусть голоса орга́на снова грянут,
Как первая весенняя гроза;
Из-за плеча твоей невесты глянут
Мои полузакрытые глаза.

Семь дней любви, семь грозных лет разлуки,
Война, мятеж, опустошенный дом,
В крови невинной маленькие руки,
Седая прядь над розовым виском.

Прощай, прощай, будь счастлив, друг прекрасный
Верну тебе твой сладостный обет,
Но берегись твоей подруге страстной
Поведать мой неповторимый бред, —

Затем, что он пронижет жгучим ядом
Ваш благостный, ваш радостный союз...
А я иду владеть чудесным садом,
Где шелест трав и восклицанья муз.

Август 1921

—————

Damned if I will. Neither by glance nor by groan
Will I touch your cursed soul,
But I vow to you by the garden of angels,
By the miraculous icon I vow
And by the fiery passion of our nights—
I will never return to you.

July 1921
Petersburg

———

Let the voice of the organ again burst forth,
Like the first spring thunderstorm;
From behind the shoulder of your bride glance
My half-closed eyes.

Seven days of love, seven terrible years of separation,
War, revolution, a devastated home,
Innocent blood on delicate hands,
Over the rosy temple a gray strand.

Good-bye, good-bye, be happy, handsome friend,
I'm returning your sweet vow,
But beware of revealing to your passionate one
My inimitable delirium—

Because that would spread burning venom
Through your blessed, your joyful union...
But a miraculous garden I go to claim,
Where the grass rustles and the Muse exclaims.

August 1921

———

Чугунная ограда,
Сосновая кровать.
Как сладко, что не надо
Мне больше ревновать.

Постель мне стелют эту
С рыданьем и мольбой;
Теперь гуляй по свету,
Где хочешь, Бог с тобой!

Теперь твой слух не ранит
Неистовая речь,
Теперь никто не станет
Свечу до утра жечь.

Добились мы покою
И непорочных дней...
Ты плачешь — я не стою
Одной слезы твоей.

27 августа 1921
Царское Село

———

А Смоленская нынче именинница,
Синий ладан над травою стелется
И струится пенье панихидное,
Не печальное нынче, а светлое.
И приводят румяные вдовушки
На кладбище мальчиков и девочек
Поглядеть на могилы отцовские,
А кладбище — роща соловьиная,
От сиянья солнечного замерло.
Принесли мы Смоленской Заступнице,

*

Cast-iron fence,
Pine bed.
How sweet to be
Beyond jealousy.

They made up this bed for me
With sobbing and prayers;
Now go anywhere in the world
You want, Godspeed!

Now your ears won't be wounded
By frenzied haranguing,
Now no one will burn
A candle till morning.

We've achieved peace
And immaculate days...
You're weeping—I'm not worth
A single one of your tears.

August 27, 1921
Tsarskoye Selo

———

Today is the nameday of Our Lady of Smolensk,
Dark blue incense drifts over the grass,
And the flowing of the Requiem
Is no longer sorrowful, but radiant.
And the rosy little widows lead
Their boys and girls to the cemetery
To visit father's grave.
But the graveyard—a grove of nightingales,
Grows silent from the sun's bright blaze.
We have brought to the Intercessor of Smolensk,

*

Принесли Пресвятой Богородице
На руках во гробе серебряном
Наше солнце, в муке погасшее —
Александра, лебедя чистого.

Август 1921

Zh. 280

О. А. *Глебовой-Судейкиной*

Пророчишь, горькая, и руки уронила,
Прилипла прядь волос к бескровному челу,
И улыбаешься — о, не одну пчелу
Румяная улыбка соблазнила
И бабочку смутила не одну.

Как лунные глаза светлы, и напряженно
Далеко видящий остановился взор.
То мертвому ли сладостный укор,
Или живым прощаешь благосклонно
Твое изнеможенье и позор?

27 августа 1921

Zh. 281

Не бывать тебе в живых,
Со снегу не встать.
Двадцать восемь штыковых,
Огнестрельных пять.

We have brought to the Holy Mother of God,
In our hands in a silver coffin
Our sun, extinguished in torment—
Alexander, pure swan.

August 1921

———

—to O.A. Glebova-Sudeikina

You prophesy, bitter one, then let your arms fall,
A lock of hair sticks to your bloodless brow,
And you smile—oh, more than one bee
Has been tempted by that rosy smile
And it has troubled more than one butterfly.

How bright the lunar eyes, and tensely
The far-off gaze has come to rest.
Is it a sweet reproach to the one who died,
Or are you graciously forgiving the living
For your impotence and infamy?

August 27, 1921

———

You are no longer among the living,
You cannot rise from the snow.
Twenty-eight bayonets,
Five bullets.

Горькую обновушку
Другу шила я.
Любит, любит кровушку
Русская земля.

16 августа 1921

Zh. 282

Пока не свалюсь под забором
И ветер меня не добьет,
Мечта о спасении скором
Меня, как проклятие, жжет.

Упрямая, жду, что случится,
Как в песне случится со мной, —
Уверенно в дверь постучится
И, прежний, веселый, дневной,

Войдет он и скажет: «Довольно,
Ты видишь, я тоже простил», —
Не будет ни страшно, ни больно...
Ни роз, ни архангельских сил.

Затем и в беспамятстве смуты
Я сердце мое берегу,
Что смерти без этой минуты
Представить себе не могу.

30 августа 1921

A bitter new shirt
For my beloved I sewed.
The Russian earth loves, loves
Droplets of blood.

August 16, 1921

———

Until I collapse by the fence
And the wind deals me the final blow,
The dream of salvation close at hand
Will burn me like an oath.

Stubborn, I wait for it to happen,
As a poem happens to me—
Confidently he will knock at the door
And, casual, cheerful, just as before,

He will enter and say: "Enough.
You see, I have forgiven too"—
It will not be frightful or painful...
Neither roses nor hosts of archangels.

So even in the frenzy of delirium
I spare my heart from torment,
For I cannot imagine death
Without this moment.

August 30, 1921

———

На пороге белом рая,
Оглянувшись, крикнул: «Жду!»
Завещал мне, умирая,
Благостность и нищету.

И когда прозрачно небо,
Видит, крыльями звеня,
Как делюсь я коркой хлеба
С тем, кто просит у меня.

А когда, как после битвы,
Облака плывут в крови,
Слышит он мои молитвы
И слова моей любви.

Июль 1921

Я гибель накликала милым,
И гибли один за другим.
О, горе мне! Эти могилы
Предсказаны словом моим.
Как вороны кружатся, чуя
Горячую свежую кровь,
Так дикие песни, ликуя,
Моя насылала любовь.

С тобою мне сладко и знойно,
Ты близок, как сердце в груди.
Дай руки мне, слушай спокойно.
Тебя заклинаю: уйди.
И пусть не узнаю я, где ты.

*

On the white threshold of paradise,
Glancing back, he cried: "I will wait!"
Dying, he bequeathed to me,
Blessedness and poverty.

And when the sky is clear,
He watches, with resounding wings,
How I share my crust of bread
With those who ask it of me.

And when, as after battle,
The clouds float in blood,
He will hear my prayers
And my words of love.

July 1921

———

I brought disaster to my dear ones,
And one after another they died.
Oh, woe is me! These graves
Were foretold by my words.
Like circling crows smelling
Hot, fresh blood
Were those savage songs
Sent by my exultant love.

With you it is sweet and sultry,
You are close as the heart in my breast.
Give me your hands, listen carefully.
I'm warning you: Go away.
And let me not know where you are.

*

О Муза, его не зови,
Да будет живым, невоспетым
Моей не узнавший любви.

Осень 1921
Петербург

Zh. 285

Долгим взглядом твоим истомленная,
И сама научилась томить.
Из ребра твоего сотворенная,
Как могу я тебя не любить?

Быть твоею сестрою отрадною
Мне завещано древней судьбой,
А я стала лукавой и жадною
И сладчайшей твоею рабой.

Но когда замираю, смиренная,
На груди твоей снега белей,
Как ликует твое умудренное
Сердце — солнце отчизны моей!

25 сентября 1921

Zh. 286

КЛЕВЕТА

И всюду клевета сопутствовала мне.
Ее ползучий шаг я слышала во сне
И в мертвом городе под беспощадным небом,

*

O Muse, don't call him,
Let him live unsung,
Unaware of my love.

August 1921
Petersburg

———

Exhausted by your long, fixed gaze,
I myself learned how to torment.
Created from your rib,
How could I not love you?

To be your comforting sister
Is my pre-ordained fate,
And I became cunning and greedy,
And the sweetest of your slaves.

But when I sink, submissive,
To your breast of white snow,
How it will glow, your enlightened
Heart—sun of my fatherland!

September 25, 1921

———

Slander

And slander has accompanied me everywhere.
In my sleep I hear her creeping tread
And in the dead city under merciless skies

*

Скитаясь наугад за кровом и за хлебом.
И отблески ее горят во всех глазах,
То как предательство, то как невинный страх.
Я не боюсь ее. На каждый вызов новый
Есть у меня ответ достойный и суровый.
Но неизбежный день уже предвижу я, —
На утренней заре придут ко мне друзья,
И мой сладчайший сон рыданьем потревожат,
И образок на грудь остывшую положат.
Никем не знаема тогда она войдет,
В моей крови ее неутоленный рот
Считать не устает небывшие обиды,
Вплетая голос свой в моленья панихиды.
И станет внятен всем ее постыдный бред,
Чтоб на соседа глаз не мог поднять сосед,
Чтоб в страшной пустоте мое осталось тело,
Чтобы в последний раз душа моя горела
Земным бессилием, летя в рассветной мгле,
И дикой жалостью к оставленной земле.

1 (14) января 1922

III

ГОЛОС ПАМЯТИ

Zh. 287

Широко распахнуты ворота,
Липы нищенски обнажены,
И темна сухая позолота
Нерушимой вогнутой стены.

I wander aimlessly for shelter and bread.
And her reflection burns in every eye,
Now as treachery, now as innocent fear.
I'm not afraid of her. For each new accusation
I have an answer, dignified and severe.
But already I foresee the inescapable day—
In the light of dawn, friends will come to me
And disturb my sweetest dream with sobs,
And place an icon on my cold breast.
Then, unknown to anyone, she will enter,
Her unquenchable mouth bloody with my blood,
Listing my imagined offenses,
Mingling her voice in the prayers for the dead.
And her shameful raving will reach everyone,
So that neighbors will avoid each other's eyes,
So that my body will be abandoned in a terrible void,
So that for the last time my soul will burn
With earthly frailty, flying, in the mist of dawn,
To the just-abandoned earth in fierce compassion.

January 1 (14), 1922

———

III

THE VOICE OF MEMORY

The gates are thrown wide open,
The lindens are naked beggars,
And there is dark dried gilding
On the impregnable, concave wall.

Гулом полны алтари и склепы,
И за Днепр широкий звон летит.
Так тяжелый колокол Мазепы
Над Софийской площадью гудит.

Всё грозней бушует, непреклонный,
Словно здесь еретиков казнят,
А в лесах заречных, примиренный,
Веселит пушистых лисенят.

15 сентября 1921

———

Zh. 288

Почернел, искривился бревенчатый мост,
И стоят лопухи в человеческий рост,
И крапивы дремучей поют леса,
Что по ним не пройдет, не блеснет коса.
Вечерами над озером слышен вздох,
И по стенам расползся корявый мох.

Я встречала там
Двадцать первый год,
Сладок был устам
Черный, душный мед.

Сучья рвали мне
Платья белый шелк,
На кривой сосне
Соловей не молк.

На условный крик
Выйдет из норы,
Словно леший дик,
А нежней сестры.

The altars and crypts are rumbling,
And beyond the Dnieper the wide sound rolls.
Thus the heavy bell of Mazepa
Over Sophia Square tolls.

Ever more dreadful it thunders, inexorable,
As if they were executing heretics here,
And in the woods across the river, mollified,
It amuses the fluffy young foxes.

September 15, 1921

———

The log bridge is blackened and twisted,
And the burdocks stand shoulder high,
And the forest of dense nettles sings
That the sickle will never pass through it, flash through it.
In the evenings over the lake there's an audible sigh,
And gnarled moss has crawled along the walls.

There I met
My twenty-first year,
Sweet to the lips
Was the dark, sultry honey.

Twigs tore my
White silk dress,
In the crooked pine
The nightingale never ceased.

At the conventional cry
It flits from its lair,
Shy as a woodland sprite,
But more tender than a sister.

Ná гору бегом,
Через речку вплавь,
Да зато потом
Не скажу: оставь.

1917

———

Zh. 289

Тот август как желтое пламя,
Пробившееся сквозь дым,
Тот август поднялся над нами,
Как огненный серафим.

И в город печали и гнева
Из тихои Корельской земли
Мы двое — воин и дева —
Студеным утром вошли.

Что сталось с нашей столицей,
Кто солнце на землю низвел?
Казался летящей птицей
На штандарте черный орел.

На дикий лагерь похожим
Стал город пышных смотров,
Слепило глаза прохожим
Сверканье пик и штыков.

И серые пушки гремели
На Троицком гулком мосту,
А липы еще зеленели
В таинственном Летнем саду.

Running up the hill,
Swimming the stream,
But then, afterwards,
I won't tell: Let me be.

1917

———

That August was like a yellow flame
Piercing through smoke,
That August rose over us
Like fiery seraphim.

And into this city of sorrow and wrath
From the quiet Karelian earth,
We two—a soldier and a maid—
On one chill morning walked.

What had happened to our capital?
Who had lowered the sun to the earth?
The black eagle on its standard
Seemed like a bird in flight.

This city of splendid vistas
Began to resemble a savage camp,
The eyes of the strollers were dazzled
By the glint of bayonet and lance.

And gray cannons thundered
Across Trinity Bridge,
As the lindens greened
In the mysterious Summer Garden.

И брат мне сказал: настали
Для меня великие дни.
Теперь ты наши печали
И радость одна храни.

Как будто ключи оставил
Хозяйке усадьбы своей,
А ветер восточный славил
Ковыли приволжских степей.

1915

———

Zh. 290

ПРИЗРАК

Зажженных рано фонарей
Шары висячие скрежещут,
Всё праздничнее, всё светлей
Снежинки, пролетая, блещут.

И, ускоряя ровный бег,
Как бы в предчувствии погони,
Сквозь мягко падающий снег
Под синей сеткой мчатся кони.

И раззолоченный гайдук
Стоит недвижно за санями,
И странно царь глядит вокруг
Пустыми светлыми глазами.

Зима 1919

———

And my brother told me: Now begin
My momentous days.
Now you alone must preserve
Our sorrows and our joys.

It was as if he were leaving the keys
With the housekeeper of his country place,
And the east wind sang the praises
Of the Volga steppe's feather grass.

1915

———

Apparition

The round, hanging lanterns,
Lit early, are squeaking,
Ever more festively, ever brighter,
The flying snowflakes glitter.

And, quickening their steady gait,
As if sensing some pursuit,
Through the softly falling snow
Under a dark blue net, the horses race.

And the gilded footman
Stands motionless behind the sleigh,
And the tsar looks around strangely
With light, empty eyes.

Winter 1919

———

ТРИ СТИХОТВОРЕНИЯ

Zh. 291

1

А. Л.

Да, я любила их, те сборища ночные, —
На маленьком столе стаканы ледяные,
Над черным кофеем пахучий, тонкий пар,
Камина красного тяжелый, зимний жар,
Веселость едкую литературной шутки
И друга первый взгляд, беспомощный и жуткий.

Zh. 292

2

Соблазна не было. Соблазн в тиши живет,
Он постника томит, святителя гнетет

И в полночь майскую над молодой черницей
Кричит истомно раненой орлицей.

А сим распутникам, сим грешницам любезным
Неведомо объятье рук железных.

Zh. 293

3

Не оттого ль, уйдя от легкости проклятой,
Смотрю взволнованно на темные палаты?
Уже привыкшая к высоким, чистым звонам,
Уже судимая не по земным законам,
Я, как преступница, еще влекусь туда,
На место казни долгой и стыда.
И вижу дивный град, и слышу голос милый,
Как будто нет еще таинственной могилы,
Где, день и ночь, склонясь, в жары и холода,
Должна я ожидать Последнего Суда.

Январь 1917

THREE VERSES

1

A.L.

Yes, I loved them, those nightly gatherings —
The icy glasses on the little table,
Over the black coffee a fine, fragrant steam,
The red fire's roaring, winter heat,
The merriment of caustic literary jests,
And a lover's first glance, terrifying and helpless.

2

There was no temptation. Temptation lives in silence,
It torments anchorites, oppresses saints,

And on a midnight in May it cries as piercingly
As a wounded eagle to the young nun.

But to these libertines, to these obliging sinners,
The embrace of its iron arms is unknown.

3

Isn't it to escape from this damned easy life
That I peer uneasily into dark chambers?
Already accustomed to high, pure chimes,
Already beyond the judgment of earthly laws,
I, like a criminal, am still drawn there,
To that place of slow execution and shame.
And I see a marvelous town, and I hear a beloved voice,
As if there were not also a mysterious grave,
Where, day and night, bowing down, in heat and cold,
I must await the Judgment Day.

January 1917

Zh. 294

КОЛЫБЕЛЬНАЯ

Далеко в лесу огромном,
Возле синих рек,
Жил с детьми в избушке темной
Бедный дровосек.

Младший сын был ростом с пальчик, —
Как тебя унять,
Спи, мой тихий, спи, мой мальчик,
Я дурная мать.

Долетают редко вести
К нашему крыльцу,
Подарили белый крестик
Твоему отцу.

Было горе, будет горе,
Горю нет конца,
Да хранит святой Егорий
Твоего отца.

1915

───────

Zh. 295

Заплаканная осень, как вдова
В одеждах черных, все сердца туманит...
Перебирая мужнины слова,
Она рыдать не перестанет.
И будет так, пока тишайший снег

*

Lullaby

Far off in the enormous forest,
Near the dark blue river,
There lived in a dark hut with his children
A poor woodcutter.

The youngest son was as big as a thumb—
How can I calm you,
Sleep, my little boy, sleep, my quiet one,
I'm a bad mother.

News rarely flies
As far as our porch,
On your father they bestowed
A little white cross.

Sorrow behind, sorrow ahead,
Sorrow without end,
Now St. George watches over
Your father.

1915

———

The tear-stained autumn, like a widow
In black weeds, clouds every heart...
Recalling her husband's words,
She sobs without ceasing.
And thus it will be, until the most quiet snow

*

Не сжалится над скорбной и усталой...
Забвенье боли и забвенье нег —
За это жизнь отдать не мало.

15 сентября 1921
Царское Село

Zh. 296

Буду черные грядки холить,
Ключевой водой поливать;
Полевые цветы на воле,
Их не надо трогать и рвать.

Пусть их больше, чем звезд зажженных
В сентябрьских небесах, —
Для детей, для бродяг, для влюбленных
Вырастают цветы на полях.

А мои — для святой Софии
В тот единственный светлый день,
Когда возгласы литургии
Возлетят под дивную сень.

И, как волны приносят на сушу
То, что сами на смерть обрекли,
Принесу покаянную душу
И цветы из Русской земли.

Лето 1916
Слепнево

Takes pity on the sorrowful and weary one . . .
Oblivion of pain and oblivion of bliss —
To give up life for this is no small thing.

September 15, 1921
Tsarskoye Selo

———

I will tend these rich, black beds,
With spring water I will sprinkle them;
The flowers of the field are free,
There's no need to touch or pick them.

Let them be more plentiful than stars kindled
In the September skies —
For children, for wanderers, for lovers
They grow, those wild flowers.

But mine — are for Saint Sophia
On that one bright day
When prayers and responses
Soar from beneath the marvelous canopy.

And, as the waves wash to the shore
That which they themselves condemned to death,
I bring my penitential soul
And flowers from the Russian earth.

Summer 1916
Slepnyovo

———

Zh. 297

НОВОГОДНЯЯ БАЛЛАДА

И месяц, скучая в облачной мгле,
Бросил в горницу тусклый взор.
Там шесть приборов стоят на столе,
И один только пуст прибор.

Это муж мой, и я, и друзья мои
Встречаем новый год.
Отчего мои пальцы словно в крови
И вино, как отрава, жжет?

Хозяин, поднявши полный стакан,
Был важен и недвижим:
«Я пью за землю родных полян,
В которой мы все лежим»!

А друг, поглядевши в лицо мое,
И вспомнив Бог весть о чем,
Воскликнул: «А я за песни ее,
В которых мы все живем!»

Но третий, не знавший ничего,
Когда он покинул свет,
Мыслям моим в ответ
Промолвил: «Мы выпить должны за того,
Кого еще с нами нет».

1923

Zh. 298

О, знала ль я, когда в одежде белой
Входила Муза в тесный мой приют,
Что к лире, навсегда окаменелой,
Мои живые руки припадут.

New Year's Ballad

And the moon, bored in the cloudy gloom,
Threw a dim gaze into the room.
There were six places set at the table
And only one empty chair.

It is my husband and I and my friends
Greeting the New Year.
Why do my fingers look bloody,
Why does the wine, like poison, burn?

The host, raising a full glass,
Was serious and motionless:
"I drink to the earth of our native glades,
In which we will all lie!"

And a friend, looking into my face
And remembering God knows what,
Exclaimed: "And I to her songs,
In which we will all live."

But the third, totally unaware
Of when he had abandoned this world,
Muttered, as an answer to my thought:
"We ought to drink to the one
Who is not here with us yet."

1923

———

Oh, if only I'd known, when, dressed in white,
The Muse entered my narrow room,
That my living hands would cling
To a lyre turned to stone.

О, знала ль я, когда неслась, играя,
Моей души последняя гроза,
Что лучшему из юношей, рыдая,
Закрою я орлиные глаза.

О, знала ль я, когда, томясь успехом,
Я искушала дивную судьбу,
Что скоро люди беспощадным смехом
Ответят на предсмертную мольбу.

1925

Zh. 299

МНОГИМ

Я — голос ваш, жар вашего дыханья,
Я — отраженье вашего лица,
Напрасных крыл напрасны трепетанья, —
Ведь все равно я с вами до конца.

Вот отчего вы любите так жадно
Меня в грехе и в немощи моей;
Вот отчего вы дали неоглядно
Мне лучшего из ваших сыновей;
Вот отчего вы даже не спросили
Меня ни слова никогда о нем
И чадными хвалами задымили
Мой навсегда опустошенный дом.
И говорят — нельзя теснее слиться,
Нельзя непоправимее любить . . .

Как хочет тень от тела отделиться,
Как хочет плоть с душою разлучиться,
Так я хочу теперь — забытой быть.

Сентябрь 1922

Oh, if only I'd known, when my soul's latest storm
Was playing, rushing overhead,
That, sobbing, I would close the eagle eyes
Of the best of the young men.

Oh, if only I'd known, when, bored with success,
I tempted divine providence,
That soon people would answer
My deathbed entreaty with merciless laughter.

1925

To the Many

I—am your voice, the warmth of your breath,
I—am the reflection of your face,
The futile trembling of futile wings,
I am with you to the end, in any case.

That's why you so fervently love
Me in my weakness and in my sin;
That's why you impulsively gave
Me the best of your sons;
That's why you never even asked
Me for any word of him
And blackened my forever-deserted home
With fumes of praise.
And they say—it's impossible to fuse more closely,
Impossible to love more abandonedly...

As the shadow from the body wants to part,
As the flesh from the soul wants to separate,
So I want now—to be forgotten.

September 1922

Notes

INTRODUCTION

The sources of these Notes are many, and most are specifically cited. However, we are especially indebted to Viktor Zhirmunsky, whose notes to Anna Akhmatova, *Stikhotvoreniya i poemy;* Anna Akhmatova, *Poems and Long Poems* (Biblioteka poeta, Bolshaya seriya. 2nd ed. Leningrad: Sovetskii pisatel, 1979) we have frequently adapted, or used in their entirety, for this edition. We thank VAAP, the Soviet copyright agency, for kind permission to make use of Zhirmunsky's notes in this manner.

The poems in VOLUME I of this edition are, with a few exceptions, the poems numbered 1 to 299 by Zhirmunsky. These represent Akhmatova's first five collections, which were published essentially as she composed them. We have used the Struve-Filipoff text for a few poems that Zhirmunsky, because of censorship, could not print in their entirety. These are: in *Plantain, Zh. 236,* a poem describing the confusion and decadence of pre-World War I Russia; and in *Anno Domini, Zh. 239* and *277,* which mention the Bible and God respectively.

The poems in VOLUME II are organized as follows: first come *Reed* and *Seventh Book* (Zhirmunsky numbers 300 to 484), the collections Akhmatova composed but was never able to publish as separate books. Again, we have substituted the Struve-Filipoff text for poems Zhirmunsky had to exclude, in whole or in part, due to censorship. In *Seventh Book, Zh. 341* describes the persecution of Osip Mandelstam, *Zh. 441* reflects on suffering and separation, and *Zh. 480* is missing the epigraph by an emigré poet. Zhirmunsky also included only four of the 17 sections of *Requiem* in the volume *Reed.*

The remainder of VOLUME II is a roughly chronological arrangement of the poems Akhmatova did not collect into books, including Epic and Dramatic Fragments and Long Poems and *Poem Without a Hero.* These poems come from three main sources: Zhirmunsky, Struve-Filipoff, and Chernykh. See the *Index to Poems—By Source* for complete bibliographic information on these editions.

The notes are keyed to the source-citations of the poems to be found on the Russian side of the texts of the poems. These citations appear in small, italic type at the left margin; e.g., *Zh. 1,* or *S-F. II, 19,* or *Ch. 306.* When poems to be found within this edition are cited within the text of these Notes, they are also cited using italic type, in the same fashion. The reader having trouble locating poems mentioned in these Notes or elsewhere should consult the *Index to Poems—By Source.*

★   ★   ★

The following text, as well as the introductions to each of the books which follow, was condensed and adapted for the present edition from the Introduction to the Notes of Anna Akhmatova, Stikhotvoreniya i poemy, *edited by Viktor Zhirmunsky (Leningrad: Biblioteka Poeta, 1979), pp. 451–452, 455, 460, 468, 470–471, 476, 480, 493 and 503.*

Akhmatova devoted much thought to the composition of her collections (or "books"). Each represented, structurally and thematically, a single artistic whole. Her first five collections (*Evening, Rosary, White Flock, Plantain,* and *Anno Domini MCMXXI*) were published as separate volumes. Censorship and other circumstances prevented her from publishing separately the collections which followed, the first of which was *Reed.* However, in subsequent published volumes of her poetry—*From Six Books* (Leningrad, 1940), *Poems* (Moscow, 1961), and *The Flight of Time* (Leningrad, 1965)—Akhmatova continued, whenever length allowed, to preserve their division according to "books."

Akhmatova emphasized the grouping of her poems by cycles within the books. In the end, these cycles, such as the Petersburg or Tashkent cycles, turned into independent sections of a "book." Comparing published and unpublished collections of her poems, numerous manuscript tables of contents and plans for collections conceived by her, offers abundant evidence of the constant attention she gave this question of cycles and allows one to establish a series of sequential regroupings within the general compositional framework of a "book." In some cases (for example, Dark Dream in *Anno Domini*), only the manuscript edition of the collection allows one to restore the unity of a conceived cycle, which is so essential for reflecting the personal and poetic biography of the author. Therefore the compiler [Zhirmunsky] paid a great deal of attention to the arrangement of the poems within the corresponding "books," adhering to the author's desire and at the same time characterizing certain unrealized plans in the notes.

The broadest group of Akhmatova's poetry appeared in her collections. These poems in the present [that is, Zhirmunsky] edition compose the basic section of seven "books"—from *Rosary* to *Seventh Book*—which were printed in *The Flight of Time*.

A significant portion of Akhmatova's works appeared in literary journals, newspapers, and other periodicals before being included in collections. Some poems from periodicals were never in collections, for one reason or another, and, therefore, completely forgotten by readers. A number of late publications also were not part of collections during the poet's lifetime. Others from her last years were published posthumously.

Some draft versions of poems from various periods were restored according to manuscripts from Akhmatova's archive and from collections by her friends. Successive draft versions reveal Akhmatova's poetic process. Changes in the text, as a rule, occurred in the transition from a journal edition of the text to its first appearance in a collection. In the final, "classical" form of the poem Akhmatova did little reworking. An exception is the *Poem Without a Hero*.

From the beginning of her career, Akhmatova dated her poems; in the first draft editions, apparently almost all of her poems had precise reference to the time and place of writing, giving them a "diary-like" quality. However, from edition to edition, Akhmatova dated the same poem with different degrees of precision, without any apparent motives or general rules. Frequently, she supplemented and refined collections of her poems given to friends with written notes; she also provided handwritten tables of contents for the collections of P.N. Luknitsky and N.L. Dilaktorskaya. The compiler [Zhirmunsky] decided to note the place where the poem was written and its date beneath the text, if this was definitely known. Verification is confirmed where sources from different periods coincide. In a small number of cases, for personal reasons, Akhmatova intentionally gave a poem a fictional date. These dates are corrected in the text according to documented sources. In ordering her poems, Akhmatova grouped them according to thematic relationships, often violating chronological order. This authorial principle has been faithfully preserved.

The greater portion of Akhmatova's literary archive is preserved in the Central State Archive of Literature and Art (Leningrad) and in the Manuscript Section of the Saltykov-Shchedrin State Public Library (Leningrad). For the private collections of Akhmatova's manuscripts, the archive of poet and translator Mikhail Lozinsky deserves special recognition. Also very valuable because of its completeness is the collection of Akhmatova's poems which was typed for her in 1945–46 by the poet's friend N.L. Dilaktorskaya from dictation by the author and from handwritten copies. In it were a certain number of unpublished poems as well as tables of contents with dates indicating when they were written, as designated by Akhmatova. A large number of poetic manuscripts from different periods are in the possession of friends. Some of these materials were given to the compiler of the [Zhirmunsky] edition and used by him in preparing the commentary on the texts (material of N. Glen, V. Ivanov, Vl. Orlov, etc.). Other poems in the possession of friends of the poet have not yet been published.

EVENING (1912)

The first book of Akhmatova's poems was published in 1912 by the Poets' Guild (actually, apparently, by the author herself). The title was *Evening. Poems,* with a preface by Mikhail Kuzmin, and a frontispiece decorated by Evgeny Lansere.

The book contained 46 lyric poems, of which 15 had been published earlier in journals. The 300 copies sold out very quickly. Reviews (more than ten in 1912–13) were, for the most part, sympathetic although colored by the unfolding arguments about the new poetic school, the Acmeists, and by conversations about "women's" lyrics. The reviewers, including Valery Bryusov, Georgy Chulkov, and Sergey Gorodetsky, did not anticipate the great role Akhmatova would play in Russian poetry.

Akhmatova, especially in her later years, referred disparagingly to her early poems. When *Evening* appeared she was so distressed, she said, that she went to Italy that spring and, sitting in a tram looking at her neighbors, thought: "How happy they are—they haven't had a little book published."

Akhmatova never republished her first collection as a separate book. Instead she included "Poems from the book, *Evening*" in her next collection, *Rosary* (1914). In the first editions of *Rosary,* the number of selected poems from *Evening* is 30. Excluded were stylizations of poetry from the eighteenth century (*Zh. 30–32*) and others which appeared fragmentary to the author (*Zh. 11, 36, 42*), imitative (*Zh. 40*) or too personal and, therefore, incomprehensible or not very interesting to the reader. Other poems were rearranged. The concluding poem was changed to "The park was filled with light mist..." (*Zh. 41*), the elegiac meditation devoted to Vera Ivanova-Shvarsalon. In later collections of poems, verses from *Evening* remained an independent section, but fewer were reprinted.

At the same time, Akhmatova began to include poems from her working notebooks of 1910–11, poems that had not been published earlier (about 10 works). This material has been included in the section of "Additions," since it was impossible to establish where the author would have placed these poems within the structure of the first collection. The structure of *Evening* frequently changes in subsequent collections, right up to *The Flight of Time* (1965).

★   ★   ★

Epigraph
From a poem, "La vigne en fleur," by the French poet André Theuriet (1833–1907). It first appeared in *From Six Books.*

Zh. 2
Tsarskoye Selo—literally, "the tsar's village," is near Petersburg. Akhmatova grew up there. It is a town with huge parks and allées of splendid lindens. The imperial summer residence, Catherine's Palace, was located there and the lycée within the palace was attended by Pushkin. Tsarskoye Selo was renamed Pushkin in 1937, to mark the centenary of the poet's birth.

Zh. 4
Line 1, The "dark-skinned youth" is Pushkin, whose ancestry included Prince Hannibal of Abyssinia, a Negro and protégé of Peter the Great. See Pushkin's story, "The Negro of Peter the Great," for a semi-fictional version of his ancestor.
Line 7, Parny—Evariste-Désiré de Parny (1753–1814), French author of elegant amorous, mock-epic and neoclassical verse. He had a very strong influence on Pushkin during his lyceum period.

Zh. 5
Akhmatova said that this poem was written under the influence of Mikhail Kuzmin (Lidiya Chukovskaya, *Entretiens avec Anna Akhmatova*, p. 132; Chukovskaya, *Zapiski: ob Anne Akhmatovoi* [Paris: YMCA Press, 1976], Vol. I, p. 50; diary entry for 8 August 1940. *Note:* the French-language edition of Chukovskaya is in one volume, while the Russian edition is in two volumes.)
Kuzmin—See note to *Zh. 473.*

Zh. 9
Line 3, Snow Maiden—In Russian folklore, the Snow Maiden is the daughter of Beautiful Spring and Father Frost, who has been concealing her from his enemy, Yarilo the Sun. Yarilo takes revenge by shining only briefly on the enchanted kingdom of the Berendeys. At last, the Snow Maiden falls in love with a mortal, Mizgir, and wishes to enter the world of humans. On her wedding day Yarilo melts her with his rays and she disappears. Satisfied, he continues to wage war on the Berendey kingdom. This legend was the basis of a play by Alexander Ostrovsky and an opera by Nicholay Rimsky-Korsakov.
Line 11, Epiphany Eve—The custom of fortune-telling is also related in Pushkin, *Evgeny Onegin,* poem V.4: "Epiphany in solemn manner/ They still observed there as of old,/ When all the serf-maids fortunes told/ For the young ladies of the manor. . ." (*Eugene Onegin,* trans. Walter Arndt. New York: E.P. Dutton & Co., 1963, p. 116)

Zh. 15
Lines 5, 6—". . . According to one proverb, seven women have collectively but one soul, and according to a still more ungallant saying, women have no souls at all, but only a vapor." Sir Donald Mackenzie Wallace, *Russia* (London, 1877), reprinted in *Readings in Russian History,* compiled and edited by Warren B. Walsh (Syracuse University Press, 1950), p. 310.

Zh. 16
M. A. Zmunchilla—a cousin of Akhmatova's and the wife of her older brother Andrey Gorenko. Akhmatova was staying with her in Kiev from 1906–1907 after she finished her studies at the Funduleevsky Gymnasium there.

Zh. 21
This is one of the poems written in the peasant-woman persona that Akhmatova sometimes adopted. See also *Zh. 23, 34* and *45.*
Line 13, "low moans"—echoes line 1 of Sergey Gorodetsky's poem, "Monastery Spring," so popular at that time, written in the same meter (folk song trochaic). The poem is from the collection entitled *The Ravine* (1907).

Zh. 23
Wendy Rosslyn suggests that this poem relates to the passage in Matthew: "Is there a man among you who will offer his son a stone when he asks for bread, or a snake when he asks for fish?" (*The Prince, The Fool and the Nunnery: The Religious Theme in the Early Poetry of Anna Akhmatova* [Amersham, England: Avebury Publishing Co., 1984], p. 43)

Zh. 24
Line 8, water nymph—In Russian folklore, one of the beliefs about water nymphs was that they were the souls of unbaptized children, those who had drowned, or women who had committed suicide. In the Russian ritual calendar, the week before Trinity Sunday is devoted to water nymphs, who leave the water at this time and go into the fields. Rimsky-Korsakov's opera *May Night* has a lovely scene in which the nymphs swing through the birches and dance in the moonlight.

Zh. 25
Title—White nights are the term for the summer weeks in Leningrad when there are only a few hours of darkness.

Zh. 28
Line 15, Sirin—a heavenly bird-girl, similar to the firebird, who descends to earth to charm people with her singing. The sirin is a favorite motif in Russian folk art. See *Zh. 491*, a poem on a similar theme.

Zh. 30
Line 3, Pierrette—heroine of a La Fontaine fable, "The Broken Pitcher." A statue of Pierrette in a Tsarskoye Selo park was celebrated by Pushkin in a poem as well as by Akhmatova in *Zh. 149*.

Zh. 34
This is one of Akhmatova's most popular poems and was set to music by Sergey Prokofiev.

Zh. 37
The lines are intentionally "unfinished." The third stanza has only four lines instead of the expected five.

Zh. 40
Innokenty Annensky (1856–1909)—poet, literary critic and classical philologist, also the director of the Gymnasium in Tsarskoye Selo. Of the poetic works of Annensky, the ones that had the most influence on contemporaries were *The Cypress Box* (1910), a collection of lyrics published just after his death and the poetic tragedy *Thamyras, The Lyre Player* (1913). The Acmeist poets honored him as their teacher; Akhmatova read his manuscript of *The Cypress Box*, given to her by Gumilyov, straight through and said of the experience: "I stopped seeing and hearing, I was spellbound. I repeated these poems day and night . . . They opened a new harmony for me" (*Entretiens*, p. 94; and *Zapiski*, Vol. I, p. 106). On another occasion she remarked to Chukovskaya: "One could say that all the poets came out of him—Mandelstam, Pasternak, I and even Mayakovsky." (*Entretiens*, p. 120; and *Zapiski*, Vol. I, p. 135) Later, Akhmatova wrote a poem to Annensky, "Teacher" (*Zh. 346*), as part of the cycle Wreath to the Dead.
This is one of several poems Akhmatova wrote using a male persona. See also *Zh. 146, 241, 242, 490, 494, 497, 505,* and *528*.

Zh. 41
Vera Ivanova-Shvarsalon (1890–1920)—daughter of the writer L.D. Zinovyeva-Annibal, stepdaughter and later the wife of the famous Symbolist poet Vyacheslav Ivanov.

Zh. 47–56
Although written contemporaneously with the other poems of *Evening*, these poems were not published as part of the first edition. They appeared in various journals and were reprinted as part of *Evening* in later collections of Akhmatova's poems, some in *Poems 1958*, some in *Poems 1961*, and all of them in *The Flight of Time* (1965).

Zh. 51
Ty—In Russian, as in many European languages, there is a distinction between the infor-
mal "you"' *(ty)* and the formal *(vy)*. A sign that you have reached a more intimate
stage in a friendship is when you are referred to as *ty*.
Lines 7–8, "forty fond sisters"—In Act V, Scene i, Hamlet compared his love to that
of Laertes for Ophelia: "Forty thousand brothers/ Could not (with all their quan-
tity of love)/ Make up my sum."

Zh. 56
This is an example of Akhmatova's habit of redating some of her poems for various per-
sonal reasons. It first appeared in *Plantain* in 1921 and then was put into the section
Evening in *The Flight of Time* (1965) with the date changed from 1914 to 1911. In *Poems
1958* it appeared under the title, "In the Nursery."

ROSARY (1914)

The unusual success of this collection placed Akhmatova in the front ranks of contem-
porary Russian poetry. In the first edition, *Rosary* contained 52 poems, of which 28 had
been published earlier in journals. Several changes in the arrangement of the poems were
introduced in subsequent editions, especially in the 3rd edition (Petrograd, 1916). We
follow the order of the first publication, placing poems added later into the "Additions"
section.

★   ★   ★

Epigraph
From the poem "Justification" by Evgeny Baratynsky (1800–1844). Many of the poems
which appear in this collection were first published in *Hyperborean*, a monthly of
poems and the critical organ of the Poets' Guild published in St. Petersburg in
1912–13 with Mikhail Lozinsky as editor. The epigraph first appeared in *From Six
Books*.

Zh. 62
This poem is set in the cabaret called the Stray Dog, where Akhmatova often read her
poems in the early, spectacular years of her success. The Stray Dog, a meeting place
for poets, painters, artists and bohemians, was in a cellar on Mikhailovsky Square
(now the Square of the Arts) in Petersburg. Its walls had been painted by Sergey
Sudeikin. In her memoirs, Akhmatova recalls "the gate which we entered in order
to descend the winding cellar staircase into the multicolored, smoky, always some-
what mysterious Stray Dog."
Line 15, "that woman dancing"—According to Max Hayward in his essay "Anna
Akhmatova" (*Writers in Russia, 1917–1978*, Harcourt Brace Jovanovich, p. 251, 2),
this woman was Olga Glebova-Sudeikina, an actress and a friend of Akhmatova's
who sometimes danced on the small stage at the Stray Dog, and the tone of despair
in this poem was caused by the recent suicide of Vsevolod Knyazev, a young poet
and Officer of the Guard who was in love with Sudeikina. Knyazev's suicide, which
involved Sudeikina, Blok and, somehow, Akhmatova, was the catalyst for
Akhmatova's longest poem, *Poem Without a Hero*. See note to the First Dedication,
Poem Without a Hero. Other poems written about Knyazev are *Zh. 76, 77* and *79*.

Zh. 66
Line 3, "my solitude here in Tver"—After her marriage to Nikolay Gumilyov in 1910, Akhmatova spent almost every summer at her mother-in-law's estate at Slepnyovo, near the town of Bezhetsk in the province of Tver. Her son Lev was raised here. See *Zh. 239.*

Zh. 69
In a manuscript copy of Akhmatova's poems, this one is dedicated to Mikhail Lozinsky (1886–1955), poet, translator and lifelong friend of Akhmatova's. He was a member of the Poets' Guild, but did not join the Acmeists although in his own poetry (*Mountain Spring*, Moscow-Petersburg, 1916) he shared the classicist tendencies of several of them. Lozinsky was on the editorial board of the literary-artistic journal *Apollon,* which printed many of Akhmatova's early poems. He owned the publishing house Hyperborean and put out a monthly poetry journal of the same name which also took many of Akhmatova's poems. He was the literary editor of her second and third books, *Rosary* and *White Flock,* and helped edit the 1940 collection of her poems, *From Six Books.* In 1946, Lozinsky was awarded a Stalin prize for his translation of Dante's *Divine Comedy.* Other poems dedicated to him by Akhmatova are *Zh. 78, 124* and *300.* She considered his poem to her, "Not Forgotten" (in *Mountain Spring*) one of the best of the dozens written to her in the decade of the 1910's. Shortly before her death, Akhmatova completed a memoir of Lozinsky.

Zh. 76–77
These poems reflect the theme of suicide by a young man in love. See also *Zh. 79* and *Poem Without a Hero,* which relates to the year 1913.

Zh. 78
M. Lozinsky—See note to *Zh. 69.*

Zh. 79
Olga Glebova-Sudeikina (1885–1945)—dramatic actress, singer and dancer, wife of the artist and set designer Sergey Sudeikin. Akhmatova was a very close friend, and would frequently watch Sudeikina perform in the cabaret, the Stray Dog. Akhmatova lived with her from 1921–1924 after the break-up of her marriage to Shileiko. Glebova-Sudeikina emigrated to Paris with the composer Artur Lourié in 1924. In the role of the "Colombine of the 1910's" she is, as the double of Akhmatova, one of the main characters in *Poem Without a Hero* (*Zh. 648*). This long poem is based on memories of the 1913, prerevolutionary Petersburg society to which they both belonged.
Line 8, "The one who broke your spell for white death"—an allusion to the suicide of Vsevolod Knyazev, a young poet and Officer of the Guard. His death is one of the major themes in *Poem Without a Hero.* His book, *Poems,* was published posthumously in 1914.

Zh. 85
Akhmatova was traveling through Italy in 1912.

Zh. 86
This poem was originally published in *Hyperborean,* No. 5 (February 1913) under the title "Return." Akhmatova spent every summer from 1896–1903 with her parents near Sebastopol not far from Khersones.

Zh. 87
Line 3, Princess Eudoxia (died in 1407)—the wife of Prince Dmitry Donskoy (see note

to *Zh. 312*). She entered a convent and became a canonized saint of the Russian Orthodox Church.

Line 7, "hysteric"—In Russian culture the *klikusha*, like the "holy fool," her male counterpart, was gifted by God with prophecy, which took the form of hysterical fits. Alyosha's mother in Dostoevsky's *Brothers Karamazov* is a *klikusha*.

Line 12, "the door of Paradise"—The icon screen in the Orthodox Church was considered the boundary between earth and heaven. The "doors of Paradise" are in the center of the icon screen and are open at various moments in the service, such as during Communion, to reveal the altar.

Zh. 89

Line 4, "it's your nameday"—November 8 is the day of the Archangel Michael on the church calendar. This poem and the next probably allude to Mikhail Lozinsky. The *imeninnyi* or "name day" of a Russian is the day on the church calendar devoted to the saint after whom he is named, and is celebrated much more festively than the person's birthday.

Zh. 93

Lines 3–4, "And a dark prayer stole/ Covered my head . . ."—In the act of confession in the Russian Orthodox Church, the priest places his stole over the head and shoulders of the penitent, who stands with bowed head before him.

Zh. 94

This poem reflects Akhmatova's first meeting with her future husband, Nikolay Gumilyov.

Zh. 95

Line 1, *Agrafena-Kupalnitsa* (Agrafena the Bather)—St. Agrippina and her day, June 23, were connected in the old Russian villages with ritual bathing for purification, probably because it was also the evening before the day of John the Baptist (*Ivan Kupala*). This evening is also Midsummer Night. June 23 was Akhmatova's birthday.

Zh. 100

Line 1, Cathedral of St. Isaac of Dalmatia, under construction from 1818 to 1858, was designed by Richard de Montferrand, and is an example of the Empire style adapted to the original Russian Orthodox church. It became one of the major landmarks of Petersburg.

Line 4, "the horse of Peter the Great"—the famous statue of Peter the Great by Etienne-Maurice Falconet commissioned by Catherine the Great. It has become one of the main symbols of Petersburg, now Leningrad.

Zh. 101

The first stanza is almost identical to the last four lines of *S-F. 22, III, 29*, a poem probably referring to Sergey Sudeikin.

Line 3, Galernaya Arch—the arch connecting the buildings of the former Senate and Synod on Decembrist Square. Built in classical style by Karl Rossi at the beginning of the nineteenth century, it led from Winter Palace Square to Nevsky Avenue, Petersburg's most important street.

Zh. 103

In the summer of 1912, Akhmatova and Gumilyov made a journey to northern Italy.

Line 1, "A golden dovecote"—Venice, the Cathedral of St. Mark; flocks of pigeons are fed on the square in front of the cathedral. The lion is the coat of arms of Venice, and associated with St. Mark, the patron saint of the city.

Zh. 106
Alexander Blok (1880–1921)—the leading Russian Symbolist poet. His first volume of
    verse (1904) celebrated the semi-mystical "Beautiful Lady," a vision partly inspired
    by Vladimir Soloviev's "Holy Sophia." In his later verse, Blok bitterly mocked his
    own romantic delusions, but in his great poem about the Revolution, "The Twelve,"
    written in 1918, he reverted to his visionary manner. He died broken and disillu-
    sioned.
Other poems alluding to Blok are *Zh. 279, 467–469, 510* and *527.* He is also an impor-
    tant character in *Poem Without a Hero.*
Akhmatova visited Blok on 15 December 1913. This poem was in response to Blok's
    "To Anna Akhmatova" appearing in the same issue of the journal, *Love for Three
    Oranges,* published by Vsevolod Meyerhold. Blok was the editor of the poetry section.
For supplementary articles on Akhmatova and Blok, see: V.N. Toporov, *Akhmatova i
    Blok. Modern Russian Literature and Culture,* V. Berkeley: Berkeley Slavic Specialties,
    1981; V.M. Zhirmunsky, "Anna Akhmatova i Aleksandr Blok," *Russkaya literatura*
    (1970), 57–83; and Anna Akhmatova, "Vospominaniya ob Al. Bloke," Struve-Filipoff,
    II, pp. 191–197.
Last line—In the last years of his life, Blok lived on Ofitserskaya Street (now the Street
    of the Decembrists); from his apartment there was a view of the sea.

Zh. 107–111
Although written contemporaneously with the other poems of *Rosary,* these poems were
    added in later editions.

WHITE FLOCK (1917)

Soon after the February Revolution, the first edition of *White Flock* was issued by the
publishing house Hyperborean. Mikhail Lozinsky assumed a major part in collecting
and preparing the poems for print, as he had in Akhmatova's previous books. The col-
lection was significantly larger than *Rosary* and *Evening*; it contained 83 poems in four
sections as well as a long poem, *At the Edge of the Sea.*

Sixty-five poems had previously been published in journals, in patriotic publica-
tions during the war, etc. This indicates Akhmatova's growing popularity with the
general, as well as the literary, public.

The first edition of *White Flock* had 1,422 copies and quickly sold out, in spite of the
difficulties of publishing during the war and the Revolution. The second was brought
out in 1918 by the publisher Prometheus; it contained four new poems corresponding
to the number of poems deleted. In the third edition the poema *At the Edge of the Sea*
was missing. (It was republished separately, by Alkonost, 1921.) The fourth edition, sup-
plemented (Berlin: Petropolis and Alkonost, 1923), included three new poems. In the
collections of poems from later periods, *White Flock,* even in abbreviated form, continued
to occupy first place in size.

Because of the turbulent times in which it appeared, *White Flock* had significantly
fewer reviews as compared to previous collections.

*   *   *

Epigraph
From the poem "Darling," by Innokenty Annensky. See note to *Zh. 40.* It first appeared in *From Six Books.*

Zh. 119
Line 2, "ocarina"—A folk instrument, also called "the Italian flute," made from baked clay.

Zh. 120
Valeriya Sreznevskaya—the wife of V.V. Sreznevsky, a professor of military medicine. She was a friend from Akhmatova's days at the gymnasium and remained a close friend for life. After Akhmatova broke up with Gumilyov, she lived with the Sreznevsky family from early 1917 until autumn 1918. See also *Zh. 482,* written on the day of Sreznevskaya's death, 9 September 1964.

Zh. 123
Lines 3–4 of this poem were included in an inscription by Akhmatova to Boris Anrep on a copy of *Evening* which she had given him as a gift, 13 February 1916.

Zh. 124
M. Lozinsky—See note to *Zh. 69.*

Zh. 126
Line 2, "poetry"—the Russian word, "pesnopenya," has religious associations and means "psalm" as well as "poem."

Zh. 127
N.V.N.—Nikolay Vladimirovich Nedobrovo (1884–1919), a close friend of Akhmatova's. In the poetic circles of pre-World War I Petersburg, Nedobrovo was known as a man of great taste, a leading connoisseur of classical Russian poetry. He wrote poetry and criticism; his review of Akhmatova's poetry in 1915 in the periodical *Russkaya mysl (Russian Thought)* was considered by Akhmatova to be the best response to her early work. It is reprinted in English in *Russian Literature Triquarterly,* No.9, Spring 1974. In it, Nedobrovo says in part: "Other people walk in the world, exult, fall, collide with one another, but it all takes place here, in the middle of the world's circle; but Anna Akhmatova belongs to those who have reached its edge—are they to turn back and come again into the world? No, they struggle painfully and hopelessly close to the frontier and cry and weep." This poem seems to be a response to his words. Akhmatova saw Nedobrovo for the last time in 1916. He died of tuberculosis at Yalta in 1919. Other poems dedicated to him are *Zh. 132, 135, 149–151,* and *189.* It was Nedobrovo who introduced Akhmatova to Boris Anrep.

Zh. 128
In the autumn of 1916, when Akhmatova wrote this poem, she was in the Crimea being treated for tuberculosis.

Zh. 130
V.A. Komarovsky—Vasily Alekseevich Komarovsky (1881–1914), a poet highly esteemed by Akhmatova and her circle, author of *First Pier* (1913) and many posthumously published lyrics in the classicist style. He suffered from schizophrenia. Akhmatova's poem is apparently a reply to Komarovsky's poem "To Anna Akhmatova" (1914), published after his death in *Apollon,* no. 8 (1916).

Zh. 131
Akhmatova, although born near Odessa on the Black Sea, regarded Petersburg, on the Neva River, as her "blissful cradle."

Line 7, "solium"—the raised platform before the icon screen in a Russian Orthodox church. See also *S-F. 34, III, 35*. The poem is included in VOLUME II.

Zh. 132

In the "Draft Notebook" (*Chrenaya tetrad*), an authorized typewritten manuscript collection of Akhmatova's works in the Central State Archive of Literature and Art, Leningrad (TsGALI), this poem appears with a dedication to N.V.N[edobrovo].

Zh. 133

Line 5, "The black angels' wings are sharp"—a reference to the figures of black angels on the arch between the Senate and the Synod buildings in Petersburg. In 1910, Osip Mandelstam dedicated a poem to Akhmatova called "Black Angel." She may be referring to the poem as well.

Line 7, "bonfires bloom"—During bitter cold times in prerevolutionary Petersburg, bonfires were lit in the streets and on the frozen canals. Coachmen waiting for their masters, among others, warmed themselves there. See *Poem Without a Hero*, Chapter Two, line 300.

Zh. 134

Line 4, "Psalm Singer"—King David

Zh. 135

N.V.N.—See note to *Zh. 127*. The dedication to Nedobrovo first appeared in *From Six Books* (1940).

Zh. 136

Line 3—Vladimir, the Great Prince of Kiev from 980 to 1015, converted his whole nation, ancient Rus, to Christianity in 988. His statue with its raised cross stands in Kiev overlooking the Dnieper River.

Zh. 137

Line 4, "not built by human hands"—According to James H. Billington in *The Icon and the Axe, An Interpretive History of Russian Culture* (New York: Knopf, 1970), p. 29: "A sixth century legend that the first icon was miraculously printed by Christ himself out of compassion for the leper king of Edessa became the basis for a host of Russian tales about icons 'not created by human hands.'"

Pushkin wrote a poem, "The Monument," at the end of his life, when it was becoming increasingly difficult to gain proper recognition for his work, referring to his poetry as the monument "made without human hands" which he built for himself and which would outlast any others.

Zh. 141

Line 11, "the Chinese Pavilion"—also known as the Grand Caprice, built in the form of a pagoda on a stone overpass in Tsarskoye Selo. It was part of the Chinoiserie, the Chinese style popular under Catherine the Great at the end of the eighteenth century. See also *Zh. 189, 309,* and *573*.

Zh. 142

Dedicated to Boris Anrep (1883–1969), an artist (mosaicist) and art critic whom Akhmatova met through Nedobrovo. Poems dedicated to him in *White Flock* include *Zh. 159, 179, 180, 183, 188* and *191*. Anrep returned from abroad to take part in World War I; apparently two poems on the theme of emigration are also addressed to him, *Zh. 583* and the poem "When in suicidal anguish..." (*S-F. I, 378*). After 1917, Akhmatova and Anrep did not meet again until 1965, in Paris, when she came to the West to receive her honorary degree from Oxford.

Zh. 143
Huvinkka—tuberculosis sanatorium near Helsinki where Akhmatova spent the autumn of 1915. Two of her sisters died of the disease, Irina at the age of four, when Anna was five, and Iya at 27.

Zh. 146
This is one of several poems Akhmatova wrote using a male persona. See note to *Zh. 40*.

Zh. 147
Olga A. Kuzmina-Karavayeva—The family Kuzmin-Karavayev lived in Beriozki, near Slepnyovo, where Akhmatova often spent her summers on her mother-in-law's estate.

Zh. 149
N.V.N.—See note to *Zh. 127*.
The poem refers to a statue by P.P. Sokolov in Tsarskoye Selo Park, which was also the subject of a poem by Pushkin written in 1830. The poem reflects the frozen moment captured eternally in the work of art:

Having dropped the urn of water, the maid smashed it on the rock.
   The maid sits sadly, holding her useless crock.
A miracle! the water does not stop flowing, while pouring out of the smashed urn;
   The maiden sits eternally sad over the eternal stream.

Also see *Zh. 30*.

Zh. 150
Line 4, Bakhchisarai—a city of many fountains in the Crimea, an area annexed to Russia during the reign of Catherine the Great. Here the poet remembers the city, then returns in memory from Bakhchisarai to Tsarskoye Selo, and to the palace with bronzed gates and eagle emblems.
Line 10, "Catherine's eagle"—In 1787, on the order of Potemkin, conquerer of the Crimea, the route of Catherine II's visit to the Crimea was marked by columns, each decorated with a gilded Catherine eagle. One of these was erected in a grove of Bakhchisarai not far from the Khan's palace.

Zh. 151
N.V.N.—See note to *Zh. 127*.
Line 15, "the Lyre Player"—the statue of Apollo the Lyre Player in Pavlovsk Park. The image of the singer-lyre player was connected by Akhmatova and her contemporaries with Innokenty Annensky's "Bacchic drama" entitled *Thamyras, the Lyre Player*. (See note to *Zh. 40*.) In the drama the blind singer is accompanied in his wanderings by his mother, who was turned by the gods into a bird because of her incestuous passion for her son. The instrument was, in fact, a kithara, the most important musical instrument in ancient Greece, and it resembles a lyre. The statue of Apollo the Lyre Player was made by F. Gordeyev at the end of the 18th century, and was based on an ancient model.

Zh. 153
In the first publication of *White Flock,* this poem appeared with an epigraph with words from Psalm 6, line 7. The indicated text is: "Every night I flood my bed with tears; I drench my couch with weeping."

Zh. 155
Line 8, Martha—Novgorod was for centuries an independent and wealthy city-state, with strong traditions of "republican" government. Mayors were elected by a fairly

broad-based political constituency, usually from the large merchant class. Martha Boretskaya was an unofficial mayor who led the Novgorodians in sustained battle to maintain their independence against the encroaching Great Princes of Muscovy. Novgorod was conquered and stripped of its charters in 1478.

Line 8, Arakcheyev—Alexei Arakcheyev (1769–1834), from an old Novgorodian family, was famous for the punitive discipline with which he organized the armed forces of Alexander I. In order to be able to mobilize troops more quickly, Arakcheyev founded military colonies. Whole villages, including children, were put under a rigorous drill and supervision, and all men were required to wear uniforms. Participants in the system detested it, but revolts were brutally crushed.

Akhmatova was in Novgorod to see Gumilyov, who was training in preparation for being sent to the front.

Zh. 156

Line 15, "her white mantle"—a reference to the legend that the Mother of God appeared in a church in Constantinople in the tenth century. According to the legend, the Madonna materialized in the center of the church and extended her veil over the people. The holiday celebrating this event, Pokrov, was very popular in Russia and symbolized the Madonna as intercessor for the people.

Zh. 157

Line 12—The Roman soldiers, waiting for Christ to die on the cross, cast lots for his garments.

Zh. 159

In a manuscript copy, this poem is dedicated to Boris Anrep. See note to *Zh. 142*.

Zh. 160

This poem was enormously popular in the First World War and was reprinted in many collections of patriotic poetry.

Zh. 161

Written in Darnitsa, near Kiev, where Akhmatova was living with her mother in a dacha at the beginning of the war. The voice is that of Akhmatova's peasant-woman persona.

Zh. 162

Day of the Holy Ghost, the seventh Sunday after Easter, is a Christian holiday celebrating the descent of the Holy Ghost (the Holy Spirit) to the Apostles, bringing them, according to scripture, the gift of tongues.

Zh. 172

Lines 7–8, "There's a drop of Novgorod blood in me"—Akhmatova's mother, Inna Erazmovna Gorenko (ca. 1852–1930) was a descendant from an ancient noble family, the Stogovs, who traced their origin from the Novgorod nobility.

Zh. 173

World War I began on 19 July 1914.

Zh. 174

Published in a journal with a dedication to N. G. Chulkova, the wife of Georgy Chulkov. Chulkov was a poet and critic associated with the journal *Apollon*. The Chulkovs kept a salon for artists and writers.

Zh. 176

It was a Russian folk custom to release a bird from captivity on Annunciation Day.

Line 8, "a miraculous icon frame"—*riza,* an embossed metal cover over an icon, with spaces left for parts of the icon to show. It appeared relatively late in the development of the icon, and became very elaborate in the seventeenth century, when precious gems would be set in the embossed metal.

Zh. 177

Line 5, "the tsarina's garden"—refers to Catherine's Park in Tsarskoye Selo.

Zh. 179

One of the poems dedicated to Anrep.

Zh. 180

One of the poems dedicated to Anrep.

Zh. 183

One of the poems dedicated to Anrep. Anrep writes that he and Akhmatova met frequently in the year 1915. During one of these conversations he mentioned not being very religious. Akhmatova reproached him, saying the guarantee of happiness was on the path to faith. "It's impossible without faith," she said. Anrep notes the poem was written in association with this conversation. (See Struve-Filipoff, III, p. 440.)

Zh. 187

See note to *Zh. 162.* In the "Draft Notebook," this poem was dedicated to Anrep. He was on duty in England and was expecting to return to Russia at this time but was detained until December 1916.

Zh. 188

One of the poems dedicated to Anrep.

Zh. 189

Line 7, "little city"—Tsarskoye Selo. See note to *Zh. 141.* This poem is dedicated to Nedobrovo. See note to *Zh. 127.*

Zh. 190

Yunya Anrep, wife of Boris Anrep. According to Amanda Haight (*Anna Akhmatova: A Poetic Pilgrimage,* p. 45), "In December 1916 she [Akhmatova] stayed at Belbek as the guest of Yunya Anrep, Boris Anrep's estranged wife, who was probably then at home on leave from her work as a nurse in the war."

Zh. 191

One of the poems dedicated to Anrep.

Zh. 193–205

Although written contemporaneously with the other poems of *White Flock,* these poems were added in later editions.

Zh. 194

Line 17—Anrep says that he had given Akhmatova a wooden altar cross which he had found in a half ruined, abandoned church in the Carpathian Mountains in Galicia. In August, when she was forced to go south for her health, she took the cross with her. (Struve-Filipoff, III, p. 442.)

Zh. 201

Line 8, "Jonah's Monastery"—the Jonah Trinity Monastery, Kiev.

PLANTAIN (1921)

Plantain is the shortest of Akhmatova's collections. The word as translated here refers to the common temperate zone weed, rather than the tropical plant. In Russian it means literally, "by-the-road." In the first edition *Plantain* contained 38 poems, including one translation—"To Zara (from the Portuguese)." The majority were written in 1916–1917 and conclude the biographical themes of *White Flock* and *Rosary*; individual poems refer to a much earlier period but for various reasons had not been included in preceding collections.

Eighteen of the poems were published earlier, mainly in newspapers. *Plantain* was republished twice as the third part of the book *Anno Domini MCMXXI*. In *Poems 1909–1960* (1961), the poems in this collection were combined with *Anno Domini* under the general title Plantain (29 poems in all). In *The Flight of Time*, the section Plantain has 23 poems. Two were transferred on a chronological basis to *Rosary* and *Evening*, three based on biographical cycles into *Anno Domini*, and poem #630 was combined with two others connected thematically into the cycle Epic Motifs. In the present edition these three poems (*Zh. 629–631*) have been transferred to the section of Epic and Dramatic Fragments and Long Poems.

⋆　⋆　⋆

Epigraph
From the dedication of Pushkin's "Poltava." It first appeared in *Anno Domini.*

Zh. 206
One of the poems dedicated to Boris Anrep in a manuscript copy.
Line 9, "secret ring"—Before Anrep went to the front in 1916, Akhmatova gave him
    a ring as a souvenir. See *Zh. 266*, "The Tale of the Black Ring."

Zh. 207
One of the poems dedicated to Boris Anrep in a manuscript copy. See note to *Zh. 142.*
Line 1, "green island"—Great Britain, where Anrep was going in 1917, leaving
    Akhmatova and Russia behind.
Line 5, "dashing man of Yaroslavl"—Anrep was born in Yaroslavl.

Zh. 210
Line 1, "moving upon the water"—See John, 5: "For an angel of the Lord went down
    at a certain season into the pool, and troubled the water. Whoever stepped in first
    after the troubling of the water was healed of whatever disease he had."

Zh. 211–212
Also dedicated to Boris Anrep.

Zh. 214
According to folklore, the cuckoo responds by crying out once for each year remaining
    in the questioner's life.

Zh. 215
In the "Draft Notebook," it is devoted to B. A[nrep].

Zh. 218
Dedicated to Boris Anrep in a manuscript copy.

Zh. 222
Line 7, "insomnia"—The word "insomnia" is used in both the 1979 Zhirmunsky edi-
    tion and in *The Flight of Time*. In the 1976 Zhirmunsky edition, the text reads "lover."

Zh. 225
Line 7, "the white one"—death

Zh. 228
Line 3, Karelia—Akhmatova called the area around Slepnyovo "the Karelian earth" since it was settled by Finns in the 17th century. Karelia is the lake region bordering Finland.

Zh. 229
Line 4, Palm Sunday Eve—In 1913, Palm Sunday occurred on 6 April. Akhmatova may be recalling the time when she became acquainted with Nedobrovo (Chernykh: Anna Akhmatova, *Sochineniya,* p. 405).

Zh. 231
Line 3, "Catherine's days"—Catherine the Great ruled Russia from 1762 to 1796.

Zh. 232
The lack of personal pronouns in this poem (peculiar even for Russian) suggests that the protagonist is looking into a mirror. When first published in a journal in 1914, the poem was titled "The Woman in Lilac," and later, in *Poems 1961,* it was called "In the Mirror."

Zh. 233
The first letters of each line (in the Russian) spell out BORIS ANREP.

Zh. 235
Also dedicated to Boris Anrep.

S-F. I, 378 (Zh. 236)
The Zhirmunsky edition has only the last 12 lines of this poem. The version used here is found in the Struve-Filipoff edition of Akhmatova's *Works,* Volume I, p. 378. It was first published in 1918 in the weekly newspaper, *Volya naroda (The People's Will)* in an even more truncated version, lines 9 through 16. According to Zhirmunsky, the poem was originally dedicated to Boris Anrep. The lines missing in the Zhirmunsky edition have subsequently appeared, as a note to this poem, in Soviet editions of Akhmatova's works, including *Anna Akhmatova: Stikhotvoreniya i poemy,* edited by I.I. Slobozhan, with notes compiled by M.M. Kralin (Leningrad: Lenizdat, 1989), p. 576.

Zh. 237
Akhmatova's first translation and the only one included in a collection of her poems. The author is Portuguese poet Antero de Kental (1842–1891).
Zara—the sister of the poet Jacino de Arugio; she died at 16.

ANNO DOMINI MCMXXI (1922)

The first edition appeared in 1922 under the title *Anno Domini MCMXXI* ("In the year of our Lord 1921"). It consisted of three parts: 14 poems in a section called MCMXXI; 15 poems in a section called The Voice of Memory; and the republication of *Plantain* with one added poem. Of the first 29 poems, only six had been published earlier. With a few exceptions, all new poems in the collection were written in 1921, a year of great productivity in Akhmatova's career.

The second edition was printed in 1923 in Berlin by the publishers Petropolis and Alkonost under the title, *Anno Domini. Poems.* The title of the collection lost its former chronological significance with the inclusion of the large first section of "New Poems" written in 1922 and also some poems of an earlier period. Of them, 12 had been published in periodicals. The two remaining sections were reprinted as they appeared in the first edition.

From Six Books reproduces *Anno Domini* very completely. In *Poems 1909–1960* this section is combined with *Plantain,* while in *The Flight of Time* the books *Plantain* and *Anno Domini* are again separated, and several poems from the 1920s are added to *Anno Domini.* Over the years, poems written at various periods, Biblical Poems, The Tale of the Black Ring, Epic Motifs, Three Poems, excerpts from the Tsarskoye Selo *poema,* and The Russian Trianon, were included in the book. The broad biographical cycle Black Dream, also including poems of various years, was removed. This tendency for extensive grouping of all poems into cycles, connected by theme and time, culminated in the table of contents of the collection of *Anno Domini,* composed by Akhmatova around 1961 and listing 55 poems. (The table of contents has been preserved in several lists in the material belonging to M.S. Petrovykh in the Saltykov-Shchedrin State Public Library.)

In view of the significant broadening of the collection, we have reproduced its contents according to the manuscript and table of contents of *The Flight of Time.* The Epic Motives and The Russian Trianon were transferred to the section of Epic and Dramatic Fragments.

★   ★   ★

Epigraph
From a poem entitled "I already knew her then. . ." by Fyodor Tyutchev (1803–1873).

Zh. 238
Petrograd—The city of Petersburg became Petrograd during World War I. Petersburg
    sounded too German to patriotic Russians, and the old Slavic word for city, "grad,"
    was used to name "Peter's city." After Lenin's death in 1924 the name of the city
    was changed to Leningrad, "Lenin's city."

S-F. I, 214 (Zh. 239)
Since this poem is published in the Zhirmunsky edition without lines 5–8, we have used
    the more complete version.
Bezhetsk—See note to *Zh. 66.*

Zh. 240
8 May (25 April) is the anniversary of Akhmatova's wedding.

Zh. 241–242, The Voice of Another
These two poems are presumably written in the persona of Nikolay Gumilyov
    (1886–1921), Akhmatova's first husband. They were married in 1910 and divorced
    in 1918. Gumilyov wrote a series of articles for the literary magazine *Apollon* which
    helped to establish his rationale for organizing the Poets' Guild in 1911 and opposing the Symbolist poetry movement with one called Acmeism (1912–1913). He published a series of reviews in *Apollon* (1909–1916), including one on the poems of
    Akhmatova, that developed the canons of taste and craftsmanship defining Acmeism.
    His concept of the poet as craftsman is enhanced by his fellow poet Kuzmin's image
    of the poet as architect and by the ideal of the Freemasons building monuments to
    "both the heavens and the earth."
        Gumilyov's own poetry went from Symbolism (the early collections) through

poetry of romantic adventure and masculine heroism drawn from his travels in Abyssinia after 1911 to the more psychologically and stylistically complex poems of his last three years in the collections *The Pyre*, 1918 and *The Pillar of Fire*, 1921. In addition to writing poetry and criticism and teaching, Gumilyov made several major translations, including Villon's *Testaments*, Coleridge's "Rime of the Ancient Mariner" and the Babylonian epic of *Gilgamesh*.

Gumilyov was born in Kronstadt, the son of a naval surgeon, raised in Petersburg and attended the Tsarskoye Selo Lyceum, where he met Annensky. In 1914, one month after the Russian declaration of war, he enlisted as a volunteer in the Life-Guard Uhlan Regiment of the Empress Alexandra Fyodorovna. He fought heroically and was decorated twice for bravery. Toward the end of the war, he spent time in London and Paris, where he met the leading literary figures of the day.

After the Revolution he served as an instructor in creative writing in the literary studio of the House of Arts in Petrograd. He was shot in August 1921, after he was accused of being involved in the Tagantsev affair, an alleged anti-Bolshevik conspiracy. Akhmatova saw Gumilyov for the last time in the Club of Poets. She found out about Gumilyov's arrest at Blok's funeral, 10 August, and 1 September she read about his execution while she was in Tsarskoye Selo. Gumilyov was executed 25 August 1921 and the requiem took place in the Kazan Cathedral, Petersburg, 9 September 1921.

Akhmatova wrote many poems to him and he to her, though they never managed to live together comfortably. They had one son, Lev Gumilyov, born in 1912. Other poems Akhmatova wrote using a male persona are given in the note to *Zh. 40.*

Zh. 241

Line 8, "the stray bullet"—a reference to Gumilyov's poem "The Workman." Below are stanzas 4 and 5, in Dimitry Obolensky's plain prose translation in *The Heritage of Russian Verse* (Indiana University Press, 1976):

The bullet he [the German workman] has cast will whistle above the white-foamed Divina; the bullet he has cast will seek out my breast—it has come for me.

I shall fall in mortal anguish, I shall see the past as it really was, and my blood will gush like a fountain onto the dry, dusty and trampled grass.

Zh. 246–251, Dark Dream

The poems of this cycle were composed at different periods, but are unified by a biographical theme—Akhmatova's relationship with her second husband, Vladimir Shileiko (1891–1930). Shileiko was a leading scholar, a specialist in ancient cuneiform languages, Sumerian, Akkadian and Babylonian. He wrote the introduction to the Russian translation of *Gilgamesh* by Nikolay Gumilyov.

Shileiko also wrote poetry and was published in leading journals. He frequently visited the Stray Dog, where he met Akhmatova and other members of her circle. They were married in 1918, and according to what Akhmatova told several sources, Shileiko forbade her to write poetry at this time. They broke up in 1921 and were officially divorced in 1928.

Zh. 245

Line 8, "Like wormwood smells the bread of strangers"—Anatoly Naiman suggests that this phrase comes from Dante's *Divine Comedy*:

*Tu proverai si come sa di sale
Lo pane altrui, e com'e duro calle
Lo scendere de'l salir per altrui scale*

You know yourself how bitter
Is alien bread and how difficult
To descend and ascend another's staircase.

(Anatoly Naiman, *Rasskazy o Anne Akhmatovoi*
   [Moscow: Khudozhestvennaya literatura, 1989], p. 33.)

Zh. 246

The setting for this poem was very likely the Stray Dog. Tamara Shileiko, "Legendy, mify i stihki," *Novy mir*, no. 4 (April 1986), suggests the poem was written in reply to a poem Shileiko had written to Akhmatova.

Zh. 250

In the autumn of 1918, Akhmatova moved with Shileiko to Moscow, to 3 Zatchatevsky Street, near the present Kropotkin Street, where they lived until January 1919. Then, they moved back to Petrograd to the Marble Palace, where Shileiko had two rooms, as an employee of the Academy of Material Culture.

Zh. 260–262, Biblical Verses

All three poems begin with the conjunction "and" in correspondence with the style of Biblical narration.

Zh. 261

In the manuscript copy in the archives, the poem is dated "1924, Kazanskaya, 2." Akhmatova lived on Kazanskaya (now Plekhanov Street) from November 1923 to March 1924.

Zh. 263

Valentina Shchegoleva (1878–1931)—actress and wife of the Pushkin scholar P.E. Shchegolev. Akhmatova stayed at their dacha near Leningrad in the 1920's.

Line 3, "God's fool" (Holy Fool)—In the Russian Orthodox church certain men are believed to be blessed by God with the gift of prophecy but often appear as deranged. It was common to see them wander the countryside wearing heavy chains. The reverence for the Holy Fool is manifest in Pushkin's play *Boris Godunov*, where the only one who dares accuse the tsar of the murder of the heir to the throne is the Holy Fool, whom Tsar Boris respects and fears.

Line 13, Seraphim—(1760–1833), a monk of the Sarov hermitage, a Christian saint.

Line 15, Anna—the wife of prince Mikhail Yaroslavich of Tver (1271–1319), punished by the Tatar khan. After her husband's death Anna became a nun and moved to Kashin to live with her son, Prince Vasily. She died in 1338 and was canonized in 1650.

Zh. 266

According to Akhmatova's story, her Tatar grandmother, whose family name she took as her pseudonym, originated from the khan of the Golden Horde; he was called Akhmat (or Akhmet) and was killed soon after the unsuccessful campaign on Moscow in 1480, a historical event considered the end of the "Tatar yoke" in Rus.

   In Russian aristocratic geneologies the family name Akhmatov is mentioned for the first time during the campaign of Ivan the Terrible against Kazan in 1544. Akhmatova's great-grandmother Praskovya Egorovna Akhmatova married a Simbirsk landowner, Egor Motovilov. Akhmatova's grandmother was his daughter, Anna Egorovna Motovilova.

See *Zh. 206.*

Zh. 268
Natalya Rykova (1897–1928)—wife of Professor G. A. Gukovsky; she was an admirer
and close friend of Akhmatova's. In 1919–1920, Akhmatova visited the Rykov family
several times on a farm in Tsarskoye Selo. Natalya Rykova's father, Professor V. I.
Rykov, an agronomist, was the director of the farm.

Zh. 269
In a copy of the poem in the archive the poem is dated "1921. Spring. Sergievskaya, 7."
In the spring of 1921 Akhmatova was living in Petrograd on Sergievskaya Street
(now Tchaikovskaya Street).
Line 1, "Dear traveler"—the moon

Zh. 272
When this poem was first published, it appeared without the fourth stanza.
Gumilyov was executed 25 August 1921.

S-F. I, 205–206 (Zh. 277)
In the Zhirmunsky edition, stanza 2, which was published in the first edition of *Anno
Domini*, appears in the notes and variants section.

Zh. 279
Blok died 7 August 1921 and was buried in the Smolensk cemetery in Petrograd on 10
August. The day of the burial coincided with the religious holiday of the Smolensk
Madonna. Blok is now buried in the Volkov Cemetery in Leningrad.

Zh. 280
A poetic description of the portrait of Olga Glebova-Sudeikina in the title role of
Belyaev's play *Confusion*; the portrait was painted by her husband, Sergey Sudei-
kin. See note to *Zh. 79* and the second dedication to *Poem Without a Hero*.

Zh. 287–299
In earlier editions of *Anno Domini MCMXXI*, the third section, titled The Voice of Mem-
ory, included an epigraph from a Gumilyov poem of 1921, "The Drunken Dervish":
"The world is only a ray from the face of a friend. Everything else—its shadow."
(M. D. Elzon, ed., *Nikolay Gumilyov, Stikhotvoreniya i poemy*. Biblioteka Poeta, Bol-
shaya seriya, third edition. Leningrad: Sovetskii pisatel, 1988, p. 335)

Zh. 287
Line 7, Mazepa—The hetman Mazepa was the Ukrainian national leader who
attempted to throw off the rule of the Muscovite tsars and was defeated (with his
ally, Charles XII of Sweden) by Peter I at Poltava in 1709. The bell was constructed
in 1706 and called the Mazeppa bell.
Line 8, St. Sophia—The cathedral of St. Sophia in Kiev (built from the 10th to the 12th
centuries) is the splendidly decorated mother church of ancient Rus.

Zh. 289
Russia entered World War I in August 1914.
Line 6, "Karelian earth"—see *Zh. 228.*
Line 18, Trinity Bridge—now the Kirovsky Bridge in Leningrad.

Zh. 291
Dedicated to Artur Lourié (1892–1966), composer, a pupil of A. K. Glazunov. Lourié
set to music a series of Akhmatova's early poems. She wrote a scenario to a ballet
by Lourié; entitled "Snow Masks—in the style of Blok," it has not been preserved.
In 1921, Akhmatova stayed with Lourié and Olga Sudeikina at No. 18, on the

Fontanka. They begged her to come to Paris with them when they emigrated, but Akhmatova refused.

Zh. 294

Line 15, St. George—Gumilyov was twice awarded the Cross of St. George for bravery at the front.

Zh. 296

St. Sophia—the mother church of ancient Rus built in Kiev by Yaroslav the Wise, the leader of Rus, in the 11th century. It was built soon after the acceptance of Christianity. A holiday for St. Sophia (8 September) was celebrated with a service honoring the birth of the Madonna.

Zh. 299

According to Amanda Haight: "Although it had a profound effect on her public in 1922, this poem was never included in a collection of Akhmatova's poems, and disappeared so completely that in 1966 it was still unknown to so precise and devoted a collector of the poet's work as Lidiya Chukovskaya: it was Akhmatova who drew it to her attention, complaining that it had been excluded from her collected works." *Anna Akhmatova, A Poetic Pilgrimage*, note, p. 67.

Index of Proper Names

This index covers both volumes. It includes artists whose portraits of Akhmatova appear in this edition, and a few places and cultural terms, selectively referenced. Akhmatova is not indexed. The references from each volume appear following a **boldface** roman numeral (**I, II**). Illustrations are noted by use of *italics*.

Acmeism, Acmeists, *I:* 2, 32, 40, 44, 53, 54, 56, 69, 87; *II:* 14, 32
Adamovich, Georgy, *I:* 58, 60, 84, 105, 150, 151
Alekseev, Mikhail, *I:* 146, 151
Aliger, Margarita, *I:* 26, 112
Altman, Natan, *I: 59*
Annenkov, Yury, *I: 58,* 82, *83,* 148, *533*
Annensky, Innokenty, *I:* 11, 42–43, 44, 45, 132, 162, 627*n*; *II:* 34, 40, 43
Anrep, Boris, *I:* 74–76, 77–78, 88–89, 150–151, 633*n*; *II:* 16, 28
Antokolsky, Pavel, *I: 123*
Ardov, Victor, *I:* 106; *II:* 34
Ballets Russes, *I:* 37, 58, 66
Balmont, Konstantin, *II:* 34
Baratynsky, Evgeny, *II:* 41
Baudelaire, Charles-Pierre, *I:* 1, 36, 63; *II:* 17, 33, 40
Bely, Andrey, *I:* 49, 61; *II:* 34, 40
Belyaev, Yury, *I:* 61, 63, 142
Berggolts, Olga, *I:* 110, *111, 123*; *II:* 34
Berlin, Isaiah, *I:* 5, 11, 121, 133, 135; *II:* 21, *24*
Blok, Alexander, *I:* 9, 11, 26, 31, 37, *39,* 40, 48, 53, 57, 61, 66–67, 68, 70, 71, 82, 84–85, 92, 104, 119-I, 132, 142, 631*n*; *II:* 32, 40
Bobyshev, Dmitry, *I:* 129, 130, *154, 155*
Brik, Lily, *I:* 61

Brodsky, Joseph, *I:* 106, 129, *129,* 130, 150, *154, 155*; *II:* 39, 52
Bryusov, Valery, *I:* 29, 31, 38, 48, 54, 87
Bulgakov, Mikhail, *II:* 755*n*
Bunin, Ivan, *I:* 56
Byron, George Gordon, Lord, *I:* 52; *II:* 34
Chagall, Marc, *I:* 34
Chaplin, Charlie, *I:* 22
Chekhov, Anton, *I:* 119; *II:* 31, 37
Chukovskaya, Lidiya, *I:* 4, 13, 29, 45, 103, 104, 112, 113, 115, 124, 125, 133, 137, 175; *II:* 34
Chukovsky, Korney, *I:* 3, 4, 7, 25, 44, *58,* 61, 64, 80–81, 82, 84, 85, 93, 95, 104, 126, 131, 141, 143; *II:* 15, 41–42
Chulkov, Georgy, *I:* 26, 37, 45, 93, *100*
Colette, Sidonie, *I:* 3
Constructivism, Constructivists, *I:* 48
Czapski, Joseph, *I:* 113–114, 131
Danko, Elena, *I:* 101; *II:* 395
Dante Alighieri, *I:* 52, 99, 118, 119; *II:* 17
Derzhavin, Gavril, *II:* 131
Diaghilev, Sergey, *I:* 37, 82
dolnik, I: 48
Dostoevsky, Fyodor, *I:* 2, 46, 64, 125, 134, 145; *II:* 32
Dudin, Mikhail, *I: 123*
Duboucher, Elena, *I:* 78
Eikhenbaum, Boris, *I:* 4, 64, 93

Eliot, T.S., *I:* 22, 135, 143; *II:* 32, 40
Evpatoriya, *I:* 26
Frost, Robert, *I:* 146
Futurism, Futurists, *I:* 40, 48, 54, 57, 61, 65, 94, 96; *II:* 14
Garshin, Vladimir, *I:* 11, 103, *103,* 114–115, 116–117, 133; *II:* 758*n*
Gershtein, Emma, *I:* 125, *127;* *II:* 34
Goethe, Johann Wolfgang von, *I:* 45; *II:* 34
Golenishchev-Kutuzov, Vladimir, *I:* 30–31
Gorenko, Andrey (Akhmatova's father), *II:* 13, 157–158
Gorenko, Andrey (Akhmatova's brother), *I:* 33
Gorenko, Inna (Stogova), *I:* 23, 33, 635*n*
Gorenko, Iya, *I:* 33
Gorenko, Victor, *I:* 24, 33
Gorky, Maxim, *I:* 80; *II:* 29, 42
Gorodetsky, Sergey, *I:* 1, 2, 53
Gumilyov, Lev, *I:* 4, 5, 51, 52, *71,* 79, 89, 98, 115–116, 121, 125–126, *155, 156; II:* 14, 19, 31, 50–51
Gumilyov, Nikolay, *I:* 1, 2, 4, 8, 10, 30–34, *32,* 42, 43, 44, 49, 50, 51, 52, 53, 70, *71,* 72–73, 78–79, 84–87, 90, 99, 119, 126, 132, 639–640*n; II:* 14, 16, 29, 32, 33, 34
Haight, Amanda, *I:* 149
Halpern, Salomea, *I:* 149; *II:* 28, 33
Homer, *I:* 56
Ivanov, Georgy, *II:* 43
Ivanov, Vyacheslav, *I:* 1, 40–41, 61, 94; *II:* 33–34, 40, 47
Joyce, James, *II:* 32
Kafka, Franz, *II:* 32
Kaminskaya, Anna, *I:* 121, *149, 155*
Karsavina, Tamara, *I:* 58, 66

Khardzhiev, Nikolay, *I:* 106, 115; *II:* 34
Khlebnikov, Velimir, *I:* 40, 54; *II:* 41
Khodasevich, Vladislav, *I:* 82, 86
Khrushchev, Nikita, *I:* 125
Knyazev, Vsevolod, *I:* 65, 136, 137, 138, 139–141, *139*
Kollontay, Alexandra, *I:* 93
Komarovsky, Vasily, *I:* 632*n*
Kommisarzhevskaya, Vera, *I:* 61
Korobova, Era, *I:* 154, *155*
Kuzmin, Mikhail, *I:* 43–44, 53, 58, 63, 92, 136–141, 143; *II:* 760*n*
Lelevich, Grigory, *I:* 4, 94
Lenin, Vladimir, *I:* 14
Leningrad, *see* Petersburg
Leopardi, Giacomo, *II:* 22, 40
Lermontov, Mikhail, *II:* 41
Livshits, Benedikt, *I:* 54, 57, *58,* 60
Lourié, *I:* Artur, *81,* 82, 95, 96, 105, 115, 642–643*n*
Luknitsky, Pavel, *I:* 52, 98, 118
Lozinsky, Mikhail, *I:* 53, 629*n;* *II:* 34
Mallarmé, Stéphane, *I:* 63
Mandelstam, Nadezhda, *I:* 4, 19, 64, 79, 96, 99, 100, 102, 115, *127,* 134, 137, 141, 144; *II:* 43
Mandelstam, Osip, *I:* 1, 2, 8, 10, 11, 30, 40, 45, 46, 53, 58, *58,* 60–61, 64, 78, 87–88, 99, 100–103, *101,* 119, 120, 141; *II:* 14, 18, 19, 28, 29, 30, 32, 33, 34, 39, 40, 43, 47, 746*n*
Mariinsky Theatre, *I:* 25
Mayakovsky, Vladimir, *I:* 10, 54–56, *55,* 60–61, 70, 93, 94, 98, 119; *II:* 39, 40, 42, 751*n*
Meyerhold, Vsevolod, *I:* 57, 63, 142
Modigliani, Amedeo, *I:* 8, 35, *35,* 150; *II:* 14, 28, 49, 51
Mussorgsky, Modest, *I:* 107

Naiman, Anatoly, *I:* 129, *129,* 130, *154*; *II:* 46
Narbut, Vladimir, *I:* 2, 53; *II:* 752*n*
Nedobrovo, Nikolay, *I:* 73–76, 78, 151, 632*n*; *II:* 16, 48
Nekrasov, Nikolay, *I:* 1, 25, 41, 106; *II:* 13, 43, 764*n*
Nicholas II (Romanov), *I:* 22
Olshanskaya, E.M., *II:* 323
Olshevskaya (Ardov), Nina, *I:* 116, 125
Ovid, 56, 120
Pasternak, Boris, *I:* 1, 2, 10, 101, 102, 105, 107–109, *108,* 112, 121, *123,* 124–125, 145; *II:* 32–33, 34, 36, 37, 39, 40–41, 43, 760*n*
Petersburg (Petrograd, Leningrad), *I:* 41, 64–65, 68, 82–84, 168 *287–297*; *II:* 25, 47–48, 137–145
Petrov-Vodkine, Kuzma, *I:* 493
Petrovykh, Maria, *I:* 100; *II:* 39, 50
Picasso, Pablo, *II:* 51
Pilniak, Boris, *II:* 747*n*
Plekhanov, Georgy, *I:* 38
Poets' Guild, *I:* 1, 53–54, 67; *II:* 14
Prokofiev, Sergey, *I:* 50
Pronin, Boris, *I:* 57, 60
Punin, Nikolay, *I:* 4, 10, 11, 96–98, *97,* 103–104, 115, 119, 125; *II:* 19, 33, 758*n*
Punina, Irina, *I:* 126, 147–148, *155*
Pushkin, Alexander, *I:* 4, 5, 11, 22, 45, 48–49, 50–51, 54, 65, 66, 68, 71–72, 81, 85, 96, 118, 121, 125, 131, 132, 133, 136, 145, 146, 152, 176; *II:* 17, 18, 21, 32, 34, 41
Radlova, Anna, *I:* 95
Rein, Evgeny, *I:* 129, *154, 155*
Remizov, Aleksey, *I:* 101
Rimbaud, Arthur, *I:* 63; *II:* 33
Romanov, Boris, *I:* 63
Rykova, Natalya, *I:* 642*n*

Sassoon, Siegfried, *I:* 149, *II:* 38
Shaginyan, Marietta, *I:* 69, 93, 95
Shakespeare, William, *II:* 18
Shelley, Percy Bysse, *II:* 40
Shileiko, Vladimir, *I:* 9, 58, 61, 79–81, *79,* 82, 90–91, 96–98; *II:* 33
Shklovsky, Viktor, *I:* 61
Shostakovich, Dmitry, *I:* 128
Shtein, Sergey von, *I:* 29–31
Silver Age, *I:* 38; *II:* 14
Slepnyovo, *I:* 36, 70, 77, 89
Sologub, Fyodor, *I:* 37, 61, 141; *II:* 34
Solovyov, Vladimir, *I:* 38
Sreznevskaya, Valeriya, *I:* 11, 22, 34, 77, 632*n*
Stalin, Joseph, *I:* 1, 4, 9, 10, 14, 99, 101, 120–121, 125, *II:* 37–38, 43
Stray Dog cabaret, *I:* 2, 13, 57–61, 66, 84, 90, 119, 135, 136, 137, 141
Sudeikin, Sergey, *I:* 58, 63
Sudeikina, Olga, *I:* 14, 58, 61–63, *62,* 65, 82, 95, 136, 137, 138–141, *140,* 142, 148, 629*n*
Surikov, Vasily, *I:* 107; *II:* 322, 762, 784
Sverchkova, Alexandra, *I:* 52–53
Symbolism, Symbolists, *I:* 1, 2, 31, 38, 40, 42, 45, 48, 49, 53, 54, 58, 61, 64–65, 66, 87, 141; *II:* 14, 33
tanopis (secret writing), *I:* 145
Tarkovsky, Arseny, *I:* 145, *155*
Tashkent, *I:* 113, *114*
Tcherepnin, Nikolay, *I:* 142
Tikhonov, Nikolay, *I:* 123
Tolstoy, Aleksey, *I:* 114; *II:* 30, 42
Tolstoy, Lev, *I:* 22, 25, 46, 54, 64; *II:* 31–32
Trotsky, Leon, *I:* 95
Tsarskoye Selo, *I:* 22, 41, 50–51, 89, 118–119, 132–133, *199–209*

Tsvetaeva, Marina, *I:* 1, 2, 25, 87, 95, 105–106, *105,* 112–113, *II:* 33, 39, 761*n*
Turgenev, Ivan, *I:* 46
Tyrsa, Nikolay, *II: 69*
Tyutchev, Fyodor, *I:* 64
Valéry, Paul, *II:* 40
Verhaeren, Emile, *II:* 33
Verlaine, Paul, *I:* 1, 35, 63; *II:* 33
Vinogradov, Viktor, *I:* 47–48, 93

zaum language, 54
Zenkevich, Mikhail, *I:* 2, 53
Zhdanov, Andrey, *I:* 5, 124–125, 129, 135; *II:* 31
Zhirmunsky, Victor, *I:* 7, 8, 13, 42; *II:* 34, 35
Zmunchilla, Nanichka, *I:* 52
Znamenskaya, V.A., *I:* 75
Zoshchenko, Mikhail, *I:* 11, 124, 126; *II:* 20, 759*n*